THE HOLMAN

BIBLE

CONCORDANCE FOR KIDS

THE HOLMAN

BIBLE

CONCORDANCE
FOR KIDS

**A Personal Guide
Through The Word
For Kids Who
Want Answers**

with
TRACYE WILSON WHITE

Acknowledgment

I know God gave me the idea for this concordance from my many years of working with nine-year old children. His timing was perfect and His constant presence allowed me to complete the manuscript.

At the time I submitted the proposal to Broadman & Holman, my husband was diagnosed with metastatic melanoma. He endured extensive chemotherapy and radiation yet died ten months after the cancer was discovered. His support and encouragement during his struggle to live gave me the strength to keep working, even after his death.

I dedicate this book to the memory of my life-mate, Homer White.

—Tracye Wilson White, May 1999

Production Staff

Executive Editor: David Shepherd
Editor: Steve Bond
Project Editor: Lloyd Mullens
Design Team: Wendell Overstreet, Stephen Phanco, Anderson Thomas Design
Production: Kevin Kunce

Library of Congress Cataloging-in-Publication Data
White, Tracye Wilson, 1940–
Holman Bible Concordance for Kids/ Tracye Wilson White
p. cm.
Includes bibliographical references.
ISBN 0-80549-373-5
1. Bible concordances, English juvenile literature.
[1. Bible concordances. 2. Bible dictionaries.] I. Title. II. Title: Holman Bible Concordance.
BS425.W49 1999
220.5' 2033–dc21 99-29740
CIP

Printed in the United States
1 2 3 4 5 02 01 00 99
D

TABLE OF CONTENTS

HOW TO USE THIS BOOK

HOW TO USE THIS BOOK

A concordance is a book in which the words are listed in alphabetical order. A Bible concordance contains words that are in the Bible. It lists the Scripture verses where you can find those words. Some concordances are exhaustive. That means they contain every word in the Bible and every occurrence of that word.

The *Holman Bible Concordance for Kids* is more selective than an exhaustive concordance. Words have been selected that will be of special interest to children and new Christians. For example, here is one of the words listed and the information about that word.

Debt (DEHT)
Something which is owed, such as money.
2 Kings 4:7 Go, sell the oil, and pay thy *d*

As you can see, with each word the following features are provided:
* Pronunciation
* brief definition
* Bible verse reference
* Words either before or after the key word

Notice that the word *debt* is not typed out in the verse. Only the initial letter, *d*, appears.

Hear what God told Joshua about the Bible as it existed in his time: "Study this Book of the Law continually. Meditate on it day and night so you may be sure to obey all that is written in it. Only then will you succeed" (Joshua 1:8, New Living Translation). May you hear and obey God's Word just as Joshua did.

Teachers and Parents of Children

The idea for this *Holman Bible Concordance for Kids* originated about five years ago as a teacher of nine-year old children saw them struggling with the use of an exhaustive concordance. Overwhelmed with the number of Scripture entries, the children quickly lost interest. The teacher discovered that no concordance had been written expressly for children.

Many activities and learning situations for children call for them to use their Bibles. For most children, the Bible is a mystery. They may be able to locate Genesis and Revelation, the first and last books, or open their Bibles to the middle and find Psalms. But how do they find a Bible verse that tells about being a good friend, or the importance of obeying their parents?

The Holman Bible Concordance for Kids was written so that boys and girls can learn how to explore their Bibles and find the wonderful surprises inside. You will notice that each word has a pronunciation, a definition or meaning, followed by one or more Scripture verses with that word included in the verse. Scattered throughout the book are pictures or illustrations that will create interest and encourage Bible study.

For the most part, each definition is based on the biblical concept. Proper and place names include information about the person or place that would be of interest to children.

The Scripture selections are from the King James Version of the Bible. In some instances, the New International Version of the Bible has been used for clarification. Those verses are marked (NIV) to show that they are not from the King James Version.

If you have ever tried to find a particular verse by looking in an exhaustive concordance,

you will appreciate the choices that were made for those words that contain many Scripture references. Select verses were chosen that would relate to the Bible studies of children, as well as their understanding of certain Bible principles.

I wish to acknowledge the following sources that were my constant companions during the writing of this material. You may wish to explore them further: pronunciations of words are based on *Pronouncing Bible Names*, by W. Murray Severance. Other sources include *Holman Bible Dictionary*, *Holman Student Bible Dictionary*, by Karen Dockrey and Johnnie and Phyllis Godwin, *Bible Dictionary for Young Readers*, by William N. McElrath, *Webster's New Young American Dictionary*, *Children's Writer's Word Book*, by Alijandra Mogilner, *Roget's Superthesaurus*, by Marc McCutcheon, and *Strong's Exhaustive Concordance of the Bible*.

With around 1600 entries, it is my hope that children will enjoy using the *Holman Bible Concordance for Kids*, and that this resource will help them unlock the mysteries of their Bibles so they can grow "in wisdom and stature, and in favor with God and man" (Luke 2:52).

BOYS AND GIRLS

This *Holman Bible Concordance for Kids* was written for you. From Aaron, the brother of Moses, to Zipporah, the wife of Moses, you will find names of people, cities and towns, rivers, and mountains. And in between you will discover words you know as well as new ones. These words are those you would read as you study your Bible.

Each word tells you how to say it, gives a definition or meaning, and one or more Bible verses with that word in it. Only part of the Bible verse is used. You will notice that the Bible verse has a letter in italics. That letter stands for the word in the verse. For example, the word "love" is not spelled out in the Bible verse. It will look like this:

Matthew 5:43 Thou shalt *l* thy neighbor

Many versions of the Bible are in print today. Each one may use different words or phrases than those you will find in the King

James Version of the Bible. Nearly all of the verses are from the King James Version. A few verses have been written using the New International Version of the Bible. Sometimes the King James Version is not easy to understand. Verses using the New International Version will be marked (NIV).

In the King James Version, some words are written in the old way of writing. For example, Jesus said to Peter, "Lovest thou me more than these?" In the language we use today, we would say "Do you love me . . . ?" Another example is in 1 Peter 5:7 where Peter writes, "for he careth for you." The way we would write it today is, "for he cares for you."

In the New Testament, the first four books, called "The Gospels," tell about the birth, life, death, and resurrection of Jesus, God's Son. Some of the books may have the same stories. Many of the verses from the Gospels will have

the same words.

Other things you will find in this concordance are maps to help you locate certain towns, rivers, and seas; and pictures and drawings related to Bible places and things. Bible books are listed in alphabetical order with the other words in the book. Each listing gives information about the book and in which division in the Old Testament or the New Testament you will find it.

The author and the publisher of this *Holman Bible Concordance for Kids* hope that this book will be a tool to help you find the hidden treasures in your Bible.

Aaron (EHR uhn)

The brother of Moses and the first high priest for Israel. God used Aaron to speak for Moses but God spoke to Moses first. Aaron died before the Israelites crossed over into the Promised Land.

Exodus 6:20 she bare him **A** and Moses
Exodus 15:20 Miriam the prophetess, the sister of **A**

Abandon (uh BAN duhn)

To leave, give up, desert.

Deuteronomy 4:31 he will not **a** or destroy you (NIV)

Abed-nego (uh BED-nih goh)

A friend of Daniel. His Hebrew name was Azariah. Abednego was among many young Jews who were taken to Babylon as captives. He and two others were put into a fiery furnace because they would worship only the LORD God. They survived because the LORD protected them.

Daniel 1:7 and to Azariah, of **A**
Daniel 3:19 was furious with Shadrach, Meshach, and **A** (NIV)
Daniel 3:26 Shadrach, Meshach, and **A** came forth

Abel (AY buhl)

The name means "breath, vapor, meadow." He was the brother of Cain, the second son of Adam and Eve. God was pleased with his offering but God rejected the offering of his brother, Cain. Cain was so jealous that he killed Abel.

Genesis 4:2 she again bare his brother **A**
Genesis 4:4 the LORD had respect unto **A**
Genesis 4:8 Cain rose up against **A** his brother

Abhor (ab HOR)

To hate.

Psalm 119:163 hate and **a** lying: but thy law do I love
Romans 12:9 **A** that which is evil, cleave to that

Abide (uh BIGHD)

To live; remain; wait for.

Psalm 15:1 LORD, who shall **a** in thy tabernacle
Luke 19:5 for today, I must **a** at thy house
Luke 24:29 saying, **A** with us; for it is
John 14:16 Comforter, that he may **a** with you
John 15:7 If ye **a** in me, and my words **a** in you

9

Abel

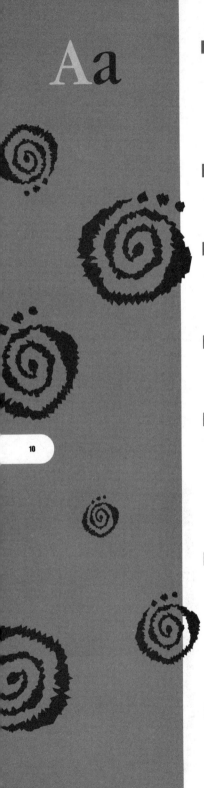

Aa

Abideth (uh BIGHD eth)
The old way of writing "abides." It is the plural for "abide."

Psalm 119:90 thou hast established the earth, and it *a*
Ecclesiastes 1:4 but the earth *a* for ever
1 Corinthians 13:13 now *a* faith, hope, charity
1 John 2:17 doeth the will of God *a* for ever

Abiding (uh BIGHD ing)
Living, remaining, waiting for.

Luke 2:8 shepherds *a* in the fields, keeping watch
Acts 16:12 we were in that city *a* certain days

Ability (uh BIL ih tee)
Power, skill, talent.

Ezra 2:69 They gave after their *a* unto the treasure
Matthew 25:15 every man according to his several *a*
Acts 11:29 every man according to his *a*

Abimelech (uh BIM uh lek)
The name means "My father is king." He was a king of the Philistines during Abraham's time.

Genesis 26:1 Isaac went unto *A* king of the Philistines

Able (AY buhl)
Can, capable, qualified.

Daniel 3:17 Our God whom we serve is *a* to deliver
Daniel 6:20 thou servest continually, *a* to deliver
Matthew 9:28 Believe ye that I am *a* to do this
1 Corinthians 10:13 tempted above that ye are *a*
Ephesians 3:20 Now unto him that is *a* to do
2 Timothy 1:12 and am persuaded that he is *a*

Abomination (uh BAHM ih na shun)
Hatred, disgust, to detest. God detested the way the Israelites were constantly turning to worship other gods. The things God's people do that go against his teachings cause the people to be an abomination to God.

Proverbs 12:22 Lying lips are *a* to the LORD
Proverbs 15:9 way of the wicked is an *a* to the LORD
Proverbs 15:26 The thoughts of the wicked are an *a*

Abound (uh BOWNED)
To overflow; more than enough; plentiful.

Romans 15:13 believing, that ye may *a* in hope
2 Corinthians 9:8 God is able to make all grace *a*
1 Thessalonians 3:12 you to increase and *a* in love

10

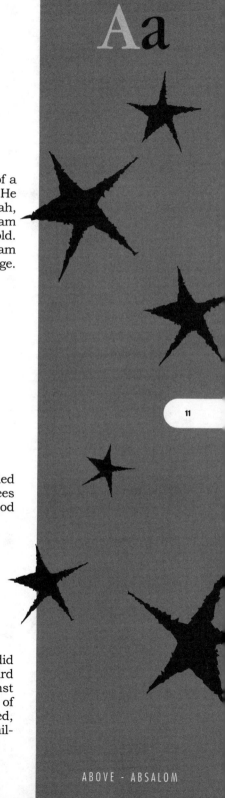

Above (uh BUHV)
Higher, over.

Psalm 57:11 Be thou exalted, O God, *a* the heavens
Psalm 96:4 he is to be feared *a* all gods
Psalm 103:11 For as the heaven is high *a* the earth
Matthew 10:24 The disciple is not *a* his master
1 Corinthians 10:13 be tempted *a* that ye are able
Philippians 2:9 a name which is *a* every name
James 1:17 every perfect gift is from *a*

Abraham (AY bruh ham)
The name means "exalted father" or "father of a multitude." It is the longer form of Abram. He became the first Hebrew. He and his wife, Sarah, became parents to a son, Isaac, when Abraham was 100 years old and Sarah was 90 years old. Isaac was the son God had promised Abraham and Sarah. Abraham lived to be 175 years of age.

Genesis 17:5 Abram, but thy name shall be *A*
Genesis 18:11 Now *A* and Sarah were old and
Genesis 21:5 *A* was an hundred years old, when
Genesis 22:1 Some time later God tested *A* (NIV)
Genesis 22:7 And Isaac spake unto *A* his father
Genesis 22:8 *A* said, My son, God will provide
Genesis 22:13 *A* looked up and there in a thicket (NIV)
Genesis 25:7 *A* lived a hundred and seventy-five years (NIV)
Romans 4:3 *A* believed God, and it was credited (NIV)
Hebrews 11:8 By faith *A*, when he was called to go
Hebrews 11:17 By faith *A*, when he was tried

Abram (AY bruhm)
The name means "father is exalted." God called Abram to leave his home in Ur in the Chaldees and go to a place He would show him. Later God changed his name to Abraham.

Genesis 11:31 Terah took *A* his son, and Lot
Genesis 12:1 LORD had said unto *A*, Get thee
Genesis 12:4 *A* departed as the LORD had spoken
Genesis 13:8 *A* said unto Lot, Let there be no
Genesis 14:19 Blessed be *A* of the most high God
Genesis 17:1 when *A* was ninety-nine years old (NIV)

Absalom (AB suh luhm)
The name means "father of peace." His name did not describe who he really was. He was the third son of David, king of Israel. He rebelled against his father, attempted to become king in place of David, had his half-brother, Amnon, murdered, and was himself murdered by Joab, David's military commander.

2 Samuel 3:3 the third, *A*, the son of Maacah

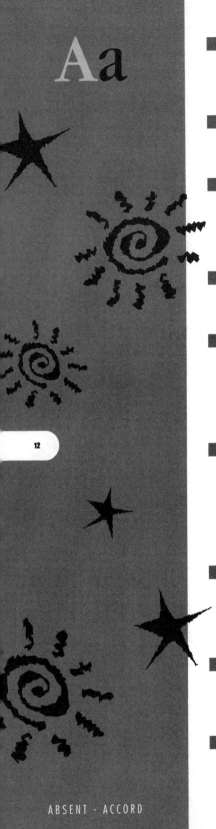

Aa

Absent (AB sent)
Away, gone, not here.

Genesis 31:49 when we are *a* one from another
Colossians 2:5 though I be *a* in the flesh

Abstain (AB stayn)
To give up, quit, refuse, go without.

1 Thessalonians 5:22 **A** from all appearance of evil

Abundance (uh BUN duns)
Plenty.

1 Kings 18:41 for there is a sound of *a* of rain
Mark 12:44 They did cast in of their *a*; but she
Luke 21:4 all these have of their *a* cast in

Abundant (uh BUN duhnt)
More than enough.

1 Peter 1:3 which according to his *a* mercy

Abundantly (uh BUN duhnt lee)
Plentiful.

Genesis 1:20 Let the waters bring forth *a* the
Exodus 1:7 were fruitful, and increased *a*, and
John 10:10 that they might have it more *a*
Ephesians 3:20 him that is able to do exceeding *a*

Acceptable (ak CEP tuh buhl)
To be good enough to earn honor or respect; pleasing.

Psalm 19:14 meditation of my heart, be *a* in thy sight,
Proverbs 10:32 lips of the righteous know what is *a*
Romans 12:1 living sacrifice, holy, *a* unto God
Romans 12:2 prove what is that good and *a*, and

Accepted (ak CEP tid)
Past tense of "accept." To accept is to receive, take, get.

Luke 4:24 No prophet is *a* in his own country
2 Corinthians 6:2 Behold, now is the *a* time

Access (AK sess)
To admit; an entry or way; to be able to come near.

Romans 5:2 By whom also we have *a* by faith
Ephesians 2:18 through him we both have *a* by one

Accord (uh KORD)
To agree; to go willingly; to be united in thought or purpose.

Acts 1:14 These all continued with one *a* in prayer

Acts 2:1 They were all with one *a* in one place
Acts 4:24 lifted up their voice to God with one *a*

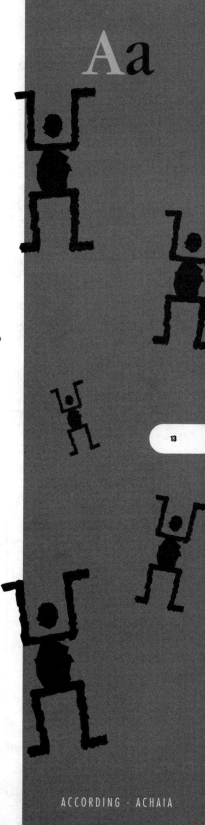

Aa

■ According (to) (uh KORD eeng)
To be in agreement with; to follow the rules of.

Genesis 6:22 did Noah; *a* to all that God commanded
Exodus 12:35 Israel did *a* to the word of Moses
Psalm 25:7 *a* to thy mercy remember thou me
Psalm 62:12 for thou renderest to every man *a*
Matthew 16:27 reward every man *a* to his works
Acts 11:29 every man *a* to his ability
2 Corinthians 9:7 Every man *a* as he purposeth
1 John 5:14 If we ask any thing *a* to his will, he

■ Account (uh COWNT)
Reason, cause; to explain, answer for.

Matthew 12:36 they shall give *a* thereof in the day
Romans 14:12 of us shall give *a* of himself to God

■ Accounted (uh COWNT id)
Past tense of "account." To think about, to study on.

Luke 22:24 which of them should be *a* the greatest
Galatians 3:6 and it was *a* to him for righteousness

■ Accusation (a kyoo ZAY shun)
To blame someone for doing wrong.

Matthew 27:37 his head his *a* written, THIS IS JESUS
Luke 6:7 that they might find an *a* against him
John 18:29 What *a* bring ye against this man

■ Accuse (a KYOOZ)
To blame or charge another with wrong doing.

Matthew 12:10 that they might *a* him
Luke 23:2 And they began to *a* him

■ Accused (a KYOOZD)
Past tense of "accuse."

Mark 15:3 The chief priests *a* him of many things
Luke 23:10 and scribes stood and vehemently *a* him

■ Accusers (a KYOOZ erz)
Those who blame others or bring charges against another person.

John 8:10 Woman, where are those thine *a*

■ Achaia (uh KAY yuh)
A part of southern Greece that was a Roman province. The capital of Achaia was Corinth (see

Aa

map on page 341).

Acts 18:27 When Apollos wanted to go to **A** (NIV)
Acts 19:21 he had passed through Macedonia and **A**
1 Thessalonians 1:7 that believe in Macedonia and **A**

■ **Acknowledge (ak NALL idj)**
To accept, admit, recognize, give an answer to.

Psalm 51:3 For I **a** my transgressions: and
Proverbs 3:6 In all thy ways **a** him, and he shall

■ **Acknowledged (ak NALL idjd)**
Past tense of "acknowledge."

Psalm 32:5 I **a** my sin unto thee, and mine iniquity

■ **Acquainted (uh QYAYNT id)**
Past tense of "acquaint." To get to know, to become familiar with.

Psalm 139:3 and art **a** with all my ways
Isaiah 53:3 man of sorrows, and **a** with grief

■ **Acts (AKTS)**
The things one does; deeds.

Deuteronomy 11:7 have seen all the great **a** of the LORD
Psalm 106:2 Who can utter the mighty **a** of the LORD
Psalm 145:4 and shall declare thy mighty **a**
Psalm 150:2 Praise him for his mighty **a**

■ **Acts, Book of (AKTS)**
The fifth book in the New Testament and the only book in the division of History. The author is Dr. Luke, who also wrote the third Gospel by his name. Where the book of Luke tells about the works of Jesus, Acts tells about the works of the apostles as they told the world about Jesus. Acts has been called the "history of the early church" because it tells how the early church grew and spread. Some main people in Acts were Peter, Paul, Silas, Barnabas, and Timothy, to name a few.

■ **Adam (AD uhm)**
The name means "man." The first man, created in God's image. Adam, and Eve, his wife, chose to disobey God and they had to leave the Garden of Eden.

Genesis 2:19 and brought them unto **A** to see
Genesis 2:20 And **A** gave names to all cattle, and to
Genesis 3:8 And **A** and his wife hid themselves
Genesis 3:20 **A** called his wife's name Eve
Genesis 5:5 days that **A** lived were nine hundred and

Adam

Aa

Added (AD uhd)
Make to be more; in addition to.

Matthew 6:33 all these things shall be *a* unto you
Luke 12:31 all these things shall be *a* unto you
Acts 2:41 and the same day there were *a* unto them
Acts 2:47 The Lord *a* to the church daily such
Acts 11:24 and much people was *a* unto the Lord

Adjure (a JYOOR)
To beg, plead, order, or charge a person to give the right facts. To be under an oath to tell the truth.

Matthew 26:63 I *a* thee by the living God, that thou
Mark 5:7 I *a* thee by God, that thou torment me not

Adorn (uh DORN)
To make beautiful, to decorate.

1 Timothy 2:9 that women *a* themselves in modest

Adultery (uh DUHL tur ee)
The act of a married person being unfaithful to one's spouse (wife or husband). Worshiping idols or other gods is being unfaithful to God. This is called "spiritual adultery."

Exodus 20:14 Thou shalt not commit *a*

Advantaged (ad VAN tijd)
Past tense of "advantage." To be able to benefit from something or to gain from it.

Luke 9:25 What is a man *a*, if he gain the whole world

Adversity (ad VUHR sih tee)
Trouble, difficult times, great need.

Proverbs 17:17 and a brother is born for *a*

Advice (ad VIGHS)
Counsel, warning, or suggestions about a problem or concern.

1 Samuel 25:33 And blessed by thy *a*, and blessed be
Proverbs 12:15 but a wise man listens to *a* (NIV)
Proverbs 13:10 wisdom is found in those who take *a* (NIV)
Proverbs 19:20 Listen to *a* and accept instruction (NIV)
Proverbs 20:18 Make plans by seeking *a* (NIV)

Advise (ad VIGHZ)
To guide, suggest, to warn ahead of time.

Acts 5:38 in the present case I *a* you: Leave (NIV)

Affection (uh FEK shun)
A fondness for, warm feelings toward, to like.

Colossians 3:2 Set your *a* on things above

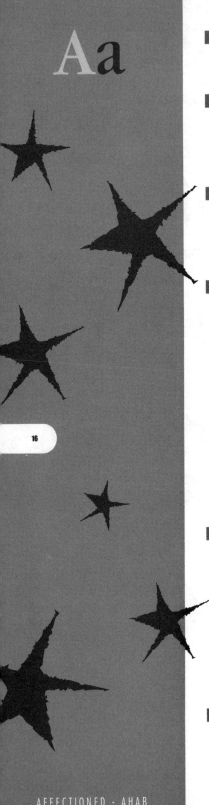

Aa

Affectioned (uh FEK shund)
Past tense of "affection."

Romans 12:10 Be kindly *a* one to another

Afflicted (uh FLIK tuhd)
Past tense of "afflict." To have trouble, be in distress or misery; to suffer.

Psalm 82:3 fatherless: do justice to the *a* and needy
Isaiah 53:7 He was oppressed, and he was *a*

Affliction (uh FLIK shun)
Being in trouble; having suffering or pain.

Exodus 3:7 I have surely seen the *a* of my people
Acts 7:34 I have seen the *a* of my people
Hebrews 11:25 Choosing rather to suffer *a* with the

Afraid (uh FRAYD)
To be scared, full of fear.

Genesis 3:10 thy voice in the garden, and I was *a*
Genesis 26:24 Do not be *a*, for I am with you (NIV)
Deuteronomy 1:21 Do not be *a*; do not be discouraged (NIV)
1 Samuel 3:15 He was *a* to tell Eli (NIV)
Psalm 27:1 my life; of whom shall I be *a*
Psalm 56:3 What time I am *a*, I will trust in thee
Psalm 56:11 I will not be *a* what man can do unto
Proverbs 3:24 thou liest down, thou shalt not be *a*
Isaiah 12:2 I will trust, and not be *a*
Matthew 14:27 Be of good cheer; it is I; be not *a*
Matthew 28:10 Jesus said unto them, Be not *a*
Luke 2:9 round about them: and they were sore *a*
John 14:27 heart be troubled, neither let it be *a*

Agrippa (uh GRIP uh)
His great-grandfather was Herod the Great. Agrippa was the Jewish king who listened to Paul and was almost persuaded to become a Christian. Agrippa listened to Paul's argument about the charges some Jews had made that he had been preaching false teachings. Agrippa found Paul innocent.

Acts 25:13 And after certain days king **A** and
Acts 26:1 Then **A** said unto Paul, Thou art
Acts 26:28 **A** said unto Paul, Almost thou persuadest

Ahab (AY hab)
The name means "father's brother." A powerful and evil king who married Jezebel, a woman from Phoenicia. Ahab ruled Israel for 22 years. His wife brought Baal worship to the country

16

and Ahab worshiped the idol. He also worshiped God. He would not stand up for the right things nor would he encourage the Israelites to worship God only. He was warned on many occasions by the prophets, mainly Elijah. He was present at the contest on Mount Carmel with Elijah and the prophets of Baal.

1 Kings 16:30 **A** the son of Omri did evil in the sight
1 Kings 16:33 **A** did more to provoke the LORD God of
1 Kings 18:41 Elijah said unto **A**, Get thee up
1 Kings 18:42 **A** went up to eat and drink
1 Kings 18:44 **A**,, Prepare thy chariot, and get thee
1 Kings 18:45 And **A** rode, and went to Jezreel
1 Kings 19:1 **A** told Jezebel all that Elijah had
1 Kings 21:16 **A** heard that Naboth was dead

Ahasuerus (uh haz-yoo EHR uhs)
Another name for him was Xerxes. He was a Persian king who chose Esther, a young, beautiful Jewish woman, as his queen.

Esther 1:1 it came to pass in the days of **A**
Esther 2:16 So Esther was taken unto king **A**
Esther 3:1 After these things did king **A** promote
Esther 3:12 in the name of King **A** was it written
Esther 7:5 king **A** answered and said unto Esther

Ahaz (AY haz)
The name means "he has grasped." He was a wicked king of Judah who encouraged idol worship. He refused to listen to the warnings and advice of the prophet, Elisha.

2 Kings 15:38 **A** his son reigned in his stead
2 Kings 16:2 Twenty years old was **A** when he

Alabaster (AL uh bas tuhr)
A smooth stone, creamy in color. It is easily carved, and small containers or jars could be made from it. These bottles would hold perfumes and precious ointments.

Matthew 26:7 an **a** box of very precious ointment
Mark 14:3 woman having an **a** box of ointment
Luke 7:37 brought an **a** box of ointment

Alexandria (al egg ZAN drih uh)
A city in Egypt which was the capital of Egypt (see map on page 341). It was built by Alexander the Great in 330 B.C. The city was located on the west side of the Nile delta near the Mediterranean Sea. Students came from all over the known world to study in the schools of the

Aa

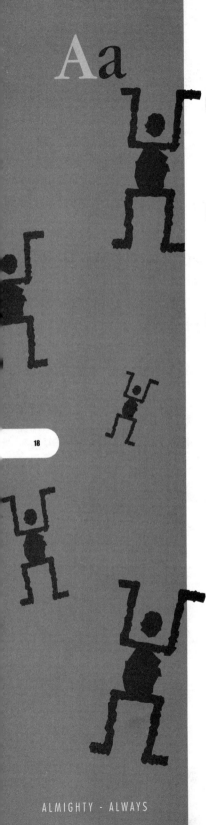

Aa

city. It was famous for its museums, and a library that contained over 500,000 books.

Acts 18:24 A certain Jew named Apollos, born at **A**

■ Almighty (ahl MIH tee)
A name for God. To be mighty and powerful in all things.

Genesis 35:11 God said unto him, I am God **A**
Psalm 91:1 shall abide under the shadow of the **A**
Revelation 4:8 Holy, holy, holy, Lord God **A**

■ Alms (AHLMZ)
An offering of money or possessions given to help the poor.

Matthew 6:1 heed that ye do not your **a** before men
Matthew 6:3 But when thou doest **a**, let not
Matthew 6:4 That thy **a** may be in secret, and

■ Alphaeus (al FEE uhs)
He was the father of the apostle, James.

Matthew 10:3 James the son of **A**, and Thaddaeus
Mark 3:18 and Thomas, and James the son of **A**
Luke 6:15 James the son of **A**, and Simon called
Acts 1:13 James the son of **A**, and Simon Zelotes

■ Altar (ALL tuhr)
A place where animal sacrifices were made to God. Some altars were merely piles of stones. Others were built with specific directions from God. Read Exodus 27:1-8 to learn about one of the altars. A modern day altar might be a table or a place that is raised, like a platform.

Genesis 8:20 Noah builded an **a** unto the LORD
Exodus 17:15 And Moses built an **a**, and called it
1 Samuel 14:35 And Saul built an **a** unto the LORD
1 Kings 18:30 And he repaired the **a** of the LORD
Matthew 5:23 bring thy gift to the **a**
Acts 17:23 I found an **a** with this inscription

■ Always (AHL wayz)
Constantly, forever.

Psalm 16:8 I have set the LORD **a** before me
Proverbs 28:14 Happy is the man that feareth **a**
Matthew 28:20 and, lo, I am with you **a**
Philippians 4:4 Rejoice in the Lord **a**
Colossians 4:6 Let your speech be **a** with grace
1 Corinthians 1:4 I thank my God **a** on your behalf
1 Thessalonians 1:2 We give thanks to God **a** for
1 Peter 3:15 be ready **a** to give an answer to

Ambassadors (am BASS uh dorz)
To work in place of another so as to represent that person.

2 Corinthians 5:20 Now then we are *a* for Christ

Amos, Book of (AY muhs)
The name means "a load," or "burden bearer." He was a shepherd who lived and farmed in a little village named Tckoa, south of Bethlehem, in Judah. He prophesied in Israel about 750 B.C., mainly to the wealthy because they got their wealth from the poor by being dishonest. They also worshiped other gods. Amos' message was for them to repent, put away the false gods, and turn back to God. He also stressed that unless they obeyed God, they would face God's judgment. His book is the third book of the division, Minor Prophets, in the Old Testament.

Amram (AM ram)
His name means "exalted people." The name of his wife was Jochebed and his children were Moses, Aaron, and Miriam.

Exodus 6:20 **A** married his father's sister Jochebed (NIV)
Numbers 26:59 and she bare unto **A** Aaron and Moses

Ananias (an uh NIGH uhs)
The name means "Yahweh has dealt graciously." Three different men with this name are mentioned in the New Testament.
1. A Christian who lied to Peter and the Holy Spirit about the money he received when he sold a certain piece of property. When Peter told him about the lie, he died immediately. Later, his wife came in and told the same lie and she died quickly, too.

Acts 5:1 But a certain man named **A**, with Sapphira
Acts 5:3 **A**, why hath Satan filled thine heart to lie
Acts 5:5 **A** hearing these words fell down, and

2. A man in Damascus whom God used to help Paul receive his sight. He was a disciple of Christ who obeyed God even though he was afraid.

Acts 9:10 a certain disciple at Damascus, named **A**
Acts 9:13 Then **A** answered, Lord, I have heard
Acts 9:17 **A** went his way, and entered into the house

3. The high priest who questioned Paul, trying to get him to shut up and not say any more about Jesus. Paul had been accused of trying to

Amos

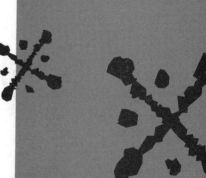

19

Aa

cause the people to rebel against the Roman government. Ananias was interested in the charges because he wanted to keep the Roman officials from becoming upset at him.

Acts 23:2 **A** commanded them that stood by him to smite
Acts 24:1 And after five days **A** the high priest

Andrew (AN droo)
One of the twelve disciples who was first a disciple of John the Baptist. He brought his brother, Simon Peter, to hear Jesus. His home was in Bethsaida, a little town on the Sea of Galilee.

Matthew 4:18 Simon called Peter, and **A** his brother
Matthew 10:2 who is called Peter, and **A** his brother
Mark 3:18 And **A**, and Philip, and Bartholomew
Luke 6:14 and **A**, his brother, James and John,
John 6:8 **A**, Simon Peter's brother, saith unto him
John 12:22 Philip cometh and telleth **A**

Angel (AYN juhl)
A heavenly being whom God created. Angels serve on earth by bringing messages from God to people. They also serve God in heaven. No one knows for sure what they look like although there are some descriptions of angels in the Bible.

Exodus 3:2 the **a** of the LORD appeared unto him
Judges 6:11 And there came an **a** of the LORD, and
1 Kings 19:5 behold, then an **a** touched him, and
Matthew 1:20 behold, the **a** of the Lord appeared
Luke 1:13 But the **a** said unto him, Fear not
Luke 1:28 the **a** came in unto her, and said
Luke 2:10 And the **a** said unto them, Fear not
Luke 2:13 there was with the **a** a multitude

Angels (AYN juhlz)
Plural for "angel."

Psalm 8:5 made him a little lower than the **a**
Psalm 91:11 he shall give his **a** charge over thee
Hebrews 13:2 some have entertained **a** unawares

Anger (AYNG uhr)
To feel rage or fury, to be greatly annoyed or bothered.

Psalm 37:8 Cease from **a** come and forsake wrath
Psalm 103:8 merciful and gracious, slow to **a**
Proverbs 15:1 but a harsh word stirs up **a** (NIV)
Proverbs 16:32 He that is slow to **a** is better than
Jonah 4:2 gracious God, and merciful, slow to **a**
Nahum 1:3 The LORD is slow to **a**, and great
Colossians 3:21 provoke not your children to **a**

Angry (AYNG ree)
To show anger by words or action; to be cross or mad.

Proverbs 22:24 Make no friendship with an *a* man
Proverbs 29:22 An *a* man stirreth up strife, and
Matthew 5:22 whosoever is *a* with his brother
Ephesians 4:26 Be ye *a*, and sin not

Anna (AN uh)
The name means "grace." A woman prophet (prophetess) who recognized the baby, Jesus, as the long awaited Messiah. She was eighty-four years old when she saw Jesus. She had been a widow for a long time, having been married only seven years before her husband died. She spent her days in the Temple praying to, and worshiping, God.

Luke 2:36 there was one *A*, a prophetess

Annas (AN uhs)
The name means "merciful." He had been a high priest and still had a lot of power during Jesus' ministry. He was one of the people who heard the charges against Jesus before Jesus was crucified. It was this same Annas who questioned Peter and other church leaders after Pentecost.

Luke 3:2 *A* and Caiaphas being the high priests
John 18:13 And led him away to *A* first
John 18:24 Now *A* had sent him bound unto
Acts 4:6 And *A* the high priest, and Caiaphas,

Anoint (uh NOYNT)
To bless or choose. To pour oil on was a sign of giving a person a special appointment. David was anointed by Samuel, the prophet, to show he would become king after King Saul. Priests who would serve God in the tabernacle were also anointed.

Exodus 30:30 And thou shalt *a* Aaron and his sons
1 Samuel 15:1 The LORD sent me to *a* thee to be king
1 Samuel 16:3 thou shalt *a* unto me him whom I name
1 Samuel 16:12 And the LORD said, Arise, *a* him
Luke 7:46 My head with oil thou didst not *a*

Anoint

Anointest (uh NOYNT ist)
An old way of expressing that something is being done. Example: "you anoint."

Psalm 23:5 thou *a* my head with oil; my cup
Psalm 23:5 You *a* my head with oil; my cup (NIV)

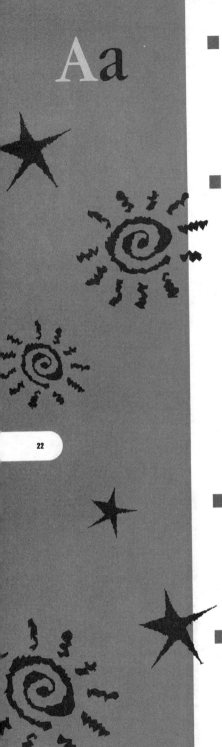

Aa

Answer (AN ser)
To give a reply.

Psalm 27:7 have mercy also upon me, and ***a*** me
Psalm 91:15 call upon me, and I will ***a*** him
Proverbs 15:1 A soft ***a*** turneth away wrath
Jeremiah 33:3 Call unto me, and I will ***a*** thee
Colossians 4:6 know how ye ought to ***a*** every man
1 Peter 3:15 be ready always to give an ***a*** to

Antioch (AN tih ahk)
The name of two cities during New Testament times where Jews lived and were faithfully worshiping God. **1.** A city in Syria, the place where Jesus' followers were first called Christians (see map on page 341). Paul and Barnabas, the first missionaries, were sent from this city.

Acts 11:22 Barnabas, that he should go as far as ***A***
Acts 11:26 were called Christians first in ***A***
Acts 15:35 Paul also and Barnabas continued in ***A***

2. A city in Pisidia, an area in Galatia, in central Asia Minor (now southwestern Turkey). Paul preached here, began a church, and was persecuted here (see map on page 341). The book of Galatians in the New Testament was written to these Christians.

Acts 13:14 Perga, they came to ***A*** in Pisidia
Acts 14:19 certain Jews from ***A*** and Iconium
2 Timothy 3:11 which came unto me at ***A***

Apollos (uh PAHL uhs)
The name means "destroyer." A Christian Jew from the city of Alexandria in Egypt. He was a good teacher and many people came to know Jesus as Savior because of him. Aquila and Priscilla taught him more about Jesus so he could become a better teacher.

Acts 18:24 A certain Jew named ***A***, born at Alexandria

Apostle (uh PAHS uhl)
A messenger sent to give a message for someone else. A disciple is one who learns. When he begins to tell what he has learned, he becomes an apostle. Jesus' disciples learned from Him and became His apostles when they took the message of salvation to others.

1 Corinthians 1:1 Paul, called to be an ***A*** of Jesus
Ephesians 1:1 Paul, an ***A*** of Jesus Christ

22

Apostles (uh PAHS uhlz)
Plural for "apostle."

Matthew 10:2 the names of the twelve *a* are
Luke 6:13 twelve, whom also he named *a*
Luke 17:5 the *a* said unto the Lord
Acts 2:43 signs were done by the *a*
1 Corinthians 12:29 Are all *a*? Are all prophets
Ephesians 4:11 And he gave some, *a*; and some

Appear (uh PIR)
To come forward, to arrive.

Genesis 1:9 and let the dry land *a*: and it was so
1 Samuel 1:22 bring him, that he may *a* before the LORD
2 Corinthians 5:10 we must all *a* before the judgment

Appearance (uh PIR uhns)
The way a thing looks; attitude (the way one feels about something).

Numbers 9:16 day, and the *a* of fire by night
1 Samuel 16:7 man looketh on the outward *a*
1 Thessalonians 5:22 Abstain from all *a* of evil

Apple (A puhl)
A tasty fruit which grows on trees. "Apple of the eye" refers to something that is very dear or valuable.

Psalm 17:8 Keep me as the *a* of the eye
Proverbs 7:2 my law as the *a* of thine eye

Apply (uh PLIGH)
To use; to pay attention (as when studying).

Proverbs 2:2 and *a* thine heart to understanding
Proverbs 22:17 and *a* thine heart unto my knowledge
Proverbs 23:12 **A** thine heart unto instruction

Appointed (uh POYN tid)
Past tense of "appoint." Chosen or named.

Psalm 104:19 He *a* the moon for seasons
Hebrews 9:27 it is *a* unto men once to die

Approved (uh PRUVD)
Past tense of "approve." Tested, tried, proven.

2 Timothy 2:15 Study to show thyself *a* unto God

Aquila (uh KWIL uh)
A friend of Paul. He was the husband of Priscilla. Aquila made tents. He and his wife helped Apollos understand about Jesus.

Acts 18:2 found a certain Jew named **A**

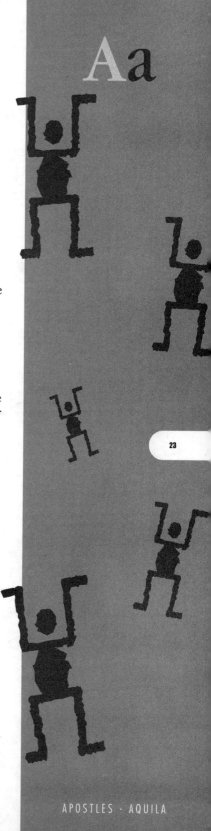

Aa

23

Aa

Acts 18:26 whom when **A** and Priscilla had heard

Ararat (EHR uh rat)
A region in western Asia with many mountains, some as high as 17,000 feet above sea level. The area where the Bible states that the ark rested after the flood.

Genesis 8:4 of the month, upon the mountains of **A**

Areopagus (ehr ih AHP uh guhs)
A rocky hill called Mars' Hill, located in Athens, Greece. A council that met in this place called themselves the Areopagus. It was to this group that Paul explained who the Unknown God was that the Greeks were worshiping.

Acts 17:19 took him, and brought him unto **A**

Ashamed (uh SHAYMD)
To feel embarrassment or guilt; to be uneasy.

Psalm 25:20 let me not be **a**; for I put my trust
Psalm 31:1 I put my trust; let me never be **a**
Romans 1:16 For I am not **a** of the gospel of
Romans 9:33 believeth on him shall not be **a**
2 Timothy 2:15 workman that needed not to be **a**

Astonished (uh STAHN isht)
Past tense of "astonish." To be surprised with no warning.

Matthew 7:28 the people were **a** at his doctrine
Mark 10:24 the disciples were **a** at his words
Luke 2:47 all that heard him were **a**

Astray (uh STRAY)
Off, wrong.

Isaiah 53:6 All we like sheep have gone **a**

Augustus (aw GUHS tuhs)
The name means "reverend." A Roman emperor, named Caesar Augustus, who ruled at the time of Jesus' birth. Augustus was also a title for other Roman rulers. When Paul was on trial for preaching about Jesus, he said he wanted to have his case brought before Caesar Augustus, in Rome. At that time, Nero was the Roman ruler.

Luke 2:1 There went out a decree from Caesar **A**
Acts 25:21 to be reserved unto the hearing of **A**
Acts 25:25 he himself hath appealed to **A**

Author (AW thur)
One who creates or writes.

1 Corinthians 14:33 God is not the *a* of confusion
Hebrews 5:9 he became the *a* of eternal salvation
Hebrews 12:2 Jesus, the *a* and perfecter of our faith (NIV)

Awe (AW)
To have fear, reverence (worship), or wonder, or a mixture of all three at the same time.

Psalm 4:4 Stand in *a*, and sin not
Psalm 33:8 inhabitants of the world stand in *a*
Psalm 119:161 my heart standeth in *a* of thy word

Baal (BAY uhl)
A god worshiped by the Canaanites. They thought the god provided fruitfulness to the land. The Israelites also worshiped Baal, causing God much distress because of the way the god was worshiped.

1 Kings 18:25 Elijah said to the prophets of *B*
2 Kings 10:18 Ahab served *B* a little; but Jehu
2 Kings 23:4 all the vessels that were made for *B*
Jeremiah 23:27 fathers have forgotten my name for *B*

Babes (BAYBZ)
Plural of "babe." A baby or infant.

1 Peter 2:2 As newborn *b*, desire the sincere milk

Babylon (BAB ih lahn)
The capital city of Babylonia. Babylon is situated on the Euphrates River in southern Mesopotamia (see map on page 339). It is about 50 miles south of the modern city of Baghdad in Iraq. The Babylonians were considered enemies of Judah and Israel during ancient times. Judah was ruled by Babylon at one time. In 586 B.C., Jerusalem was destroyed by Babylon.

2 Kings 24:1 Nebuchadnezzar King of *B* came up
2 Kings 24:15 into captivity from Jerusalem to *B*
1 Chronicles 9:1 away to *B* for their transgressions
Ezra 7:6 This Ezra went up from *B*
Nehemiah 13:6 thirtieth year of Artaxerxes king of *B*
Daniel 1:1 came Nebuchadnezzar king of *B*
Daniel 2:24 Destroy not the wise men of *B*

Banner (BAN uhr)
A special flag or streamer.

Bb

Baptize

Exodus 17:15 altar and called it The LORD is my **B** (NIV)
Numbers 2:2 each man under his standard with the **b** (NIV)
Psalm 60:4 has given a **b** to them that fear thee

■ Banners (BAN uhrz)
Plural of "banner."

Psalm 20:5 name of our God will we set up our **b**

■ Baptism (BAP tiz uhm)
A person is immersed (or dipped) into water. This is like a person who has died and has been buried. Baptism also shows that the person has turned away from the way he used to live. When he comes out of the water, it is like a dead person coming up from a grave. This shows he has new life that will last forever. Every person will die at some time. Baptism is also a picture that those who believe in Jesus will be resurrected (raised) from the grave at a future time. A person is not saved by being baptized. Baptism shows he has received the salvation of Jesus and that he is being obedient to Christ.

Romans 6:4 we are buried with him by **b**

■ Baptist (BAP tist)
This term, "Baptist," was given to John, the cousin of Jesus, because he baptized those who professed belief in the Jesus about whom he preached.

Matthew 3:1 In those days came John the **B**
Matthew 16:14 some say thou art John the **B**
Mark 6:14 he said, That John the **B** was risen
Luke 7:20 John the **B** hath sent us unto thee

■ Baptize (BAP tighz)
A ceremony where a person is dipped in water or water is sprinkled on him (See "Baptism" above).

Matthew 3:11 He will **b** you with the Holy Spirit (NIV)
Luke 3:16 He will **b** you with the Holy Spirit (NIV)
John 1:26 saying, I **b** with water: but there

■ Barabbas (buh RAB uhs)
He was a murderer and robber who had been jailed before Jesus' arrest and crucifixion. The crowd, who was angry about the work Jesus had done, asked Pilate to release Barabbas instead of Jesus.

Matthew 27:16 a notable prisoner, called **B**
Matthew 27:26 Then released he **B** unto them
Luke 23:18 this man, and release unto us **B**
John 18:40 Not this man, but **B**. Now **B** was

Barnabas (BAHR nuh buhs)

The name means "son of encouragement." His father was named Levi. Barnabas gave generously and saw good in others. He became a friend to Saul and introduced Saul to the Jerusalem believers. Later he went with Paul on some of his missionary journeys.

Acts 4:36 Joses, who by the apostles was named **B**
Acts 9:27 **B** took him and brought him to the apostles
Acts 13:46 Then Paul and **B** waxed bold, and said
Acts 14:14 when the apostles, **B** and Paul heard
Acts 15:35 Paul also, and **B**, continued in Antioch

Bartholomew (bahr THAHL uh myoo)

One of the twelve disciples of Jesus. Nothing else is known about him. He might have had another name, Nathanael. Some Bible students think his name was Nathanael Bartholomew.

Matthew 10:3 Philip and **B**; Thomas and Matthew
Mark 3:18 Andrew, and Philip, and **B**
Luke 6:14 James and John, Philip and **B**
Acts 1:13 Andrew, Philip, and Thomas, **B**

Bartimaeus (BAHR tih MEE uhs)

He was a blind beggar who sat on the roadside near Jericho. He was waiting for Jesus to come by. When he knew Jesus was near, Bartimaeus called out for Jesus to have pity on him. Jesus healed him of his blindness and he followed Jesus.

Mark 10:46 blind **B**, son of Timaeus, sat by

Baruch (BAY rook)

He was the scribe who wrote for Jeremiah. He was also the friend of Jeremiah. His name means "blessed." After he wrote down the words Jeremiah dictated, Baruch read them to the counselors of King Jehoakim. The king burned the scroll as it was read to him. Then God told Jeremiah to write the words again and to add more to them. Baruch wrote all the words Jeremiah spoke.

Jeremiah 36:4 Jeremiah called **B** the son of Neriah
Jeremiah 36:8 **B** the son of Neriah did according to
Jeremiah 36:10 Then read **B** in the book the words
Jeremiah 36:32 another roll, and gave it to **B**

Battle (BAA tuhl)

An argument, fight, or war.

Psalm 24:8 and mighty, the LORD mighty in **b**

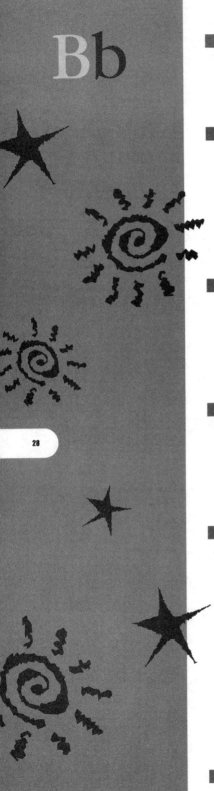

Bb

Beautiful (BYOO tih fuhl)
Fair, lovely, pretty. Something one enjoys looking at.

Genesis 29:17 but Rachel was *b* and well-favoured
Ecclesiastes 3:11 hath made every thing *b* in his

Beer-sheba (bee ehr-SHEE buh)
A Canaanite city located in the southern part of Canaan (see map on page 336). People traveling from Egypt into Canaan and areas north passed through Beer-sheba. This city was important to the Israelites when they settled Canaan after they had left Egypt.

Genesis 21:33 Abraham planted a grove in *B*
1 Kings 19:3 went for his life, and came to *B*

Beginning (bee GHIN eeng)
The place or time where something starts.

Genesis 1:1 In the *b* God created the heaven
Psalm 111:10 fear of the LORD is the *b* of wisdom
Psalm 119:160 Thy word is true from the *b*
Proverbs 1:7 fear of the LORD is the *b* of
Revelation 1:8 I am Alpha and Omega, the *b* and

Begotten (bee GAH tuhn)
A form of the word "beget." Something that is created and is the only one of its kind. A thing that is truly special.

John 3:16 that he gave his only *b* Son, that
John 3:18 in the name of the only *b* Son of God
1 John 4:9 God sent his only *b* Son into the

Believe (bee LEEV)
To trust that something is true; to have faith in something. When a person believes that Jesus is God's Son, he wants to obey Him and do as He directs. To believe in Jesus means you trust Him to give you eternal life. Then you want to live like Him.

Matthew 9:28 *B* ye that I am able to do this
Mark 1:15 Repent ye, and *b* the gospel
Mark 5:36 Be not afraid, only *b*
Mark 9:24 and said with tears, Lord I *b*
Acts 8:37 I *b* that Jesus Christ is the Son of
Acts 16:31 *B* on the Lord Jesus Christ, and
Romans 10:9 shalt *b* in thine heart that God
Romans 10:14 how shall they *b* in him of whom

Believeth (bee LEEV ith)
The old way of writing or saying "believes," the

plural for "believe."

Mark 16:16 He that **b** and is baptized shall be
John 3:16 whosoever **b** in him should not perish
John 3:18 He that **b** on him is not condemned
John 11:25 he that **b** in me, though he were
Romans 10:11 whosoever **b** on him shall not be
1 Corinthians 13:7 **b** all things, hopeth all
1 John 5:1 whosoever **b** that Jesus is the Christ

Belteshazzar (bel tih SHAZ uhr)

The name given to Daniel by King Nebuchadnezzar of Babylon. Belteshazzar meant "may he protect his life," or "protect the king's life." Bel was the name of a Babylonian god but it was the LORD God of Israel who protected Daniel.

Daniel 1:7 he gave unto Daniel the name of **B**
Daniel 4:19 Then Daniel, whose name was **B**
Daniel 5:12 same Daniel, whom the king named **B**
Daniel 10:1 unto Daniel, whose name was called **B**

Benjamin (BEN juh min)

The youngest son of Jacob and the second son of Rachel, Jacob's favorite wife. The name Benjamin means "son of the right hand." The smallest of the twelve tribes of Israel was Benjamin. The first king of Israel, Saul, was from this tribe, as was the apostle Paul.

Genesis 35:18 his father called him **B**
Genesis 35:24 sons of Rachel; Joseph, and **B**
Genesis 42:4 **B**, Joseph's brother, Jacob sent not
Genesis 43:16 when Joseph saw **B** with them
Genesis 45:14 threw his arms around his brother **B** (NIV)
Philippians 3:5 stock of Israel, of the tribe of **B**

Berea (buh REE uh)

The name means "place of many waters." The city is located in Macedonia, now a part of northern Greece (see map on page 341). This is the city to which Paul and Silas fled when a riot occurred in Thessalonica. Some of the Jews in Thessalonica became angry at Paul's preaching.

Acts 17:10 Paul and Silas by night unto **B**
Acts 17:13 word of God was preached of Paul at **B**

Beseech (bee SEECH)

To ask or beg.

Numbers 12:13 Heal her now, O God, I **b** thee
Nehemiah 1:5 I **b** thee, O LORD God of heaven
Psalm 116:4 O LORD, I **b** thee, deliver my soul

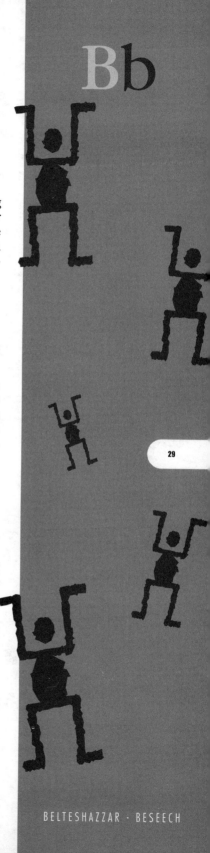

Bb

29

BELTESHAZZAR · BESEECH

Romans 12:1 | *b* you therefore, brethren, by
Ephesians 4:1 Lord, *b* you that ye walk worthy

■ Bethany (BETH uh nih)

A village located about two miles south and east of Jerusalem (see map on page 340). It is situated on the eastern part of the Mount of Olives. Bethany means "house of figs." It was in this village where Jesus spent a lot of time with his friends, Lazarus, Mary, and Martha, when he was in the area of Jerusalem.

Matthew 21:17 and went out of the city unto *B*
Matthew 26:6 Now when Jesus was in *B*
Mark 11:1 and *B*, at the mount of Olives
Mark 11:11 he went out unto *B* with the twelve
Mark 14:3 in *B* in the house of Simon the
Luke 24:50 he led them out as far as to *B*
John 11:1 man was sick, named Lazarus, of *B*
John 11:18 Now *B* was nigh unto Jerusalem

■ Bethel (BETH-uhl)

The name means "house of God." The village was begun in this place because of numerous springs, making it possible to grow crops. Bethel was about eleven or twelve miles north of Jerusalem, just over the border when the northern kingdom broke off from Judah (see map on page 340). Jerusalem was the main place of worship for the Israelites, but King Jereboam built a temple in Bethel so the people would not have to go to Jerusalem to worship.

Genesis 28:19 called the name of that place *B*
Genesis 35:1 Jacob, Arise, go up to *B*, and dwell
2 Kings 2:2 for the LORD hath sent me to *B*

■ Bethesda (buh THEZ duh)

The name means "house of mercy." It is spelled "Beth-zatha" in some of the older New Testament writings. A pool in Jerusalem was named Bethesda. It was believed that an angel stirred the waters. After the waters had been stirred, the first person into the waters would be healed. It was at this pool where Jesus healed the man who had been crippled for thirty-eight years.

John 5:2 which is called in the Hebrew tongue *B*

■ Bethlehem (BETH lih hem)

The name means "house of bread." The city was located about five miles to the south and west of Jerusalem (see map on page 340). David and Jesus were both born in Bethlehem. David was

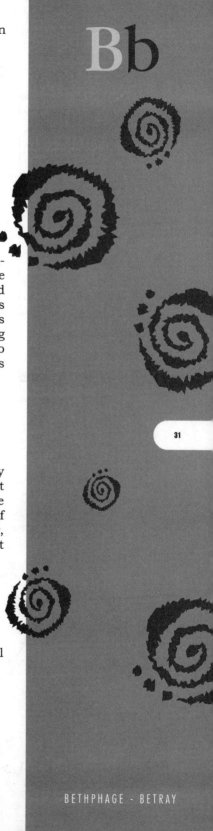

also anointed there. Bethlehem became known as the "city of David."

Genesis 35:19 way to Ephrath, which is **B**
Ruth 1:19 they two went until they came to **B**
Ruth 2:4 behold, Boaz came from **B**
1 Samuel 20:6 that he might run to **B** his city
2 Samuel 23:15 drink of the water of the well of **B**
Micah 5:2 But thou, **B** Ephratah, though thou be
Matthew 2:1 Now when Jesus was born in **B**
Matthew 2:5 said unto him, In **B** of Judaea
Matthew 2:8 And he sent them to **B**, and said
Luke 2:4 city of David, which is called **B**
Luke 2:15 Let us now go even unto **B**

Bethphage (BETH fuh jee)
The name means "house of unripe figs." A village located close by Bethany, on the east side of the mount of Olives. It lies just off the road that comes into Jerusalem from Jericho. It was in this village where Jesus told two disciples they would find a colt tied. They were to bring the colt to Jesus because he would ride into Jerusalem on its back. This would be called His "triumphal entry."

Matthew 21:1 Jerusalem and were come to **B**
Mark 11:1 nigh to Jerusalem, unto **B** and
Luke 19:29 when he was come nigh to **B**

Bethsaida (beth-SAY ih duh)
The name means "house of fish." This village lay on the northeast shore of the Sea of Galilee, not far from where the Jordan River flows into the Sea of Galilee (see map on page 340). Three of Jesus' disciples were from Bethsaida: Peter, Andrew, and Philip. It was near this village that Jesus fed the 5,000 with the loaves and fishes.

Mark 6:45 go to the other side before unto **B**
Mark 8:22 And he cometh to **B**; and they
John 1:44 Now Philip was of **B**, the city of

Betray (be TRAY)
To go against one's word to keep a secret; to sell out another.

Matthew 26:16 he sought opportunity to **b** him
Matthew 26:21 that one of you shall **b** me
Matthew 26:46 he is at hand that doth **b** me
Mark 14:10 chief priests, to **b** him unto them
Mark 14:11 sought how he might conveniently **b** him
Luke 22:6 and sought opportunity to **b** him
John 13:2 Judas Iscariot, Simon's son, to **b** him

31

Bb

Birthright

John 13:11 For he knew who should **b** him
John 13:21 that one of you shall **b** me

■ Betrayed (be TRAYD)
Past tense of "betray."

Matthew 10:4 and Judas Iscariot, who also **b** him
Matthew 26:2 Son of man is **b** to be crucified
Matthew 26:45 Son of man is **b** into the hands
Mark 3:19 And Judas Iscariot, which also **b** him
Mark 14:44 he that **b** him had given them a token

■ Birthright (BURTH right)
The firstborn son in a family was given certain rights because he was born first in the family. One of the privileges was receiving a larger part of all that his father owned. He would also receive a special blessing from the father. Esau traded his birthright to his brother, Jacob, for a bowl of stew.

Genesis 25:31 Sell me this day thy **b**
Genesis 25:32 What profit shall this **b** do to me
Genesis 25:33 and he sold his **b** unto Jacob
Genesis 27:36 he took away my **b**

■ Blaspheme (blass FEEM)
To speak in a way that does not show respect or reverence to God or Jesus; to say things that are not true about God or Jesus. Cursing God or Jesus or using their names in a bad way is to blaspheme Them.

Mark 3:28 blasphemies wherewith soever they shall **b**
Mark 3:29 he that shall **b** against the Holy Ghost

■ Blasphemy (BLASS feh mee)
The act of saying or doing things that would dishonor God or Jesus or anything about either one of Them. The Pharisees accused Jesus of blasphemy because He said He was the Son of God. A person can receive forgiveness if he blasphemes God or Jesus but not if he blasphemes the Holy Spirit.

Matthew 12:31 All manner of sin and **b** shall be forgiven
Matthew 12:31 but the **b** against the Holy Ghost shall not
Matthew 26:65 rent his clothes, saying, He hath spoken **b**
Matthew 26:65 behold, now ye have heard his **b**
Mark 14:64 Ye have heard the **b**: what think ye?

■ Bless (BLEHS)
To give something good, wish something good to another person, to praise or honor God; to

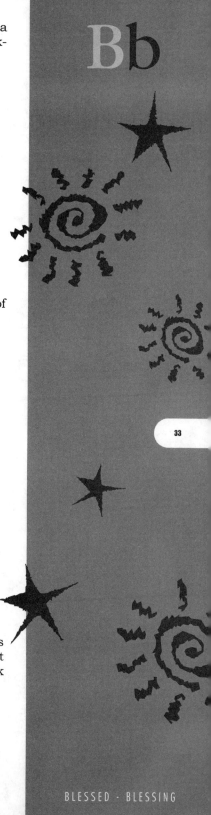

thank. To bless God is to worship Him. When a person blesses his food at a meal, he is thanking God for providing for him.

Genesis 12:3 I will *b* them that *b* thee, and
Genesis 26:24 I am with thee, and will *b* thee
Numbers 6:24 The LORD *b* thee, and keep thee
Psalm 16:7 I will *b* the LORD, who hath given
Psalm 34:1 I will *b* the LORD at all times
Psalm 63:4 Thus will I *b* thee while I live
Psalm 100:4 be thankful unto him, and *b* his
Psalm 103:1 *B* the LORD, O my soul; and all
Psalm 103:1 that is with in me, *b* his holy name
Psalm 103:2 *B* the LORD, O my soul, and forget
Psalm 145:2 Every day will I *b* thee; and I
Matthew 5:44 Love your enemies, *b* them that
Luke 6:28 *B* them that curse you, and pray

Blessed (BLEST; or BLESS ihd)

Past tense of "bless." To be happy because of something God has done.

Genesis 1:28 And God *b* them, and God said
Genesis 2:3 And God *b* the seventh day, and
Genesis 9:1 And God *b* Noah and his sons
Genesis 22:18 nations on earth will be *b*, because (NIV)
Genesis 28:6 Esau saw that Isaac had *b* Jacob
Psalm 18:46 The LORD liveth; and *b* be my rock
Psalm 33:12 *B* is the nation whose God is the LORD
Psalm 84:12 *b* is the man that trusteth in thee
Psalm 112:1 *B* is the man that feareth the LORD
Psalm 118:26 *B* be he that cometh in the name of
Proverbs 8:32 *b* are they that keep my ways
Proverbs 8:34 *B* is the man that heareth me
Matthew 5:3 *B* are the poor in spirit: for
Mark 6:41 he looked up to heaven, and *b* them
Mark 10:16 put his hands upon them, and *b* them
Luke 19:38 *B* be the king that cometh in the
John 20:29 *b* are they that have not seen, and
Acts 20:35 It is more *b* to give than to receive

Blessing (BLESS eeng)

To have blessed, to receive something that was not expected. Once a blessing was spoken, it would come to pass. It could not be taken back or changed.

Genesis 39:5 and the *b* of the LORD was upon all
Deuteronomy 11:26 I set before you this day a *b*
Deuteronomy 11:27 A *b*, if ye obey the commandments
Luke 24:53 in the temple, praising and *b* God
Revelation 5:12 and honour, and glory, and *b*

33

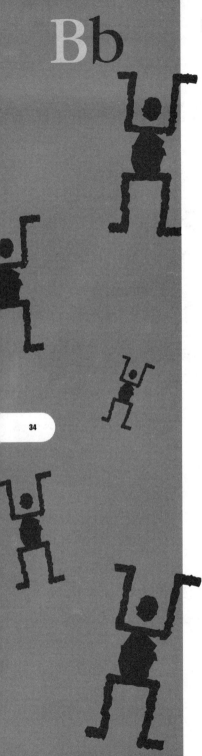

Bb

■ Blood (BLUD)
The fluid necessary for both animals and humans to live. Sometimes the word "blood" is used to represent life. In the Old Testament, the blood of the animals was the main element in the sacrifices the people were required to give. In the New Testament, Jesus talked about His blood as the sacrifice that would give us eternal life.

Matthew 26:28 This is my *b* of the new testament which
Mark 14:24 This is my *b* of the new testament
1 Corinthians 11:25 cup is the new testament in my *b*

■ Boast (BOWST)
To brag or show pride. It is good to boast about God or to show praise to Him. It is not good to brag about oneself.

Psalm 44:8 In God we *b* all the day long
Proverbs 27:1 Do not *b* about tomorrow, for you (NIV)
Ephesians 2:9 not of works, lest any man should *b*

■ Boaz (BOH az)
The name may mean "lively." He was a rich landowner who lived in Bethlehem. He was also kind and helpful. He was a relative of Elimelech, Naomi's husband. Naomi's daughter-in-law, Ruth, a widow like Naomi, picked up grain from the fields of Boaz. Boaz married Ruth and he became an ancestor of David and of Jesus.

Ruth 2:1 family of Elimelech; and his name was *B*
Ruth 2:8 Then said *B* unto Ruth, Hearest thou not
Ruth 3:2 And now is not *B* of our own kindred
Ruth 4:1 Then went *B* up to the gate, and sat
Ruth 4:21 Salmon begat *B*, and *B* begat Obed

■ Bold (BOWLD)
To be brave, have courage, or be fearless.

Acts 13:46 Paul and Barnabas waxed *b*, and said
1 Thessalonians 2:2 we were *b* in our God to speak

■ Boldly (BOWLD lee)
See "Bold."

Mark 15:43 and went in *b* unto Pilate, and
Acts 9:27 how he had preached *b* at Damascus
Acts 13:46 Then Paul and Barnabas answered them *b*
Acts 18:26 And he began to speak *b* in the
Hebrews 4:16 Let us therefore come *b* unto the

■ Boldness (BOWLD niss)
See "Bold."

Acts 4:13 Now when they saw the *b* of Peter and
Acts 4:31 and they spake the word of God with *b*

Born (BORN)

To have life as a result of birth; to be created.

Ecclesiastes 3:2 A time to be *b*, and a time to die
Isaiah 9:6 For unto us a child is *b*, unto us a son
Matthew 2:1 Now when Jesus was *b* in Bethlehem
Matthew 2:2 Where is he that is *b* King of the Jews
Matthew 2:4 demanded of them where Christ should be *b*
Luke 2:11 For unto you is *b* this day in the city
John 3:3 Except a man be *b* again, he cannot see
John 3:5 Except a man be *b* of water and of the
1 John 3:9 whosoever is *b* of God doth not commit
1 John 4:7 every one that loveth is *b* of God

Bread (BREHD)

Loaves, either flat or round, made from flour, usually barley or wheat, and baked in an oven or over an open fire. In biblical times, a person broke or pulled a piece of bread from the loaf. Bread was a necessary part of the diet in biblical times. Barley and wheat could be ground into flour and sold or the grain could be used to buy things a person needed.

Jesus said He was the "bread of life." At the Last Supper, He broke the bread and gave it to His disciples. He told them the bread was like His body which He was giving for them so they could have eternal life.

Genesis 25:34 Then Jacob gave Esau *b* and pottage
Genesis 41:54 in all the land of Egypt there was *b*
Exodus 12:8 roast with fire, and unleavened *b*
Matthew 4:4 Man shall not live by *b* alone
Matthew 6:11 Give us this day our daily *b*
Matthew 26:26 Jesus took *b*, and blessed it, and
Luke 4:4 Man shall not live by *b* alone
John 6:35 Jesus said unto them, I am the *b*
1 Corinthians 11:26 For as often as ye eat this *b*

Brick (BRIK)

Rectangular blocks made from clay while the clay is moist. The forms are left in the sun to dry and harden. Sometimes straw was used in the bricks made in Egypt. The clay had to be dug from the earth and then mixed with water to soften it. After that, the blocks were shaped. Making bricks was very hard work.

Exodus 1:14 hard bondage, in mortar, and in *b*, and
Exodus 5:7 no more give the people straw to make *b*
Exodus 5:16 they say to us, make *b*: and, behold

35

Bb

Brother (BRUH thur)
A male relative or family member, all of whom have the same mother and father.

Genesis 4:8 Cain talked with Abel his ***b***
Genesis 4:8 Cain rose up against Abel his ***b***
Genesis 4:9 LORD said unto Cain, Where is Abel thy ***b***
Proverbs 18:24 a friend that sticketh closer than a ***b***
Matthew 18:15 if thy ***b*** shall trespass against thee
Matthew 18:35 hearts forgive not every one his ***b***
Luke 15:27 he said unto him, thy ***b*** is come
Luke 15:32 be glad: for this thy ***b*** was dead, and
1 John 2:10 He that loveth his ***b*** abideth in
1 John 4:21 he who loveth God love his ***b*** also

Bulrushes (BUL rush iz)
Bulrush is a reed plant that grew at the water's edge along the Nile River and Lake Huleh. Its stems were used to make boats and baskets. The mother of Moses made a small boat, painted it with tar to keep it from taking in water, and after she placed him in the boat, she put the boat in the water along the edges of the Nile River. It was in this little boat that Pharaoh's daughter found him and rescued him.

Another word for bulrush is "papyrus." Papyrus was pounded flat and the edges pasted together to make the long scrolls on which much of the Bible is recorded.

Exodus 2:3 she took for him an ark of ***b***

Burden (BEHR din)
A load or weight, usually heavy or hard to carry.

Psalm 55:22 Cast thy ***b*** upon the LORD, and he shall
Matthew 11:30 For my yoke is easy, and my ***b*** is light

Bush (BUHSH)
A plant or shrub. The bush that Moses saw burning in the desert might have been a thorny bush like those found in the area around Sinai.

Exodus 3:2 flame of fire out of the midst of a ***b***
Exodus 3:2 he looked, and, behold, the ***b*** burned
Exodus 3:2 fire, and the ***b*** was not consumed
Exodus 3:3 great sight, why the ***b*** is not burnt
Exodus 3:4 called to him out of the midst of the ***b***

Business (BIZ nihs)
A job, trade, or work; one's own affairs.

Luke 2:49 I must be about my father's ***b***
1 Thessalonians 4:11 be quiet, and to do your own ***b***

Caesar (SEE zuhr)

The name used by many Roman emperors after Julius Caesar. The name came to be used sometime after 44 B.C., the year Julius Caesar was assassinated (murdered).

Matthew 22:17 Is it right to pay taxes to **C** (NIV)
Matthew 22:21 Give to **C** what is Caesar's, and (NIV)
Luke 2:1 went out a decree from **C** Augustus
Luke 3:1 fifteenth year of the reign of Tiberius **C**
John 19:12 Anyone who claims to be a king opposes **C** (NIV)

Caesarea (SESS uh REE uh)

A city located on the Mediterranean Sea. Caesarea lies 23 miles south of Mount Carmel. The city was built by Herod the Great and was named for Caesar Augustus. Caesarea was the Roman capital of Judea (see map on page 340).

Acts 9:30 brought him down to **C**, and sent him
Acts 10:1 was a certain man in **C** called Cornelius
Acts 10:24 The following day he arrived in **C** (NIV)
Acts 11:11 the house where I was, sent from **C**
Acts 18:22 And when he had landed at **C**

Caesarea-Philippi (SESS uh REE uh-FIL ih pigh)

The city is located on a plateau about 25 miles north of the Sea of Galilee in a mountainous area. Philip, the son of Herod the Great, ruled the city and rebuilt it, later changing the name to honor Tiberius Caesar, the Roman emperor at the time. Jesus and His disciples spent some time in this area (see map on page 340).

Matthew 16:13 Jesus came into the coasts of **C** Philippi
Mark 8:27 his disciples, into the towns of **C** Philippi

Caiaphas (KIGH uh fuhs)

The name means "rock." He was the high priest who led others in a plot to have Jesus arrested and crucified. He was also involved in the trials of Peter and John.

Matthew 26:3 the high priest, who was called **C**
Matthew 26:57 laid hold on Jesus led him away to **C**
Luke 3:2 Annas and **C** being the high priests

Caesarea

John 11:49 of them, named **C**, being the high priest
John 18:14 **C** was he, which gave counsel to the Jews
John 18:24 Annas had sent him bound unto **C**
John 18:28 led they Jesus from **C** unto the hall

Cain (KAYN)

The first son born to Adam and Eve. The name means "acquisition" or to acquire (get). He was a farmer. Cain became jealous and angry when God accepted the offering his brother, Abel, gave, and God rejected the offering Cain gave. Cain killed his brother and then lied to God about it.

Genesis 4:2 but **C** was a tiller of the ground
Genesis 4:5 **C** and to his offering he had not respect
Genesis 4:8 **C** talked with Abel his brother
Genesis 4:8 **C** attacked his brother Abel and killed (NIV)
Genesis 4:16 **C** went out from the presence of the LORD

Calf (CAFF)

Young animals born to cows or to animals close-ly related to cows.

Exodus 32:4 into an idol cast in the shape of a **c** (NIV)
Exodus 32:19 that he saw the **c**, and the dancing
Exodus 32:35 the people, because they made the **c**
Luke 15:23 Bring the fattened **c** and kill it (NIV)

Call (CAWL)

1. (verb) To cry out or ask someone to do some-thing; shout or yell.

2 Samuel 22:4 I will **c** on the LORD, who is worthy
1 Kings 18:24 I will **c** on the name of the LORD
Psalm 18:3 I will **c** upon the LORD, who is worthy
Psalm 86:7 day of my trouble I will **c** upon thee
Psalm 91:15 He shall **c** upon me, and I will answer
Psalm 105:1 thanks unto the LORD; **c** upon his name
Psalm 145:18 them that **c** upon him, to all that **c**
Isaiah 65:24 before they **c**, I will answer
Jeremiah 33:3 **C** unto me, and I will answer thee
Matthew 1:21 and thou shalt **c** his name JESUS
Luke 1:31 a son, and shalt **c** his name JESUS
Romans 10:13 For whosoever shall **c** upon the name

2. (noun) When God appoints or invites a person to serve Him. The person might be a pastor, teacher, missionary, or a mother.

Matthew 9:13 not come to **c** the righteous, but sinners
Mark 2:17 came not to **c** the righteous, but sinners
Luke 5:32 I came not to **c** the righteous, but sinners
Acts 2:39 as many as the Lord our God shall **c**

Called (CAWLD)
Past tense of the verb "call." To be named.

Isaiah 9:6 name shall be **c** Wonderful, Counselor
Matthew 1:25 and he **c** his name JESUS
Matthew 18:2 Jesus **c** a little child unto him
Matthew 21:13 My house shall be **c** the house of prayer
Matthew 27:33 they were come unto a place **c** Golgotha
Mark 6:7 And he **c** unto him the twelve
Mark 11:17 My house shall be **c** of all nations the
Luke 2:21 his name was **c** JESUS, which was so
Luke 15:19 am no more worthy to be **c** thy son
Luke 23:33 come to the place, which is **c** Calvary
John 1:42 son of Jona: thou shalt be **c** Cephas
John 12:17 when he **c** Lazarus out of his grave
John 19:17 which is **c** in the Hebrew Golgotha

Calvary (KAL vuh rih)
The name means "a bare skull." The site where the crucifixion of Jesus took place. The Greek word is Golgotha, which also means "skull." The site is located outside the city walls of Jerusalem.

Luke 23:33 come to the place, which is called **C**

Camel (KAM uhl)
Large animals used to ride or carry heavy loads. The animals have a hump back which contains fat to help them on long trips. Their bodies are strong and their feet padded, which help them endure long journeys across the hot desert land.

Matthew 19:24 easier for a **c** to go through the eye
Mark 10:25 easier for a **c** to go through the eye of
Luke 18:25 easier for a **c** to go through a needle's

Camel's hair (KAM uhlz hair)
A rough material or fabric made from the hair taken from the back and hump of a camel. A mantle or long robe was worn on the outside, over a tunic. This kind of mantle, made from hair of the camel, was part of the clothing worn by a prophet. John the Baptist wore such clothing, as did Elijah and Elisha.

Matthew 3:4 John's clothes were made of **c** hair (NIV)
Mark 1:6 John wore clothing made of **c** hair (NIV)

Canaan (KAY nuhn)
The area of land bordered by the Mediterranean on the west, the Jordan River on the east, and stretching from the Sea of Galilee to south of the Dead Sea. Also known as "The Promised Land,"

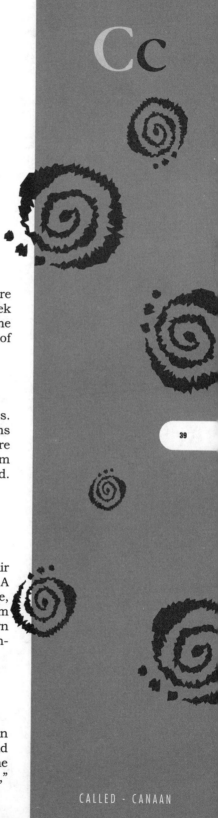

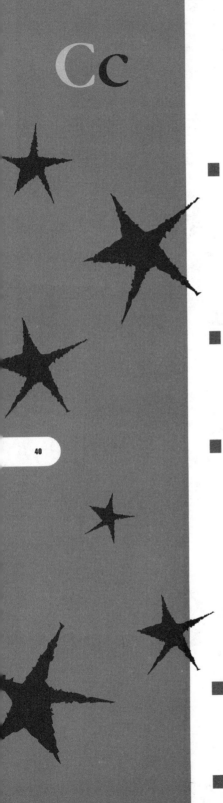

Cc

to which God led Abraham, and later the Israelites after they left their slavery in Egypt.

Genesis 12:5 went forth to go into the land of **C**
Genesis 13:12 Abram dwelled in the land of **C**
Genesis 45:17 go, get you into the land of **C**
Deuteronomy 32:49 behold the land of **C**, which I give
Joshua 5:12 did eat of the fruit of the land of **C**

■ Candle (CAN duhl)
The reference in the Bible usually means "lamp." The wax candles we use today may not have been in use then. The purpose of the candle or lamp was to give light.

Matthew 5:15 Neither do men light a **c**, and put it
Mark 4:21 Is a **c** brought to be put under a bushel
Luke 8:16 when he hath lighted a **c**, covereth it
Luke 11:33 when he hath lighted a **c**, putteth it in
Luke 15:8 lose one piece, doth not light a **c**, and

■ Candlestick (CAN duhl stik)
Something that holds a candle.

Matthew 5:15 put it under a bushel, but on a **c**
Mark 4:21 under a bed? and not to be set on a **c**
Luke 8:16 under a bed; but setteth it on a **c**
Luke 11:33 neither under a bushel, but on a **c**

■ Capernaum (kuh PUHR nay uhm)
The name means "village of Nahum." The city is located on the northwest shore of the Sea of Galilee (see map on page 340). Just west of the city, the Jordan River flows into the lake. Jesus used this city as His "home base." Not many people of Capernaum believed in Jesus although He did many miracles and much teaching in the area.

Matthew 8:5 And when Jesus was entered into **C**
Matthew 17:24 And when they were come to **C**
Mark 2:1 he entered into **C** after some days
Luke 7:1 of the people, he entered into **C**
John 2:12 After this he went down to **C**
John 6:17 and went over the sea toward **C**

■ Care (KAIR)
To have concern for; to worry about.

Mark 4:38 Teacher, don't you **c** if we drown (NIV)
Luke 10:40 Lord, dost thou not **c** that my sister
1 Peter 5:7 Casting all your **c** upon him; for he

■ Careful (KAIR fuhl)
To worry or have concern; to be aware so as to

prevent problems.

Luke 10:41 Martha, thou are *c* and troubled about
Philippians 4:6 Be *c* for nothing; but in every

■ Careth (KAIR ith)
The old way of saying "cares." Plural for "care."

1 Peter 5:7 your care upon him; for he *c* for you

■ Carmel (KAHR muhl)
The name means "garden-land" or "fruitful land." Mount Carmel is 1,750 feet above sea level. The summit (top) is a few miles from the Mediterranean Sea. This is the mountain where Elijah invited the prophets of Baal to come in order to prove who was the one true God.

1 Kings 18:19 gather to me all Israel unto Mount *C*
1 Kings 18:42 Elijah went up to the top of *C*
2 Kings 4:25 unto the man of God to mount *C*

■ Cast (KAST)
To throw, toss, pitch; to drop.

Exodus 4:3 And he said, *C* it on the ground
Psalm 51:11 *C* me not away from thy presence
Psalm 55:22 *C* thy burden upon the LORD, and
Ecclesiastes 3:6 time to keep, and a time to *c* away
John 6:37 that cometh to me I will in no wise *c* out
John 21:6 *C* the net on the right side of the ship

■ Casting (KAST eeng)
Pitching, throwing, tossing.

Matthew 4:18 and Andrew his brother, *c* a net into
Matthew 27:35 they divided up his clothes by *c* lots (NIV)
Mark 10:50 *c* away his garment, rose, and came to
Luke 21:1 and saw the rich men *c* their gifts
Luke 21:2 saw also a certain poor widow *c* in
1 Peter 5:7 *C* all your care upon him; for he

■ Centurion (sen TYOOR ee uhn)
A Roman officer in charge of 100 soldiers. A centurion was highly respected. The New Testament mentions several centurions who showed faith that Jesus was the Son of God.

Matthew 8:5 there came to him a *c*, beseeching
Matthew 27:54 Now when the *c*, and they that were
Mark 15:39 And the *c*, which stood over against
Luke 7:6 the *c* sent friends to him, saying
Luke 23:47 Now when the *c* saw what was done
Acts 10:22 they said, Cornelius the *c*, a just man
Acts 28:16 the *c* delivered the prisoners to the

Centurion

41

Cc

Cephas (SEE fuhs)
The name means "rock" or "stone." Jesus gave this name to Peter probably because he would become a strong leader in the church. He was already somewhat of a leader among the twelve disciples.

John 1:42 son of Jona: thou shalt be called **C**

Chaldees (kal DEEZ)
Chaldeans. A tribe of people who lived near the Babylonians. They eventually overtook the Babylonians and became a very strong nation. They were later called Babylonians as well as Chaldeans. Ur, a city of the Chaldees, is where Abram lived before God called him to go to the area of Canaan.

Genesis 11:28 of his nativity, in Ur of the **C**
Genesis 15:7 that brought thee out of Ur of the **C**
Nehemiah 9:7 broughtest him forth out of Ur of the **C**

Charge (CHARJ)
A command or order; a task or responsibility.

Psalm 91:11 he shall give his angels **c** over thee
Matthew 4:6 shall give his angels **c** concerning thee
Matthew 26:63 I **c** you under oath by the living God (NIV)
Mark 9:25 spirit, I **c** thee, come out of him, and
Luke 4:10 He shall give his angels **c** over thee

Chariot (CHAIR ee uht)
A cart with two wheels, pulled by one or more horses. They were used during times of war, to hunt animals for food, or to carry visitors or other important people. Kings David and Solomon used chariots in their battles and won many battles because of the usefulness and swiftness of the chariot.

Genesis 46:29 And Joseph made ready his **c**, and
Exodus 14:6 And he made ready his **c**, and took his
Exodus 14:25 And took off their **c** wheels, that
1 Kings 18:44 say unto Ahab, Prepare thy **c** and
2 Kings 2:11 behold, there appeared a **c** of fire
Acts 8:28 sitting in his **c** read Esaias the prophet
Acts 8:38 and he commanded the **c** to stand still

Chariots (CHAIR ee uhtz)
Plural for "chariot."

Exodus 14:7 And he took six hundred chosen **c**
Exodus 14:28 waters returned, and covered the **c**
Exodus 15:4 Pharaoh's **c** and his host hath he cast

Chariot

42

Psalm 20:7 Some trust in **c**, and some in horses

Charity (CHAIR ih tee)
Love. Many versions of the Bible use the word "love" rather than "charity." An act of kindness or love shown toward others.

1 Corinthians 13:1 and of angels, and have not **c**
1 Corinthians 13:4 **C** suffereth long, and is kind
1 Corinthians 13:4 **c** envieth not
1 Corinthians 13:8 **C** never faileth: but whether
1 Corinthians 13:13 faith, hope, **c**, these three
1 Corinthians 13:13 but the greatest of these is **c**

Cheek (CHEEK)
A part of the face located on either side of the nose and mouth below the eye.

Matthew 5:39 shall smite thee on thy right **c**
Luke 6:29 him that smiteth thee on the one **c**

Cheer (CHEEHR)
The way one thinks and feels; to encourage another; to offer comfort or hope.

Matthew 9:2 Son, be of good **c**; thy sins be forgiven
Matthew 14:27 Be of good **c**; it is I; be not afraid
Mark 6:50 Be of good **c**: it is I; be not afraid

Cheerful (CHEEHR fuhl)
Happy, agreeable, friendly.

Proverbs 15:13 a happy heart makes the face **c** (NIV)
2 Corinthians 9:7 for God loveth a **c** giver

Child (CHIGHLD)
A kid or youth. Usually a person between infancy and youth.

Exodus 2:2 saw him that he was a goodly **c**
1 Samuel 2:21 the **c** Samuel grew before the LORD
Proverbs 20:11 Even a **c** is known by his doings
Proverbs 22:6 Train up a **c** in the way he should
Isaiah 9:6 For unto us a **c** is born, unto us a
Matthew 1:23 Behold, a virgin shall be with **c**
Matthew 2:8 Go and search diligently for the **c**
Matthew 2:9 and stood over where the young **c** was
Matthew 18:2 Jesus called a little **c** unto him
Luke 1:80 And the **c** grew and became strong in (NIV)
Luke 18:17 receive the kingdom of God as a little **c**

Children (CHIL drehn)
Plural of "child."

Matthew 5:9 they shall be called the **c** of God

43

Matthew 19:14 Let the little **c** come to me (NIV)
Luke 18:16 Suffer little **c** to come unto me, and
Ephesians 6:1 **C**, obey your parents in the Lord

■ Choose (CHOOZ)
To pick, select, or take.

Joshua 24:15 **c** you this day whom ye will serve
1 Kings 18:25 **C** you one bullock for yourselves
Proverbs 1:29 and did not **c** the fear of the LORD

■ Christ (KRIGHST)
The name means "anointed" or "anointed one." This title tells us that Jesus has been anointed as the Son of God. He is the Messiah, the Savior for all people in the world.

Matthew 1:18 Now the birth of Jesus **C** was on this
Matthew 2:4 demanded of them where **C** should be born
Matthew 16:16 Thou art the **C**, the Son of the living
Luke 2:11, a Saviour, which is **C** the Lord
Luke 4:41 Thou art **C**, the Son of God
Luke 9:20 Peter answering said, The **C** of God
John 11:27 I believe that thou art the **C**
John 20:31 ye might believe that Jesus is the **C**
Acts 8:37 I believe that Jesus **C** is the Son of God
Romans 5:6 in due time **C** died for the ungodly
Romans 5:8 while we were yet sinners, **C** died for us
Philippians 4:13 I can do all things through **C**
Colossians 3:13 even as **C** forgave you, so also do
Hebrews 13:8 Jesus **C** the same yesterday, and today

■ Christian (KRISS chuhn)
The name given to a person who is a follower of Jesus. Jesus' followers were called Christians for the first time in Antioch of Syria because everything they did was like that of Christ. When the name was given to the believers, it was meant to make fun of them. But followers are proud to use the name.

Acts 26:28 Almost thou persuadest me to be a **C**
1 Peter 4:16 Yet if any man suffer as a **C**

■ Christians (KRISS chuhnz)
Plural for "Christian."

Acts 11:26 the disciples were called **C** first in Antioch

■ Chronicles, 1, 2, Books of (KRAHN ih kuhls)
The eighth and ninth books in the Old Testament division of History. At one time they were one book. The Chronicles give a short history of Israel from Adam to King David, as well as specific detail

44

about Judah, the Southern Kingdom. They show God's greatness, that He was faithful, and that He still keeps his promises no matter what happens. These books also tell about King David's desire to build a temple to God and how he prepared for his son, Solomon, to build this house of God.

Cleopas (KLEE oh puhs)
A follower of Jesus. Luke 24 tells how Cleopas and another follower walked with Jesus on the evening after the resurrection. The two people did not recognize Jesus until He broke the bread as they shared a meal.

Luke 24:18 whose name was **C**, answering said

Closet (CLAW zet)
Jesus talked about a closet, a small room in the home, where He urged people to go to pray.

Matthew 6:6 when thou prayest, enter into thy **c**

Cloud (CLOWD)
Fog, mist, vapor. God used a cloud to allow the people of Israel to know He was near. The cloud also hid His face from the people. The cloud protected the Israelites as they left Egypt. It kept the Egyptians from coming near them.

Genesis 9:13 I do set my bow in the **c**
Exodus 13:21 before them by day in a pillar of a **c**
Exodus 16:10 glory of the LORD appeared in the **c**
Exodus 34:5 And the LORD descended in the **c**
1 Kings 18:44 ariseth a little **c** out of the sea

Coat (KOHT)
A jacket; a garment worn over clothing, usually to provide warmth.

Genesis 37:3 and he made him a **c** of many colours
1 Samuel 2:19 his mother made him a little **c**
Matthew 5:40 and take away thy **c**, let him have
Luke 6:29 cloak forbid not to take thy **c** also

Cock (KAHK)
A word used in the New Testament for rooster. The male bird is the one of the species that crows, or makes the loud sounds that can be heard for quite a distance. Roosters crowed twice during the night: at midnight, and again about three in the morning. The Roman soldiers used the rooster's crow as a guide to help them change the guard because the crowing times were so true. Jesus told Peter he would deny

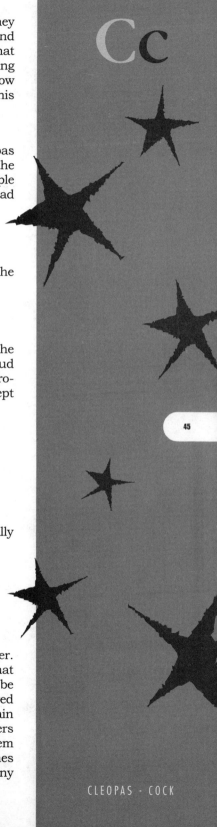

45

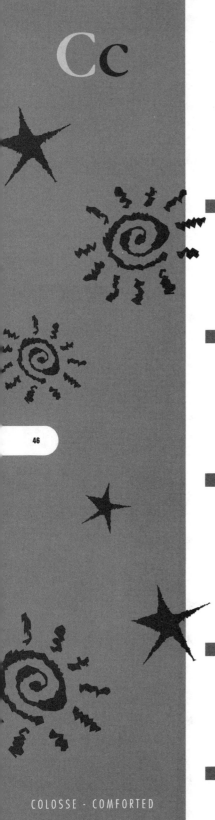

Cc

Him three times before the second crowing of the cock.

Matthew 26:34 before the *c* crow, thou shalt deny
Matthew 26:74 And immediately the *c* crew
Mark 14:30 even in this night, before the *c* crow
Mark 14:72 And the second time the *c* crew
Luke 22:34 Peter, the *c* shall not crow this day
Luke 22:60 while he yet spake, the *c* crew
John 13:38 I say unto thee, the *c* shall not crow
John 18:27 denied again: and immediately the *c* crew

Colosse (koh LAHS sih)
A city in Asia, in Phrygia, in the area that is now Turkey (see map on page 341). Paul started a church in the city of Colosse. It was to those Christians that he wrote the letter called Colossians.

Colossians 1:2 brethren in Christ which are at *C*

Colossians, Book of (kuh LAHSH uhnz)
The seventh book in the division, Paul's Letters, in the New Testament. People who lived in Colosse. Paul wrote this letter encouraging them to not listen to the false teachers. He stressed that they live and work together in unity and to act in the love of Christ. He may have been under house arrest in Rome at the time of this writing.

Colt (KOHLT)
A young male donkey, camel, or horse.

Zechariah 9:9 on a *c*, the foal of a donkey (NIV)
Matthew 21:2 donkey tied there, with her *c* by her (NIV)
Matthew 21:7 They brought the donkey and the *c* (NIV)
Mark 11:2 ye shall find a *c* tied, whereon never
Mark 11:7 And they brought the *c* to Jesus
Luke 19:30 ye shall find a *c* tied, whereon never
Luke 19:35 they cast their garments upon the *c*
John 12:15 king is coming, seated on a donkey's *c* (NIV)

Comfort (KUHM fuhrt)
To bring calm or peace; to provide cheer.

Psalm 23:4 thy rod and thy staff they *c* me
Matthew 9:22 be of good *c*; thy faith hath made
Mark 10:49 Be of good *c*, rise; he calleth thee
Luke 8:48 be of good *c*: thy faith hath made thee
John 11:19 to *c* them concerning their brother

Comforted (KUHM fuhr tid)
Past tense of "comfort."

46

Matthew 5:4 they that mourn: for they shall be *c*
John 11:31 and *c* her, when they saw Mary, that

■ Comforter (KUHM fuhr tuhr)

This is a name given to the Holy Ghost (or Holy Spirit). The Holy Spirit gives comfort and strength and advice to Christians. The Comforter is a helper to the Christians on earth. He came after Jesus went back to heaven. Jesus helps us in heaven by speaking to God for us.

John 14:16 he shall give you another *C*
John 14:26 But the *C*, which is the Holy Ghost
John 15:26 the *C* is come, whom I will send
John 16:7 if I go away, the *C* will not come

■ Comfortless (KUHM fuhrt less)

To have no peace or hope; to feel alone (based on the definition of "comfort").

John 14:18 I will not leave you *c*: I will come

■ Commandment (kah MAND mint)

A law or a rule. The commandments which God has given us are important and they are to be obeyed.

Psalm 19:8 the *c* of the LORD is pure
Proverbs 6:20 keep thy father's *c*, and forsake not
Matthew 22:36 which is the great *c* in the law
Matthew 22:38 This is the first and great *c*
Mark 12:30 thy strength: this is the first *c*
John 13:34 A new *c* I give unto you, That ye
John 15:12 This is my *c*, That ye love one another
Ephesians 6:2 which is the first *c* with a promise

■ Commandments (kah MAND mintz)

Plural of "commandment." Usually refers to the Ten Commandments but includes all the laws God gave for our benefit. Some of the commandments help us get along with others. Several commandments help us know how to get in touch with God and how to keep ourselves right with Him.

Exodus 20:6 them that love me, and keep my *c*
Leviticus 22:31 Therefore shall ye keep my *c*
Psalm 111:7 all his *c* are sure
Psalm 119:47 I will delight myself in thy *c*
Psalm 119:151 and all thy *c* are truth
Ecclesiastes 12:13 Fear God, and keep his *c*
Matthew 22:40 on these two *c* hang all the law
John 14:15 If ye love me, keep my *c*
John 14:21 He that hath my *c*, and keepeth them

Commandments

Cc

■ **Commit (kahm MIHT)**
To do, to promise. To commit oneself to God, a person promises to let God show him or her the right things to do, or say, or think.

Psalm 31:5 Into thine hand I **c** my spirit
Psalm 37:5 **C** thy way unto the LORD: trust also
Proverbs 16:3 **C** to the LORD whatever you do (NIV)

■ **Committed (kahm MIH tid)**
Past tense for "commit."

2 Timothy 1:12 keep that which I have **c** unto him

■ **Compassion (kahm PASH uhn)**
To comfort, to feel sorry for; an emotional expression to show another how you feel.

Psalm 86:15 But thou, O LORD, art a God full of **c**
Psalm 111:4 the LORD is gracious, and full of **c**,
Psalm 112:4 he is gracious, and full of **c**
Matthew 14:14 and was moved with **c** toward them
Matthew 20:34 So Jesus had **c** on them, and touched
Luke 7:13 when the Lord saw her, he had **c** on her
Luke 15:20 his father saw him, and had **c**, and

■ **Compassions (kahm PASH uhz)**
Plural for "compassion."

Lamentations 3:22 not consumed, because his **c** fail not

■ **Compel (kahm PELL)**
To cause, control, force, or order a person to do something.

Matthew 5:41 whosoever shall **c** thee to go a mile
Mark 15:21 And they **c** one Simon a Cyrenian
Luke 14:23 **c** them to come in, that my house

■ **Condemn (kuhn DEM)**
To blame, charge, find guilty, or sentence. God will be the final judge for all the wrongs we have done. But Jesus' death on the cross can keep the believer from receiving a terrible sentence, a sentence of eternal death. The believer can instead receive eternal life, by placing his faith and trust in Jesus Christ, God's only Son.

Matthew 20:18 and they shall **c** him to death
Mark 10:33 and they shall **c** him to death
Luke 6:37 **c** not, and ye shall not be condemned
John 3:17 sent not his Son into the world to **c**

■ **Confess (kuhn FESS)**
To admit that you have done wrong. To tell God

or another person about the wrong things you have done. To say that you are going to do a thing, especially to walk with Jesus Christ.

Matthew 10:32 Whosoever shall **c** me before men
Matthew 10:32 him will I **c** before my Father
Luke 12:8 whosoever shall **c** me before men
Luke 12:8 him shall the Son of man also **c**
Romans 10:9 if thou shalt **c** with thy mouth
Romans 10:10 it is with your mouth that you **c** (NIV)
Romans 14:11 and every tongue shall **c** to God
Philippians 2:11 every tongue should **c** that Jesus
1 John 1:9 If we **c** our sins, he is faithful
1 John 4:15 Whosoever shall **c** that Jesus is the

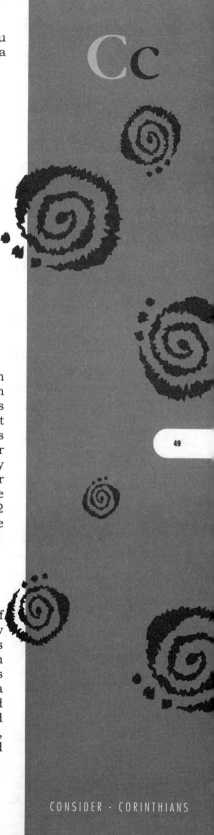

Consider (kuhn SIH duhr)
To think about, to wonder.

Psalm 8:3 When I **c** thy heavens, the work of thy
Matthew 6:28 **C** the lilies of the field, how they
Luke 12:24 **C** the ravens: for they neither sow
Luke 12:27 **C** the lilies how they grow

Corinth (KAWR inth)
The city of Corinth is located in the southern part of Greece (see map on page 341). Corinth became the Roman capital of Achaia and was situated on a hill 1,886 feet above sea level. It was easy to defend. However, the city was burned in 146 B.C. and rebuilt 100 years later by Julius Caesar. It became an important city for shipping cargo. The Romans worshiped their gods as well as the Greek gods. Corinth became known for its wickedness. Paul wrote 1,2 Corinthians to the Christians at Corinth and he wrote Romans while he was in Corinth.

Acts 18:1 Paul departed from Athens, and came to **C**

Corinthians, 1, 2, Books of (koh RIN thih uhns)
These two books are numbers two and three of the division, Paul's Letters, in the New Testament. They were written to the Christians at Corinth. (The people who lived in Corinth were called Corinthians.) Although Corinth was a Greek city, it became the capital of Achaia, a Roman province. This city was very wicked and much false worship took place within. Paul tried to teach the Corinthians about Christian love, the Holy Spirit, the resurrection of Jesus, and the importance of giving.

Cc

Cornelius (kawr NEE lih uhs)
A Roman centurian who lived in Caesarea. An angel told him in a dream to send for Peter. Peter came and told him about Jesus. Cornelius and his whole family became believers of Jesus. He may have been the first non-Jew (Gentile) to become a follower of Christ.

Acts 10:1 a man in Caesarea called **C**, a centurion
Acts 10:7 the angel which spake unto **C** was departed
Acts 10:21 men which were sent unto him from **C**
Acts 10:30 And **C** said, Four days ago I was
Acts 10:31 And said, **C**, thy prayer is heard, and

Correct (kawr EKT)
To guide or teach another; to direct; to punish.

Proverbs 29:17 **C** thy son, and he shall give thee

Correction (kawr EK shun)
See "Correct."

Proverbs 23:13 Withhold not **c** from the child
2 Timothy 3:16 reproof, for **c**, for instruction in

Counselor (KOWN suh luhr)
Also spelled "counsellor." A person who gives advice to others. Kings often had counselors to help them know how to decide things. God and Jesus the Messiah are often referred to as counselors. The Holy Spirit is also known as a counselor.

Isaiah 9:6 His name shall be called Wonderful, **C**
Mark 15:43 Joseph of Arimathaea, an honourable **c**

Courage (KUR ij)
Boldness, daring; mental strength.

Deuteronomy 31:6 Be strong and of a good **c**, fear not
Joshua 1:6 Be strong and of a good **c**
Joshua 10:25 dismayed, be strong and of good **c**
Psalm 27:14 Wait on the LORD: be of good **c**
Psalm 31:24 Be of good **c**, and he shall strengthen

Covenant (KUHV uh nuhnt)
An agreement between two people or several people: a promise. God made a covenant with Abraham and those who would come after him. If they would do as God said (follow His laws), then He would take care of them and protect them. This was part of the Old Covenant. When Jesus came to earth, He established a New Covenant, that if we would have faith in Him, He would provide eternal life for us.

Genesis 6:18 But with thee will I establish my **c**
Genesis 17:2 And I will make my **c** between me and

Covet (KUV iht)

To selfishly want for yourself something that belongs to another person. That thing may not be something that is needed, only something that is wanted. A person can covet possessions, money, even other people. A person who covets refuses to believe in God and His ability to supply what he needs.

Exodus 20:17 Thou shalt not **c** thy neighbor's house
Exodus 20:17 shalt not **c** thy neighbor's wife, no

Create (kree AYT)

To construct, form, make, or produce something. God is the only one who can create something from nothing. When man creates, he takes what is available and makes it into something different.

Psalm 51:10 **C** in me a clean heart, O God; and

Created (kree AYT id)

Past tense of "create."

Genesis 1:1 In the beginning God **c** the heaven
Genesis 1:27 God **c** man in his own image
Genesis 2:3 rested from all his work which God **c**
Ephesians 2:10 we are God's workmanship, **c** in Christ (NIV)
Colossians 1:16 For by him were all things **c**
Colossians 1:16 all things were **c** by him, and for him

Creator (kree AYT uhr)

The one who creates. God is the creator of all things.

Ecclesiastes 12:1 Remember now thy **C** in the days of
Isaiah 40:28 everlasting God, the LORD, the **C** of

Creature (KREE chur)

Anything made by God that has life or breathes. A creature can be either an animal or a human.

Genesis 1:24 Let the earth bring forth the living **c**
Genesis 2:19 whatsoever Adam called every living **c**
Mark 16:15 and preach the gospel to every **c**

Crete (KREET)

A large island, made up mostly of mountains, located near the tip of Greece, in the Mediterranean Sea. It was this island that Paul sailed near as he was being taken to Rome (see map on page 341).

Acts 27:7 we sailed under **C**, over against Salmone

C c

51

Cc

Cross

■ **Cried (KRIGHD)**
Past tense of "cry."

Genesis 27:34 he **c** with a great and exceeding
Exodus 2:23 by reason of the bondage, and they **c**
Psalm 3:4 I **c** unto the LORD with my voice, and
Psalm 120:1 I **c** unto the LORD, and he heard me
Matthew 27:23 they **c** out the more, saying,
Matthew 27:46 ninth hour Jesus **c** with a loud voice
Mark 3:11 fell down before him, and **c**, saying
Mark 9:24 father of the child **c** out, and said
Mark 15:13 And they **c** out again, Crucify him
Luke 23:18 And they **c** out all at once, saying
John 11:43 he **c** with a loud voice, Lazarus, come
John 19:6 officers saw him, they **c** out, saying
John 19:15 But they **c** out, Away with him

■ **Cross (KRAWS)**
A cross was made of two wooden beams, one
beam upright, and the other beam tied level
near the top. A placard would be nailed over the
prisoner's head, stating his crime. This method
(way) of punishment was used by the Romans
and it was quite painful and very shameful. The
prisoners were either tied to the beams, or nails
were used to secure their hands and feet to the
beam. A small wooden block was placed so the
body could rest on a "seat." The person would
hang on the cross until he died, sometimes for
many days.

After Jesus had been crucified and resurrected, the cross represented a person being willing
to obey Jesus, even if it meant death for the person. The cross was the way Jesus made it possible to forgive the sins of all people. All four
Gospel books tell different things about the crucifixion of Jesus.

Matthew 16:24 and take up his **c**, and follow me
Matthew 27:32 him the compelled to bear his **c**
Mark 8:34 and take up his **c**, and follow me
Mark 10:21 come, take up the **c**, and follow me
Luke 9:23 take up his **c** daily, and follow me
Luke 23:26 on him they laid the **c**, that he might
John 19:17 bearing his **c**, went forth into a place
Philippians 2:8 obedient unto death, even death on a **c**

■ **Crown (KROWN)**
A special decoration worn on the head. Early
crowns were made of cloth, wrapped around the
head. Metal crowns, often with precious jewels,
were worm by kings and the high priest of Israel.

Roman soldiers made fun of Jesus and made a crown of thorny twigs to place on His head.

Matthew 27:29 when they had platted a **c** of thorns
Mark 15:17 and platted a **c** of thorns, and put it
John 19:2 and the soldiers platted a **c** of thorns
John 19:5 came Jesus forth, wearing the **c** of thorns

Crucified (KROO suh fighd)

Past tense of "crucify." To die on a cross. Jesus was crucified in order that our sins be forgiven and so we could spend eternity with Him (see "Cross," above). This was a very painful and shameful way to die. Men as well as women were crucified.

Matthew 26:2 Son of man is betrayed to be **c**
Matthew 27:22 all say unto him, Let him be **c**
Matthew 27:26 he delivered him to be **c**
Matthew 28:5 ye seek Jesus, which was **c**
Mark 15:15 he had scourged him, to be **c**
Mark 16:6 Jesus of Nazareth, which was **c**
Luke 24:20 condemned to death, and have **c** him
John 19:16 therefore unto them to be **c**
John 19:18 where they **c** him, and two other
Acts 2:36 whom ye have **c**, both Lord and Christ

Crucify (KROO suh figh)

To place someone on a cross so that person would die. A punishment for crimes committed against the government. Before a person was crucified, he would be beaten with a whip that had sharp bones or metal pieces tied to the ends. After the beating, often the person would be made to carry his cross to the site where the crucifixion would take place. The person's hands and feet would be nailed to the cross. Sometimes ropes were used along with the nails. The nails used on Jesus may have been made from iron and were about six inches long. The person might hang on the cross for several days before he died of starvation, suffocation (could not breathe), or his heart stopped beating. If the person hung there too long, the soldiers would break his or her legs. This terrible pain would cause the person to die quickly.

Matthew 20:19 to scourge, and to **c** him: and the
Matthew 27:31 and led him away to **c** him
Mark 15:27 And with him they **c** two thieves
Luke 23:21 they cried, saying, **C** him, **c** him
John 19:6 they cried out, saying, **C** him, **c** him

53

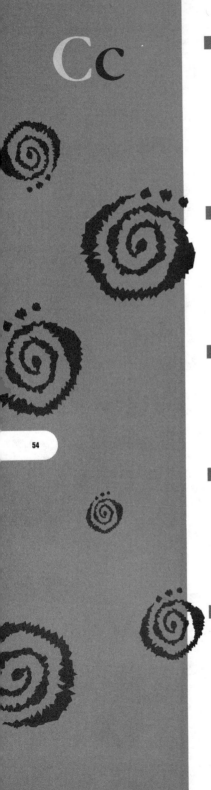

Cc

■ Cry (KRIGH)
To sob or weep; to shout or yell; call out.

Exodus 2:23 their **c** came up unto God by reason of
Exodus 3:7 have heard their **c** by reason of their
Exodus 12:30 there was a great **c** in Egypt
Psalm 17:1 listen to my **c**. Give ear to my prayer (NIV)
Psalm 39:12 prayer, O LORD, and give ear unto my **c**
Psalm 55:17 and at noon, will I pray, and **c** aloud
Mark 10:47 began to **c** out, Jesus, thou son of David
Luke 19:40 the stones would immediately **c** out

■ Crying (KRIGH eeng)
Calling out. John the Baptist was calling out for all to hear the message of repentance.

Matthew 3:3 The voice of one **c** in the wilderness
Matthew 9:27 blind men followed him, **c**, and saying
Mark 1:3 The voice of one **c** in the wilderness
Luke 3:4 The voice of one **c** in the wilderness
John 1:23 I am the voice of one **c** in the wilderness

■ Cubit (KYOO bit)
A measure of length, taken from the elbow to the tip of the middle finger. This could vary from 18 to 21 inches.

Genesis 6:16 in a **c** shalt thou finish it above
Matthew 6:27 can add one **c** unto his stature
Luke 12:25 can add to his stature one **c**

■ Cubits (KYOO bitz)
Plural of "cubit." The ark would be 450 feet long, 75 feet wide, and 45 feet high. A football field is 360 feet long and 150 feet wide. Thus, the ark was longer than a football field and half as wide.

Genesis 6:15 of the ark shall be three hundred **c**
Genesis 6:15 the breadth of it fifty **c**
Genesis 6:15 and the height of it thirty **c**

■ Cup (KUHP)
Like a glass or a mug. In biblical times, a cup was made from clay that was hardened by drying and then placed in a very hot fire. Bronze and other metals, like gold or silver, were also used. The word "cup" could refer to something that was not easy to do. The "cup" that Jesus drank just before His arrest and crucifixion represented the suffering He would face. The cup could also represent blessing. The psalmist talked about his "cup running over" (Psalm 23:5). This meant that the cup had more good things than it could hold.

54

Genesis 44:2 put my *c*, the silver *c*, in the sack's
Psalm 23:5 head with oil; my *c* runneth over
Matthew 20:22 Are ye able to drink of the *c* that I
Matthew 26:27 And he took the *c* and gave thanks
Mark 14:23 And he took the *c*, and when he had
Luke 22:17 And he took the *c*, and gave thanks
Luke 22:20 This *c* is the new testament in my blood

Curse (KUHRS)

A curse was given to tell someone that bad may come to him. A curse could also be given to an event. Once spoken, a curse could not be taken back. Old Testament people took a curse seriously.

Matthew 5:44 Love your enemies, bless them that *c* you
Luke 6:28 Bless them that *c* you, and pray for them
Romans 12:14 which persecute you: bless, and *c* not

Curses (KUHR sihs)

Plural for "curse."

Exodus 21:17 Anyone who *c* his father or mother must (NIV)
Matthew 15:4 Anyone who *c* his father or mother must (NIV)
Mark 7:10 Anyone who *c* his father or mother must (NIV)

Custom (KUH stuhm)

A habit; a thing that is usually done. Also, in biblical times, a kind of tax.

Matthew 9:9 named Matthew, sitting at the receipt of *c*
Mark 2:14 son of Alphaeus, sitting at the receipt of *c*
Luke 2:27 Jesus, to do for him after the *c* of the law
Luke 4:16 as his *c* was, he went into the synagogue
Luke 5:27 Levi, sitting at the receipt of *c*
John 18:39 ye have a *c*, that I should release unto you

Cyprus (SIGH pruhs)

A large mountainous island in the eastern Mediterranean Sea about 200 miles northwest of Caesarea in Samaria (see map on page 341). Barnabas was born in Cyprus. Paul visited the island on his first missionary journey. A large number of Jewish Christians lived on the island.

Acts 4:36 a Levite, and of the country of **C**
Acts 13:4 and from thence they sailed to **C**
Acts 15:39 Barnabas took Mark, and sailed unto **C**
Acts 27:4 we sailed under **C**, because the winds

Cyrene (sigh REE nee)

A city in Northern Africa that was the capital city of a Roman district (see map on page 341). Many Greek-speaking Jews lived in the city dur-

ing the first thirty or forty years of the first century. A man named Simon, of Cyrene, was forced to carry the cross of Jesus to Golgotha.

Matthew 27:32 found a man of **C**, Simon by name
Mark 15:21 A certain man from **C**, Simon (NIV)
Luke 23:26 they seized Simon from **C**, who was (NIV)

■ Cyrenius (sigh REE nih uhs)
He was a Roman official when the birth of Jesus took place.

Luke 2:2 first made when **C** was governor of Syria

■ Daily (DAY lee)
A thing that is done or happens every day.

Exodus 16:5 be twice as much as they gather d
Matthew 6:11 Give us this day our d bread
Matthew 26:55 d with you teaching in the temple
Mark 14:49 I was d with you in the temple teaching
Luke 9:23 deny himself, and take up his cross d
Luke 11:3 Give us day by day our d bread
Luke 19:47 And he taught d in the temple
Luke 22:53 When I was d with you in the temple
Acts 2:47 Lord added to the church d such as

■ Damascus (duh MASS kuhs)
The capital city of Syria. It is located 2300 feet above sea level and about 60 miles from the Mediterranean Sea. Two major highways went through the city. People have lived in Damascus for over 4,000 years. Saul (Paul) was converted to Christianity as he traveled the highway to Damascus (see map page 340).

Acts 9:2 letters to **D** to the synagogues
Acts 9:3 as he journeyed, he came near **D**
Acts 9:8 by the hand, and brought him to **D**
Acts 9:10 there was a certain disciple at **D**
Acts 9:22 confounded the Jews which dwelt at **D**
Acts 9:27 preached boldly at **D** in the name of

■ Daniel (DAN yuhl)
The name means "God is judge" or "God is my judge." A young Jew who was taken captive to Babylon and trained to serve the Babylonian kings. He would do nothing that would go

Daniel

56

against the teachings of God, which he had learned as a child. Daniel's name was changed to "Belteshazzar" by King Nebuchadnezzar. Belteshazzar means "protect the king's life." Because Daniel honored God, God helped Daniel escape death and finally one of the kings gave him a high office.

Daniel 1:6 the children of Judah, **D**, Hananiah
Daniel 1:7 gave unto **D** the name of Belteshazzar
Daniel 1:8 **D** resolved not to defile himself with (NIV)
Daniel 1:9 God had brought **D** into favour and tender
Daniel 1:17 **D** had understanding in all visions and
Daniel 1:19 Among them all was none found like **D**
Daniel 2:48 Then the king made **D** a great man
Daniel 5:29 they clothed **D** with scarlet, and
Daniel 6:16 brought **D**, and cast him into the den
Daniel 6:16 **D**, thy God whom thou servest
Daniel 6:23 **D** was taken up out of the den, and
Daniel 6:26 tremble and fear before the God of **D**

Daniel, Book of (DAN yuhl)

The fifth book in the division, Major Prophets, in the Old Testament. The book shows that Daniel was true to God even when he was in danger. It shows the problems he had because he chose to obey God and how God protected him. God expects us to obey Him, too.

David (DAY vid)

The name means "beloved" or "favorite." His father was Jesse, and David had many older brothers. He was a shepherd and was anointed to become king by Samuel even before King Saul died. David played a harp and often played and sang to comfort King Saul. Saul became jealous of David because he was talented and the people really liked David. Saul tried to kill David many times but God protected him.

David wrote many of the Psalms. He is known as the "best king Israel ever had."

1 Samuel 16:13 the spirit of the LORD came upon **D**
1 Samuel 16:19 Send me **D** thy son, which is with
1 Samuel 16:23 **D** took a harp, and played with
1 Samuel 17:43 Philistine said unto **D**, Am I a dog
1 Samuel 17:49 **D** put his hand in his bag, and
1 Samuel 17:50 So **D** prevailed over the Philistine
1 Samuel 18:5 Whatever Saul sent him to do, **D** did (NIV)
1 Samuel 18:12 Saul was afraid of **D**, because the
1 Samuel 18:30 **D** behaved himself more wisely than
1 Chronicles 18:14 So **D** reigned over all Israel

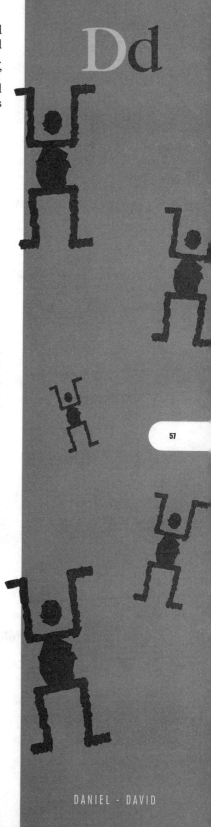

Dd

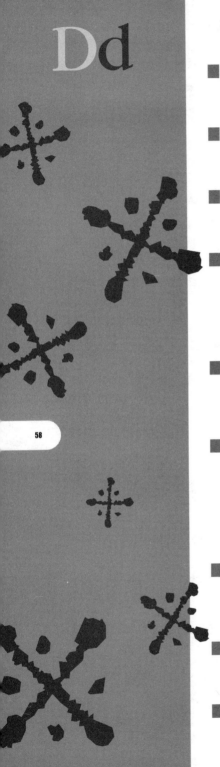

Dd

Matthew 9:27 saying, Thou son of **D**, have mercy
Mark 10:47 say, Jesus, thou son of **D**, have mercy

Debt (DEHT)
Something which is owed, such as money.

2 Kings 4:7 Go, sell the oil, and pay thy **d**

Debtors (DEHT ohrs)
Those who owe a debt.

Matthew 6:12 forgive us our debts, as we forgive our **d**

Debts (DEHTS)
Plural for "debt."

Matthew 6:12 And forgive us our **d**, as we forgive

Deceive (dee SEEV)
To cheat, fool, or trick someone; to lie to a person.

Matthew 24:4 Take heed that no man **d** you
Mark 13:5 Take heed lest any man **d** you
1 John 1:8 say we have no sin, we **d** ourselves

Deceived (dee SEEVD)
Past tense for "deceive."

Luke 21:8 Watch out that you are not **d** (NIV)
Galatians 6:7 Be not **d**; God is not mocked

Declare (dee KLAIR)
To announce, claim, or say.

1 Chronicles 16:24 **D** his glory among the heathen
Psalm 19:1 The heavens **d** the glory of God
Psalm 96:3 **D** his glory among the heathen
Psalm 97:6 The heavens **d** his righteousness
Acts 17:23 ye ignorantly worship, him **d** I unto

Declared (dee KLAIRD)
Past tense for "declare."

Exodus 9:16 that my name may be **d** throughout
Luke 8:47 she **d** unto him before all the people

Decree (dee KREE)
Official law or rule; an order.

Luke 2:1 went out a **d** from Caesar Augustus

Deed (DEED)
An act, action, or work. A deed can be good, or it can be bad.

Colossians 3:17 Whatsoever you do in word or **d**, do

Dd

Deeds (DEEDZ)
Plural for "deed."

Psalm 66:3 Say to God, How awesome are your ***d*** (NIV)
Psalm 86:10 you are great and do marvelous ***d*** (NIV)
Habakkuk 3:2 I stand in awe of your ***d***, O LORD (NIV)
Matthew 5:16 that they may see your good ***d***, and (NIV)
John 3:19 than light, because their ***d*** were evil

Delight (dee LIGHT)
Happiness, joy, pleasure.

Psalm 1:2 his ***d*** is in the law of the LORD
Psalm 37:4 ***D*** thyself also in the LORD; and he
Proverbs 15:8 the prayer of the upright is his ***d***
Proverbs 29:17 he shall give ***d*** to thy soul
Romans 7:22 in my inner being, I ***d*** in God's law (NIV)

Delights (dee LIGHTS)
Plural of "delight."

Proverbs 3:12 loves, as a father the son he ***d*** in (NIV)
Proverbs 12:22 but he ***d*** in men who are truthful (NIV)

Deliver (dee LIH vuhr)
To rescue or set free; to give salvation to.

Matthew 6:13 lead us not into temptation, but ***d*** us
Luke 11:4 lead us not into temptation, but ***d*** us from

Delivered (dee LIH vurhd)
Past tense for "deliver."

Psalm 34:4 he heard me, and ***d*** me from all my fears

Denied (dee NIGHD)
Past tense for "deny."

Luke 22:57 he ***d*** him, saying, Woman I know him not
John 13:38 not crow, till thou has ***d*** me thrice
John 18:25 He ***d*** it, and said, I am not

Deny (dee NIGH)
To refuse, say no to, turn down. It can also mean not to believe or care about.

Matthew 16:24 him ***d*** himself, and take up his cross
Matthew 26:34 before the cock crow, thou shalt ***d*** me
Matthew 26:35 die with thee, yet will I not ***d*** thee
Mark 8:34 let him ***d*** himself, and take up his cross
Mark 14:30 before the cock crow twice, thou shalt ***d*** me
Luke 9:23 let him ***d*** himself, and take up his cross
2 Timothy 2:12 if we ***d*** him, he also will ***d*** us

59

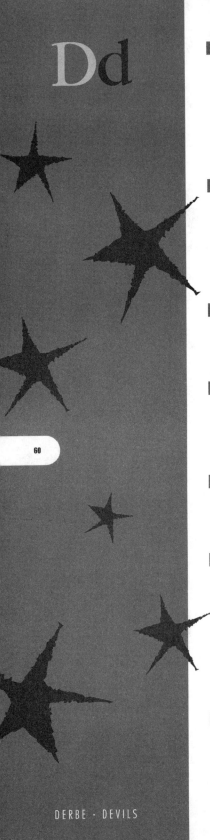

Dd

Derbe (DUHR bih)
This was a city located in Galatia (now a part of south central Turkey). Paul visited this town during three of his missionary journeys (see map on page 341).

Acts 14:6 and fled unto Lystra and **D**, cities
Acts 14:20 and he departed with Barnabas to **D**
Acts 16:1 Then came he to **D** and Lystra

Despise (dih SPIGHZ)
To hate, look down on, dislike very much.

Proverbs 3:11 My son, do not **d** the LORD's discipline (NIV)
Proverbs 23:22 **d** not thy mother when she is old
Matthew 6:24 will hold to the one, and **d** the other
Luke 16:13 he will hold to the one, and **d** the other
1 Timothy 4:12 Let no man **d** thy youth

Despised (dih SPIGHZD)
Past tense of "despise."

Genesis 25:34 thus Esau **d** his birthright
Isaiah 53:3 He is **d** and rejected of men;

Destroy (dih STROEE)
To crush, wipe out, destruct.

Matthew 5:17 I am not to come to **d**, but to fulfill
Mark 11:18 and sought how they might **d** him
Luke 19:47 chief of the people sought to **d** him

Destruction (dih STRUK shun)
Ruin; the failure of something; downfall.

Proverbs 16:18 Pride goeth before **d**, and
Matthew 7:13 broad is the way that leadeth to **d**

Deuteronomy, Book of (DOO tuh RAHN uh mih)
The fifth book of the Old Testament and the fifth book in the division of Law. Moses spoke the words in the book but they were probably written down after he died. He had anointed and appointed Joshua as the new leader to take the Israelites into Canaan, the Promised Land. Moses reminded the people of the laws God had given and urged them to be obedient to God.

Devils (DEV uhlz)
A devil is a supernatural being who tries to stop the things God is doing for people. God always tries to make people happy. Other words for the devil are Satan, demon, or the evil one. A devil always tries to confuse, change, or tell lies about

God's word or God himself. A devil will try to tempt people to do or say things that cause them to sin.

Mark 1:34 divers diseases, and cast out many ***d***
Luke 8:33 Then went the ***d*** out of the man and
James 2:19 the ***d*** also believe, and tremble

■ Dip (DIHP)
To dunk or lower a thing in a liquid.

Ruth 2:14 and ***d*** thy morsel in the vinegar

■ Dipped (DIHPT)
Past tense of "dip."

2 Kings 5:14 and ***d*** himself seven times in Jordan
John 13:26 I shall give a sop, when I have ***d*** it
John 13:26 when he had ***d*** the sop, he gave it to

■ Dippeth (DIH puth)
An old way of saying "dips," plural for "dip."

Matthew 26:23 that ***d*** his hand with me in the dish
Mark 14:20 one of the twelve, that ***d*** with me

■ Disciple (dih SIGH puhl)
The word means "learner" or "pupil." As the person learned, he passed on his knowledge to others.
John 20:4 and the other ***d*** did outrun Peter

■ Disciples (dih SIGH puhlz)
This word is most often connected to those who followed Jesus. Jesus used various ways to teach the ones He called His disciples. The twelve men, to whom Jesus said, "Follow me," are called disciples. But anyone who listened to Jesus, and then shared His teachings, was also called His disciple.

Matthew 9:37 saith he unto his ***d***, The harvest
Matthew 14:19 gave the loaves to his ***d***, and the ***d***
Matthew 14:26 the ***d*** saw him walking on the water
Matthew 26:18 the passover at thy house with my ***d***
Matthew 26:36 Gethsemane, and saith unto the ***d***
Matthew 26:56 Then all the ***d*** deserted him and fled (NIV)
Mark 6:1 his hometown, accompanied by his ***d*** (NIV)
Mark 14:13 And he sendeth fort two of his ***d***
Luke 6:1 his ***d*** plucked the ears of corn
Luke 9:14 And he said to his ***d***, Make them sit
Luke 11:1 ***d*** said unto him, Lord, teach us to pray
John 6:8 of his ***d***, Andrew, Simon Peter's brother
John 13:35 my ***d***, if ye have love one to another
Acts 11:26 ***d*** were called Christians first in Antioch

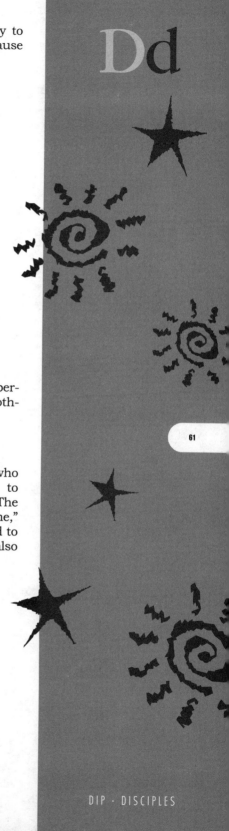

Dd

61

Dd

Distress (diss TREHS)
Can mean misery, suffering, sadness, worry.
Distress can be the result of one's problems or
troubles.

2 Samuel 22:7 In my *d* I called upon the LORD
Psalm 18:6 In my *d* I called upon the LORD
Psalm 118:5 I called upon the LORD in *d*
Psalm 120:1 In my *d* I cried unto the LORD

Divide (dih VIGHD)
To cut, part, or separate.

Exodus 14:16 thine hand over the sea, and *d* it

Divided (dih VIGH did)
Past tense of "divide."

Genesis 1:4 and God *d* the light from the darkness
Exodus 14:21 the sea dry land, and the waters were *d*
Mark 6:41 and the two fishes *d* he among them all

Doer (DOO uhr)
A person who does.

James 1:23 a hearer of the word, and not a *d*

Doers (DOO uhrz)
Plural of "docr."

James 1:22 be ye *d* of the word, and not hearers only

Doeth (DOO ith)
Old way of writing or saying "does."

Proverbs 17:22 merry heart *d* good like a medicine

Doings (DOO eengz)
Ones actions or deeds.

Proverbs 20:11 Even a child is known by his *d*

Door (DAWR)
Entrance, opening. In the New Testament,
Christ was often referred to as a door because
He made it possible for man to enter into eternal
life.

Matthew 6:6 and when thou hast shut thy *d*
Mark 11:4 and found the colt tied by the *d*
Mark 15:46 and rolled a stone unto the *d* of the
John 10:9 I am the *d*: by me if any man enter in
Revelation 3:20 I stand at the *d*, and knock

Dorcas (DAWR kuhs)
The name means "gazelle." She was from
Joppa and did many good things for others

because she was a Christian. When she died, her friends asked Peter to come to Joppa. He prayed for her and her life was restored. Many people believed in Jesus as a result of this miracle by an apostle.

Acts 9:36 which by interpretation is called **D**
Acts 9:39 the coats and garments which **D** made

Dove (DUV)
A bird similar to the smaller pigeons. Doves are mentioned several times in the Bible. Noah let a dove fly from the ark to see if dry land had appeared after the flood. The four Gospel writers write that a dove landed on Jesus after He was baptized. Doves are gentle and faithful to their mates. In Leviticus, God had told Moses that two doves could be used as a sacrifice if a person could not afford a lamb (see "Turtles," page 303. Turtles is another name for "turtledoves"). Mary brought two doves for her sacrifice after Jesus was born.

Genesis 8:8 he sent forth a **d** from him
Matthew 3:16 saw the Spirit of God descending like a **d**
Mark 1:10 the Spirit like a **d** descending upon him
Luke 3:22 descended in a bodily shape like a **d**
John 1:32 Spirit descending from heaven like a **d**

Drink (DRINGK)
To sip or swallow a liquid.

Proverbs 20:1 Wine is a mocker, strong **d** is raging
Proverbs 25:21 if he be thirsty, give him water to **d**
Matthew 6:25 about your life, what you will eat or **d** (NIV)
Matthew 25:35 I was thirsty, and ye gave me **d**
Matthew 25:42 I was thirsty, and ye gave me no **d**
Romans 12:20 if he thirst, give him **d**: for in so
1 Corinthians 11:25 oft as ye **d** it, in remembrance

Dwell (DWEL)
To live; stay; the place where a person lives.

Psalm 15:1 who shall **d** in thy holy hill
Psalm 23:6 I will **d** in the house of the LORD
Psalm 27:4 that I may **d** in the house of the LORD

Dwelleth (DWEL ith)
The old way of saying or writing "dwells."

Psalm 91:1 He that **d** in the secret place of the

Dove

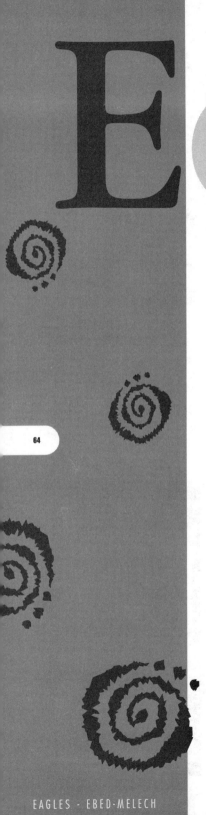

Eagles (EE guhlz)
In the Bible, "eagle" refers to the largest bird to fly in Palestine. It builds large nests in the mountains, is a powerful bird with good eyesight, and flies quite fast. Eagles are very careful to protect their young. The eagle is a picture of how God loves and cares for His people.

Isaiah 40:31 They will soar on wings like **e** (NIV)

Earth (URTH)
Can either be defined as the whole planet or as a certain area of land. Opposite of heaven, as "heaven and earth."

Genesis 1:1 God created the heaven and the **e**
Psalm 8:1 how excellent is thy name in all the **e**
Psalm 24:1 The **e** is the LORD's, and the fullness
Psalm 33:8 Let all the **e** fear the LORD
Psalm 37:11 But the meek shall inherit the **e**
Matthew 5:5 meek: for they shall inherit the **e**
Matthew 5:13 Ye are the salt of the **e**
Matthew 6:10 Thy will be done in **e**, as it is
Mark 13:31 Heaven and **e** shall pass away: but
Luke 2:14 on **e**, peace, good will toward men
Luke 23:44 darkness over all the **e** until the
Acts 1:8 and unto the uttermost part of the **e**

East (EEST)
The direction from which the sun rises. The word also refers to the land east of Palestine.

Exodus 10:13 The LORD brought an **e** wind upon
Exodus 10:13 the **e** wind brought the locusts
Exodus 14:21 the sea to go back by a strong **e** wind
Psalm 103:12 As far as the **e** is from the west
Matthew 2:1 came wise men from the **e** to Jerusalem
Matthew 2:2 we have seen his star in the **e** and
Matthew 2:9 the star, which they saw in the **e**

Easy (EE zee)
No problem, simple, not hard; restful.

Proverbs 14:6 knowledge is **e** unto him that
Matthew 11:30 my yoke is **e**, and my burden is light

Ebed-melech (EE bed-MEE lek)
The name means "servant of the king." He was a court official for King Zedekiah of Judah. When Ebed-melech heard that Jeremiah was

64

in the well and would starve, he helped rescue Jeremiah. God then promised to protect Ebed-melech.

Jeremiah 38:7 Now when **E**, the Ethiopian, one
Jeremiah 38:10 Then the king commanded **E** the Ethiopian
Jeremiah 38:11 **E** took the men with him, and went
Jeremiah 39:16 Go and speak to **E** the Ethiopian

Ecclesiastes, Book of (ih KLEE zih ASS teez)

The fourth book in the division of Poetry and Wisdom in the Old Testament. The author is uncertain, referred to only as The Preacher. This book stressed the importance of a person fearing and honoring God in order for life to have meaning and purpose. Wisdom is learned when one realized that life has limits. Chapter 12, verse 13, reads, "Fear God, and keep his commandments: for this is the whole duty of man."

Eden (EE duhn)

The garden where Adam and Eve lived after they were created by God. Eden has been called the "garden of delight" or "paradise." It is thought that Eden was located between the Euphrates and Tigris Rivers in what is now Iraq.

Genesis 2:8 planted a garden eastward in **E**
Genesis 2:15 put him into the garden of **E** to
Genesis 3:23 God sent him forth from the garden of **E**

Effective (ih FEK tiv)

An action that causes an exact reaction or result; successful.

James 5:16 prayer of a righteous man is powerful and **e** (NIV)

Effectual (ih FEK choo uhl)

An action that can cause an exact reaction or result.

James 5:16 The **e** fervent prayer of a righteous man

Egypt (EE jipt)

A land located in northern Africa (see map on page 336). It is one of the oldest nations in the world. The Sinai Wilderness separates Egypt from Palestine. The Nile River flows through Egypt, providing water to grow crops. Egypt is mostly desert. Jacob's youngest son, Joseph, was sold into slavery in Egypt. Later, Jacob and his whole family moved to the northern

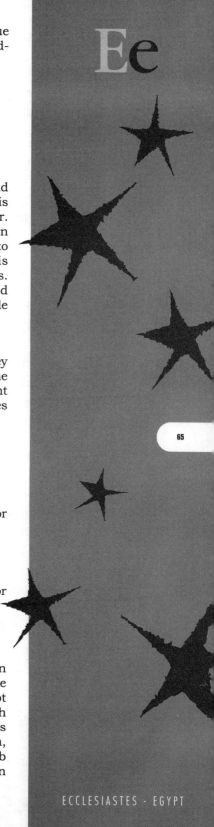

Ee

65

Ee

part of Egypt. Four hundred years later, Moses was born in Egypt and helped free the Israelite people from slavery.

Genesis 37:28 and they brought Joseph into **E**
Genesis 41:29 plenty throughout all the land of **E**
Genesis 41:41 have set thee over all the land of **E**
Genesis 42:1 Jacob saw there was corn in **E**
Genesis 45:9 God hath made me lord of all **E**
Genesis 45:18 give you the good of the land of **E**
Exodus 4:19 Moses in Midian, Go, return into **E**
Exodus 13:14 The LORD brought us out from **E**
Matthew 2:13 flee into **E**, and be thou there until
Matthew 2:19 appeareth in a dream to Joseph in **E**

Eli (EE ligh)

His name meant "high." Eli was the priest at Shiloh. The boy, Samuel, was brought by his mother to live at the place of worship in Shiloh. She had promised to dedicate a son to God if He would give her one. Eli did not train his own sons to do right, but he did help Samuel to know how to listen to God and to obey Him.

1 Samuel 1:9 Now **E** the priest sat upon a seat by
1 Samuel 1:17 Then **E** answered and said, Go in peace
1 Samuel 2:11 child did minister unto the LORD before **E**
1 Samuel 3:8 Then **E** realized that the LORD was (NIV)
1 Samuel 3:16 Then **E** called Samuel, and said,

Elder (ELL duhr)

An older person in a family or group. In Old Testament times, an elder was the leader of a clan or group. Elders were often respected because of their experiences and wisdom as they helped make decisions and rules for the Israelite nation. In the New Testament, elders served on a panel to help make decisions for the church.

Luke 15:25 Now his **e** son was in the field: and

Elders (EL duhrz)

Plural of "elder."

Ruth 4:9 And Boaz said unto the **e**, and
Matthew 26:3 scribes, and the **e** of the people
Matthew 26:59 priests, and **e**, and all the council
Matthew 27:12 was accused of the chief priests and **e**
Mark 8:31 and be rejected of the **e**, and of the
Luke 9:22 and be rejected of the **e** and chief priests
Luke 22:66 the **e** of the people and the chief priests

Elijah (ih LIGH juh)

His name means "my God is Yah." "Yah" is a short form of Yahweh, the Hebrew name for God. Elijah lived in Tishbe of Gilead in Israel, the Northern Kingdom. Elijah trusted God. Even though kings didn't like Elijah, he gave God's message to them. The favorite story about Elijah is when he faced the 450 prophets of Baal and the 400 prophets of Asherah on Mount Carmel. He proved that God was the one true God. Elijah did not die but was taken to heaven in a whirlwind or wind storm. Elisha, the man to follow Elijah, saw the whirlwind take Elijah to heaven.

Elijah

1 Kings 17:1 and **E** the Tishbite, who was of the
1 Kings 17:13 And **E** said unto her, Fear not, go and
1 Kings 17:22 And the LORD heard the voice of **E**
1 Kings 17:24 woman said to **E**, Now by this I know
1 Kings 18:21 **E** came unto all the people, and said
1 Kings 18:31 **E** took twelve stones, according to
1 Kings 18:42 **E** went up to the top of Carmel; and he
1 Kings 18:46 And the hand of the LORD was on **E**
1 Kings 21:17 word of the LORD came to **E** the Tishbite
2 Kings 2:8 **E** took his mantle, and wrapped it
2 Kings 2:9 **E** said to Elisha, Ask what I shall do
2 Kings 2:11 **E** went up by a whirlwind into heaven

Elim (EE lim)

Place name meaning "trees." One place where the Israelites camped after Moses led them out of Egypt. At Elim, there were twelve water wells and seventy palm trees.

Exodus 15:27 they came to **E**, where were twelve wells
Numbers 33:9 and came unto **E**: and in **E** were twelve

Elimelech (ih LIM uh lek)

The name means "my God is king." He was the husband of Naomi. He took Naomi and their two sons to Moab during a famine. After he arrived in Moab, he died. He was a relative of Boaz.

Ruth 1:2 the name of the man was **E**, and the name of
Ruth 1:3 **E** Naomi's husband died; and she was left
Ruth 2:1 of the family of **E**; and his name was Boaz
Ruth 2:3 Boaz, who was of the kindred of **E**

Elisabeth (ih LIZ uh beth)

The name means "my God is good fortune" or "God is my oath." She was the wife of Zacharias and the mother of John the Baptist. She was also related to Mary, the mother of Jesus.

Ee

Luke 1:13 thy wife **E** shall bear thee a son, and thou
Luke 1:36 And, behold, thy cousin **E** she hath also
Luke 1:41 and **E** was filled with the Holy Ghost

Elisha (ih LIGH shuh)

His name means "my God is salvation." Elisha was a prophet who came after Elijah. Before Elijah went up into heaven in the whirlwind, Elisha asked for a "double portion" of Elijah's spirit. After that, Elisha was able to perform many miracles. He also gave advice to many kings.

1 Kings 19:16 anoint **E** son of Shaphat from Abel (NIV)
2 Kings 2:9 **E** said, I pray thee, let a double portion
2 Kings 2:12 **E** saw it and cried, My father, my
2 Kings 4:2 **E** said unto her, What shall I do for thee
2 Kings 4:32 when **E** was come into the house, behold,
2 Kings 5:8 when **E** the man of God had heard that
2 Kings 6:17 **E** prayed, and said, LORD, I pray thee
2 Kings 8:4 all the great things that **E** hath done

Elkanah (el KAY nuh)

The name means "God created." He was the father of Samuel.

1 Samuel 1:1 and his name was **E**, the son of
1 Samuel 1:8 Then said **E** her husband to her, Hannah
1 Samuel 2:20 And Eli blessed **E** and his wife

Emmanuel (ih MAN yoo el)

The name means "God with us." It is also sometimes spelled "Immanuel" (see "Immanuel," page 115). Isaiah foretold that a son would be born and this would be his name. We know that Jesus was that son.

Matthew 1:23 a son, and they shall call his name **E**

Emmaus (eh MAY uhs)

The name means "hot baths." This village lay about seven miles from Jerusalem (see map on page 340). Two disciples walked to Emmaus the day Jesus was resurrected. Jesus walked with them but they did not know it was the risen Christ until He broke the bread at the meal.

Luke 24:13 went that same day to a village called **E**

Endure (in DAWR)

To allow; bear, suffer; last, remain, stay.

Psalm 9:7 the LORD shall **e** for ever
Psalm 30:5 weeping may **e** for a night, but joy
Psalm 72:17 His name shall **e** for ever

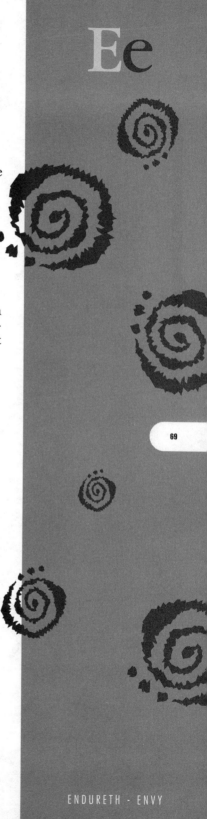

Endureth (in DAWR ith)

The old way of saying or writing, "endures."

1 Chronicles 16:34 for his mercy **e** for ever
Psalm 100:5 his truth **e** to all generations
Psalm 107:1 for his mercy **e** for ever
Matthew 10:22 he that **e** to the end shall be saved
1 Corinthians 13:7 hopeth all things, **e** all things

Enemies (IN ih meez)

Plural for "enemy." The Bible teaches us to love our enemies, not hate them.

Psalm 18:3 So shall I be saved from mine **e**
Psalm 23:5 table before me in the presence of mine **e**
Psalm 59:1 Deliver me from mine **e**, O my God
Matthew 5:44 Love your **e**, bless them that curse you
Luke 6:35 But love ye your **e**, and do good

Enemy (IN ih mee)

One who does not like, or who hates another. An enemy will try to hurt the one he hates. It is natural for us to hate those we call our enemy, but Jesus taught us to love them.

Proverbs 24:17 Do not gloat when your **e** falls (NIV)
Proverbs 25:21 If thine **e** be hungry, give him bread
Matthew 5:43 love thy neighbor, and hate thine **e**
Romans 12:20 If thine **e** hunger, feed him

Enter (IN tuhr)

To admit, go in, start.

Psalm 100:4 **E** into his gates with thanksgiving
Matthew 6:6 when thou prayest, **e** into thy closet
Matthew 7:13 **E** through the narrow gate. For wide (NIV)
Matthew 19:24 for a rich man to **e** into the kingdom
Mark 9:25 out of him, and **e** no more into him
Mark 10:25 than for a rich man to **e** into the
Luke 13:24 effort to **e** through the narrow door (NIV)
Luke 22:40 Pray that ye **e** not into temptation
Luke 22:46 rise and pray, lest ye **e** into temptation

Entreat (en TREET)

To ask, beg, plead.

Exodus 8:29 I will **e** the LORD that the swarms
Exodus 10:17 **e** the LORD your God, that he may
Ruth 1:16 **E** me not to leave thee, or to return

Envy (IN vee)

To be jealous of, or want something, that another person has. Often spite and dislike are a part of envy. Both the Old Testament and the New Testament warn about the danger of envy.

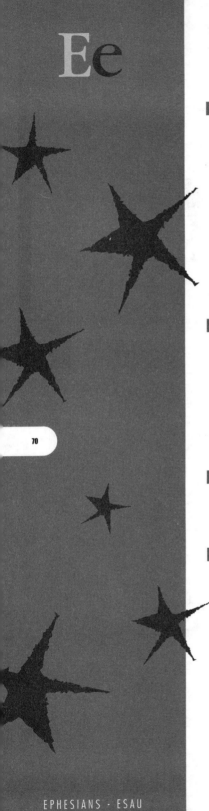

Ee

Proverbs 3:31 Do not *e* a violent man or choose (NIV)
Proverbs 23:17 Let not thine heart *e* sinners
Matthew 27:18 knew that for *e* they had delivered him
Mark 15:10 the chief priests had delivered him for *e*

■ Ephesians, Book of (ih FEE shuhnz)

The fifth book of the division, Paul's Letters, in the New Testament. He visited the city of Ephesus on his second and third missionary journeys. He stayed in Ephesus for three years so he knew the Christians there. Paul may have been in a Roman prison when he wrote this letter to the church at Ephesus. He urged the Christians to live their lives for God, not to depend on their own abilities but to do so in God's strength. He stressed the importance of faithfully following Christ's teachings in all they did, but especially to their families, and to the church.

■ Ephesus (EF uh suhs)

A large seaport city in western Asia Minor on the Aegean Sea (see map on page 341). Ephesus was controlled by Roman rule. The apostle Paul started a church in Ephesus. After his third missionary journey, he stayed for three years to teach and preach. The book of Ephesians was written to the Christians at Ephesus.

Ephesians 1:1 the saints which are at *E*, and to the

■ Ephratah (EF ruh tuh)

The name means "fruitful." It is another name for Bethlehem of Judah.

Micah 5:2 But thou, Bethlehem *E*, though thou be

■ Esau (EE saw)

The meaning of the name is not known. His name may mean "hairy." Another name given to him was Edom, which meant "red." He was one of the sons of Isaac and Rebekah and had a twin brother, Jacob. Esau was the favorite son of Isaac, and Jacob was the favorite son of Rebekah. He traded his birthright to Jacob for a bowl of stew. Later, Jacob cheated Esau out of his father's blessing. After many years of being enemies, Esau finally forgave his brother.

Genesis 25:25 and they called his name *E*
Genesis 25:27 *E* was a cunning hunter, a man of
Genesis 25:28 Isaac loved *E*, because he did eat
Genesis 25:34 Jacob gave *E* some bread and some (NIV)
Genesis 25:34 thus *E* despised his birthright

Genesis 27:11 **E** my brother is a hairy man, and
Genesis 27:32 I am thy son, thy firstborn **E**
Genesis 27:34 when **E** heard the words of his father
Genesis 27:41 **E** hated Jacob because of the blessing
Genesis 33:4 **E** ran to meet him, and embraced him

Escape (eh SKAYP)
Get away, run.

Proverbs 19:5 he that speaketh lies shall not **e**
1 Corinthians 10:13 also make a way to **e**, that ye
Hebrews 2:3 How shall we **e**, if we neglect so

Esther (ESS tuhr)
The name is Persian and means "Ishtar." Ishtar was a Mesopotamian goddess. Esther was a Jewish girl who had been in exile in Babylon with many other Israelites. Her Jewish name was "Hadassah." Esther's older cousin, Mordecai, raised her after her parents died. She became queen to King Ahasuerus, ruler in Babylon. Esther saved all the Jewish people in Babylon from being killed. The book of Esther in the Old Testament is named for her.

Esther 2:7 he brought up Hadassah, that is, **E**
Esther 4:5 Then called **E** for Hatach, one of the
Esther 4:15 Then **E** sent this reply to Mordecai (NIV)
Esther 5:2 when the king saw **E** the queen standing
Esther 6:14 unto the banquet that **E** had prepared
Esther 7:3 Then **E** the queen answered and said
Esther 8:4 So **E** arose, and stood before the king

Esther, Book of (ESS tuhr)
The book of Esther is the twelfth and last in the division, History, in the Old Testament. It tells the story of Esther and how God used her to save the Israelite people who had been taken from Canaan to Persia. It is interesting to know that the entire book never says God's name.

Eternal (life) (ee TUR nuhl lighf)
Eternal is that life after death that has no boundary. It is life that will go on forever, that will never end. One has eternal life when he asks God to forgive him of his sins and then he trusts Jesus to be his Lord and Savior.

Matthew 19:16 shall I do, that I may have **e** life
Mark 10:17 shall I do that I may inherit **e** life
Luke 10:25 what shall I do to inherit **e** life
John 3:15 should not perish but have **e** life
Romans 6:23 but the gift of God is **e** life
1 John 5:11 that God hath given to us **e** life

Esther

Ee

Eve

Ethiopia (EE thih OH pih uh)
The region in Africa south of Egypt in what is known today as Sudan (see map on page 339). It is one of the oldest nations in the world. The people who lived there had dark skin. Ebed-melech, who rescued Jeremiah from the well, was from Ethiopia. Also, the man whom Philip told about Jesus in Acts 8 was from Ethiopia.

Acts 8:27 man of **E**, an eunuch of great authority

Ethiopian (EE thih OH pih uhn)
A person from Ethiopia.

Jeremiah 38:7 Now when Ebed-melech the **E**, one of

Eunuch (YOO nuhk)
A man who does not have the physical ability to become a father. Usually the sexual organs have been removed. Eunuchs could be trusted and often worked as court officials for a king or other rulers in the ancient Near East. The Near East is the area around the Mediterranean Sea, including northeast Africa, Palestine, and Mesopotamia.

Acts 8:27 man of Ethiopia, an **e** of great authority

Euphrates (yoo FRAY teez)
The name means "bursting" or "sweet" and was called "the river" by the Hebrews. Starting in Armenia, and finally flowing into the Persian Gulf, it is the longest river in western Asia (see map on page 336). The Euphrates River formed the northern boundary of the land God would give the Israelites. One of the many cities built along the Euphrates was Babylon. Today, this river flows through or borders Turkey, Syria, Iraq, and Iran.

Joshua 1:4 even unto the great river, the river **E**

Eve (EEV)
The name meant "life." She was the first woman God created. He used one of Adam's ribs to form her. She disobeyed God and ate from the tree in the middle of the garden. Then she gave some of the fruit to Adam. She was the mother of Cain and Abel, as well as other children.

Genesis 3:20 Adam called his wife's name **E**

Evening (EEV ninhg)
Night, sundown, sunset.

Genesis 1:5 the **e** and the morning were the first

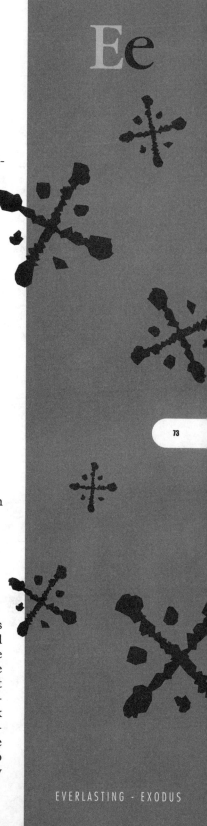

Genesis 1:8 the **e** and the morning were the second
Genesis 1:13 the **e** and the morning were the third
Genesis 1:19 the **e** and the morning were the fourth
Genesis 1:23 the **e** and the morning were the fifth
Genesis 1:31 the **e** and the morning were the sixth
Psalm 55:17 **E**, and morning, and at noon will I pray
Matthew 14:15 when it was **e**, his disciples came to

Everlasting (eh VUR LA sting)
Never ending. Usually associated with everlasting life (see "Eternal Life").

Psalm 93:2 thou art from **e**
Psalm 100:5 For the LORD is good; his mercy is **e**
Psalm 139:24 and lead me in the way **e**
John 3:16 should not perish, but have **e** life
John 4:24 believeth on him that sent me, hath **e** life

Exalt (egg ZAWLT)
To raise up, honor, praise, worship.

Exodus 15:2 my father's God, and I will **e** him
Psalm 34:3 and let us **e** his name together
Psalm 99:5 **E** ye the LORD our God, and worship
Psalm 118:28 thou art my God, I will **e** thee

Exalted (egg ZAWL tid)
Past tense of "exalt."

Psalm 18:46 let the God of my salvation be **e**
Psalm 21:13 Be thou **e**, LORD, in thine own strength
Psalm 57:5 Be thou **e**, O God, above the heavens

Exceeding (ek SEE ding)
To be more than enough; to be more than expected.

Matthew 5:12 Rejoice, and be **e** glad: for great is
Matthew 26:38 My soul is **e** sorrowful, even unto death
Mark 14:34 My soul is **e** sorrowful unto death
Luke 23:8 when Herod saw Jesus, he was **e** glad

Exodus, Book of (EK suh duhs)
The word means "mass departure." This book is the second in the division of Law, in the Old Testament. It is also the second book in the Bible. It tells how God directed Moses to lead the Israelites out of Egyptian slavery. It tells about and contains the laws which God gave the people, mainly the Ten Commandments. The book also gives details about the Israelites wanderings in the desert. God showed His presence with the people by providing a cloud by day to protect from the hot desert sun, and a fire by

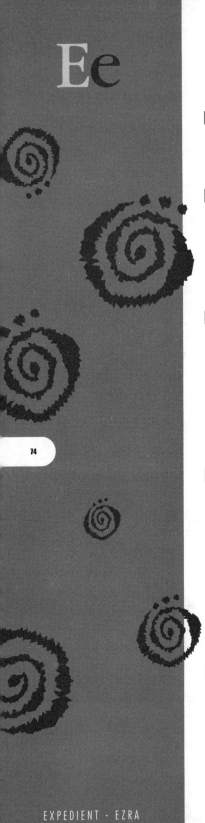

Ee

night, to provide warmth from the cold desert nights. He sent manna and quail for food, and He provided water for them and their flocks and herds of animals.

Expedient (ek SPEE dih uhnt)
Useful, worthwhile, fitting, beneficial, helpful.

John 16:7 It is **e** for you that I go away
John 18:14 it was **e** that one man should die

Ezekiel (ih ZEE kih uhl)
The name means "God will strengthen." Ezekiel was a prophet and priest in Judah. He was taken captive to Babylon in 597 B.C. He began to prophesy to those in exile as well as those left n Jerusalem in 593 B.C.

Ezekiel 1:3 word of the LORD came expressly unto **E**

Ezekiel, Book of (ih ZEE kih uhl)
The name of the fourth book of the division, Major Prophets, in the Old Testament. His book contains many visions and messages for the Jews who became captives of the Babylonians in 598 B.C. Some messages were warnings about their sinful living. Later messages offered more hope as Ezekiel tried to help the Hebrews see how God was protecting Israel, His chosen people.

Ezra (EZ ruh)
The name means "Yahweh helps." Ezra was a priest and a scribe. A scribe wrote letters and did other things a secretary might do today. He had been in exile in Babylon but returned to Jerusalem. His main work was to help the Jewish people worship God in the way they should. He was also a teacher of the laws of God.

Ezra 7:6 This **E** went up from Babylon; and he
Ezra 7:10 For **E** had prepared his heart to seek
Nehemiah 8:5 And **E** opened the book in the sight
Nehemiah 8:6 **E** blessed the LORD, the great God

Ezra, Book of (EZ ruh)
The ninth book of the division, History, in the Old Testament. It tells about the Jews who returned to Jerusalem from Babylon. This group of people rebuilt the Temple. The walls around Jerusalem had been rebuilt earlier when Nehemiah led a group from Babylon to help make Jerusalem secure. Since Ezra was a priest and scribe, the book tells how he taught

74

Scripture to the Jews to help them get back their identity (to know who they were as God's people).

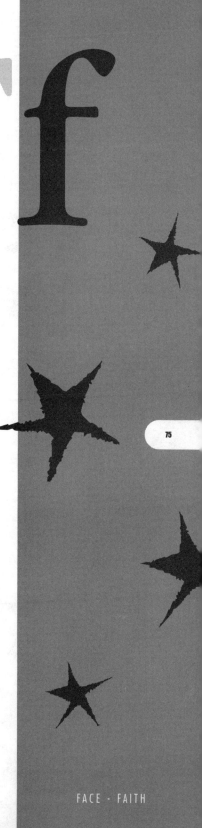

Face (FAYCE)
The front of a person's head, including his eyes, nose, mouth, and chin. Face can also refer to God's presence.

Exodus 3:6 Moses hid his *f*, for he was afraid
Exodus 10:29 I will see thy *f* again no more
Numbers 6:25 LORD make his *f* shine upon thee
Psalm 27:9 Hide not thy *f* far from me
Psalm 67:1 and cause his *f* to shine upon us
Matthew 26:39 and fell on his *f*, and prayed
Matthew 26:67 Then did they spit in his *f*
Mark 14:65 to spit on him, and to cover his *f*
Luke 5:12 who seeing Jesus fell on his *f*
Luke 22:64 they struck him on the *f*, and

Fadeth (FAY dith)
The old way of saying or writing "fades," the plural for "fade." When a thing fades, it begins to get thinner or to vanish or disappear.

Isaiah 40:8 The grass withereth, the flower *f*

Fail (FAYL)
To lose strength; forget; abandon.

Joshua 1:5 I will not *f* thee, nor forsake thee
Lamentations 3:22 because his compassions *f* not
Luke 22:32 prayed for thee, that thy faith *f* not

Faith (FAYTH)
Belief, trust in something or someone. We trust in Jesus as our Savior because we believe that he died on the cross for our sins.

Habakkuk 2:4 but the just shall live by his *f*
Matthew 9:22 thy *f* hath made thee whole
Matthew 17:20 have *f* as a grain of mustard seed
Luke 7:9 I have not found so great *f*, no, not
Luke 7:50 Thy *f* hath saved thee; go in peace
Romans 5:1 Therefore being justified by *f*
Romans 10:17 So then *f* cometh by hearing, and
1 Corinthians 13:13 And now abideth *f*, hope,
Ephesians 2:8 by grace are ye saved through *f*
Hebrews 10:38 Now the just shall live by *f*
Hebrews 11:1 Now *f* is being sure of what we hope (NIV)

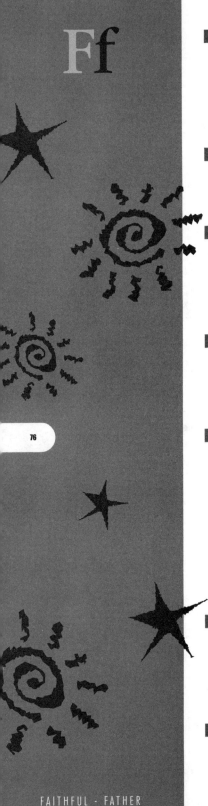

Ff

■ Faithful (FAYTH fuhl)
Loyal, true, honest. A person who is faithful is one who can be trusted to do what is right. God is faithful because He keeps His promises.

Proverbs 14:5 A **f** witness will not lie
1 John 1:9 he is **f** and just to forgive us

■ Faithfulness (FAYTH fuhl niss)
See "Faithful."

Psalm 119:90 Thy **f** is unto all generations
Lamentations 3:23 new every morning: great is thy **f**

■ False (FAWLS)
Untrue; a lie.

Exodus 20:16 Thou shalt not bear **f** witness
Deuteronomy 5:20 Neither shalt thou bear **f** witness
Matthew 19:18 Thou shalt not bear **f** witness
Romans 13:9 Thou shalt not bear **f** witness

■ Falsely (FAWLS lee)
See "False."

Leviticus 19:11 shall not steal, neither deal **f**
Leviticus 19:12 shall not swear by my name **f**
Matthew 5:11 say all manner of evil against you **f**

■ Famine (FA min)
A time when crops will not grow due to lack of rain. Insects and war can destroy crops, creating a famine. A famine means there is not enough food. People face possible starvation at a time of famine.

Genesis 12:10 And there was a **f** in the land
Genesis 41:27 east wind shall be seven years of **f**
Genesis 42: 5 the **f** was in the land of Canaan
Ruth 1:1 that there was a **f** in the land
Luke 15:14 there arose a mighty **f** in that land

■ Far (FAHR)
Distant; far away.

Psalm 22:11 Be not **f** from me; for trouble is near
Psalm 103:12 As **f** as the east is from the west
Luke 15:13 and took his journey into a **f** country
Luke 24:50 he led them out as **f** as to Bethany

■ Father (FAH thur)
The male parent. Dad. Father (with a capital "F") is one way God is addressed.

Exodus 20:12 Honor thy *f* and thy mother
Matthew 5:16 glorify your *F* which is in heaven
Matthew 6:6 pray to thy *F* which is in secret
Matthew 6:9 Our *F* which art in heaven, Hallowed
Matthew 19:19 Honor thy *f* and thy mother
Luke 11:2 when ye pray, say, Our *F* which art
Luke 22:42 prayed, *F*, if you are willing, take (NIV)
Luke 23:34 Then said Jesus, *F*, forgive them
John 14:6 no man cometh unto the *F*, but by me
John 20:21 my *F* hath sent me, even so send I you
Ephesians 6:2 Honor thy *f* and mother; which is

Faults (FAWLTZ)
Flaws, mistakes, sins, errors.

James 5:16 Confess your *f* one to another, and

Fear (fihr)
Reverence, respect, awe; to be afraid.

Exodus 14:13 *F* ye not, stand still, and see the
Deuteronomy 8:6 to walk in his ways, and to *f*
Deuteronomy 31:8 *f* not, neither be dismayed
Psalm 2:11 Serve the LORD with *f*, and rejoice
Psalm 23:4 shadow of death, I will *f* no evil
Psalm 27:1 whom shall I *f*? the LORD is the strength
Psalm 118:6 I will not *f*. what can man do unto me
Proverbs 1:7 The *f* of the LORD is the beginning of
Proverbs 3:7 *f* the LORD, and depart from evil
Ecclesiastes 12:13 *F* God, and keep his commandments
Hebrews 13:6 I will not *f* what man shall do

Feared (FIHRD)
Past tense of "fear."

1 Chronicles 16:25 he also is to be *f* above all gods
Psalm 96:4 he is to be *f* above all gods

Feareth (FIHR ith)
The old way of writing or saying "fears."

Psalm 25:12 What man is he that *f* the LORD
Psalm 112:1 Blessed is the man that *f* the LORD
Psalm 128:4 shall the man be blessed that *f* the LORD
Proverbs 28:14 Happy is the man that *f* always

Fearfully (FIHR fuhl lee)
See "Fear."

Psalm 139:14 for I am *f* and wonderfully made

Fears (FIHRZ)
Plural of "fear."

Psalm 34:4 and delivered me from all my *f*

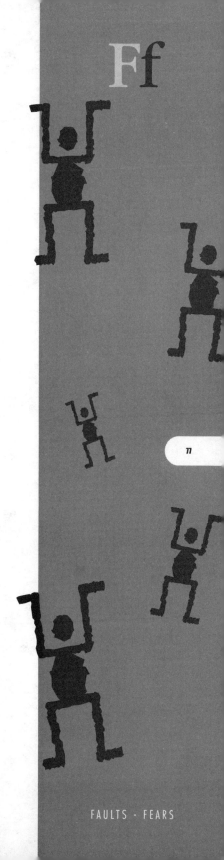

Ff

■ Feed (FEED)
To dine, eat; to give food.

John 21:15 He saith unto him, **F** my lambs
John 21:16 He saith unto him, **F** my sheep
John 21:17 Jesus saith unto him, **F** my sheep

■ Feet (FEET)
Plural of "foot." The end of the legs on which a man or animal stands.

Exodus 3:5 put off thy shoes from off thy **f**
Psalm 119:105 Thy word is a lamp unto my **f** and
Matthew 15:30 cast them down at Jesus' **f**
Matthew 28:9 they came and held him by the **f**
Mark 5:22 when he saw him, he fell at his **f**
Luke 7:38 stood at his **f** behind him weeping
Luke 8:41 and he fell down at Jesus' **f**
Luke 24:39 Behold my hands and **f**, that it is I
Luke 24:40 he showed them his hands and his **f**
John 11:2 and wiped his **f** with her hair
John 12:3 anointed the **f** of Jesus, and wiped his
John 13:5 and began to wash the disciples' **f**

■ Female (FEE mayl)
A girl or woman.

Genesis 1:27 male and **f** created he them

■ Fervent (FUHR vint)
A warm or strong feeling.

James 5:16 effectual **f** prayer of a righteous man

■ Field (FEELD)
Land which has no fences. Crops can be planted or the grasses allowed to grow as pasture for animals.

Matthew 6:28 Consider the lilies of the **f**, how
Matthew 6:30 if God so clothe the grass of the **f**

■ Fields (FEELDZ)
Plural of "field.".

John 4:35 Lift up your eyes, and look on the **f**

■ Fiery (FIGH ree)
Burning, blazing, very hot.

Daniel 3:20 cast them into the burning **f** furnace
Daniel 3:26 to the mouth of the burning **f** furnace

■ Fig (FIHG)
A sweet fruit, pear-shaped, brown when ripe, and filled with many small seeds in the center.

The tree is short with thick branches and twigs. The fruit can be flattened, dried, and stored to use later.

Genesis 3:7 and they sewed *f* leaves together
John 1:48 thou wast under the *f* tree, I saw
John 1:50 I saw thee under the *f* tree

Fight (FITE)

An attack or battle. The apostle Paul referred to his life of sharing about Jesus as though it were a fight. He had many difficulties as he went from place to place to tell about Jesus. He was stoned, was in a shipwreck, spent time in prison, and faced other problems. But he did not give up. His life work was to tell about Jesus to anyone who would listen.

John 18:36 this world, then would my servants *f*
2 Timothy 4:7 I have fought a good *f*, I have

Fill (FIHL)

To provide, supply; to place something in a container until no more can be put in.

Genesis 44:1 **F** the men's sacks with food, as much
1 Kings 18:33 **F** four barrels with water, and pour
Matthew 15:33 as to *f* so great a multitude
John 2:7 Jesus saith unto them, **F** the waterpots
Romans 15:13 Now the God of hope *f* you with all joy

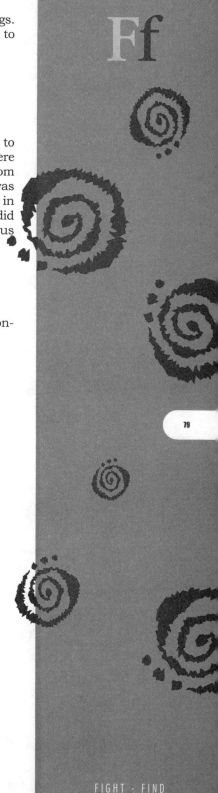

Filled (FIHLD)

Past tense of "fill."

Psalm 71:8 Let my mouth be *f* with thy praise
Matthew 5:6 after righteousness: for they shall be *f*
Matthew 14:20 And they did all eat, and were *f*
Matthew 15:37 And they did all eat, and were *f*
Matthew 27:48 took a sponge, and *f* it with vinegar
Mark 8:8 So they did eat, and were *f*
Mark 15:36 one ran and *f* a sponge with vinegar
Luke 2:40 *f* with wisdom: and the grace of God
Luke 5:7 they came, and *f* both the ships
Luke 9:17 they did eat, and were all *f*
Luke 15:16 have *f* his belly with the husks
John 6:12 When they were *f*, he said unto his
John 6:13 and *f* twelve baskets with the fragments
John 12:3 and the house was *f* with the odor
John 19:29 and they *f* a sponge with vinegar

Find (FIGHND)

To discover or locate.

Exodus 5:11 get you straw where you can *f* it

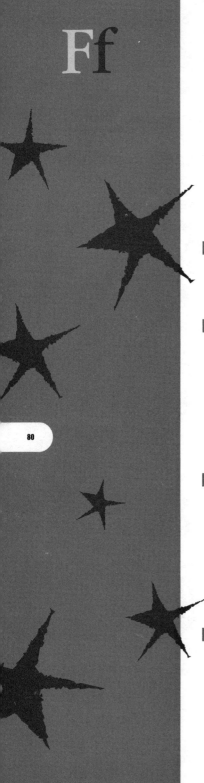

Ruth 2:2 after him in whose sight I shall *f* grace
Proverbs 20:6 but a faithful man who can *f*
Matthew 7:7 seek and ye shall *f*, knock, and
Matthew 7:14 life, and few there be that *f* it
Matthew 16:25 lose his life for my sake shall *f* it
Matthew 21:2 ye shall *f* an ass tied, and a colt
Mark 11:2 ye shall *f* a colt tied, whereon never
Luke 2:12 Ye shall *f* the babe wrapped in swaddling
Luke 6:7 that they might *f* an accusation against
Luke 15:4 after that which is lost, until he *f* it
Luke 19:30 entering ye shall *f* a colt tied
John 18:38 I *f* in him no fault at all
John 19:6 for I *f* no fault in him

■ Firm (FUHRM)
Hard, solid, steady, sure.

Exodus 14:13 Do not be afraid. Stand *f* and you (NIV)
Matthew 10:22 he who stands *f* to the end will be (NIV)

■ Firmament (FUHR mah mint)
The sky. The heavens, where the sun, moon, planets, and stars have been placed.

Genesis 1:6 Let there be a *f* in the midst of
Genesis 1:7 And God made the *f*, and divided
Genesis 1:8 And God called the *f* Heaven
Genesis 1:14 Let there be lights in the *f* of
Psalm 19:1 and the *f* showeth his handiwork
Daniel 12:3 shall shine as the brightness of the *f*

■ First (FUHRST)
Beginning, earliest, ahead.

Genesis 1:5 evening and the morning were the *f* day
Mark 12:29 Jesus answered him, The *f* of all the
Mark 12:30 strength: this is the *f* commandment
Luke 24:1 Upon the *f* day of the week, very early
John 1:41 He *f* findeth his own brother Simon
John 20:1 The *f* day of the week cometh Mary
Revelation 22:13 beginning and the end, the *f* and

■ Firstborn (FUHRST born)
The child or animal born first. In the Hebrew culture, the firstborn was the first son born to a man and his wife. This son was dedicated to God. He would receive a double portion of the father's wealth. When his father died, he would become the leader of the family and care for his mother until she died. The firstborn also included animals which were sacrificed.

Exodus 12:12 and I will smite all the *f* in the land

Exodus 12:29 at midnight the LORD smote all the *f*
Exodus 12:29 from the *f* of Pharaoh that sat on his
Exodus 12:29 and all the *f* of cattle
Matthew 1:25 she had brought forth her *f* son
Luke 2:7 And she brought forth her *f* son, and

Fishers (FIH shurz)
Those who fished; also fishermen.Compare Matthew 4:18 (KJV) with Matthew 4:18 (NIV).

Matthew 4:18 net into the sea: for they were *f*
Matthew 4:19 and I will make you *f* of men
Mark 1:16 net into the sea: for they were *f*
Mark 1:17 I will make you to become *f* of men

Five (FIGHV)
A number that is one more than four.

Matthew 14:17 We have here but *f* loaves, and two
Matthew 14:19 took the *f* loaves, and the two fishes
Matthew 14:21 eaten were about *f* thousand men
Mark 6:41 And when he had taken the *f* loaves
Mark 6:44 eat of the loaves were about *f* thousand
Mark 8:19 brake the *f* loaves among the *f* thousand
Luke 9:13 no more than *f* loaves and two fishes
Luke 9:14 For they were about *f* thousand men
Luke 9:16 Then he took the *f* loaves and the two
John 6:9 a lad here, which hath *f* barley loaves
John 6:10 men sat down, in number about *f* thousand
John 6:13 with the fragments of the *f* barley loaves

Flame (FLAYM)
Blaze, fire.

Exodus 3:2 *f* of fire out of the midst of a bush
Daniel 3:22 the *f* of the fire slew those men

Flee (FLEE)
To run away; escape.

Jonah 1:3 Jonah rose up to *f* unto Tarshish
Matthew 2:13 child and his mother, and *f* into Egypt
James 4:7 Resist the devil, and he will *f* from you

Fleece (FLEES)
A covering; skin; wool.

Judges 6:37 I will put a *f* of wool in the floor
Judges 6:38 and wringed the dew out of the *f*
Judges 6:39 let it now be dry only upon the *f*
Judges 6:40 it was dry upon the *f* only

Flies (FLIGHZ)
Plural of "fly," an insect with wings.

Ff

Fishers

81

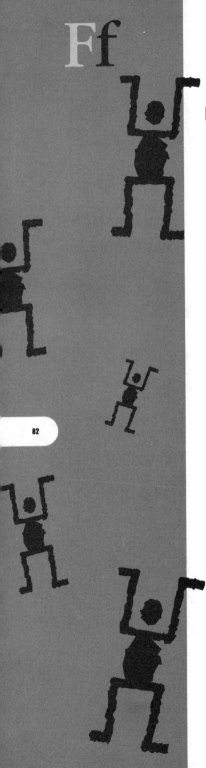

Ff

Exodus 8:21 I will send swarms of *f* upon thee
Exodus 8:22 no swarms of *f* shall be there
Exodus 8:24 swarm of *f* into the house of Pharaoh
Exodus 8:29 entreat the LORD that the swarms of *f*

Flock (FLOK)

A group of animals being watched by a shepherd. In the Bible, it usually refers to sheep or goats. Jesus sometimes called His followers a flock.

Genesis 4:4 he also brought the firstlings of his *f*
Exodus 3:1 Moses kept the *f* of Jethro his father-in-law
Luke 2:8 keeping watch over their *f* by night

Flood (FLUHD)

Too much water after a heavy rain. The flood, as described in Genesis 6-9, was sent by God to destroy those who refused to stop sinning. This flood covered all the earth. Noah and his family listened to and obeyed God. They were saved from the flood in the ark.

Genesis 6:17 do bring a *f* of waters upon the earth
Genesis 7:6 when the *f* of waters was upon the earth
Genesis 7:17 And the *f* was forty days upon the earth
Genesis 9:11 cut off any more by the waters of a *f*
Genesis 9:28 Noah lived after the *f* three hundred
Luke 6:48 foundation on a rock: and when the *f* arose

Flower (FLAUR)

A plant with blooms or a bud in bright colors. Within the flower are the seeds from which to grow more flowers.

Isaiah 40:8 The grass withereth, the *f* fadeth: but

Flowing (FLOW eeng)

To flow means to stream, or run. God told the Israelites that Canaan was a land "flowing with milk and honey." This was an example to show them the land was good and had plenty for everyone.

Exodus 3:8 unto a land *f* with milk and honey
Exodus 13:5 give thee, a land *f* with milk and honey

Foal (FOLE)

A young horse, usually less than a year old.

Zechariah 9:9 on a colt, the *f* of a donkey (NIV)
Matthew 21:5 on a colt, the *f* of a donkey (NIV)

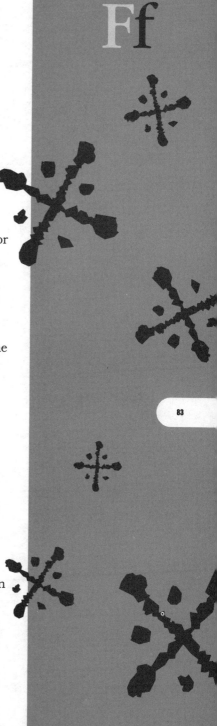

Follow (FAH low)
To mind or obey; to come after, to succeed.

Matthew 4:19 ***F*** me, and I will make you fishers
Matthew 16:24 take up his cross, and ***f*** me
Mark 2:14 said, ***F*** me. And he arose and followed
Mark 8:34 and take up his cross, and ***f*** me
Mark 10:21 and come, take up the cross, and ***f***
Mark 14:13 man bearing a pitcher of water: ***f*** him
Luke 5:27 and he said unto him, ***F*** me
Luke 9:23 take up his cross daily, and ***f*** me
Luke 22:10 bearing pitcher of water; ***f*** him
John 12:26 If any man serve me, let him ***f*** me

Folly (FAH lee)
Foolish or foolishness; a mistake. A stupid or
dumb thing to do or say.

Proverbs 13:16 But a fool exposes his ***f*** (NIV)
Proverbs 14:24 but the foolishness of fools is ***f***
Proverbs 16:22 but ***f*** brings punishment to fools (NIV)

Fool (FOOWL)
A person who acts in a careless or silly way. One
who makes poor choices.

Psalm 14:1 The ***f*** hath said in his heart
Psalm 53:1 The ***f*** hath said in his heart
Proverbs 12:15 way of a ***f*** is right in his own eyes
Proverbs 15:5 A ***f*** despiseth his father's instruction

Foolish (FOOWL ish)
A careless, dumb, silly, or unwise action.

Proverbs 14:7 Stay away from a ***f*** man, for you (NIV)
Proverbs 17:25 A ***f*** son is a grief to his father
Proverbs 19:13 A ***f*** son is his father's ruin (NIV)
Matthew 7:26 shall be likened unto a ***f*** man

Footstool (FOOT stuwl)
A stool with very short legs on which a person
can rest his feet.

Psalm 110:1 until I make your enemies a ***f*** for (NIV)

Forbid (fahr BID)
To ban, not allow, prevent, stop.

Matthew 19:14 and ***f*** them not, to come unto me
Mark 10:14 to come unto me, and ***f*** them not
Luke 18:16 children to come unto me, and ***f*** them not

Forgave (fahr GAYV)
Past tense of "forgive."

Luke 7:42 he frankly *f* them both
Luke 7:43 he, to whom he *f* most
Colossians 3:13 as Christ *f* you, so also do ye

Forget (fahr GHET)
To not remember.

Psalm 103:2 my soul, and *f* not all his benefits
Psalm 119:16 I will not *f* thy word
Psalm 119:93 I will never *f* thy precepts
Proverbs 3:1 My son, *f* not my law
Proverbs 4:5 Get wisdom, get understanding: *f* it not
Hebrews 13:2 Do not *f* to entertain strangers (NIV)

Forgetful (fahr GHET fuhl)
To easily forget.

Hebrews 13:2 Be not *f* to entertain strangers

Forgive (fahr GIHV)
To stop feeling angry or upset at another person; to pardon. When we forgive others, we still remember the act that made us angry. When God forgives us, He does not remember the wrong things we have done. When we forgive others, we must try to do it as God does.

2 Chronicles 7:14 from heaven, and will *f* their sin
Psalm 86:5 LORD, art good, and ready to *f*
Matthew 6:12 And *f* us our debts, as we *f* our debtors
Matthew 6:14 if ye *f* men their trespasses, your
Matthew 6:15 if ye *f* not men their trespasses
Matthew 6:15 neither will your Father *f* your
Mark 2:7 who can *f* sins but God only
Luke 5:21 Who can *f* sins, but God alone
Luke 6:37 *f*, and ye shall be forgiven
Luke 11:4 *f* us our sins; for we also *f* every one
Luke 23:34 Then said Jesus, Father, *f* them; for
1 John 1:9 faithful and just to *f* us our sins

Forgiven (fahr GIHV ihn)
The reason for one being angry or upset no longer exists. When we trust in Jesus as our Savior, our sins are forgiven. That means that God has forgotten forever our sins.

Matthew 9:2 be of good cheer; thy sins be *f* thee
Mark 2:5 sick of the palsy, Son, thy sins be *f*
Luke 5:20 Man, thy sins are *f* thee
Luke 6:37 forgive, and ye shall be *f*

Luke 7:47 Her sins, which are many, are *f*
Luke 7:48 And he said unto her, Thy sins are *f*

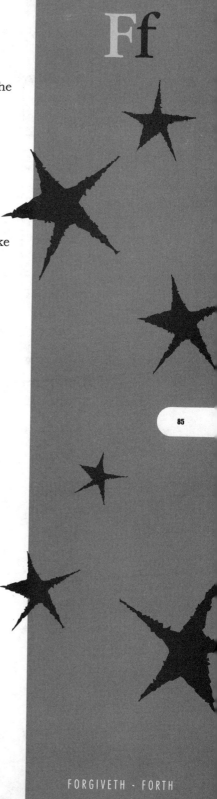

■ Forgiveth (fahr GIHV ith)
The old way of saying or writing "forgives," the plural for "forgive."

Psalm 103:3 Who *f* all thine iniquities
Luke 7:49 Who is this that *f* sins also

■ Forgiving (fahr GIHV eeng)
See "Forgive."

Ephesians 4:32 tenderhearted, *f* one another, even

■ Form (FAWRM)
The shape of a thing; how a thing looks; to make something.

Genesis 1:2 And the earth was without *f*, and void
Mark 16:12 he appeared in another *f* unto two of them
Philippians 2:6 Who, being in the *f* of God,
Philippians 2:7 took upon him the *f* of a servant

■ Formed (FAWRMD)
Past tense of "form."

Genesis 2:7 And the LORD God *f* man of the dust
Genesis 2:19 the ground the LORD God *f* every beast
Psalm 95:5 and his hands *f* the dry land

■ Forsake (fahr SAYK)
To abandon, desert, leave behind.

Deuteronomy 31:6 he will not fail thee, nor *f* thee
Deuteronomy 31:8 will not fail thee, neither *f* thee
Joshua 1:5 I will not fail thee, nor *f* thee
1 Samuel 12:22 For the LORD will not *f* his people
Psalm 38:21 *F* me not, O LORD: O my God, be not
Proverbs 1:8 *f* not the law of thy mother
Hebrews 13:5 I will never leave thee, nor *f* thee

■ Forsaken (fahr SAY kin)
See "Forsake."

Psalm 22:1 My God, my God, why hast thou *f* me
Matthew 27:46 My God, my God, why hast thou *f* me
Mark 15:34 My God, my God, why hast thou *f* me

■ Forth (FAWRTH)
Forward, outside, onward.

Genesis 1:11 Let the earth bring *f* grass
Genesis 1:20 Let the waters bring *f* abundantly
Exodus 9:23 Moses stretched *f* his rod toward

85

Ff

Fortress

Exodus 14:27 Moses stretched *f* his hand over the
Psalm 115:18 bless the LORD from this time *f*
Matthew 9:38 that he will send *f* laborers into
Mark 1:41 put *f* his hand, and touched him, and
Mark 3:5 saith unto the man, Stretch *f* thine hand
Mark 11:1 he sendeth *f* two of his disciples
Luke 2:7 And she brought *f* her firstborn son
Luke 8:27 And when he went *f* to land, there met
Luke 15:22 Bring *f* the best robe, and put it on him
John 11:43 cried with a loud voice, Lazarus, come *f*
John 19:5 came Jesus *f*, wearing the crown of thorns
John 19:17 he bearing his cross went *f* into a
John 20:3 Peter therefore went *f*, and that other

■ Fortress (FAWR triss)
A castle; shelter, fenced place.

2 Samuel 22:2 LORD is my rock, and my *f*
Psalm 18:2 The LORD is my rock, and my *f*
Psalm 71:3 for thou art my rock and my *f*
Psalm 91:2 He is my refuge and my *f*. my God

■ Forty (FAWR tee)
One more than thirty nine.

Genesis 7:4 cause it to rain upon the earth *f* days
Genesis 7:12 rain fell on the earth *f* days and *f* (NIV)
Exodus 16:35 children of Israel did eat manna *f* years
Exodus 34:28 there with the LORD *f* days and *f* nights
1 Kings 19:8 strength of that meat *f* days and *f* nights
Matthew 4:2 he had fasted *f* days and *f* nights
Mark 1:13 he was there in the wilderness *f* days
Luke 4:2 Being *f* days tempted of the devil

■ Found (FOWND)
Past tense of "find."

Matthew 8:10 I have not *f* so great faith, no
Matthew 27:32 they *f* a man of Cyrene, Simon
Mark 11:4 and *f* the colt tied by the door
Luke 1:30 for thou hast *f* favor with God
Luke 2:16 came with haste, and *f* Mary, and Joseph

■ Foundation (fown DAY shun)
A base or bottom; the ground. A house must have a strong, well-built foundation to keep it from falling in.

Luke 6:48 digged deep, and laid the *f* on a rock
Luke 6:49 without a *f* built an house upon the earth

■ Founded (FOWN did)
See "Found." Old way of writing "found" in the past tense.

Psalm 24:2 For he hath **f** it upon the seas
Matthew 7:25 for it was **f** upon a rock
Luke 6:48 for it was **f** upon a rock

Fourth (FAWRTH)
Follows the third.

Genesis 1:19 evening and the morning were the **f** day
Matthew 14:25 in the **f** watch of the night Jesus
Mark 6:48 about the **f** watch of the night he

Fowl (FOWL)
Any kind of bird or chicken.

Genesis 1:20 and **f** that may fly above the earth
Psalm 8:8 The **f** of the air, and the fish of

Fowls (FOWLZ)
Plural of "fowl."

Matthew 6:26 Behold the **f** of the air
Luke 12:24 how much more are ye better than the **f**

Foxes (FOCKS ihs)
An animal that looks like a dog. It has a long muzzle, large ears that are pointed, and a long bushy tail.

Matthew 8:20 The **f** have holes, and the birds
Luke 9:58 **F** have holes, and birds of the air have

Fragments (FRAG mince)
Plural for "fragment." Parts or pieces.

Matthew 14:20 took up of the **f** that remained twelve
Mark 6:43 took up twelve baskets full of the **f**
Mark 8:19 how many baskets full of **f** took ye up
Luke 9:17 and there was taken up of **f** that remained
John 6:12 Gather up the **f** that remain that
John 6:13 filled twelve baskets with the **f** of the

Frankincense (FRANkin since)
Resin from trees of the balsam family. It is usually ground into a powder and burned. It gives off a spicy smell. Frankincense was used in the Temple in the most holy place. One of the gifts given to Jesus by the Wise Men was some frankincense.

Matthew 2:11 unto him gifts; gold, and **f**, and myrrh

Free (FREE)
To be let go; to be loosed; to not be a slave.

Psalm 51:12 and uphold me with thy **f** spirit
John 8:32 truth, and the truth shall make you **f**

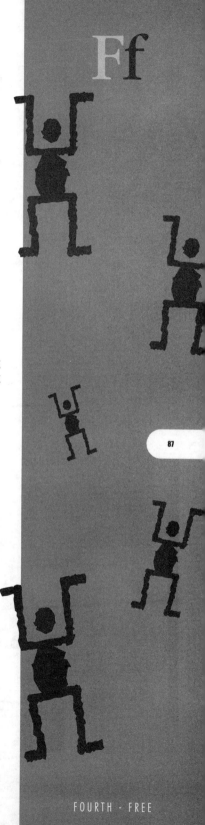

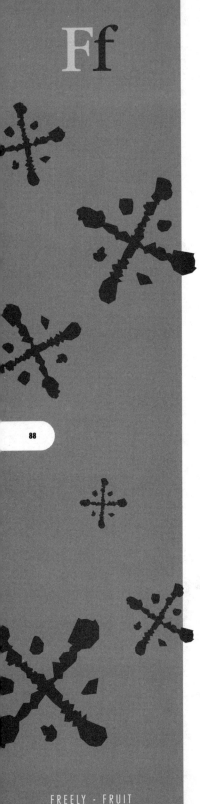

Ff

John 8:36 If the son therefore shall make you *f*
John 8:36 ye shall be *f* indeed

■ **Freely (FREE lee)**
Openly; without charge.

Genesis 2:16 any tree of the garden thou mayest *f* eat
Matthew 10:8 *f* ye have received, *f* give

■ **Friend (FRIND)**
A buddy or pal. Someone to be trusted. One who
is not an enemy.

Proverbs 17:17 A *f* loveth at all times
Proverbs 18:24 there is a *f* that sticketh closer
Matthew 26:50 And Jesus said unto him, *F*
John 11:11 saith unto them, Our *f* Lazarus sleepeth
John 19:12 let this man go, thou art not Caesar's *f*
James 2:23 and he was called the *F* of God

■ **Friendly (FRIND lee)**
Acting like a friend.

Proverbs 18:24 that hath friends must show himself *f*

■ **Friends (FRINDZ)**
Plural of "friend."

Proverbs 18:24 A man that hath *f* must show himself
John 15:13 that a man lay down his life for his *f*
John 15:14 Ye are my *f*, if ye do whatsoever I

■ **Frogs (FRAWGZ)**
An animal that can live on land and in water,
having webbed feet, smooth skin, and no tail.
One of the ten plagues that God sent Pharaoh.
Frogs were already a usual sight in Egypt.

Exodus 8:2 I will smite all thy borders with *f*
Exodus 8:5 and cause *f* to come up upon the land
Exodus 8:8 Pray to the LORD to take the *f* away (NIV)
Exodus 8:11 And the *f* shall depart from thee

■ **Fruit (FROOT)**
A crop. The part of many trees and plants that
can be eaten. In the Bible, it is sometimes
referred to as the good things a person does.

Genesis 1:11 and the *f* tree yielding *f* after
Genesis 3:2 We may eat of the *f* of the trees
Genesis 3:6 she took of the *f* thereof, and did eat
Genesis 4:3 Cain brought of the *f* of the ground
Matthew 7:17 every good tree bringeth forth good *f*
Matthew 7:18 a good tree cannot bring forth evil *f*

Matthew 26:29 I will not drink of this **f** of the vine (NIV)
Mark 14:25 will drink no more of the **f** of the vine
Luke 22:18 I will not drink of the **f** of the vine
Galatians 5:22 But the **f** of the Spirit is love

Full (FUHL)
Enough, plenty; can hold no more.

Psalm 29:4 the voice of the LORD is **f** of majesty
Psalm 33:5 earth is **f** of the goodness of the LORD
Psalm 86:15 O LORD, art a God **f** of compassion
Psalm 104:24 the earth is **f** of all thy riches
Psalm 111:4 the LORD is gracious and **f** of compassion
Matthew 14:20 fragments that remained twelve baskets **f**
Matthew 15:37 meat that was left seven baskets **f**
Mark 8:19 how many baskets **f** of fragments took ye
Mark 15:36 ran and filled a sponge **f** of vinegar
Luke 4:1 Jesus being **f** of the Holy Ghost returned
John 15:11 and that your joy might be **f**
John 16:24 shall receive, that your joy may be **f**
John 19:29 there was set a vessel **f** of vinegar
John 21:11 drew the net to land **f** of great fishes

Fulness (FUHL hiss)
Usually spelled "fullness." Being complete.

Psalm 24:1 The earth is the LORD's, and the **f** thereof
Galatians 4:4 But when the **f** of the time was come

Furnace (FUHR niss)
A large object made of brick or stone which was used like an oven. Most furnaces in biblical times were used to heat or melt metal, make pottery or bricks, or to make lime. Certain kinds were used for baking bread.

Daniel 3:6 cast into the midst of a burning fiery **f**
Daniel 3:17 able to deliver us from the burning fiery **f**
Daniel 3:19 ordered the **f** heated seven times hotter (NIV)
Daniel 3:20 cast them into the burning fiery **f**
Daniel 3:26 near to the mouth of the burning fiery **f**

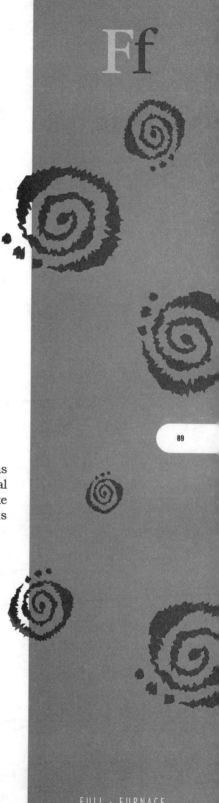

Ff

89

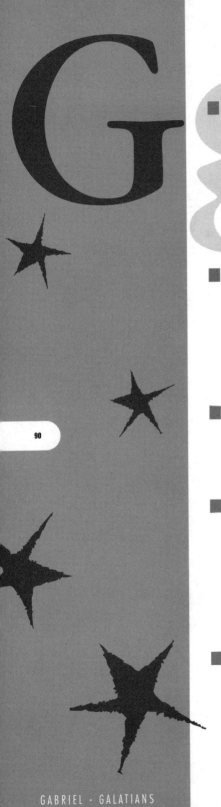

Gabriel (GAY brih el)
The name means "strong man of God." He is identified four times in the Bible. Each time he brings a message from God to a person. His appearances include two to Daniel, one to Zacharias, the father of John the Baptist, and one to Mary, the mother of Jesus.

Daniel 9:21 in prayer, *G*, the man I had seen in (NIV)
Luke 1:19 said unto him, I am *G*, that stand in
Luke 1:26 the angel *G* was sent from God

Gadarenes (GAD un reenz)
People who lived in Gadara, a village located southeast of the Sea of Galilee (see map on page 340). It was here that Jesus healed a man whose mind was controlled by demons.

Mark 5:1 of the sea, into the country of the *G*
Luke 8:26 they arrived at the country of the *G*
Luke 8:37 *G* round about besought him to depart

Gain (GAYN)
To get or win.

Matthew 16:26 if he shall *g* the whole world
Mark 8:36 profit a man, if he shall *g* the whole
Luke 9:25 if he *g* the whole world, and lose

Galatia (guh LAY shuh)
A Roman province in Asia Minor, located in what is now central Turkey (see map on page 341). Several churches were started by Paul in the cities of Galatia. The New Testament book, Galatians, was written by Paul to the people of Galatia.

Acts 16:6 throughout Phrygia and the region of *G*
Acts 18:23 went over all the country of *G* and
Galatians 1:2 with me, unto the churches of *G*

Galatians, Book of (guh LAY shuhnz)
The fourth book in the division, Paul's Letters, in the New Testament. Since Galatia was a region in a Roman province rather than a city, the letter was written so that it could be taken to each of the churches in Galatia. Paul had started churches in Antioch of Pisidia, Iconium, Lystra, and Derbe. He had visited the churches more than once to encourage them. Judaizers

(Christian Jews) were causing many problems by insisting the Gentiles (non-Jews) had to obey the law of Moses. These Jews were saying that the Gentiles could not be saved unless they were first circumcised. Paul wrote a very strong letter saying that the law of circumcision was no longer necessary since Jesus Christ had come. Now the Christian could let the Spirit guide him.

Galilean (GAL ih LEE uhn)

One who lived in Galilee. Jesus was a Galilean because He was from Nazareth. The speech of these Jews was different from the Jews in Judah. During the trial of Jesus, Peter was accused of being a Galilean because of his speech.

Mark 14:70 one of them, for you are a *G* (NIV)
Luke 22:59 also was with him: for he is a *G*
Luke 23:6 he asked whether the man were a *G*

Galilee (GAL ih lee)

The name means "circle" or "region." Galilee is located in the northern part of Palestine (see map on page 340). Samaria bordered on the south. The Jordan River and the Sea of Galilee formed the eastern border. The Mediterranean Sea formed the western border. Nazareth, where Jesus grew up, is located in Galilee. Other places in Galilee were Capernaum, Bethsaida, and the Sea of Galilee. Galilee was a Roman province during the time Jesus was living. Jesus spent most of His ministry in Galilee.

Matthew 3:13 Then cometh Jesus from *G* to Jordan
Matthew 4:18 And Jesus, walking by the sea of *G*
Matthew 4:23 And Jesus went about all *G*, teaching
Matthew 4:25 great multitudes of people from *G*
Matthew 15:29 and came nigh unto the sea of *G*
Matthew 26:69 Thou was also with Jesus of *G*
Matthew 28:10 tell my brethren that they go into *G*
Mark 1:9 that Jesus came from Nazareth of *G*
Mark 1:16 Now as he walked by the sea of *G*
Mark 14:28 I will go before you into *G*
Mark 16:7 that he goeth before you into *G*
Luke 1:26 was sent from God unto a city of *G*
Luke 3:1 and Herod being tetrarch of *G*
Luke 24:6 spake unto you when he was yet in *G*
John 2:1 there was a marriage in Cana of *G*
John 7:1 After these things Jesus walked in *G*
John 12:21 Philip, which was of Bethsaida of *G*
John 21:2 and Nathaniel of Cana in *G*

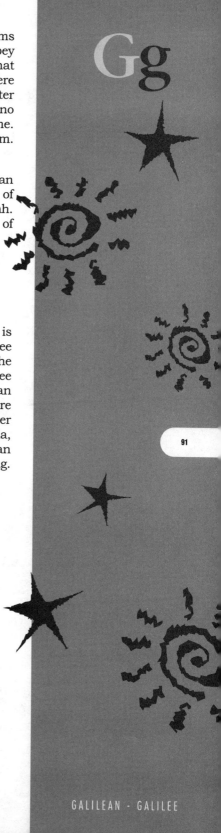

Gg

91

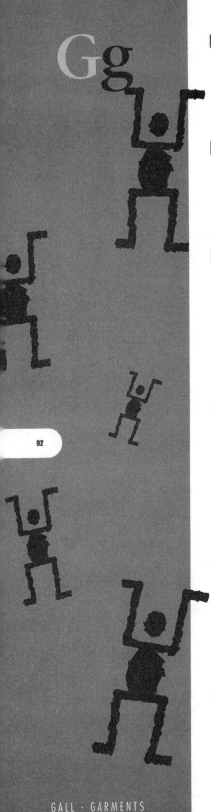

Gall (GAWL)
The juice of a bitter plant, which is poisonous. The gall offered Jesus while He was on the cross could have been something like opium. Opium is a narcotic drug.

Matthew 27:34 him vinegar to drink mingled with **g**

Gallows (GOWL ohwz)
A platform built for the purpose of hanging a person.

Esther 5:14 Let a **g** be made of fifty cubits high
Esther 7:9 Behold, also, the **g** fifty cubits high
Esther 7:10 hanged Haman on the **g** that he had

Gamaliel (guh MAY lih uhl)
The name means "God rewards with good." A respected Pharisee and member of the Sanhedrin (the Jewish council). Gamaliel defended the apostles when their lives were threatened by the council. He was the teacher of the apostle Paul.

Acts 5:34 in the council, a Pharisee, named **G**
Acts 22:3 brought up in this city at the feet of **G**

Garden (GAHR din)
A plot of land where flowers, trees, vegetables, or other plants were grown. Most gardens in biblical times had a wall or hedge around them. Some gardens were inside the house with the house surrounding the garden. A garden was a place to spend time thinking, praying, visiting with friends, eating meals, or to go to in the heat of the day,

Genesis 2:8 LORD God planted a **g** eastward in Eden
Genesis 2:15 took the man, and put him into the **g**
Genesis 2:16 Of every tree of the **g** thou mayest freely eat
Genesis 3:8 LORD God walking in the **g** in the cool
Genesis 3:23 LORD God sent him forth from the **g**
John 18:1 where was a **g**, into the which he entered
John 18:26 Did not I see thee in the **g** with him
John 19:41 where he was crucified there was a **g**
John 19:41 and in the **g** a new sepulcher

Garments (GAHR mintz)
Articles of clothing.

Psalm 22:18 They part my **g** among them, and
Matthew 27:35 they crucified him, and parted his **g**
Mark 11:7 colt to Jesus, and cast their **g** on him
Mark 11:8 many spread their **g** in the way

Mark 15:24 had crucified him, they parted his *g*
Luke 19:35 they cast their *g* upon the colt
Luke 24:4 two men stood by them in shining *g*
John 13:4 from supper, and laid aside his *g*
John 19:23 when they had crucified Jesus, took his *g*

Gate (GAYT)
An opening, door, entrance to a garden or a city.

Ruth 4:1 Boaz went up to the *g*, and sat
Matthew 7:13 Enter through the narrow *g*. For wide (NIV)
Matthew 7:14 But small is the *g* and narrow the (NIV)

Gates (GAYTZ)
Plural of "gate."

Psalm 100:4 Enter into his *g* with thanksgiving
Matthew 16:18 the *g* of hell shall not prevail

Gather (GATH uhr)
To collect, take in, bring together.

Exodus 16:4 and *g* a certain rate every day
Exodus 16:5 shall be twice as much as they *g* daily
Exodus 16:16 *G* of it every man according to his
Exodus 16:26 Six days ye shall *g* it; but on the
Matthew 6:26 do they reap, nor *g* into barns
John 6:12 *G* up the fragments that remain

Gathered (GATH uhrd)
Past tense of "gather."

Genesis 41:49 Joseph *g* corn as the sand of the sea
1 Kings 18:20 *g* the prophets together unto mount Carmel
Matthew 18:20 where two or three are *g* together in
Matthew 27:27 *g* unto him the whole band of soldiers
Mark 1:33 all the city was *g* together at the door
Mark 5:21 much people *g* unto him: and he was nigh
Mark 6:30 apostles *g* themselves together unto Jesus
Luke 15:13 the younger son *g* all together, and took
Luke 24:33 and found the eleven *g* together
John 6:13 *g* them together, and filled twelve
John 11:47 *g* the chief priests and the Pharisees

Gave (GAYV)
Past tense of "give."

Matthew 25:35 hungry and you *g* me something to eat (NIV)
Matthew 25:35 I was thirsty, and ye *g* me drink
Matthew 25:42 hungry and you *g* me nothing to eat (NIV)
Matthew 25:42 I was thirsty, and ye *g* me no drink
Matthew 27:34 *g* him vinegar to drink mingled with
Mark 14:22 blessed, and brake it, and *g* to them
Mark 15:37 with a loud voice, and *g* up the ghost

Gg

Luke 7:21 many that were blind he **g** sight
Luke 18:43 when they saw it, **g** praise unto God
Luke 22:17 took the cup, and **g** thanks, and said
Luke 22:19 he took bread, and **g** thanks, and brake
John 3:16 loved the world, that he **g** his only
John 19:30 he bowed his head, and **g** up the ghost
Galatians 2:20 who loved me, and **g** himself for me

GAZA (GAY zuh or GAH zuh)

The name means "strong." A city located about three miles from the Mediterranean Sea (see map on page 340). It was one of the Philistine cities. A major highway passed through Gaza going to Egypt. Egyptian goods were carried through Gaza to the ancient Near East and ancient Near East goods were carried through Gaza to Egypt. It was on the road to Gaza where Philip met the man from Ethiopia.

Acts 8:26 way that goeth down from Jerusalem unto **G**

Gehazi (gih HAY zigh)

The name means "valley of vision" or "goggle-eyed." He was a servant of the prophet Elisha.

2 Kings 4:12 And he said to **G** his servant,
2 Kings 4:14 **G**, Verily, she hath no child
2 Kings 5:20 But **G**, the servant of Elisha the man of God
2 Kings 5:21 So **G** followed after Naaman
2 Kings 5:25 Where have you been, **G**, Elisha asked (NIV)
2 Kings 5:25 servant didn't go anywhere, **G** answered (NIV)
2 Kings 5:27 **G** went from Elisha's presence, and he (NIV)

Gemariah (GHEM uh RIGH uh)

The name means "Yahweh has completed or carried out." He was the son of Shaphan, a court scribe. It was Gemariah's room in the Temple where Baruch read the words Jeremiah had written. Gemariah tried to persuade the king not to destroy the scroll.

Jeremiah 36:10 the chamber of **G** the son of Shaphan
Jeremiah 36:11 When Michaiah the son of **G**, the son
Jeremiah 36:25 **G** urged the king not to burn the (NIV)

Genesis, Book of (JEN ih siss)

The first book of the Bible as well as the first book in the Old Testament division of Law. As a book of beginnings, it tells about the beginning of the human race, and the beginning of a nation through Abraham in a new land (Canaan). It contains stories of the creation; the flood and saving of Noah and his family; calling of Abraham; how Jacob tricked Esau, his broth-

94

er, and how Jacob was later tricked by his father-in-law; Joseph and his life in Egypt; and many more.

The author is believed to be Moses, and it is possible he wrote the first five books of the Bible during the time the Israelites wandered in the wilderness.

◾ Gennesaret (gih NESS uh ret)
The name for the Sea of Galilee as used in the New Testament. It is referred to as a lake rather than a sea. The Old Testament used the name "Sea of Chinnereth" for this body of water (see map on page 340).

Matthew 14:34 they came into the land of **G**
Mark 6:53 they came into the land of **G**, and
Luke 5:1 word of God, he stood by the lake of **G**

◾ Gentile (JEN tighl)
Any person who is not a Jew.

Romans 2:10 to the Jew first, and also to the **G**

◾ Gentiles (JEN tighlz)
Plural of "Gentile."

Matthew 12:21 And in his name shall the **G** trust
Mark 10:33 and shall deliver him to the **G**
Luke 2:32 A light to lighten the **G**, and

◾ Gerar (geh RAHR)
The name possibly means "drag away." This city was located between Gaza and Beer-sheba, where both Abraham and Isaac made treaties with the kings of Gerar.

Genesis 26:6 And Isaac dwelt in **G**
Genesis 26:20 herdmen of **G** did strive with Isaac's
Genesis 26:26 Then Abimelech went to him from **G**

◾ Gethsemane (geth SEM uh nih)
The name means "olive press." Gethsemane is a garden and olive orchard located about a mile from Jerusalem. Jesus may have come often to this garden to spend time alone or with His disciples. It was to Gethsemane where Jesus took the disciples after they had their last supper together.

Matthew 26:36 Jesus with them unto a place called **G**
Mark 14:32 came to a place which was named **G**

◾ Gideon (GID ih uhn)
The name means "one who cuts to pieces." He

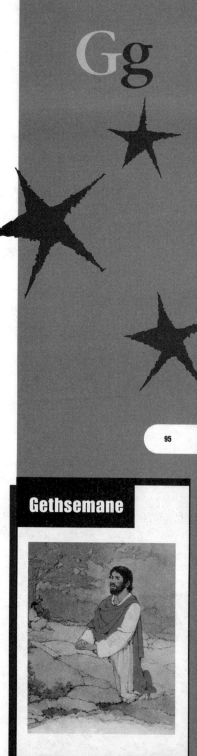

Gethsemane

Gg

was one of the major judges of the Israelites. God told him to take 300 men to defeat the Midianites.

Judges 6:11 **G** threshed wheat by the winepress
Judges 6:24 **G** built an altar there unto the LORD
Judges 6:34 the spirit of the LORD came upon **G**
Judges 7:2 And the LORD said unto **G**, The people
Judges 7:7 LORD said unto **G**, By the three hundred
Judges 7:18 The sword of the LORD, and of **G**

Gift (GIHFT)
An ability or talent; offering or present.

Matthew 5:23 if thou bring thy **g** to the altar
John 4:10 If thou knewest the **g** of God, and
Acts 2:38 And you will receive the **g** of the (NIV)
Romans 6:23 the **g** of God is eternal life
Ephesians 2:8 not of yourselves: it is the **g** of God
James 1:17 Every good **g** and every perfect **g**

Give (GIV)
To leave, offer, or present.

Psalm 18:49 Therefore will I **g** thanks unto thee
Psalm 55:1 **G** ear to my prayer, O God
Psalm 96:8 **G** unto the LORD the glory due his name
Psalm 105:1 O **g** thanks unto the LORD; call upon
Proverbs 9:9 **G** instruction to a wise man, and he
Matthew 6:11 **G** us this day our daily bread
Matthew 10:8 freely ye have received, freely **g**
Matthew 11:28 heavy laden, and I will **g** you rest
John 13:34 A new commandment I **g** unto you
Acts 20:35 It is more blessed to **g** than to receive

Given (GIV uhn)
Handed over.

Matthew 7:7 Ask, and it shall be **g** you
Matthew 28:18 All power is **g** unto me in heaven
Luke 6:38 Ask, and it shall be **g** you
Luke 22:19 This is my body which is **g** for you

Glad (GLAD)
Cheerful, happy, pleased.

Psalm 32:11 Be **g** in the LORD, and rejoice
Psalm 104:34 I will be **g** in the LORD
Psalm 122:1 I was **g** when they said unto me
Proverbs 10:1 A wise son maketh a **g** father
Proverbs 15:20 A wise son maketh a **g** father
Mark 14:11 And when they heard it, they were **g**
Luke 15:32 we should make merry, and be **g**
Luke 23:8 Herod saw Jesus, he was exceeding **g**
John 20:20 the disciples **g**, when they saw the LORD

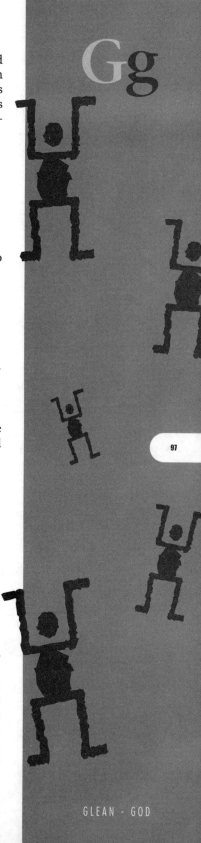

Glean (GLEEN)

It means "to gather." The law of Moses required reapers to leave a portion in the fields, or on trees or vines, so that the poor and widows could pick up the rest for their needs. This was a way of helping them feed and clothe themselves and their children.

Leviticus 19:10 And thou shalt not **g** thy vineyard
Deuteronomy 24:21 thou shalt not **g** it afterward
Ruth 2:7 I pray you, let me **g** and gather
Ruth 2:8 Go not to **g** in another field
Ruth 2:23 to **g** unto the end of barley harvest and

Glorify (GLOW rih figh)

To praise and worship; to honor; to admire; to show the good in something or someone.

Psalm 86:9 O LORD; and shall **g** thy name
Psalm 86:12 I will **g** thy name for evermore
Matthew 5:16 **g** your Father which is in heaven

Glorious (GLOW ree uhs)

Wonderful, beautiful, magnificent, grand, heavenly.

Psalm 72:19 And blessed be his **g** name for ever

Glory (GLOW ree)

1. The brilliance, beauty, and shining of the presence of God. 2. To show honor, respect, and reverence; to praise.

Exodus 16:7 then ye shall see the **g** of the LORD
1 Chronicles 16:24 Declare his **g** among the heathen
Psalm 72:19 whole earth be filled with his **g**
Psalm 96:3 Declare his **g** among the heathen
Matthew 6:13 and the power, and the **g**, for ever
Luke 2:9 the **g** of the Lord shone round about them
Luke 2:14 **G** to God in the highest, and on earth
Luke 12:27 Solomon in all his **g** was not arrayed
Luke 19:38 peace in heaven, and **g** in the highest

God (GAHD)

The Creator who has no beginning and no end. He is the one true God and the Father of our Lord Jesus Christ. He is known by many names. These names are man's way of trying to tell who God is. He reveals Himself to us in one of three ways: God the Father, God the Son, and God the Holy Spirit. He is love, mercy, and forgiveness. He is our guide, He comforts, He encourages, and He hears us when we call out to Him. To know His Son, Jesus, is to know God.

Genesis 1:1 In the beginning **G** created the heaven

97

Gg

Genesis 1:26 And **G** said, Let us make man in our
Genesis 1:27 So **G** created man in his own image
Genesis 2:3 And **G** blessed the seventh day, and
Deuteronomy 6:4 The LORD our **G** is one LORD
Psalm 18:30 As for **G**, his way is perfect
Psalm 19:1 The heavens declare the glory of **G**
Psalm 22:1 My **G**, my **G**, why has thou forsaken me
Psalm 46:1 **G** is our refuge and strength
Psalm 46:10 Be still, and know that I am **G**
Psalm 51:10 Create in me a clean heart, O **G**
Psalm 55:16 As for me, I will call upon **G**
Psalm 91:2 my **G**; in him will I trust
Psalm 100:3 Know ye that the LORD he is **G**
Psalm 139:23 Search me, O **G**, and know my heart
Proverbs 30:5 Every word of **G** is pure
Malachi 3:8 Will a man rob **G**? Yet ye have
Matthew 4:10 Thou shalt worship the Lord thy **G**
Matthew 27:54 Truly this was the Son of **G**
Mark 10:27 for with **G** all things are possible
Luke 1:37 for with **G** nothing shall be impossible
John 3:16 For **G** so loved the world, that he gave
Romans 5:8 But **G** demonstrates his own love for us (NIV)
Romans 6:23 but the gift of **G** is eternal life
Romans 8:31 If **G** be for us, who can be against us
Galatians 6:7 Be not deceived; **G** is not mocked
Ephesians 2:8 not of yourselves: it is the gift of **G**
Philippians 1:3 I thank my **G** upon every remembrance
Philippians 4:19 my **G** shall supply all your need
1 John 4:11 if **G** so loved us, we ought also to love

▌ Gold (GOHLD)

A soft, yellow metal used in jewelry and coins.
Gold has been highly valued because it is easy
to work with, beautiful, and can be melted without causing harm to it. Israel used gold to make
many items used in the tabernacle and Temple.
Gold can be hammered into very thin sheets
and placed over objects. This is called "gilding."

Exodus 20:23 neither shall ye make unto you gods of **g**
Psalm 119:127 I love thy commandments above **g**
Proverbs 16:16 better is it to get wisdom than **g**
Matthew 2:11 presented unto him gifts; **g**, and
Acts 3:6 Silver and **g** have I none; but such as I
Revelation 21:21 the street of the city was pure **g**

▌ Golgotha (GAHL guh thuh, or gahl GAHTH uh)

The name means "skull." Golgotha is located
outside the wall of Jerusalem. This is where
Jesus was crucified. Another name for Golgotha

was "Calvary."

Matthew 27:33 they were come unto a place called **G**
Mark 15:22 they bring him into the place **G**
John 19:17 which is called in the Hebrew **G**

■ Goliath (guh LIGH uhth)
The Philistine giant whom young David killed with a slingshot and stone (pebble). Goliath was reported to be nine feet tall.

1 Samuel 17:4 of the camp of the Philistines, named **G**,
1 Samuel 21:9 priest said, The sword of **G** the Philistine

■ Good (GUHD)
1. Pleasant, joyful, worthy.

Genesis 1:31 had made, and, behold, it was very **g**

2. Helpful, behaving in the right way, dependable, just.

Genesis 2:9 the tree of knowledge of **g** and evil
Psalm 34:14 Depart from evil, and do **g**
Psalm 37:3 Trust in the LORD, and do **g**
Psalm 86:5 thou LORD, art **g**, and ready to forgive
Psalm 100:5 For the LORD is **g**; his mercy is
Proverbs 3:27 Withhold not **g** from them to whom
Proverbs 17:22 A merry heart doeth **g** like a medicine
Proverbs 22:1 A **g** name is rather to be chosen
Matthew 5:16 may see your **g** works, and glorify
Luke 6:35 But love ye your enemies, and do **g**
John 10:11 I am the **g** shepherd: the **g** shepherd
Romans 12:9 Hate what is evil; cling to what is **g** (NIV)
Romans 12:21 but overcome evil with **g**
James 1:17 Every **g** gift and every perfect gift is

■ Goodness (GUHD niss)
"The quality or state of being good."

Exodus 33:19 I will make all my **g** pass before thee
Psalm 23:6 Surely **g** and mercy shall follow me

■ Goshen (GOH shuhn)
The area in the northeast part of the Nile delta in Egypt (see map on page 337). An area that was fertile because of the water available. Crops grew well and herds of animals had plenty to eat. It was this area of Egypt in which Joseph settled his family. They lived there over 400 years, until Moses helped them leave during the Exodus.

Genesis 45:10 thou shalt dwell in the land of **G**
Genesis 46:28 and they came into the land of **G**
Genesis 47:27 land of Egypt, in the country of **G**

Gg

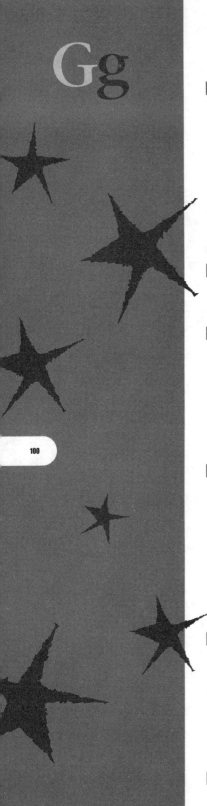

Exodus 8:22 will deal differently with the land of **G** (NIV)
Exodus 9:26 place it did not hail was the land of **G** (NIV)

Gospel (GAHS puhl)

The word means "good news." The first four books of the New Testament are called the Gospels. These books tell the good news of Jesus Christ, God's Son. It is the good news of Jesus' life, death, and resurrection that provides eternal life to everyone who will believe.

Matthew 4:23 and preaching the **g** of the kingdom
Mark 1:15 repent ye, and believe the **g**
Mark 16:15 and preach the **g** to every creature
Romans 1:16 I am not ashamed of the **g** of Christ

Government (GUV urn mint)

Authority, leadership, rulers, those in control.

Isaiah 9:6 and the **g** shall be upon his shoulder

Governor (GUV uhr nuhr)

Usually an official who was appointed to rule over an area. He would have to answer to the king. Some examples of biblical governors are Joseph under Pharaoh, Pontius Pilate under Caesar.

Genesis 42:6 Joseph was the **g** over the land
Matthew 27:2 delivered him to Pontius Pilate the **g**
Luke 2:2 first made when Cyrenius was **g** of Syria

Grace (GRAYS)

Love and acceptance we receive from God. It is God's gift to us and it is free. We cannot earn it. Grace comes to us when we accept Jesus as our Savior and Lord.

Genesis 6:8 Noah found **g** in the eyes of the LORD
Psalm 84:11 the LORD will give **g** and glory
Luke 2:40 and the **g** of God was upon him
2 Corinthians 12:9 My **g** is sufficient for thee
Ephesians 2:8 For by **g** are ye saved through faith

Gracious (GRAY shush)

Merciful, loving, forgiving; kind and courteous.

Numbers 6:25 shine upon thee, and be **g** unto thee
Psalm 86:15 a compassionate and **g** God, slow to (NIV)
Psalm 103:8 The LORD is merciful and **g**
Psalm 111:4 the LORD is **g** and full of compassion
Psalm 145:8 The LORD is **g**, and full of compassion
Luke 4:22 wondered at the **g** words which

Grain (GRAYN)

The seed of certain grasses that can be eaten.

Some examples are wheat, barley, and oats. It can also refer to sand, although sand cannot be eaten (grain of sand).

Matthew 17:20 ye have faith as a *g* of mustard seed
Luke 17:6 If ye had faith as a *g* of mustard seed

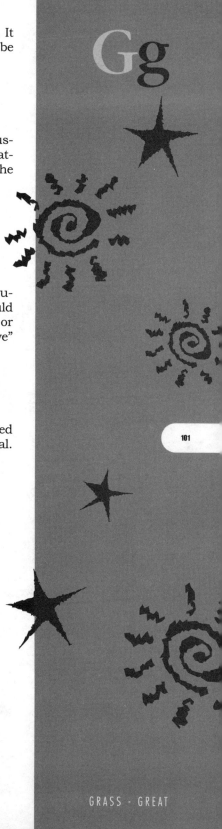

Grass (GRASS)
Green plants with stems, thin leaves, and clusters of flowers on a stalk. Animals—such as cattle, sheep, goats, and horses—graze on the grasses as part of their food.

Isaiah 40:8 The *g* withereth, the flower fadeth
Matthew 6:30 if God so clothe the *g* of the field
Luke 12:28 If then God so clothe the *g*, which
1 Peter 1:24 The *g* withereth, and the flower fadeth

Grave (GRAYV)
The place where a dead body is buried. It is usually a pit or cave. In biblical times, a grave could be a hole dug in the ground, a natural cave, or a hole dug out of a rock. Another use for "grave" is a serious look on a person's face.

John 11:17 he had lain in the *g* four days already
John 12:17 when he called Lazarus out of his *g*

Graven (GRAYV in)
Graven image is an idol that has been carved from wood or stone or formed from some metal.

Exodus 20:4 shalt not make unto thee any *g* image
Leviticus 26:1 shall make you no idols nor *g* image
Deuteronomy 5:8 Thou shalt not make thee any *g* image

Great (GRAYT)
Big, huge, many, important, or grand.

Genesis 1:16 And God made two *g* lights
Genesis 41:29 there come seven years of *g* plenty
Exodus 3:3 this *g* sight, why the bush is not burnt
Exodus 12:30 and there was a *g* cry in Egypt
Exodus 14:31 Israel saw that *g* work which the LORD
1 Kings 19:7 because the journey is too *g* for thee
1 Kings 19:11 *g* and strong wind rent the mountains
1 Chronicles 16:25 For *g* is the LORD, and greatly
Psalm 103:11 *g* is his mercy toward them that fear
Psalm 145:3 *G* is the Lord, and greatly to be praised
Proverbs 22:1 name is rather to be chosen than *g* riches
Matthew 8:10 I have not found so *g* faith
Matthew 14:14 Jesus went forth, and saw a *g* multitude
Matthew 22:38 This is the first and *g* commandment
Matthew 27:60 rolled a *g* stone to the door of the

101

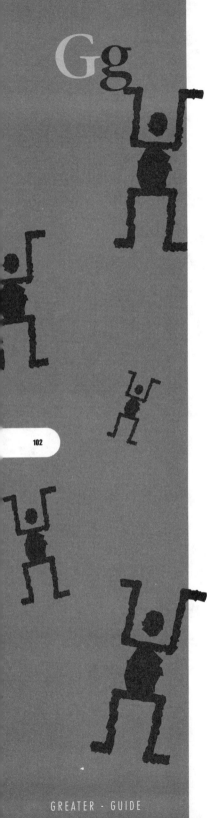

Mark 4:37 And there arose a *g* storm of wind
Mark 5:11 a *g* herd of swine feeding
Mark 16:4 rolled away: for it was very *g*
Luke 2:10 I bring you good tidings of *g* joy
Luke 2:36 she was of a *g* age, and had lived with
Luke 15:20 But when he was yet a *g* way off
Luke 22:44 his sweat was as it were *g* drops of blood
John 6:18 the sea arose by reason of a *g* wind
John 21:11 drew the net to land full of *g* fishes

■ Greater (GRAYT uhr)
More than great. See "Great."

Genesis 1:16 the *g* light to rule the day, and the
John 15:13 *G* love hath no man than this, than he
1 John 4:4 *g* is he that is in you, than he that

■ Greatly (GRAYT lee)
See "great."

Psalm 89:7 God is *g* to be feared in the assembly
Psalm 96:4 the LORD is great, and *g* to be praised
Psalm 109:30 I will *g* praise the LORD with my mouth
Psalm 145:3 Great is the LORD, and *g* to be praised
Matthew 27:14 insomuch that the governor marvelled *g*
Matthew 27:54 they feared *g*, saying, Truly this was
Mark 5:23 besought him *g*, saying, My little daughter
Mark 9:15 *g* amazed, and running to him saluted him

■ Greek (GREEK)
A language spoken in Greece. Alexander the Great is credited with spreading the language all over the known world because he had conquered much of it. The New Testament was written in Greek. A Greek is one who was born in or lives in Greece.

Luke 23:38 was written over him in letters of *G*
John 19:20 and it was written in Hebrew, and *G*, and
Romans 1:16 to the Jew first, and also to the *G*

■ Green (GREEN)
The color, which can refer to different plants, or the ripeness of fruit or vegetables.

Psalm 23:2 maketh me to lie down in *g* pastures

■ Guide (GIGHD)
To lead the way or the person who leads the way.

Psalm 25:9 The meek will he *g* in judgment
Psalm 73:24 Thou shalt *g* me with thy counsel

Habakkuk, Book of (huh BAK kuk)
The seventh book of the division, Minor Prophets, in the Old Testament. He was a prophet and his name means "to embrace." Not much else is known about him.

His book is divided into three parts: 1. Questions he asked and the answers he receives from God. 2. Concern he had about good people who have to suffer and bad people who seem to have everything they want. 3. A prayer in the form of a hymn or psalm.

Haggai, Book of (HAG igh)
The name means "festive." He may have been an old man when he returned from exile in Babylon. The people had rebuilt their homes but seemed to be unhappy. He urged them to rebuild the Temple so they could renew their relationship to God.

The book stresses the need for both work and worship in order to give peace and contentment. It is the tenth book in the division, Minor Prophets, in the Old Testament, and is made up of two very short chapters.

Hair (HAIR)
Growth on the head of a person that looks like fine thread. Humans also have hair over their bodies but it does not grow in length like the hair on the head (and face of men). The covering on animals is also hair and is often called "fur." During Old Testament days, men and women both wore long hair. During the time of Jesus, women still wore long hair but men cut theirs shorter. Much respect was given to those with grey or white hair. The way one wore his or her hair had great meaning. For example, when a person fasted, mourned or was sad, he would mess up his hair. Often a host would offer oil to put on the head of a guest. To have no hair on the head caused disgrace and shame.

Matthew 3:4 John had his raiment of camel's *h*
Matthew 5:36 thou canst not make one *h* white or black
Mark 1:6 And John was clothed with camel's *h*
John 11:2 ointment, and wiped his feet with her *h*
John 12:3 Jesus, and wiped his feet with her *h*

Hairs (HAIRZ)
Plural of "hair."

Matthew 10:30 the very *h* of your head are all numbered

Hh

Luke 7:38 and did wipe them with the **h** of her head
Luke 7:44 and wiped them with the **h** of her head
Luke 12:7 the very **h** of your head are all numbered

Hall (HAWL)
A large building, often used for government use, business, or activities. Also, a large room in a palace or other building. This room was often used to make legal decisions, meet the public, or to entertain guests at a feast or banquet.

Matthew 27:27 took Jesus into the common **h**
Mark 15:16 soldiers led him away into the **h**
Luke 22:55 kindled a fire in the midst of the **h**
John 18:28 from Caiaphas unto the **h** of judgment
John 18:33 Pilate entered into the judgment **h** again
John 19:9 into the judgment **h**, and saith unto Jesus

Hallow (HAL oh)
To make something holy; to separate things or people to be used only for use as holy; to handle something in a sacred way.

Jeremiah 17:22 but **h** ye the sabbath day, as I

Hallowed (HAL ohd)
Past tense of "hallow."

Exodus 20:11 blessed the sabbath day, and **h** it
Matthew 6:9 which art in heaven, **H** be thy name
Luke 11:2 which art in heaven, **H** be thy name

Hand (HAND)
The end of the arm that allows a person to hold things. The human hand has five fingers with which a person can grasp objects. "At hand" means the time is near for something to happen.

Exodus 8:5 Stretch forth thine **h** with thy rod
Exodus 14:16 stretch out thine **h** over the sea
Psalm 31:5 Into thine **h** I commit my spirit
Psalm 37:24 the LORD upholdeth him with his **h**
Proverbs 3:27 when it is in the power of thine **h**
Ecclesiastes 9:10 Whatsoever thy **h** findeth to do
Matthew 6:3 let not thy left **h** know what thy
Matthew 8:3 And Jesus put forth his **h**, and
Matthew 12:10 a man which had his **h** withered
Matthew 26:18 The Master saith, My time is at **h**
Matthew 26:46 he is at **h** that doth betray me
Mark 1:15 and the kingdom of God is at **h**
Mark 3:3 unto the man which had the withered **h**
Mark 3:5 saith unto the man, Stretch forth thy **h**
Luke 5:13 he put forth his **h**, and touched him
Luke 6:6 a man whose right **h** was withered

Luke 6:10 unto the man, Stretch forth thy *h*
Luke 8:54 took her by the *h*, and called
Luke 15:22 put a ring on his *h*, and shoes on
Luke 23:33 one on the right *h*, and the other on
John 10:28 shall any man pluck them out of my *h*
John 11:55 the Jews' passover was nigh at *h*
John 20:25 and thrust my *h* into his side, I
John 20:27 and reach hither thy *h*, and thrust

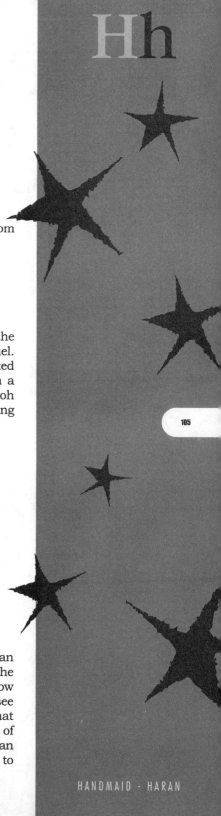

■ Handmaid (HAND mayed)
A female or woman servant.

Luke 1:38 And Mary said, Behold the *h* of the Lord

■ Hang (HANG)
To swing, or to be held with no assistance from underneath.

Esther 6:4 to speak unto the king to *h* Mordecai
Esther 7:9 the king said, *H* him thereon
Matthew 22:40 On these two commandments *h* all the law

■ Hannah (HAN uh)
The name means "grace." She was one of the two wives of Elkanah and the mother to Samuel. She prayed to God for a son and later dedicated him to the LORD. Each year she made him a coat and took it to the sanctuary at Shiloh where Samuel was serving God and learning from Eli, the priest.

1 Samuel 1:2 two wives; the name of the one was *H*
1 Samuel 1:2 but *H* had no children
1 Samuel 1:9 *H* rose up after they had eaten
1 Samuel 1:13 Now *H*, she spake in her heart
1 Samuel 2:1 And *H* prayed, and said, My heart

■ Happy (HAP ee)
Cheerful, glad, joyful, merry.

Job 5:17 *h* is the man whom God correcteth
Proverbs 3:13 *H* is the man that findeth wisdom
Proverbs 16:20 whoso trusteth in the LORD, *h* is he
Proverbs 29:18 he that keepeth the law, *h* is he

■ Haran (HAY ran)
The name means "mountaineer" or "caravan route." Haran was the name of Lot's father, the brother of Abraham. A city, in what is now southeastern Turkey, was also called Haran (see map on page 336). It was to this city that Abraham brought his family when he left Ur of the Chaldees. Many relatives stayed in Haran when Abraham continued his journey on to

Hh

Harp

Canaan, the place to which God was leading him.

Genesis 11:27 Terah begat Abram, Nahor, and *H*
Genesis 11:27 and *H* begat Lot
Genesis 11:31 and they came unto *H* and dwelt there
Genesis 11:32 And Terah died in *H*
Genesis 28:10 from Beer-sheba, and went toward *H*

◼ Harden (HAR din)
To be unbending or have no feeling toward; to say no to God's will, which can come from the person or from God.

Exodus 7:3 And I will *h* Pharaoh's heart, and
Exodus 14:4 will *h* Pharaoh's heart, that he shall

◼ Harp (HARP)
A musical instrument. Other names for the harp include lyre, psaltery, and viol. The shape of the harp varied as did the number of strings. Some harps had three strings where others might have twenty. The harp was often made from expensive woods, therefore only the wealthy could own them. The harp David played for King Saul was probably more simple.

1 Samuel 16:16 man, who is a cunning player on an *h*
1 Samuel 16:23 David took an *h*, and played with his hand
Psalm 33:2 Praise the LORD with *h*: sing unto him

◼ Harvest (HAR vist)
The time for gathering or reaping the ripe crops. Harvest time usually came just before or during special events. The first fruits or the first part of the harvest was presented to God as an offering. Part of the crop was left behind for the poor and widows to pick up. The various crops and fruits were harvested at different times during the growing season. This depended on when they were ripe.

Leviticus 19:9 And when ye reap the *h* of your land
Ruth 1:22 to Bethlehem in the beginning of barley *h*
Matthew 9:37 The *h* truly is plenteous, but the
Matthew 9:38 Pray ye therefore the Lord of the *h*
Matthew 9:38 send forth laborers into his *h*
Luke 10:2 The *h* truly is great, but the laborers
Luke 10:2 pray ye therefore the Lord of the *h*
Luke 10:2 send forth laborers into his *h*
John 4:35 yet four months, and then cometh *h*
John 4:35 fields; for they are white already to *h*

◼ Hatach (HAY tak)
The name may mean "runner" and may be of

Persian origin. He was a eunuch who served in the court of King Ahasuerus. He was Esther's servant.

Esther 4:5 Then Esther called for **H**, one of the
Esther 4:6 So **H** went forth to Mordecai unto the
Esther 4:9 **H** came and told Esther the words
Esther 4:10 Esther spake unto **H**, and gave him

Hate (HAYT)

To dislike greatly. To hate others can cause a person to do hurtful things or say angry, hurtful words. The old way is to hate our enemies but Jesus said we should love our enemies and do good to those who hate us.

Psalm 97:10 Let those who love the LORD **h** evil (NIV)
Proverbs 6:16 These six things doth the LORD **h**
Proverbs 8:13 To fear the LORD is to **h** evil (NIV)
Ecclesiastes 3:8 A time to love, and a time to **h**
Matthew 5:43 love thy neighbor and **h** thine enemy
Matthew 5:44 do good to them that **h** you
Matthew 6:24 either he will **h** the one, and love
Luke 6:22 Blessed are ye, when men shall **h** you
Luke 6:27 do good to them which **h** you

Head (HED)

The part of the body above the shoulders, on which the eyes, mouth, nose, ears, and chin are located. The head contains the brain, which is the "master control center" of the body.

Psalm 23:5 thou anointest my **h** with oil
Proverbs 25:22 will heap burning coals on his **h** (NIV)
Matthew 8:20 Son of man has no place to lay his **h** (NIV)
Matthew 10:30 very hairs of your **h** are all numbered
Matthew 27:29 thorns, they put it upon his **h**
Luke 9:58 Son of man has no place to lay his **h** (NIV)
Luke 12:7 the very hairs of your **h** are all numbered
John 19:2 crown of thorns, and put it on his **h**
John 19:30 It is finished: and he bowed his **h**, and

Heal (HEEL)

To make well, to mend, to cure.

Psalm 41:4 **h** my soul; for I have sinned
Ecclesiastes 3:3 A time to kill, and a time to **h**
Matthew 8:7 I will come and **h** him
Matthew 12:10 Is it lawful to **h** on the sabbath
Luke 4:18 hath sent me to **h** the brokenhearted
Luke 4:23 this proverb, Physician, **h** thyself
Luke 6:7 whether he would **h** on the sabbath day
Luke 14:3 Is it lawful to **h** on the sabbath day

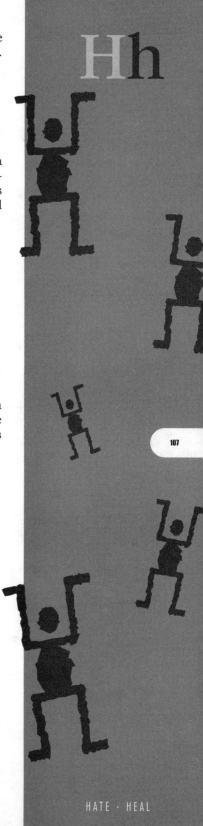

Hh

Hh

◼ Heap (HEEP)
A pile; to make into a pile; to fill fuller than full.

Exodus 15:8 the floods stood upright as an **h**
Proverbs 25:22 thou shalt **h** coals of fire upon
Romans 12:20 in so doing thou shalt **h** coals of fire

◼ Hear (HEER)
To notice sound; to listen to, pay attention to, respond to.

1 Kings 18:37 **H** me, O LORD, **h** me, that this
Psalm 4:1 **H** me when I call, O God
Psalm 4:1 have mercy upon me, and **h** my prayer
Psalm 4:3 the LORD will **h** when I call unto him
Psalm 61:1 **H** my cry, O God: attend unto my
Psalm 102:1 **H** my prayer, O LORD, and let my cry
Proverbs 1:5 A wise man will **h**, and will increase
Proverbs 1:8 My son, **h** the instruction of thy father
Proverbs 8:33 **H** instruction, and be wise, and
Mark 12:29 commandments is, **H**, O Israel; The Lord
Luke 5:15 and great multitudes came together to **h**

◼ Hearers (HEER uhrz)
Those who hear. See "Hear."

James 1:22 doers of the word, and not **h** only

◼ Heart (HART)
1. The organ, located in the upper chest, that moves blood through the body. 2. The center of something. 3. This definition is the one which is important in Bible study. It is an expression that refers to the feelings, thoughts, and moral actions. The Hebrew people would say "heart" but people today would say "mind" or "brain."

Exodus 7:13 And he hardened Pharaoh's **h**
Deuteronomy 6:5 love the LORD thy God with all thine **h**
Psalm 24:4 He that hath clean hands, and a pure **h**
Psalm 51:10 Create in me a clean **h**, O God
Psalm 119:10 With my whole **h** have I sought thee
Psalm 119:11 Thy word have I hid in mine **h**
Psalm 139:23 Search me, O God, and know my **h**
Proverbs 3:5 Trust in the LORD with all thine **h**
Proverbs 15:13 A happy **h** makes the face cheerful (NIV)
Proverbs 17:22 A cheerful **h** is good medicine (NIV)
Proverbs 23:12 Apply thine **h** unto instruction
Matthew 5:8 Blessed are the pure in **h**
Matthew 22:37 love the Lord thy God with all thy **h**
Luke 12:34 treasure is, there will your **h** be also
John 14:1 Let not your **h** be troubled
Romans 10:9 and shalt believe in thine **h**

Romans 10:10 For with the *h* man believeth

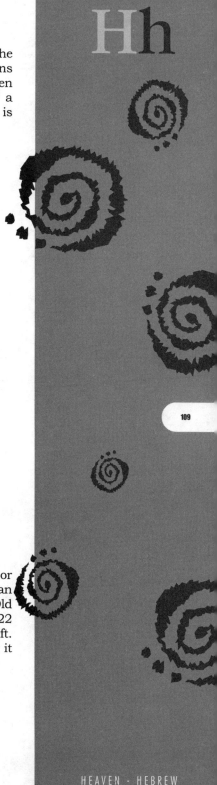

Heaven (HEH vin)

1. God placed the sun, moon, and stars in the heavens. 2. The sky. A place where Christians go after they die. We do not know where heaven is but we do know it is the place where a Christian will be with God, where everything is perfect.

Genesis 1:1 In the beginning God created the *h*
Genesis 1:8 and God called the firmament *h*
Exodus 16:4 I will rain bread from *h*
2 Chronicles 7:14 then will I hear from *h*
Psalm 69:34 Let the *h* and earth praise him
Psalm 115:15 blessed of the LORD which made *h*
Psalm 121:2 LORD, which made *h* and earth
Psalm 136:26 give thanks unto the God of *h*
Psalm 139:8 If I ascend up into *h*, thou art there
Ecclesiastes 3:1 a time to every purpose under the *h*
Matthew 5:16 for great is your reward in *h*
Matthew 5:16 glorify your Father which is in *h*
Matthew 5:48 Father which is in *h* is perfect
Matthew 6:9 Our Father which art in *h*, Hallowed
Matthew 16:19 the keys of the kingdom of *h*
Matthew 19:21 thou shalt have treasure in *h*
Matthew 28:18 All power is given unto me in *h*
Mark 3:31 *H* and earth shall pass away: but my
Luke 3:22 a voice came from *h*, which said
Acts 4:12 There is none other name under *h*
Philippians 2:10 knee should bow, of things in *h*

Heavens (HEH vinz)

Plural for "heaven."

Psalm 8:3 When I consider thy *h*, the work of thy
Psalm 19:1 The *h* declare the glory of God

Hebrew (HEE broo)

1. Abraham or one of his descendants. A Jew or Israelite are other words used in place of an Hebrew. Also, a language. Almost all of the Old Testament is written in Hebrew. Hebrew has 22 alphabet letters and is written from right to left. Most of the Hebrew words are verbs, making it a colorful language.

Genesis 39:17 The *H* servant, which thou hast brought
Genesis 41:12 young man, an *H*, servant to the captain
Exodus 2:11 spied an Egyptian smiting an *H*
Jonah 1:9 I am an *H*; and I fear the LORD

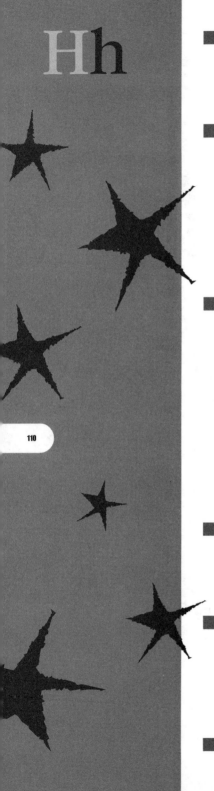

Hh

Hebrews (HEE brooz)
Plural of "Hebrew."

Genesis 40:15 stolen away out of the land of the *H*
Exodus 2:13 two men of the *H* strove together
Exodus 9:1 Thus saith the LORD God of the *H*

Hebrews, Book of (HEE brooz)
The first book in the division, General Letters, in the New Testament. The author is not known. The letter was written for those Jews who had become believers and who were thinking about giving up their belief in Jesus. They were being harassed, or picked on, because of their belief in Jesus. The writer reminded the Jewish Christians that Jesus had suffered for them and that He would be with them in their time of testing.

Hebron (HEE bruhn)
The name means "association" or "league." A city, located 19 miles southwest of Jerusalem, in the hill country of Judah and 15 miles west of the Dead Sea (see map on page 336). Because of the plentiful water supply, it is a good area for growing crops. Hebron is 3000 feet above sea level. It has been occupied since about 3300 B.C. Abraham lived there and was buried not too far from the city. David claimed Hebron as his first capital after he became king.

Genesis 13:18 in *H*, and built there an altar unto
2 Samuel 2:11 David was king in *H* over the house of
2 Samuel 5:5 In *H* he reigned over Judah seven years

Height (HIGHT)
The highest point; the tallness of a thing.

Genesis 6:15 and the *h* of it thirty cubits
1 Samuel 17:4 Goliath, of Gath, whose *h* was six
Romans 8:39 Nor *h*, nor depth, nor any other

Hell (HELL)
The place where unbelievers in Jesus Christ will go after they die. It is a place of eternal punishment. Other names for hell used in the Bible are Hades, Gehenna, Sheol, and the pit.

Psalm 139:8 I make my bed in *h*, behold, thou art there
Matthew 16:18 the gates of *h* shall not prevail against

Help (HELP)
To aid or assist; an act of giving aid.

Psalm 33:20 he is our *h* and our shield (NIV)

Psalm 46:1 strength, a very present **h** in trouble
Psalm 121:1 hills, from whence cometh my **h**
Luke 5:7 that they should come and **h** them
Luke 10:40 bid her therefore that she **h** me
Acts 16:9 Come over into Macedonia, and **h** us

Helper (HELP uhr)
One who helps.

Psalm 30:10 have mercy upon me: LORD, be thou my **h**
Psalm 54:4 Behold, God is mine **h**

Herb (ERB)
Any green plant, tender grass, or grain, used in foods to make them taste better, or as medicines to help treat illnesses.

Genesis 1:11 bring forth grass, the **h** yielding seed
Genesis 1:29 I have given you every **h** bearing seed
Exodus 9:25 and the hail smote every **h** of the field

Herdmen (HERD min)
Those who cared for herds of cattle, sheep, goats, or other animals.

Genesis 13:7 strife between the **h** of Abram's cattle
Genesis 13:8 and between my **h** and thy **h**
Genesis 26:20 **h** of Gerar did strive with Isaac's **h**

Herod (HEHR uhd)
The name of the family who ruled Palestine about fifty years before and for about fifty years after Jesus was born. These kings were evil. The four Herod's who were ruling during New Testament times will be listed separately, as shown below.

Herod the Great was king at the time of Jesus' birth. He met with the Wise Men to learn where Jesus was to have been born. When they did not come back to tell him, he had many baby boys killed in Bethlehem, hoping to kill the "King of the Jews." But God had sent Joseph and Mary to Egypt with Jesus.

Matthew 2:1 Judea, in the days of **H** the king
Matthew 2:3 When **H** the king heard these things
Matthew 2:7 Then **H**, when he had privily called
Matthew 2:12 that they should not return to **H**

Herod Antipas (AN tih puhs)
He was the son of Herod the Great. He was the one who had John the Baptist beheaded. He really admired John, but he had given a promise to Salome that she could have anything she wished

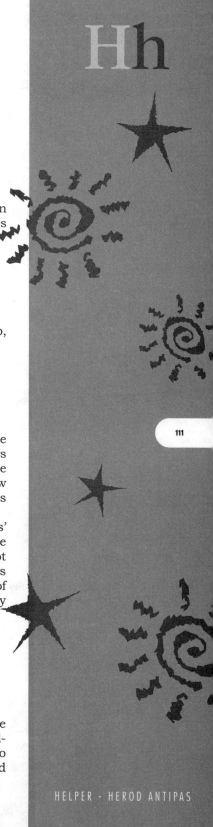

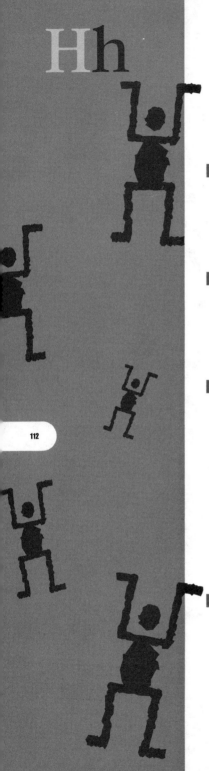

Hh

for. She asked for the head of John the Baptist on a platter. Herod could not change his promise. This Herod also held one of the trials of Jesus.

Matthew 14:1 **H** the tetrarch heard of the fame of Jesus
Matthew 14:3 For **H** had laid hold on John, and
Mark 6:18 For John had said unto **H**, It is not
Mark 6:20 **H** feared John, knowing that he was a
Luke 23:12 Pilate and **H** were made friends together

Herod Agrippa I (uh GRIP uh)
He was the son of Herod Antipas. He ordered James killed and wanted to kill Peter.

Acts 12:1 about that time **H** the king stretched
Acts 12:6 when **H** would have him brought forth
Acts 12:11 hath delivered me out of the hand of **H**

Herod Agrippa II
He was the ruler who listened to Paul after Paul was arrested for preaching about Jesus.

Acts 26:1 Then **A** said unto Paul, Thou art
Acts 26:27 King **A**, believest thou the prophets
Acts 26:28 Then **A** said unto Paul, Almost thou

Holy (HOH lee)
1. Blessed, moral, pure. 2. A person, place, or thing that is used especially for God. Sacred or godly. A Christian is to live a godly life (live as God directs him to live).

Exodus 3:5 place whereon thou standeth is **h** ground
Leviticus 11:44 ye shall be **h**; for I am **h**
1 Samuel 2:2 There is none **h** as the LORD
Psalm 11:4 The LORD is in his **h** temple
Psalm 51:11 and take not thy **h** spirit from me
Psalm 111:9 **h** and awesome is his name (NIV)
Isaiah 6:3 **H**, **h**, **h**, is the LORD of hosts
1 Peter 1:16 Be ye **h**; for I am **h**

Holy Ghost (HOH lee GOHST)
Same as the Holy Spirit. The Holy Spirit is the Spirit of God that lives within each person who has asked Jesus to be his or her Savior. He guides and teaches us through our thoughts by helping us to remember or know the right things to do. He has also been called a Comforter, one who is present when we face sad or hurtful times. Other names of the Holy Ghost include Helper and Counselor, besides being a Comforter. He is part of the Trinity: God the Father, God the Son (Jesus), and God the Holy Spirit.

Matthew 1:20 which is conceived in her is of the **HG**

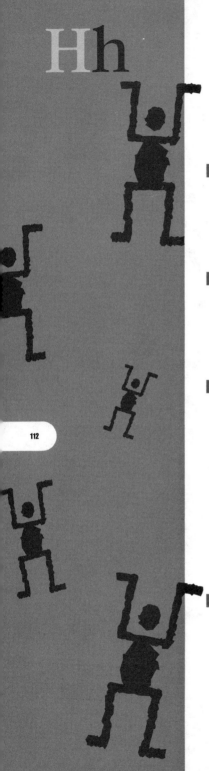

112

Matthew 12:31 blasphemy against the ***HG*** shall not be
Matthew 28:19 Father, and of the Son, and of the ***HG***
Mark 1:8 but he shall baptize you with the ***HG***
Luke 1:15 and he shall be filled with the ***HG***
Luke 2:25 and the ***HG*** was upon him
Luke 3:16 he shall baptize you with the ***HG***
Luke 12:10 blasphemeth against the ***HG*** it shall not
John 14:26 the Comforter, which is the ***HG***, whom the
Acts 1:8 power, after that the ***HG*** is come upon you

Honest (AHN ist)
Fair, just, moral, truthful in actions and words.

Acts 6:3 among you seven men of ***h*** report
2 Corinthians 13:7 ye should do that which is ***h***
Philippians 4:8 are true, whatsoever things are ***h***

Honor (AHN uhr)
Also spelled "honour." To glorify, respect, or worship; to show respect toward; to value. By obeying God or parents, we honor them.

Exodus 20:12 ***H*** thy father and thy mother
Deuteronomy 5:16 ***H*** thy father and thy mother
1 Chronicles 16:27 Glory and ***h*** are in his presence
Psalm 66:2 Sing forth the ***h*** of his name
Psalm 96:6 ***H*** and majesty are before him
Proverbs 3:9 ***H*** the LORD with thy substance
Proverbs 20:3 an ***h*** for a man to cease from strife
Matthew 19:19 ***H*** thy father and thy mother
Mark 6:4 prophet is not without ***h***, but in his own
Mark 7:10 Moses said, ***H*** thy father and thy
John 4:44 prophet hath no ***h*** in his own country
John 12:26 man serve me, him will my Father ***h***
Ephesians 6:2 ***H*** thy father and mother; which is

Hope (HOHP)
To believe, dream, expect, long for, trust; believing that God will do all that He promised. The Christian knows that as God has been faithful in the past, He will be faithful today, and in days to come. His promises never fail.

Psalm 39:7 my ***h*** is in thee
Psalm 119:81 but I ***h*** in thy word
Lamentations 3:24 therefore will I ***h*** in him
Romans 8:25 But if we ***h*** for that we see not, then
1 Corinthians 13:13 three remain: faith, ***h*** and love (NIV)

Horses (HAWRS ehz)
Animals with large hoofs used for riding, as work animals, or to pull chariots or wagons during times of war.

Psalm 20:7 some trust in chariots, and some in ***h***

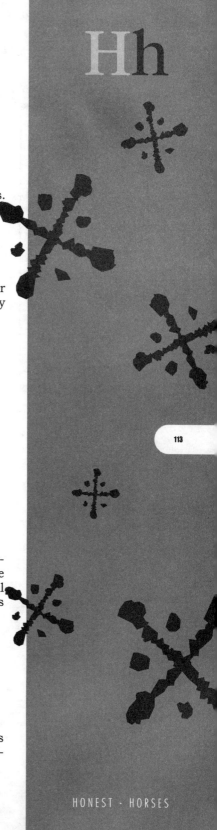

Hh

113

Hh

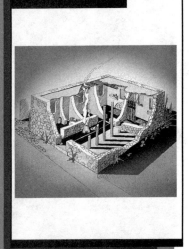

House

Hosea, Book of (hoh ZAY uh)

The name means "salvation." The book is the second in the division, Minor Prophets, in the Old Testament. He was a prophet in Israel from about 750-725 B.C., just before the end of the Northern Kingdom. Hosea wanted the people to realize that God loved them in spite of their sinfulness. He compared Israel to an unfaithful wife and how her husband would do whatever he could to get her to come back and be faithful to him. God would renew His relationship with Israel if they would repent and ask Him for forgiveness.

House (HOWCE)

A home in which people live. In biblical times, people lived in houses made from brick, mud, rocks, or other building materials. Caves could also be used as a home. Paul was a tentmaker so tents were also used to live in. In biblical times, the word "house" might also refer to a family.

1 Kings 17:15 she, and he, and her *h*, did eat
Psalm 23:6 I will dwell in the *h* of the LORD
Psalm 122:1 Let us go into the *h* of the LORD
Isaiah 56:7 mine *h* shall be called an *h* of prayer
Matthew 7:24 man, which built his *h* upon a rock
Matthew 7:26 man, which built his *h* upon the sand
Matthew 21:13 My *h* shall be called the *h* of prayer
Luke 6:48 like a man which built an *h*, and digged
Luke 6:49 without a foundation built an *h* upon
Luke 19:5 for today I must abide at thy *h*
Luke 19:9 This day is salvation come to this *h*
Luke 19:46 My *h* is the *h* of prayer
John 14:2 In my Father's *h* are many mansions

Humble (HUM buhl)

Not bold or proud; meek, modest, plain; patient.

Psalm 34:2 the *h* shall hear thereof, and be glad
James 4:6 the proud, but giveth grace unto the *h*
James 4:10 *H* yourselves in the sight of the Lord
1 Peter 5:5 the proud, and giveth grace to the *h*

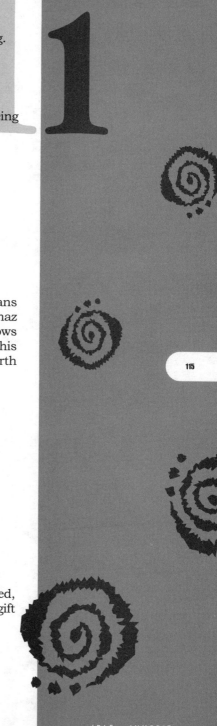

Idle (EYE duhl)

Lazy, not doing anything useful; not working.

Proverbs 19:15 and an *i* soul shall suffer hunger
Luke 24:11 words seemed to them as *i* tales

Image (IM idj)

Likeness, picture. Often refers to man being made like God.

Genesis 1:26 God said, Let us make man in our *i*
Genesis 1:27 So God created man in his own *i*
Exodus 20:4 shalt not make unto thee any graven *i*
Leviticus 26:1 shall make you no idols nor graven *i*
Deuteronomy 5:8 shalt not make thee any graven *i*
Matthew 22:20 saith unto them, Whose is this *i*
Mark 12:16 saith unto them, Whose is this *i*
Luke 20:24 Show me a penny. Whose *i* and

Immanuel (ih MAN yoo el)

The same as "Emmanuel." The name means "God is with us." Isaiah prophesied to King Ahaz that a child would be born and Matthew shows that child was Jesus, God's Son. God gave this promise to Isaiah over 700 years before the birth of Jesus.

Isaiah 7:14 a son, and shall call his name *I*
Matthew 1:23 him *I*—which means, "God with us" (NIV)

Impossible (im PAHS ih buhl)

Out of the question, cannot be done.

Matthew 17:20 and nothing shall be *i* unto you
Matthew 19:26 with men this is *i*; but with God
Mark 10:27 With men it is *i*, but not with God
Luke 1:37 For with God nothing shall be *i*
Luke 18:27 things which are *i* with men are possible
Hebrews 11:6 without faith it is *i* to please him

Inherit (ihn HAIR et)

To receive something from one who has died, usually a relative; to receive something as a gift from God.

Psalm 37:11 But the meek shall *i* the earth
Matthew 5:5 meek: for they shall *i* the earth
Mark 10:17 shall I do that I may *i* eternal life
Luke 10:25 what shall I do to *i* eternal life
Luke 18:18 what shall I do to *i* eternal life

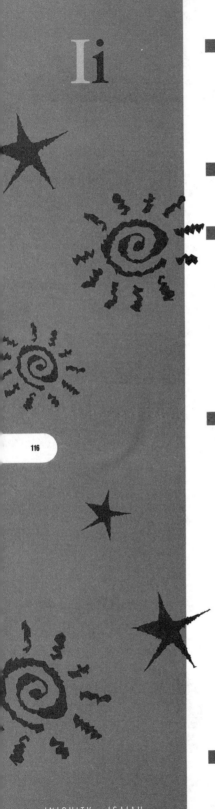

Iniquity (en IK weh tee)
Sin, wrong; ignoring laws, especially the laws of God.

Psalm 25:11 forgive my *i*, though it is great (NIV)
Psalm 38:18 I will declare mine *i*; I will be sorry
Psalm 51:2 Wash me thoroughly from mine *i*
Psalm 66:18 If I regard *i* in my heart, the LORD

Instruct (en STRUKT)
To educate, teach, train; to command or order.

Psalm 32:8 I will *i* thee and teach thee in the way

Instruction (en STRUK shun)
The act or method of teaching.

Proverbs 1:7 but fools despise wisdom and *i*
Proverbs 1:8 My son, hear the *i* of thy father
Proverbs 8:33 Hear *i*, and be wise, and refuse it not
Proverbs 9:9 Give *i* to a wise man, and he will
Proverbs 12:1 Whoso loveth *i* loveth knowledge
Proverbs 13:1 A wise son heareth his father's *i*
Proverbs 15:5 A fool despiseth his father's *i*
Proverbs 23:12 Apply thine heart unto *i*
2 Timothy 3:16 correction, for *i* in righteousness

Isaac (Igh zik)
The name means "laughter." He was the son of Abraham and Sarah, born when they were very old. God had directed Abraham, the father of Isaac, to take Isaac and offer him as a sacrifice. Abraham was ready to obey God when God provided a ram for him to sacrifice instead. Isaac married a cousin, Rebekah, and they had twin sons, Esau and Jacob. Isaac was very wealthy with many animals. When Isaac was very old and almost blind, his son, Jacob, tricked him into giving him the blessing that was meant for Esau. Isaac lived to be 180 years old.

Genesis 17:19 and thou shalt call his name *I*
Genesis 22:2 Take now thy son, thy only son *I*
Genesis 22:9 bound *I* his son, and laid him on the
Genesis 27:26 And his father *I* said unto him, Come
Genesis 27:30 soon as *I* had made an end of blessing
Genesis 27:32 and *I* his father said unto him
Genesis 27:33 And *I* trembled very exceedingly
Genesis 27:37 And *I* answered and said unto Esau

Isaiah, Book of (igh ZAY uh)
The name means "Yahweh saves." This book is the first in the division, Major Prophets, in the Old

Testament. He was a prophet in Judah from about 740-701 B.C., and five kings reigned during those years. Isaiah was well educated and quite aware of what was happening in his world. The first part of the book told why the people should be obedient to God, no matter what. He also talked about what was happening in Jerusalem before the Babylonians conquered the city and took most of the people to Babylonia. The second half of the book gave the people encouragement and hope, that God would send a Messiah (Savior). He stressed being obedient to God's laws and being faithful in their worship.

Israel (IZ ray el)

The name means "God rules" or "God heals." This is the name God gave Jacob after Jacob had wrestled with the angel. He had twelve sons and their descendants became the twelve tribes of Israel. Thus, they became the Hebrew nation. Israel was the kingdom ruled by Saul, David, and Solomon. When Israel split, it became the Northern Kingdom, and the Southern Kingdom was Judah.

Genesis 32:28 called no more Jacob, but *I*
Genesis 37:3 Now *I* loved Joseph more than all
Genesis 46:30 And *I* said unto Joseph, Now let me die
Genesis 49:28 these are the twelve tribes of *I*
Exodus 2:25 God looked upon the children of *I*
Exodus 14:29 children of *I* walked upon dry land
Exodus 16:15 when the children of *I* saw it
Exodus 16:35 children of *I* did eat manna forty years
Deuteronomy 6:4 Hear, O *I*: The LORD our God
Psalm 106:48 Blessed be the LORD God of *I*
Micah 5:2 unto me that is to be a ruler in *I*
Matthew 2:6 Governor, that shall rule my people *I*
Matthew 8:10 not found so great faith, no, not in *I*
Matthew 15:31 and they glorified the God of *I*
Matthew 27:42 If he be the king of *I*, let him
Mark 12:29 Hear, O *I*: The Lord our God is
Luke 2:25 waiting for the consolation of *I*
Luke 4:25 many widows were in *I* in the days
Luke 7:9 so great faith, no, not in *I*
John 12:13 Blessed is the King of *I* that cometh

Israelites (IZ ray el ights)

Descendants of Abraham; a Hebrew or Jew; citizens of Israel. Plural of "Israelite."

Joshua 3:17 all the *I* passed over on dry ground
1 Samuel 25:1 Samuel died; and all the *I* were

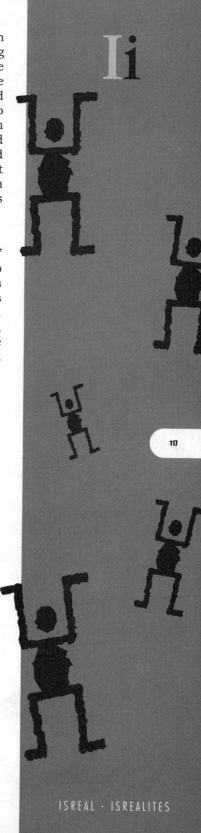

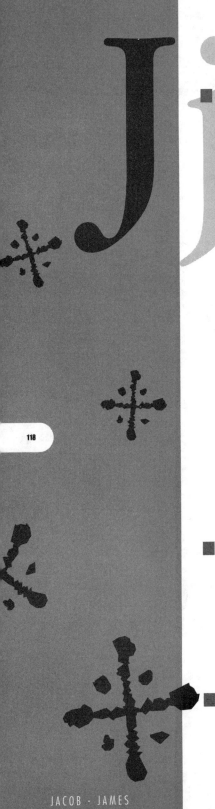

Jacob (JAY kuhb)

The name means "he grasps the heel," or "he cheats, supplants." His parents were Isaac and Rebekah. He had a twin brother, Esau, who was born first. He tricked Esau out of his birthright by trading it for a bowl of stew when Esau was so hungry. Later, he cheated Esau out of the father's special blessing to the oldest son. Jacob wore Esau's clothing and pretended to be Esau when Esau was out hunting. Jacob had two wives, Leah and Rachel, and had twelve sons and several daughters. Later God changed his name to Israel. He died in Egypt where one of his sons, Joseph, was in charge of providing food during the terrible famine.

Genesis 25:26 and his name was called *J*
Genesis 25:31 and *J* said, Sell me this day thy birthright
Genesis 25:27 *J* was a plain man, dwelling in tents
Genesis 25:33 *J* gave Esau bread and pottage of lentils
Genesis 27:19 And *J* said unto his father, I am Esau
Genesis 27:22 *J* went near unto Isaac his father
Genesis 27:30 Isaac had made an end of blessing *J*
Genesis 27:41 Esau hated *J* because of the blessing
Genesis 28:20 *J* vowed a vow, saying, If God will be
Genesis 29:18 And *J* loved Rachel; and said, I will
Genesis 29:20 *J* served seven years for Rachel
Genesis 47:7 Joseph brought in *J* his father
Genesis 47:7 before Pharaoh: and *J* blessed Pharaoh
Exodus 3:6 the God of Isaac, and the God of *J*

Jairus (JIGH ruhs)

The name means "Jah will enlighten." Jah is a short form of Yahweh, a name for God. He was an official in the synagogue who asked Jesus to heal his twelve-year-old daughter. The girl died before Jesus arrived and He brought her back to life, showing His power over death.

Mark 5:22 of the rulers of the synagogue, *J* by name
Luke 8:41 came a man named *J*, and he was a ruler

James (JAYMZ)

James is the Greek form of the Hebrew name Jacob. It is believed that more than one James is referred to in the New Testament. A few are listed here.

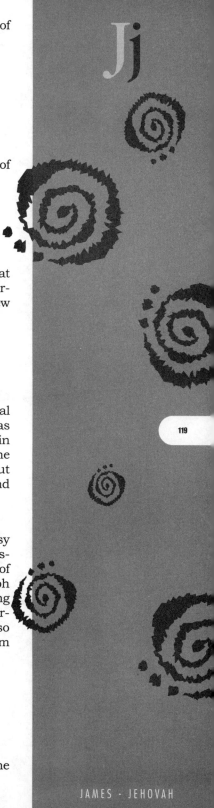

1. A disciple, the son of Zebedee and brother of John. He was a fisherman.

Matthew 4:21 **J** the son of Zebedee, and John his
Mark 3:17 **J** the son of Zebedee, and John the brother
Mark 9:2 Jesus taketh with him Peter, and **J**, and
Luke 5:10 **J**, and John, the sons of Zebedee
Luke 8:51 no man to go in, save Peter, and **J**
Luke 9:28 he took Peter and John and **J**

2. A second disciple, known as James the son of Alphaeus.

Matthew 10:3 **J** the son of Alphaeus, and Lebbeus
Mark 3:18 and Thomas, and **J** the son of Alphaeus
Luke 6:15 Thomas, **J** the son of Alphaeus
Acts 1:13 Matthew, **J** the son of Alphaeus

3. The brother of Jesus. He did not believe that Jesus was the Messiah until after Jesus' resurrection. He later became a leader in the New Testament church.

Matthew 27:56 Mary the mother of **J** and Joses
Mark 16:1 and Mary the mother of **J**
Luke 24:10 Joanna, and Mary the mother of **J**

James, Book of (JAYMZ)
The second book in the division, General Letters, in the New Testament. The author was probably James, Jesus' half brother. The main message of James' letter was to remind the Christian to not just hear the word of God but to do what it says. A Christian's actions and words must match.

Jealous (GEL uhs)
Envious, distrustful, resentful. Human jealousy often results in great anger toward others, causing one to do harm to another. The jealousy of Joseph's brothers caused them to sell Joseph into slavery. Jealous can also mean being watchful, protective, or wary. God did not tolerate His people worshiping other gods. He also tried to protect the Israelites, His people, from their enemies.

Exodus 20:5 for I the LORD thy God am a **j** God
Deuteronomy 5:9 for I the LORD thy God am a **j** God
1 Kings 19:10 I have been very **j** for the LORD
1 Kings 19:14 I have been very **j** for the LORD

Jehovah (jeh HOH vuh)
A divine or holy name for the LORD God. The

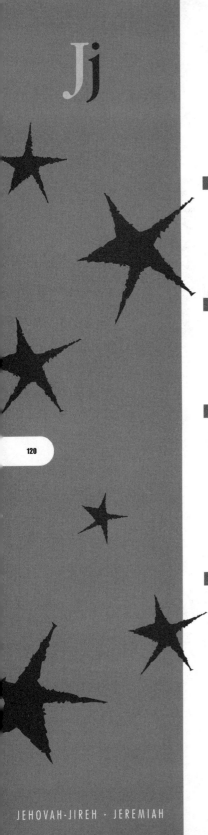

Jj

same as Yahweh. Both names were considered so sacred that they were not spoken in order to keep a person from saying the name improperly. This would be considered blaspheming the holy name of God.

Exodus 6:3 by my name **J** was I not known to them
Psalm 83:18 thou, whose name alone is **J**
Isaiah 12:2 for the LORD **J** is my strength and

▪ Jehovah-Jireh (jeh HOH vuh-JIGH reh)

The name means "Yahweh will provide." This name was given to the place where Abraham had taken Isaac to be sacrificed. God, instead, provided the right sacrifice and Isaac's life was spared.

Genesis 22:14 Abraham called the name of that place **J**

▪ Jehovah-Nissi (jeh HOH vuh-NISS igh)

The name means "Yahweh is my banner." When the Israelites defeated the Amalekites, Moses built an altar to worship and praise God for the victory. He named the altar Jehovah-Nissi.

Exodus 17:15 altar, and called the name of it **J**

▪ Jehudi (jih HYOO digh)

The name means "Judaen or Jewish." He was the messenger who read aloud the words God had Jeremiah write. King Jehoiakim cut off the pieces and threw them into the fire as he finished reading each section.

Jeremiah 36:14 the princes sent **J** the son of
Jeremiah 36:21 So the king sent **J** to fetch the roll
Jeremiah 36:21 And **J** read it in the ears of the king
Jeremiah 36:23 when **J** had read three or four leaves

▪ Jeremiah (JER ih MIGH uh)

The name means "may Yahweh lift up." He is thought to be the greatest prophet in the Old Testament. He prophesied under the last five kings of Judah. His father was Hilkiah, the priest. Jeremiah constantly warned the Israelites that God would bring judgment on their wicked living. Many times the people tried to kill him. He was taken captive with many Israelites and died in Egypt.

Jeremiah 1:1 The words of **J** the son of Hilkiah
Jeremiah 36:1 this word came unto **J** from the LORD
Jeremiah 36:4 Then **J** called Baruch the son of Neriah
Jeremiah 36:32 took **J** another roll, and gave it to Baruch
Jeremiah 38:6 took they **J**, and cast him into the dungeon

Jeremiah 38:13 So they drew up **J** with cords
Jeremiah 38:13 **J** remained in the court of the prison

Jeremiah, Book of (JER ih MIGH uh)

The second book in the division, Major Prophets, in the Old Testament. Baruch, a scribe and friend of Jeremiah, wrote the book as Jeremiah spoke the words. The book tells about the life of Jeremiah, the events that were taking place in Judah, how the sin of the people would cause them great heartache, and how God's promises to renew the people would take place.

Jericho (JER ih koh)

The name means "moon." It is thought to be the oldest city in the world. The city is located a few miles west of the Jordan River and north of the Dead Sea (see map on page 337). Jericho was the first city the Israelites conquered when Joshua led them into the Promised Land. Joshua led the people to march once around the city for six days. On the seventh day, they marched around the city seven times, gave a loud shout, and the walls fell down. This allowed them to enter the city. During Jesus' day, Zacchaeus and Bartimaeus, the blind beggar whom Jesus healed, lived in Jericho.

Joshua 2:1 saying, Go view the land, even **J**
Joshua 6:2 I have given into thine hand **J**
Mark 10:46 And they came to **J**
Mark 10:46 as he went out of **J** with his disciples
Luke 10:30 man went down from Jerusalem to **J**
Luke 18:35 as he was come nigh unto **J**
Luke 19:1 Jesus entered and passed through **J**
Hebrews 11:30 By faith, the walls of **J** fell down

Jerusalem (jih ROO suh lem)

The name means "founded by (god) Shalem." The city is on a hill 2500 feet above sea level and is situated about 18 miles west of the Dead Sea (see map on page 338). Jerusalem is surrounded by mountains. The main source of water is the Gihon Spring at the foot of the hill. Other names for Jerusalem are "Zion," "Mount Moriah," and "the city of David." Three valleys are located on the east, west, and south of the city. Jerusalem has been occupied for over 5500 years. It was located at a crossroad, where many people traveled from east to west, north to south. David ruled Judah from Jerusalem, and Solomon built the Temple at Jerusalem. When the Romans ruled Palestine, Herod the Great

Jerusalem

Jj

rebuilt the city, adding many large buildings, including the Temple (which had been destroyed). When David was king, he made Jerusalem a Jewish city. And because the Temple was located there, the Israelites thought it the most important city in Palestine.

2 Samuel 5:5 in *J* he reigned thirty and three years
Nehemiah 1:3 the wall of *J* also is broken down, and
Nehemiah 2:11 So I came to *J*, and was there three
Nehemiah 2:17 *J* lieth waste, and the gates thereof
Nehemiah 2:17 and let us build up the wall of *J*
Nehemiah 4:7 heard that the walls of *J* were made up
Matthew 2:1 came wise men from the east to *J*
Matthew 16:21 how that he must go unto *J*, and suffer
Mark 10:33 Behold, we go up to *J*; and the Son of man
Luke 2:41 Now his parents went to *J* every year at the
Luke 2:43 the child Jesus tarried behind in *J*
Luke 10:30 certain man went down from *J* to Jericho
Luke 18:31 Behold, we go up to *J*, and all things that
John 2:13 passover was at hand, and Jesus went up to *J*
John 11:18 Now Bethany was nigh unto *J*, about fifteen
Acts 1:8 ye shall be witnesses unto me both in *J*,

Jesse (JESS ih)

The name means "man" or "manly." He was the father of King David and the grandson of Boaz. Boaz married Ruth and their son was Obed. David was the youngest of Jesse's eight sons. Jesse also had two daughters.

Ruth 4:22 Obed the father of *J*, and *J* the father of (NIV)
1 Samuel 16:5 And he sanctified *J* and his sons
1 Samuel 17:17 And *J* said unto David his son
1 Samuel 17:58 son of thy servant *J* the Bethlehemite

Jesus (JEE zuhs)

The name means "Yahweh is salvation" and "the anointed one" or "Messiah." Jesus is Greek for "Joshua," the Jewish name. His mother was Mary, a virgin, and his earthly father was Joseph, a carpenter. Jesus was born in Bethlehem about 6 B.C.

When he was twelve, his parents took him to Jerusalem and he stayed behind when it was time to go home. Jesus learned from Joseph to be a carpenter and he worked as a carpenter until he was thirty years of age. At that time, he left Nazareth, his childhood home, had his cousin John the Baptist baptize him in the Jordan River, and began to preach and choose His disciples.

During the three years of his ministry, he

Jesus

preached, healed, raised people from the dead, and taught about God's kingdom. Most of His ministry was in Galilee, but he also went to Samaria and east of the Jordan River. He didn't spend much time in the area around Jerusalem because of the Jewish religious leaders. These leaders were jealous of Jesus and did not like His teachings since the people followed Him everywhere to hear Him and to see His miracles. Many people hoped that Jesus was the Messiah who would rescue them from the terrible Roman rule. Thus, the leaders tried to figure out how to get rid of Him.

During Passover week in A.D. 30, Jesus was betrayed by Judas Iscariot, one of the twelve disciples. He was arrested, had a mock trial, was beaten and humiliated, and crucified on a cross as though He were a criminal. When He died, His body was placed in a borrowed tomb. On the first day of the week, a Sunday morning, three days after he died, He arose from the grave and appeared to many disciples, commanding them to go "into all the world and preach the gospel" (Mark 16:15). Forty days after his resurrection, he returned to heaven to be with God, His Father.

Matthew 1:18 Now the birth of **J** Christ was on this
Matthew 1:21 Son, and thou shalt call his name **J**
Matthew 3:13 Then cometh **J** from Galilee to Jordan
Matthew 4:1 Then was **J** led up of the Spirit into
Matthew 4:18 **J**, walking by the sea of Galilee
Matthew 4:23 And **J** went about all Galilee
Matthew 14:25 **J** went unto them, walking on the
Matthew 16:24 Then **J** said unto his disciples
Matthew 18:2 **J** called a little child unto him
Matthew 20:30 when they heard that **J** passed by
Matthew 20:34 So **J** had compassion on them, and
Matthew 26:6 **J** was in Bethany, in the house of
Matthew 26:26 **J** took bread, and blessed it, and
Matthew 27:37 THIS IS **J** THE KING OF THE JEWS
Mark 1:9 **J** came from Nazareth of Galilee
Mark 2:17 When **J** heard it, he saith unto them
Mark 5:21 When **J** was passed over again by ship
Mark 10:47 he heard that it was **J** of Nazareth
Mark 12:41 **J** sat over against the treasury
Mark 14:22 they did eat, **J** took bread, and
Mark 14:53 they led **J** away to the high priest
Mark 15:34 the ninth hour, **J** cried with a loud
Mark 15:37 And **J** cried with a loud voice, and
Mark 16:6 Ye seek **J** of Nazareth, which was

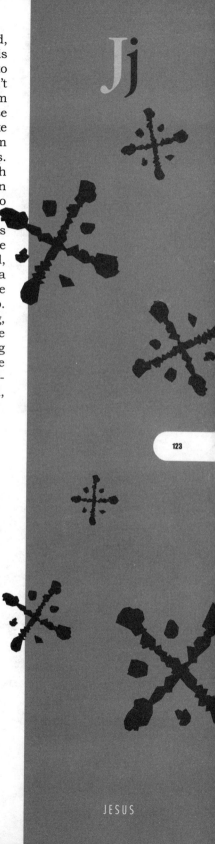

Jj

123

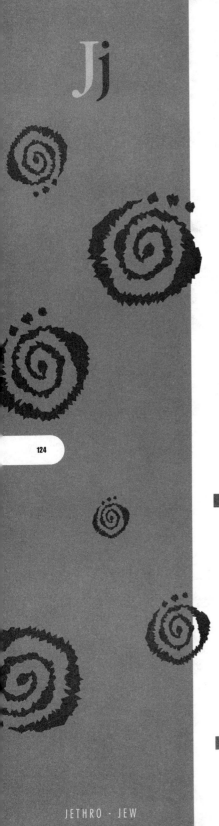

Jj

Luke 5:10 **J** said unto Simon, Fear not; from
Luke 8:45 And **J** said, Who touched me
Luke 10:30 **J** answering said, A certain man
Luke 18:37 him, that **J** of Nazareth passeth by
Luke 19:35 And they brought him to **J**: and they
Luke 19:35 upon the colt, and they set **J** thereon
Luke 23:46 **J** had cried with a loud voice
Luke 24:36 **J** himself stood in the midst of them
John 1:42 brought him to **J**. And when **J** beheld
John 5:8 **J** saith unto him, Rise, take up thy bed
John 6:5 When **J** lifted up his eyes, and saw a
John 6:10 **J** said, Make the men sit down
John 6:11 **J** took the loaves; and when he had
John 6:19 they see **J** walking on the sea, and
John 9:11 man that is called **J** made clay, and
John 11:5 **J** loved Martha, and her sister, and
John 11:39 **J** said, Take ye away the stone
John 18:12 the Jews took **J**, and bound him
John 19:18 either side one, and **J** in the midst
John 19:19 **J** OF NAZARETH THE KING OF THE JEWS
John 19:23 when they had crucified **J**, took his
John 19:40 took they the body of **J**, and wound
John 20:14 turned herself back, and saw **J**
John 20:14 and knew not that it was **J**
John 20:21 Then said **J** to them again, Peace
Acts 9:5 Lord said, I am **J** whom thou persecutest
Acts 16:31 Believe on the Lord **J** Christ, and
Philippians 2:10 name of **J** every knee should bow
Philippians 2:11 tongue should confess that **J** Christ

◼ Jethro (JETH roh)

The name means "excess" or "superiority." He
was the father-in-law of Moses. Another name
used to identify Jethro is the name "Reuel."
Jethro was a priest in the land of Midian, the
place where Moses fled when he hurriedly left
Egypt. After Moses led the Israelites out of
Egypt, Jethro came to visit and gave him some
good advice.

Exodus 3:1 kept the flock of **J** his father-in-law
Exodus 4:18 returned to **J** his father-in-law
Exodus 4:18 **J** said to Moses, Go in peace
Exodus 18:2 **J**, Moses' father-in-law, took
Exodus 18:9 **J** rejoiced for all the goodness
Exodus 18:10 **J** said, Blessed be the LORD, who

◼ Jew (JOO)

The word came into use from the tribe of Judah,
after the Northern Kingdom of Israel had been
destroyed. Other words are Hebrew and

Israelite. Any person who is a descendant of Abraham is considered a Jew. Also, anyone who worships God in the way the Jews worship is considered a Jew.

Esther 2:5 a certain **J**, whose name was Mordecai
John 4:9 How is it that thou, being a **J**, askest
Acts 18:2 found a certain **J** named Aquila
Romans 1:16 to the **J** first, and also to the Greek

Jezebel (JEZ uh bel)

The name means "where is the Prince?" She was the wife of Ahab, king of Israel. She was from Phoenicia and brought Baal worship to the Israelites. Jezebel was very wicked and was determined to have her way, no matter what. She tried to destroy all of God's prophets and put in place the prophets of Baal. On Mount Carmel, Elijah showed that these Baal prophets were false and they were all killed. Jezebel became very angry at Elijah and threatened his life. Later she had Naboth killed so Ahab could have Naboth's vineyard.

1 Kings 16:31 he also married **J** daughter of Ethbaal (NIV)
1 Kings 19:1 Ahab told **J** all that Elijah had done
1 Kings 21:14 **J**, saying, Naboth is stoned, and is dead

Jezreel (JEZ reel)

The name means "God sows." It is the name of a valley and the city in which King Ahab had a summer palace (see map on page 338). Ahab liked living in this city. The valley is well-watered and things grow quite well in the area. Naboth's vineyard was located in Jezreel next to the palace lands.

1 Kings 18:45 And Ahab rode, and went to **J**
1 Kings 18:46 ran before Ahab to the entrance of **J**
1 Kings 21:1 had a vineyard, which was in **J**

Joash (JOH ash)

The name means "Yahweh gives." This Joash was the baby son of King Ahaziah of Judah. His aunt, sister to Joash's slain father, hid him for six years. His grandmother was executed when he was seven and he was made king. Jehoida, the priest, was a great influence on the young king, helping him learn the things he would need to know to become a good king. Joash helped rid Judah of idol worship. But after Jehoida died, Joash stopped doing those things that pleased God. Judah once again worshiped idols. Some Scripture references have the word

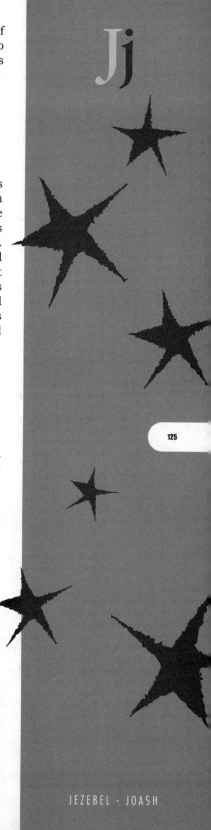

125

Jj

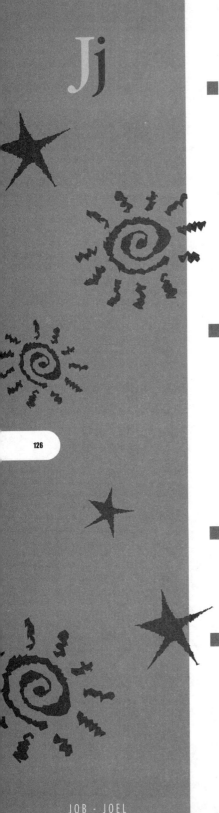

"Jehoash." This is the same Joash.

2 Kings 11:2 sister of Ahaziah, took **J** the son of

Job (JOHB)

A man in the Old Testament who was wealthy and trusted God. God allowed Satan to test him. Over a period of time, Job lost his sons and daughters and all he owned. He asked God many questions and ordered him to give the answers. In all his loss, pain, anger and frustration, he continued to trust God. When the testing time was over, God restored his wealth and he had more sons and daughters.

Job 1:1 land of Uz, whose name was **J**
Job 1:9 Does **J** fear God for nothing (NIV)
Job 42:10 the LORD gave **J** twice as much
Job 42:12 LORD blessed the latter end of **J** more
Job 42:16 **J** lived an hundred and forty years

Job, Book of (JOHB)

An Old Testament book that is the first in the division of Poetry and Wisdom. The author is unknown. The book tells how God allowed Satan to take away all of Job's possessions and children, and to cause him to be ill. As his friends sat with him, Job would not blame God for all that had happened. Job cries out to God for the answers to his questions, his faith in God assuring him of an answer. He showed that God cares when we suffer and that only God can be trusted when things go wrong. Job got back all the things he had lost and had more children.

Joel (JOH el)

The name means "Yah is God." He was a prophet who probably lived in Jerusalem. His message was to encourage the people to worship God alone.

Joel 1:1 The word of the LORD that came to **J**

Joel, Book of (JOH el)

The second Old Testament book in the division of Minor Prophets. He foretold that God would send a large swarm of locusts which would eat everything in sight. The people would be left hungry because of a drought. If the people, from the lowly farmer to the priest, would repent and turn back to God, He would prevent the locusts from coming. He also said a time would come when God's Spirit would be in all people, and they would not have to depend on the prophets to give them the messages of God. That promise came true at Pentecost when Peter preached and the Holy Spirit entered the lives of the believers.

John (JAHN)

The name means "Yahweh has been gracious." He was one of the twelve apostles. He was one of Zebedee's sons. His brother was James and they were fishermen on the Sea of Galilee. They worked with Peter and Andrew. John has been referred to as "the beloved disciple" of Jesus. He wrote five New Testament books: John, 1,2,3 John, and Revelation.

Matthew 10:2 son of Zebedee, and **J** his brother
Matthew 17:1 Peter, James, and **J** his brother
Mark 1:29 Simon and Andrew, with James and **J**
Mark 14:33 taketh with him Peter and James and **J**
Luke 6:14 and Andrew his brother, James and **J**
Luke 22:8 he sent Peter and **J**, saying, Go and
Acts 4:13 they saw the boldness of Peter and **J**

John the Baptist (JAHN thuh BAP tist)

A cousin of Jesus. His parents, Zachariah and Elizabeth, were very old when he was born. His father was a priest. John wore camel's hair clothing and a leather belt, ate locusts and wild honey, and lived in the desert until he began preaching repentance of sins. He told all who listened that Messiah was coming. Herod Antipas had him beheaded.

Matthew 3:1 In those days came **J** the Baptist
Matthew 3:4 same **J** had his raiment of camel's hair
Matthew 3:14 **J** forbad him saying, I have need to
Matthew 4:12 had heard that **J** was cast into prison
Mark 1:4 **J** did baptize in the wilderness, and
Mark 1:6 **J** was clothed with camel's hair, and
Mark 1:9 and was baptized of **J** in Jordan
Mark 1:14 Now after that **J** was put in prison
Luke 1:13 and thou shalt call his name **J**
Luke 1:63 and wrote, saying, His name is **J**
Luke 3:2 the word of God came unto **J** the son
Luke 3:16 **J** answered, saying unto them all
Luke 3:20 that he shut up **J** in prison
John 1:6 man sent from God, whose name was **J**
John 1:15 **J** bare witness of him, and cried,
John 1:26 **J** answered them, saying, I baptize
John 1:29 The next day **J** seeth Jesus coming
John 1:35 **J** stood, and two of his disciples

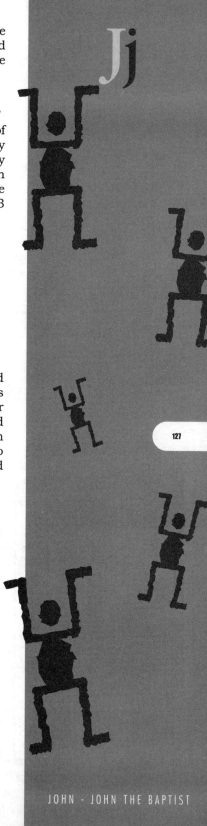

127

Jj

John, Book of (JAHN)
The fourth book in the New Testament division of Gospels. The book, written by John the apostle, tells about the work Jesus did in Samaria and Judaea. He stresses how Jesus is the Son of God and that salvation is in Him. He has much detail about the arrest, trial, death, and resurrection of Jesus.

John, 1,2,3, Books of (JAHN)
Books five, six, and seven of the New Testament division of General Letters. The author was probably John the Apostle. Each letter has a different point. First John stresses love for one another, to be aware of false teachers, and to not fall into sin. Second John warns the believers to not listen to false teachers because they cause confusion. Third John recognizes a man named Gaius (GAY yuhs) who had treated kindly other Christians and visitors (missionaries).

Jonah (JOH nuh)
The name means "dove." He lived in a small town near Nazareth and was a prophet in Israel about 750 B.C. God sent Jonah to Nineveh to preach repentance and judgment. Jonah got on a boat headed for Tarshish (possibly in Spain), thinking he could run away from God. After spending three days in the belly of a large fish, Jonah went to Nineveh, preached, and the people repented. He has been called an unwilling messenger.

Jonah 1:1 word of the LORD came unto **J**
Jonah 1:3 **J** rose up to flee to Tarshish
Jonah 1:17 prepared a great fish to swallow **J**
Jonah 1:17 **J** was in the belly of the fish three
Jonah 2:1 Then **J** prayed unto the LORD his God
Jonah 3:3 **J** arose, and went unto Nineveh
Jonah 4:1 But it displeased **J** exceedingly

Jonah, Book of (JOH nuh)
The book is the fifth in the division, Minor Prophets, in the Old Testament. After Jonah finally agreed to preach and the entire city repented, he was angry because he wanted God's judgment to fall on wicked Nineveh. Most of the book talks about Jonah, but it shows that God loves all people.

Jonathan (JAHN uh thuhn)
The name means "Yahweh gave." He was the oldest son of King Saul and a good friend to

Jonah

David. David became king after Saul died. Jonathan was willing to stand up for David and learned that King Saul was jealous of David. Saul wanted to kill David. Jonathan was a good soldier. He and his brothers died in the same battle in which King Saul died. Fourteen other men by the name of Jonathan are mentioned in the Bible.

1 Samuel 14:49 sons of Saul were **J**, and Ishui, and
1 Samuel 18:1 soul of **J** was knit with the soul of
1 Samuel 18:3 Then **J** and David made a covenant
1 Samuel 20:18 **J** said to David, Tomorrow is the
1 Samuel 20:28 **J** answered Saul, David earnestly
1 Samuel 20:34 **J** arose from the table in fierce
1 Samuel 20:35 **J** went out into the field at the
1 Samuel 20:37 **J** cried after the lad, and said
1 Samuel 20:42 **J** said to David, Go in peace
1 Samuel 31:2 the Philistines slew **J** and
2 Samuel 1:4 Saul and **J** his son are dead also

Joppa (JAHP uh)

The name means "beautiful." A city located on the Mediterranean Sea. It is thirty-five miles northwest of Jerusalem (see map on page 340). Cedar logs were rafted down the coast to Joppa for King Solomon's Temple. Jonah fled to Joppa to get on a ship to take him away from Nineveh, where God wanted him to go. Dorcas, a woman gifted in sewing, was one of the first Christians in Joppa.

Jonah 1:3 went down to **J**; and he found a
Acts 9:36 at **J** a certain disciple named Tabitha
Acts 10:5 send men to **J** and call for one Simon
Acts 10:23 certain brethren from **J** accompanied
Acts 10:32 Send therefore to **J**, and call hither
Acts 11:5 I was in the city of **J** praying
Acts 11:13 Send men to **J**, and call for Simon

Jordan (JAWR duhn)

The name means "the descender." This river divided the eastern and western tribes of Israel (see map on page 340). It begins at the foot of Mount Herman, empties into the Sea of Galilee, and continues flowing south from the Sea of Galilee until it reaches the Dead Sea. It is 70 miles from the Sea of Galilee to the Dead Sea but the twists and turns of the river make it over 200 miles long. From the place where the river begins to where it empties into the Dead Sea, the river drops 2300 feet, almost one-half mile in distance. Joshua led the Israelites across the

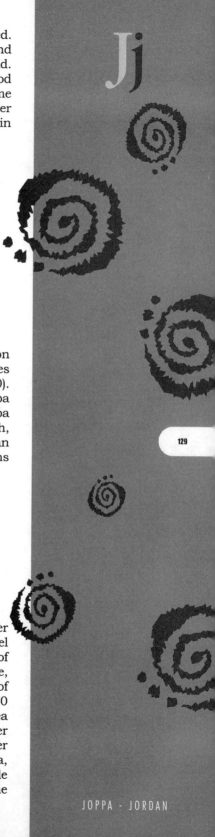

Jordan into the Promised Land and John the Baptist baptized Jesus in the Jordan River.

Deuteronomy 3:27 for thou shalt not go over this **J**
Deuteronomy 11:31 Ye shall pass over **J** to go in to
Joshua 3:15 they that bare the ark were come unto **J**
1 Kings 17:3 by the brook Cherith, that is before **J**
Matthew 3:5 and all the region round about **J**
Matthew 3:6 And were baptized of him in **J**
Matthew 3:13 cometh Jesus from Galilee to **J**
Mark 1:5 were all baptized of him in the river of **J**
Mark 1:9 and was baptized of John in **J**
Luke 3:3 And he came into all the country about **J**
Luke 4:1 being full of the Holy Ghost returned from **J**
John 3:26 he that was with thee beyond **J**

◼ Joseph (JOH zif)

The name means "adding." Three of the Joseph's in the Bible will be included here.

1. The eleventh son of Jacob. His mother was Rachel. Jacob favored Joseph over his other sons, and they were jealous of him. His father gave him a "coat of many colors." Joseph had dreams that he shared with his family. In his dreams, his family would be under his rule. Dreams were very important in Biblical times. When he was about seventeen years of age, Joseph was sold as a slave to an Egyptian ruler. Later he became an important official for Pharaoh, and Joseph's father and brothers did have to come to him for help in a famine. Joseph moved his family to Goshen in Egypt.

Genesis 37:3 Israel loved **J** more than all his
Genesis 37:5 **J** dreamed a dream, and he told it
Genesis 37:23 **J** was come unto his brethren
Genesis 37:23 they stripped **J** out of his coat
Genesis 37:28 lifted up **J** out of the pit, and
Genesis 39:1 And **J** was brought down to Egypt
Genesis 39:2 And the LORD was with **J**, and he
Genesis 39:21 But the LORD was with **J**
Genesis 41:46 And **J** was thirty years old when
Genesis 42:6 **J** was the governor over the land
Genesis 45:4 he said, I am **J** your brother
Genesis 47:7 **J** brought in Jacob his father

2. The carpenter, the earthly father of Jesus. He was the husband of Mary. He may have already died by the time Jesus was a grown man.

Matthew 1:18 Mary was pledged to be married to **J** (NIV)
Matthew 1:24 When **J** woke up, he did what the angel (NIV)

Luke 1:27 pledged to be married to a man named *J* (NIV)
Luke 2:4 And *J* also went up from Galilee
Luke 2:16 found Mary and *J*, and the babe lying in

Joseph of Arimathaea

3. A wealthy man, a member of the Jewish Sanhedrin, and a secret follower of Jesus. He buried Jesus in his own tomb, the one he had carved out of a rock for himself and his family.

Matthew 27:57 rich man of Arimathea, named *J*
Matthew 27:59 when *J* had taken the body, he
Mark 15:43 *J* of Arimathea, an honourable
Mark 15:45 of the centurion, he gave the body to *J*
Luke 23:50 there was a man named *J*, a counselor
John 19:38 *J* of Arimathea, being a disciple

Joshua (JAHSH yoo uh)

The name means "Yahweh delivered." His father was named Nun. Joshua and Caleb were among the twelve spies sent into Canaan to spy out the land and bring back a report to Moses. These two men were the only ones who believed that Israel could take the land. They were the only two allowed to live long enough to see the Promised Land. He became the leader of the Israelites before Moses died. It was Joshua who led the people into the Promised Land. He was born in Egypt. After the Israelites were led out of Egypt, Moses made Joshua the general of the Israelite troops. He was a good military leader and spiritual leader for the people.

Deuteronomy 3:28 But charge *J*, and encourage him
Deuteronomy 31:3 and *J*, he shall go over before thee
Deuteronomy 31:23 he gave *J* the son of Nun a charge
Deuteronomy 34:9 *J* the son of Nun was full of the Spirit
Joshua 3:6 *J* spake unto the priests, saying, Take up
Joshua 3:7 LORD said unto *J*, This day will I begin to
Joshua 4:4 Then *J* called the twelve men, whom he
Joshua 4:5 *J* said unto them, Pass over before the
Joshua 4:9 *J* set up twelve stones in the midst
Joshua 6:2 LORD said unto *J*, See, I have given into
Joshua 6:16 *J* said unto the people, Shout; for the
Joshua 6:27 So the LORD was with *J*; and his fame was

Joshua, Book of (JAHSH yoo uh)

The first book in the division, History, in the Old Testament. Tells how Joshua led the Israelites across the Jordan River and how they settled their new land. The book also stresses how God showed His mighty power.

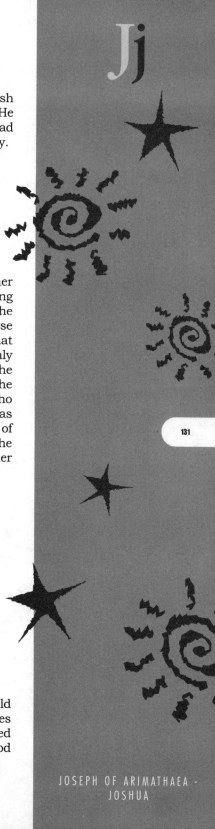

Jj

Josiah

Josiah (joh SIGH uh)

The name means "Yahweh heals." He became king when he was eight years old. When he was sixteen (his eighth year to reign), he began to ask God to guide him. During his twelfth year as king, at the age of twenty, he began to remove all the idols and their altars from places around Judah. A "Book of the Law" was found when repairs were being made on the Temple. Josiah had been king for eighteen years at this time. The book encouraged him to make many changes to help the people return to worshiping God only. After he died, he became known as the greatest king Judah had. He ruled Judah for thirty-one years.

2 Kings 22:1 **J** was eight years old when he
2 Kings 22:3 in the eighteenth year of king **J**
2 Chronicles 34:1 **J** was eight years old when
2 Chronicles 34:33 **J** removed all the detestable idols (NIV)

Jot (JAHT)

Refers to the smallest letter in the Greek alphabet, like "iota," or the Hebrew letter, "yod." In the English, the "i" is the smallest letter.

Matthew 5:18 one **j** or one tittle shall in no wise

Joy (JOYEE)

Gladness, happiness, pleasure; a happy feeling.

Nehemiah 8:10 for the **j** of the LORD is your strength
Psalm 30:5 for a night, but **j** cometh in the morning
Psalm 126:5 sow in tears will reap with songs of **j** (NIV)
Luke 2:10 I bring you good tidings of great **j**

Joyful (JOYEE fuhl)

Feeling happy, showing pleasure.

Psalm 66:1 Make a **j** noise unto God, all ye lands
Psalm 98:4 Make a **j** noise unto the LORD, all the
Psalm 100:1 Make a **j** noise unto the LORD, all ye

Judaea (joo DEE uh)

Also spelled "Judea." The name means "Jewish." The territory surrounding the city of Jerusalem (see map on page 340). The boundaries of Judea changed depending on who was ruling at the time. Herod the Great was king of Judea at the time Jesus was born. The eastern boundary was the Dead Sea, and the western boundary was the Mediterranean Sea.

Matthew 2:1 Jesus was born in Bethlehem of **J**
Matthew 2:5 said unto him, in Bethlehem of **J**

Matthew 3:1 preaching in the wilderness of *J*
Matthew 4:25 and from Jerusalem, and from *J*
Mark 3:7 from Galilee followed him, and from *J*
Luke 1:5 in the days of Herod, the king of *J*
Luke 3:1 Pontius Pilate being governor of *J*
John 4:3 He left *J*, and departed again into Galilee
John 4:54 when he was come out of *J* into Galilee
Acts 1:8 both in Jerusalem, and in all *J*

Judah (JOO duh)

The name means "Praise Yahweh." The name of Jacob's fourth son. His mother was Leah. The descendants of Judah became one of the twelve tribes of Israel. The area given to the tribe of Judah when they entered the Promised Land was just west of the Dead Sea, and included Jerusalem (see map on page 338). The territory of Judah later became the Southern Kingdom. King David and Jesus were from the tribe of Judah.

Genesis 29:35 therefore she called his name *J*
1 Kings 12:20 house of David, but the tribe of *J*
Micah 5:2 thou be little among the thousands of *J*

Judas (JOO duhs)

Also, Jude (JOOD). The Greek form of the Hebrew name Judah, which means "Praise Yahweh." The name Judas was used very often. Jesus had a half brother named Judas. One of Jesus' disciples was Judas who had a brother named James. The Judas most people know about is Judas Iscariot, a disciple of Jesus, the one who betrayed Him. He was the treasurer for the disciples. Once he had received the 30 pieces of silver for the betrayal, he later tried to return it to the religious leaders. The Bible says he then hanged himself.

Matthew 10:4 and *J* Iscariot, who also betrayed him
Matthew 26:14 *J* Iscariot, went unto the chief priests
Matthew 26:25 *J*, which betrayed him, answered and
Mark 3:19 *J* Iscariot, which also betrayed him
Mark 14:10 *J* Iscariot, one of the twelve, went unto
Mark 14:43 while he yet spake, cometh *J*, one of the
Luke 6:16 *J* Iscariot, which also was the traitor
Luke 22:48 *J*, betrayest thou the Son of man with a
John 18:2 *J* also, which betrayed him, knew the
John 18:3 *J* then, having received a band of men
John 18:5 *J* also, which betrayed him, stood with

Jude, Book of (JOOD)

The eighth, and last letter, of the division,

Jj

General Letters of the New Testament. It is the next to last book of the New Testament. Jude contains only twenty-five verses. The author is one of Jesus' half brothers. He wrote the letter to encourage the Christians to be aware of false teachers and to continue to live godly lives.

■ Judge (JUDJ)
To make a decision. One who listens to a witness and then decides the outcome; an official.

Exodus 18:13 Moses sat to *j* the people
Ecclesiastes 3:17 God shall *j* the righteous and the
Matthew 7:1 *J* not, that ye be not judged
Matthew 7:2 the same way you *j* others, you will be (NIV)
Luke 6:37 *J* not, and ye shall not be judged

■ Judges, Book of (JUH jihz)
The seventh book in the Old Testament and the second book in the division of History. The author is unknown. It tells how the Israelites settled into the land of Canaan after Joshua died, and their gradual acceptance of the gods and morals of the Canaanite people. The Israelites ignored God as their king. Since they had no earthly king, they began to do as they pleased. As they got into trouble and cried out to God, He would send a deliverer or judge who would help them find their way back to God.

■ Judgment (JEJ ment)
1. A sentence on persons or nations decreed by God.

Exodus 12:12 Against all the gods of Egypt I will execute *j*
1 John 4:17 May have boldness in the day of *j*
Revelation 18:10 for in one hour is thy *j* come

2. Discernment or decisionmaking by human beings.

Psalm 119:66 teach me good *j* and knowledge

■ Just (JUHST)
Fair, honest, right; moral.

Genesis 6:9 Noah was a *j* man and perfect in his
Proverbs 9:9 teach a *j* man, and he will increase in
Habakkuk 2:4 but the *j* shall live by his faith
Matthew 1:19 Then Joseph her husband, being a *j* man
Matthew 5:45 sendeth rain on the *j* and on the unjust
Mark 6:20 Herod feared John, knowing that he was a *j* man
Luke 2:25 Simeon; and the same man was *j* and devout
Luke 23:50 and he was a good man, and a *j*

Acts 10:22 Cornelius the centurion, a *j* man, and one
Romans 1:17 The *j* shall live by faith

Justice (JUHS tuhs)
Fairness, lawfulness; doing or acting in the right way.

Proverbs 1:3 receive the instruction of wisdom, *j*
Proverbs 21:3 To do *j* and judgement is more acceptable

Justified (JUHS ti fighd)
Past tense of "justify."

Romans 3:24 being *j* freely by his grace through
Romans 5:1 being *j* by faith, we have peace with God

Justly (JUHST lee)
Fairly, honestly, truly; to be right morally.

Micah 6:8 the LORD require of thee, but to do *j*
Luke 23:41 we indeed *j*; for we receive the due reward

Keep (KEEP)
To hold on to, save; obey, regard, respect; protect, care for.

Exodus 20:8 Remember the sabbath day, to *k* it holy
Psalm 91:11 to *k* thee in all thy ways
Psalm 34:13 *K* thy tongue from evil, and thy lips from
Psalm 119:34 Give me understanding, and I shall *k* thy law
Proverbs 8:32 blessed are they that *k* my ways
Ecclesiastes 3:6 time to *k*, and a time to cast away
Ecclesiastes 3:7 time to *k* silence, and a time to speak
Ecclesiastes 12:13 Fear God, and *k* his commandments
Matthew 26:18 I will *k* the passover at thy house
Luke 4:10 angels charge over thee, to *k* thee
Luke 11:28 hear the word of God, and *k* it
John 14:15 If ye love me, *k* my commandments
John 14:23 If a man love me, he will *k* my words

Keeper (KEE puhr)
One who takes care of something; a guard.

Genesis 4:2 And Abel was a *k* of sheep
Genesis 4:9 Am I my brother's *k*
Genesis 39:22 *k* of the prison committed to Joseph's
Psalm 121:5 The LORD is thy *k*
Acts 16:27 And the *k* of the prison awakening
Acts 16:36 *k* of the prison told this saying to Paul

Kk

Kill (KIHL)
To take the life of an animal or human being; murder.

Genesis 37:21 and said, Let us not **k** him
Exodus 20:13 Thou shalt not **k**
Deuteronomy 5:17 Thou shalt not **k**
Matthew 5:21 of old time, Thou shalt not **k**
Matthew 26:4 arrest Jesus in some sly way and **k** him (NIV)
Mark 10:34 shall spit upon him, and shall **k** him
Luke 22:2 scribes sought how they might **k** him
John 5:18 the Jews sought the more to **k** him
John 8:40 But now ye seek to **k** me, a man that
Acts 10:13 Rise, Peter; **k**, and eat

Kind (KIND)
A type or group; gentle, warm, caring.

Genesis 1:11 fruit tree yielding fruit after his **k**
Genesis 1:24 forth the living creature after his **k**
Luke 6:35 he is **k** unto the unthankful and to the
1 Corinthians 13:4 Love is patient, love is **k** (NIV)
Ephesians 4:32 be ye **k** one to another, tenderhearted

King (KING)
Emperor or ruler who is a man.

Exodus 1:8 a new **k** over Egypt, which knew not Joseph
1 Samuel 8:5 make us a **k** to judge us like all the
1 Samuel 8:22 Listen to them and give them a **k** (NIV)
1 Samuel 11:15 and there they made Saul **k** before them
2 Samuel 2:4 there they anointed David **k** over the
Psalm 10:16 The LORD is **K** for ever and ever
Psalm 47:6 sing praises unto our **K**, sing praises
Psalm 47:7 For God is the **K** of all the earth
Matthew 2:1 of Judea in the days of Herod the **k**
Matthew 2:2 where is he that is born **K** of the Jews
Matthew 27:37 THIS IS JESUS THE **K** OF THE JEWS
Mark 15:26 THE **K** OF THE JEWS
Luke 19:38 Blessed be the **K** that cometh in the
Luke 23:37 thou be the **k** of the Jews, save thyself
Luke 23:38 THIS IS THE **K** OF THE JEWS
John 19:14 saith unto the Jews, Behold your **K**
John 19:15 priests answered, we have no **k** but Caesar
John 19:19 NAZARETH THE **K** OF THE JEWS

Kingdom (KING dum)
A land governed or controlled by a ruler, such as a king or queen. Jesus taught about the kingdom of God, in which God would be the ruler.

Psalm 145:13 Thy **k** is an everlasting **k**
Matthew 3:2 Repent ye: for the **k** of heaven is at

King

Matthew 4:23 and preaching the gospel of the **k**
Matthew 5:3 spirit: for theirs is the **k** of heaven
Matthew 6:10 Thy **k** come. Thy will be done in earth
Matthew 6:13 thine is the **k**, and the power, and
Matthew 6:33 Seek ye first the **k** of God
Mark 1:15 and the **k** of God is at hand: repent ye
Mark 12:34 Thou art not far from the **k** of God
Luke 1:33 and of his **k** there shall be no end
Luke 11:2 Thy **k** come. Thy will be done, as in
Luke 18:16 the **k** of God belongs to such as these (NIV)
Luke 18:17 receive the **k** of God like a little child (NIV)
Luke 23:42 remember me when thou comest into thy **k**
John 18:36 My **k** is not of this world

Kings, 1, 2, Books of (KINGZ)

The sixth and seventh books in the division, History, in the Old Testament. The author is unknown but some think it was Jeremiah. These books record the last events of King David, Solomon's reign as King, and the division of Israel into two kingdoms: the Northern Kingdom of Israel, and the Southern Kingdom of Judah. The Kings also tell about the kings of both kingdoms and how their evil ways caused the people to sin. God finally allowed the Northern Kingdom to fall in 722 B.C. and the Southern Kingdom fell in 586 B.C. Even though the people were in exile, God would show His mercy and love, and bless the Israelite people again.

Kinsman (KINZ muhn)

A family member, usually related by birth. In the Old Testament, a kinsman had certain responsibilities. If a man died without a son, the man's brother or closest relative would marry the widow. Her first son born would then take the name of the widow's former husband and the son would inherit any property. If a man had to sell all he had because he was poor, the kinsman would buy it back for him. Also, if a person had a wrong done to them, other family members (kinsmen) would take it upon themselves to punish the one who had done wrong. The story of Ruth in the Old Testament shows what a kinsman is supposed to do. Jesus Christ became the kinsman for all of mankind, to buy us back from our sinful ways.

Ruth 2:1 And Naomi had a **k** of her husband's, a mighty
Ruth 3:9 for thou art a near **k**

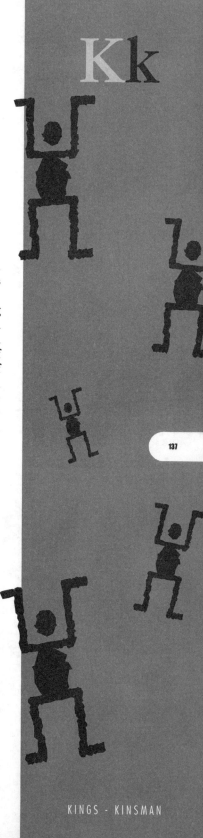

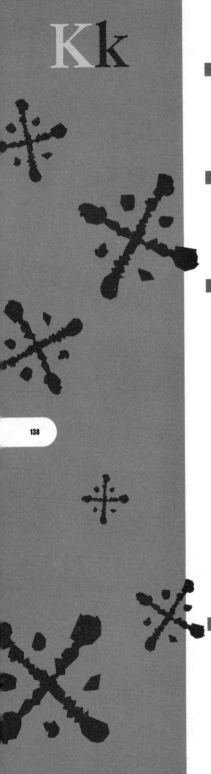

Kk

Ruth 4:1 the *k* of whom Boaz spake came by
Ruth 4:8 Therefore the *k* said unto Boaz, Buy it for

◼ Knee (NEE)
The joint connecting the thigh and lower leg, allowing the leg to bend.

Isaiah 45:23 That unto me every *k* shall bow
Romans 14:11 saith the LORD, every *k* shall bow
Philippians 2:10 at the name of Jesus every *k* shall bow

◼ Knock (NOK)
To bang, rap, or tap. To make noise by pounding with the fist or hand.

Matthew 7:7 *k*, and it shall be opened unto you
Luke 11:9 *k*, and it shall be opened unto you
Revelation 3:20 Behold, I stand at the door, and *k*

◼ Know (NO)
To understand, remember, to know in a personal way.

1 Kings 18:37 people may *k* that thou art the LORD God
Psalm 46:10 Be still, and *k* that I am God
Psalm 100:3 *K* ye that the LORD he is God
Psalm 139:23 Search me, O God, and *k* my heart
Psalm 139:23 try me, and *k* my thoughts
Matthew 9:6 ye may *k* that the Son of man hath power
Matthew 26:70 saying, I *k* not what thou sayest
Matthew 26:72 with an oath, I do not *k* the man
Matthew 26:74 and to swear, saying, I *k* not the man
Matthew 28:5 Fear not ye: for I *k* that ye seek Jesus
Mark 14:68 he denied, saying, I *k* not, neither
Mark 14:71 and to swear, saying, I *k* not this man
Luke 22:57 he denied him, saying, Woman, I *k* him not
Luke 22:60 Peter said, Man, I *k* not what thou sayest
Luke 23:34 forgive them; for they *k* not what they do
John 20:2 and we *k* not where they have laid him
John 20:13 and I *k* not where they have laid him
John 21:24 and we *k* that his testimony is true

◼ Knowledge (NAH lidj)
Learning and understanding received through experience.

Psalm 119:66 Teach me good judgment and *k*
Proverbs 1:7 fear of the LORD is the beginning of *k*
Proverbs 10:14 Wise men lay up *k*
Proverbs 12:1 whoso loveth instruction loveth *k*
Colossians 1:9 be filled with the *k* of his will
Colossians 1:10 and increasing in the *k* of God

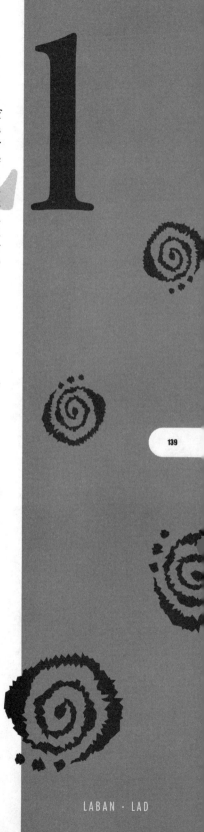

Laban (LAY buhn)
The name means "white." He was the brother of Rebekah, wife of Isaac. When Jacob tricked his brother, Esau, out of the blessing reserved for the first born son, Jacob fled to Haran to live with his uncle Laban. Laban had two daughters, Leah and Rachel. Jacob loved Rachel and worked seven years in order to marry her. But Laban tricked Jacob into marrying Leah because she was the oldest daughter. Jacob had to work another seven years for Rachel. Many years later, Laban and Jacob agreed to stop tricking one another.

Genesis 24:29 Rebekah had a brother, and his name was ***L***
Genesis 27:43 flee thou to ***L*** my brother to Haran
Genesis 29:16 And ***L*** had two daughters
Genesis 29:21 Jacob said unto ***L***, Give me my wife

Labor (LAY buhr)
Same as "labour." Effort or work. It usually means physical effort.

Exodus 20:9 Six days shalt thou ***l***, and do all
Deuteronomy 5:13 Six days thou shalt ***l***, and do
Matthew 11:28 Come unto me, all ye that ***l*** and are

Laborers (LAY buhr urz)
Those who do work that requires physical effort.

Matthew 9:37 is plenteous, but the ***l*** are few
Matthew 9:38 he will send forth ***l*** into his harvest
Luke 10:2 harvest truly is great, but the ***l*** are few
Luke 10:2 he would send forth ***l*** into his harvest
1 Corinthians 3:9 For we are ***l*** together with God

Lack (LAK)
To need or want.

Genesis 18:28 thou destroy all the city for ***l*** of five
Exodus 16:18 he that gathered little had no ***l***
Proverbs 28:27 giveth unto the poor shall not ***l***
Matthew 19:20 I kept from my youth up: what ***l*** I
James 1:5 If any of you ***l*** wisdom, let him ask

Lad (LAD)
A boy, child, youth.

1 Samuel 20:21 behold, I will send a ***l***, saying
1 Samuel 20:36 And he said unto his ***l***, Run, find out

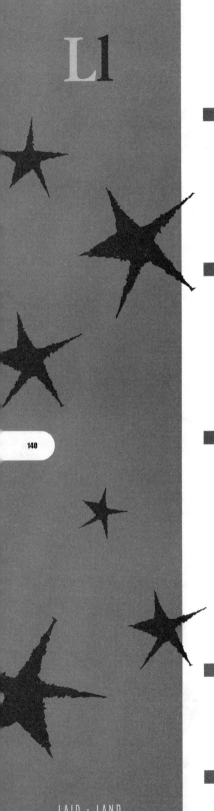

1 Samuel 20:37 Jonathan cried after the *l*, and said
1 Samuel 20:39 But the *l* knew not any thing
1 Samuel 20:41 And as soon as the *l* was gone
John 6:9 There is a *l* here, which hath five loaves

Laid (LAYD)
Past tense of "lay."

1 Kings 17:19 and *l* him upon his own bed
1 Kings 19:6 did eat and drink, and *l* him down
Isaiah 53:6 and the LORD hath *l* on him the
Matthew 26:50 came they, and *l* hands on Jesus
Matthew 27:60 And *l* it in his own new tomb
Luke 2:7 and *l* him in a manger; because there
John 11:34 And said, Where have ye *l* him

Lamb (LAM)
A young sheep which was often used in the Jewish sacrifices. Since Jesus gave His life as a sacrifice for the sins of all people, He is often called the Lamb of God.

Genesis 22:8 My son, God will provide himself a *l*
Exodus 12:5 Your *l* shall be without blemish
Isaiah 53:7 he is brought as a *l* to the slaughter
John 1:29 and saith, Behold the *L* of God
John 1:36 he saith, Behold the *L* of God

Lamentations, Book of (LA men TAY shuhnz)
The third book in the division, Major Prophets, in the Old Testament. It is thought that Jeremiah wrote the book. To lament is to cry or mourn over a great loss of some kind. Lamentations is a book of five poems that mourn the fall of Jerusalem in 587 B.C. For many, many years, God had warned the Israelites that Jerusalem would be captured and destroyed, but the people ignored the warnings of the prophets. Lamentations 3:22-23 are a reminder that God is faithful and also understanding and will have pity on His people when they repent and seek His forgiveness.

Lamp (LAMP)
A light. Lamps in biblical times were low clay bowls with a spout. The bowl held mainly olive oil, and the wick came through the spout. The wicks were made from twisted flax.

Psalm 119:105 Thy word is a *l* unto my feet

Land (LAND)
Dirt, soil, dust, or ground; the dry part of the

140

earth's surface; a country.

Genesis 1:9 and let the dry *l* appear: and it was so
Genesis 1:10 And God called the dry *l* Earth
Genesis 12:10 And there was a famine in the *l*
Genesis 41:43 him ruler over all the *l* of Egypt
Exodus 20:2 brought thee out of the *l* of Egypt
Exodus 33:3 Unto a *l* flowing with milk and honey
Deuteronomy 1:8 Behold, I have set the *l* before you
1 Kings 17:7 there had been no rain in the *l*
Matthew 14:34 they came into the *l* of Gennesaret
Matthew 27:45 there was darkness over all the *l*
Mark 15:33 there was darkness over the whole *l*
Luke 15:14 there arose a mighty famine in that *l*

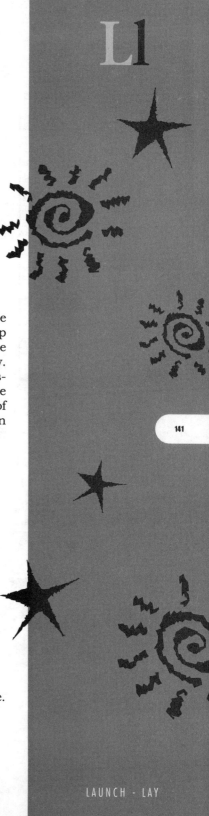

Launch (LAWNCH)
To begin, push off, start.

Luke 5:4 *L* out into the deep, and let down

Law (LAW)
Rules made by man or God that must be obeyed. The first five books of the Bible make up the division of Law because they contain the laws God gave Moses for the Israelites to obey. The laws were to remind them how God had rescued them from slavery in Egypt. Sometimes the entire Old Testament is included in the books of law. The law also refers to the Ten Commandments.

Exodus 24:12 give thee tablets of stone, and a *l*
Joshua 1:8 This book of the *l* shall not depart out
Psalm 1:2 his delight is in the *l* of the LORD
Psalm 19:7 The *l* of the LORD is perfect
Psalm 119:34 understanding, and I shall keep thy *l*
Psalm 119:97 O how I love thy *l*
Proverbs 1:8 and forsake not the *l* of thy mother
Proverbs 3:1 My son, forget not my *l*
Proverbs 6:20 and forsake not the *l* of thy mother
Proverbs 28:7 Whoso keepeth the *l* is a wise son
Matthew 5:17 not that I am come to destroy the *l*
Matthew 22:40 these two commandments hang all the *l*
John 19:7 We have a *l*, and by our *l* he ought to die
Acts 5:34 Pharisee, named Gamaliel, a doctor of the *l*

Lay (LAY)
Leave, put, rest, or set a thing in a certain place.

Exodus 16:13 in the morning the dew *l* round about
Exodus 16:14 And when the dew that *l* was gone up
Exodus 16:14 there *l* a small round thing, as small
1 Kings 18:23 cut it in pieces, and *l* it on wood

Ll

Lazarus

1 Kings 18:23 the other bullock, and *l* it on wood
1 Kings 19:5 as he *l* and slept under a juniper tree
Proverbs 10:14 Wise men *l* up knowledge
Matthew 6:19 **L** not up for yourselves treasures upon
Matthew 6:20 *l* up for yourselves treasures in heaven
Matthew 9:18 come and *l* thine hand upon her, and
Matthew 28:6 Come, see the place where the Lord *l*
Mark 2:4 the bed wherein the sick of the palsy *l*
Mark 5:23 come and *l* thy hands on her, that she may
Luke 5:25 took up that whereon he *l*, and departed
Luke 8:42 twelve years of age, and she *l* a dying
John 11:38 It was a cave, and a stone *l* upon it
John 15:13 that a man *l* down his life for his friends

▪ Lazarus (LAZ uh ruhs)

The name means "One whom God helps." A close friend of Jesus. Mary and Martha were his sisters and they lived in Bethany. Jesus spent much time in their home. When Lazarus died, Jesus raised him to life again to show God's glory.

John 11:1 a certain man was sick, named **L**
John 11:5 loved Martha, and her sister, and **L**
John 11:14 Jesus said unto them plainly, **L**, is dead
John 11:43 cried with a loud voice, **L**, come forth
John 12:9 they might see **L** also, whom he had raised

▪ Lead (LEED)

Guide, go ahead of.

Psalm 25:5 **L** me in thy truth, and teach me
Matthew 6:13 And *l* us not into temptation
Luke 11:4 and *l* us not into temptation

▪ Leadeth (LEE duth)

The old way of writing or saying "leads."

Psalm 23:2 he *l* me beside the still waters
Psalm 23:3 he *l* me in the paths of righteousness
Matthew 7:13 broad is the way, that *l* to destruction
Matthew 7:14 narrow is the way, which *l* unto life

▪ Leah (LEE uh)

The name means "wild cow" or gazelle." She was Laban's oldest daughter, and Jacob's first wife. Her sister was Rachel, the one whom Jacob loved and for whom he worked seven years so he could marry her. Laban tricked Jacob into marrying Leah. She had six sons and one daughter.

Genesis 29:16 the name of the elder was **L**
Genesis 29:23 that he took **L** his daughter
Genesis 35:23 sons of **L**; Reuben, Jacob's firstborn

Lean (LEEN)
1. Depend, rely on.

Proverbs 3:5 and *l* not unto thine own understanding

2. To be skinny.

Genesis 41:20 The *l*, ugly cows ate up the seven (NIV)

Learn (LURN)
To master or understand a thing; to study or learn by heart; discover, find.

Psalm 119:73 that I may *l* thy commandments
Matthew 11:29 Take my yoke upon you, and *l* of me

Least (LEEST)
Last, littlest.

Judges 6:15 and I am the *l* in my father's house
Matthew 5:19 breaks one of the *l* of these commandments (NIV)
Matthew 5:19 will be called *l* in the kingdom of heaven (NIV)
Matthew 25:40 done it unto one of the *l* of these

Led (LED)
Past tense of "lead."

Matthew 27:2 they had bound him, they *l* him away
Matthew 27:31 and *l* him away to crucify him
Mark 15:20 and *l* him out to crucify him
Luke 4:1 was *l* by the Spirit into the wilderness
Luke 23:1 arose, and *l* him away unto Pilate
Luke 23:26 as they *l* him away, they laid hold upon
Luke 24:50 And he *l* them out as far as to Bethany
John 18:28 Then *l* they Jesus from Caiaphas
John 19:16 And they took Jesus, and *l* him away

Lentiles (LEN tuhlz)
Small plants with tiny flowers, and pods that hold only two seeds. Beans or peas used in making a reddish-brown stew. It was this type of stew Jacob gave Esau in exchange for the birthright.

Genesis 25:34 gave Esau bread and pottage of *l*

Leper (LEH puhr)
Someone with leprosy.

Numbers 5:2 put out of the camp every *l*
Matthew 8:2 there came a *l* and worshiped him
Mark 1:40 And there came a *l* to him

Lepers (LEH puhrz)
Plural of "leper."

Matthew 10:8 Heal the sick, cleanse the *l*

L l

143

Leprosy

Luke 7:22 the lame walk, the *l* are cleansed
Luke 17:12 there met him ten men that were *l*

■ Leprosy (LEH pruh see)

A name given to several kinds of serious skin diseases. When a person had leprosy, he was isolated from others in the village or town. A person with leprosy was considered "unclean" and not able to worship. No one could touch a leper or he would be unclean too. A leper had to shout "unclean" whenever he walked where others might pass him. Before he could be considered clean again, he had to have the priest examine him. The priests had been given very specific instructions from Moses by God about how to judge the skin diseases and when the person was cured. These instructions are found in Leviticus.

Leviticus 13:8 pronounce him unclean: it is a *l*
2 Kings 5:3 for he would recover him of his *l*
Matthew 8:3 And immediately his *l* was cleansed
Mark 1:42 immediately the *l* departed from him
Luke 5:12 in a certain city, behold a man full of *l*
Luke 5:13 immediately the *l* departed from him

■ Let (LET)

To allow or permit; make or cause.

Genesis 1:3 And God said, *L* there be light
Genesis 1:26 And God said, *L* us make man in our
Exodus 5:8 *L* us go and sacrifice to our God
Exodus 7:16 *L* my people go, that they may serve
Psalm 19:14 *L* the words of my mouth, and the
Psalm 33:8 *L* all the earth fear the LORD
Psalm 95:1 *l* us make a joyful noise to the
Psalm 122:1 *L* us go into the house of the LORD
Matthew 5:16 *L* your light so shine before men
Matthew 26:39 if it be possible, *l* this cup pass
Luke 2:15 *L* us now go even unto Bethlehem
Luke 5:4 and *l* down the nets for a catch (NIV)
John 14:1 *L* not your heart be troubled: ye
Ephesians 4:26 *l* not the sun go down upon your wrath

■ Levi (LEE vigh)

The name means "a joining." Several men by the name of Levi are mentioned in the Bible. Jesus chose a disciple by the name of Levi, also known as Matthew, who was a tax collector.

Mark 2:14 he saw *L* the son of Alpheus sitting at
Luke 5:27 saw a publican, named *L*, sitting at
Luke 5:29 *L* made him a great feast in his own house

144

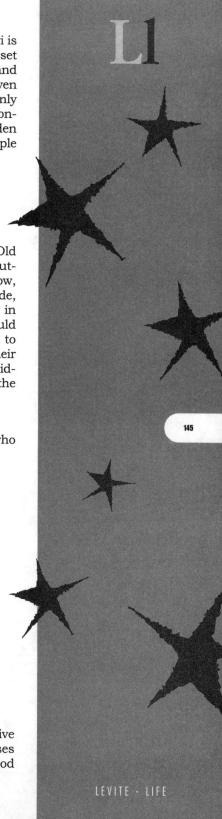

L1

Levite (LEE vight)

A member of the tribe of Levi. The tribe of Levi is descended from Jacob's son, Levi. God had set aside the Levites to help with the tabernacle and to assist the priests. The tribe of Levi was given this responsibility because they were the only ones who stood with Moses when Moses condemned the people for worshiping the golden calf. Tithes and offerings given by the people helped to support the Levites.

Exodus 4:14 Is not Aaron the *L* thy brother
Deuteronomy 12:12 the *L* that is within your gates
Luke 10:32 And likewise a *L*, when he was at the

Leviticus, Book of (lih VIT ih kuhs)

The third book in the division, Law, in the Old Testament. Moses wrote this book which outlines the duties of the priests. It describes how, and what kind of sacrifices were to be made, and stresses the holiness of God. Included in the instructions were ways the Israelites could keep a good relationship with God and what to do when they sinned so they could renew their connection to God. Leviticus 19:18 was considered by Jesus to be one of the main verses in the Old Testament.

Liar (Ligh uhr)

A person who does not tell the truth; one who cheats.

Proverbs 17:4 and a *l* giveth ear to a naughty tongue
1 John 1:10 say we have not sinned, we make him a *l*
1 John 2:4 keepeth not his commandments, is a *l*
1 John 2:22 Who is a *l* but he that denieth that Jesus
1 John 4:20 and hateth his brother, he is a *l*

Lie (LIGH)

1. To be flat or stretched out, as on a bed.

Psalm 23:2 He maketh me to *l* down in green pastures
John 5:6 When Jesus saw him *l*, and knew that he

Lie (LIGH)

2. To say something that is untrue.

Proverbs 14:5 A faithful witness will not *l*
Colossians 3:9 *L* not to one another, seeing that

Life (LIGHF)

God as the Creator is the only one who can give or take away life. Anything that grows, uses water, oxygen, and food has life. When God

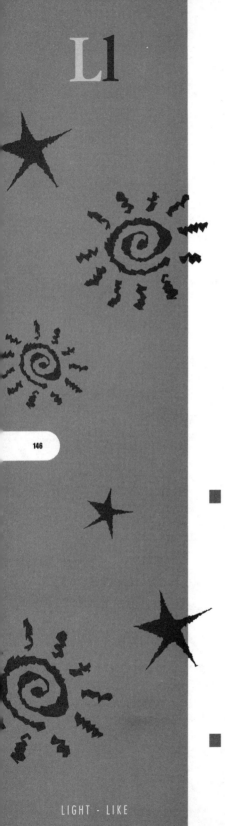

breathed into the animals and Adam, life began. Besides the physical life, humans also have a spiritual life. We can have fellowship with God, meaning we can talk to Him and He can talk to us. When we obey God, then we have true life. When Jesus died on the cross for the sins of all people, He gave us an opportunity to have eternal life. In order to have eternal life, we must believe that Jesus is God's son, ask Him to forgive our sins, and trust Him to be our Savior and Lord. We show we have trusted Jesus when we obey Him.

Genesis 2:7 breathed into his nostrils the breath of *l*
Psalm 23:6 shall follow me all the days of my *l*
Psalm 27:1 the LORD is the strength of my *l*
Matthew 7:14 narrow is the way, which leadeth unto *l*
Matthew 16:25 whosoever will save his *l* shall lose it
Matthew 16:25 whosoever will lose his *l* for my sake
Mark 8:35 whosoever will save his *l* shall lose it
Mark 8:35 whosoever shall lose his *l* for my sake
Mark 10:17 shall I do that I may inherit eternal *l*
Luke 18:18 what shall I do to inherit eternal *l*
John 3:15 should not perish, but have eternal *l*
John 3:16 not perish, but have everlasting *l*
John 10:10 I am come that they might have *l*
John 11:25 I am the resurrection, and the *l*
John 14:6 I am the way, the truth, and the *l*
John 15:13 a man lay down his *l* for his friends
Romans 6:23 gift of God is eternal *l* through Jesus

Light (LIGHT)

Opposite of darkness. Light was created by God. In Earth's solar system, the sun is our source of light. Earth's moon reflects light from the sun. Thus, Jesus as God's Son, reflects the light of God, showing us what God is like. As His children, we reflect what Jesus is like.

Psalm 27:1 The LORD is my *l* and my salvation
Psalm 119:105 a lamp unto my feet, and a *l* unto my
Matthew 5:14 Ye are the *l* of the world
Matthew 5:16 Let your *l* so shine before men
John 1:5 And the *l* shineth in darkness
John 3:19 men loved darkness rather than *l*
John 8:12 I am the *l* of the world
1 John 1:5 God is *l*, and in him is no darkness

Like (LIGHK)

To be similar to another thing.

Psalm 1:3 And he shall be *l* a tree planted
Psalm 71:19 God, who is *l* unto thee

Psalm 103:13 **L** as a father pitieth his children
Matthew 22:39 second is **l** unto it, Thou shalt
Mark 12:31 second is **l**, namely this, Thou shalt
Luke 6:48 He is **l** a man which built an house
John 7:46 answered, Never man spake **l** this man

Liken (LIGH kin)
To compare.

Isaiah 40:25 To whom then will ye **l** me
Matthew 7:24 I will **l** him unto a wise man

Lilies (LIL ees)
Refers to several types of flowers that grow in Galilee in the early spring. Many are bright red or yellow.

Matthew 6:28 Consider the **l** of the field
Luke 12:27 Consider the **l** how they grow

Linen (LIN in)
A fabric spun from the flax plant grown in Palestine. Before weaving into cloth, it is bleached. Many things were made from linen: clothing, bedding, curtains, and burial shrouds. "Fine linen" was a fabric woven very fine so that it looked like silk.

Matthew 27:59 he wrapped it in a clean **l** cloth
Mark 15:46 And he bought fine **l**, and took him
Mark 15:46 down, and wrapped him in the **l**
Luke 16:19 which was clothed in purple and fine **l**
Luke 23:53 took it down, and wrapped it in **l**
Luke 24:12 he beheld the **l** clothes laid by themselves
John 19:40 body of Jesus, and wound it in **l** clothes
John 20:6 He saw the strips of **l** lying there (NIV)
John 20:7 not lying with the **l** clothes, but wrapped

Lips (LIPS)
The edges of the mouth, formed from muscle. The Bible mentions several kinds of lips: those that flatter, lie, fear, are joyful, or righteous.

Psalm 51:15 O LORD, open thou my **l**
Psalm 63:3 my **l** shall praise thee
Psalm 141:3 keep the door of my **l**
Proverbs 12:22 Lying **l** are abomination to the LORD

Little (LIT uhl)
Small, tiny.

Psalm 8:5 made him a **l** lower than the angels
Micah 5:2 even though thou be **l** among the
Matthew 6:30 more clothe you, O ye of **l** faith
Matthew 18:3 and become as **l** children, ye shall

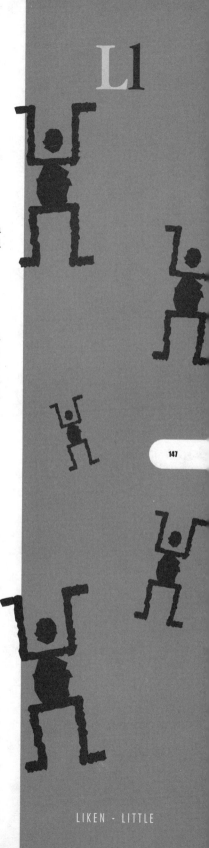

147

Matthew 19:14 Jesus said, Suffer *l* children, and
Mark 10:14 Suffer the *l* children to come unto me
Luke 12:28 will he clothe you, O ye of *l* faith
Luke 18:16 Suffer *l* children to come unto me
Luke 19:3 because he was *l* of stature
James 3:5 the tongue is a *l* member, and boasteth

■ Live (LIHV)
Be alive.

Psalm 116:2 will I call upon him as long as I *l*
Psalm 146:2 While I *l* will I praise the LORD
Proverbs 7:2 Keep my commandments, and *l*
Matthew 4:4 Man shall not *l* by bread alone
Luke 4:4 That man shall not *l* by bread alone
John 14:19 because I *l*, ye shall *l* also
Romans 1:17 The just shall *l* by faith

■ Loaves (LOHVZ)
Plural of "loaf." A loaf usually refers to the shape of bread when it is baked.

Matthew 15:34 How many *l* have ye
Matthew 15:36 he took the seven *l* and the fishes
Mark 6:38 How many *l* have ye
Mark 6:41 When he had taken the five *l* and
Mark 6:41 and blessed, and brake the *l*
Mark 6:44 eat of the *l* were about five thousand
Luke 9:13 we have no more but five *l* and
Luke 9:16 he took the five *l* and the two fishes
John 6:11 And Jesus took the *l*; and when he
John 6:13 the fragments of the five barley *l*

■ Locusts (LOH kusts)
A large insect that looks like a grasshopper. A swarm of locusts will destroy all vegetation: trees, bushes, crops. Sometimes in the Middle East, locusts can multiply into very great numbers. God used locusts in one of the ten plagues on Egypt to try and get Pharaoh to let the Israelites go free. Locusts provide a good source of protein and are eaten in the Middle East, either raw, boiled, or roasted, usually with honey. John the Baptist ate locusts and wild honey.

Exodus 10:4 tomorrow will I bring the *l* into
Exodus 10:13 morning, the east wind brought the *l*
Exodus 10:14 *l* went up over all the land of Egypt
Exodus 10:19 west wind, which took away the *l*
Matthew 3:4 his meat was *l* and wild honey
Mark 1:6 he did eat *l* and wild honey

148

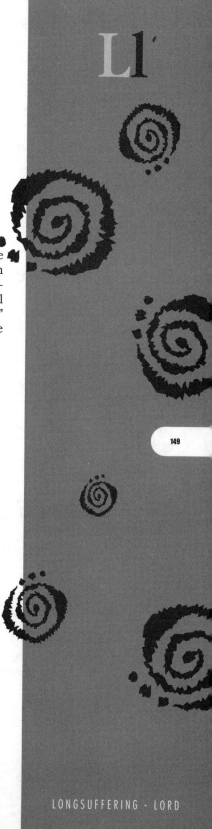

Longsuffering (LAWNG suh fer eeng)
Patient, forgiving, not easily angered.

Numbers 14:18 The LORD is *l*, and of great mercy
Psalm 86:15 full of compassion, gracious, *l*
Galatians 5:22 the Spirit is love, joy, peace, *l*

Look (LOOK)
To see, to view with the eyes.

Genesis 9:16 I will *l* upon it, that I may remember
Exodus 3:6 for he was afraid to *l* upon God
Matthew 11:3 should come, or do we *l* for another
John 4:35 Lift up your eyes, and *l* on the fields

Lord (LAWRD)
Master, ruler, one who uses his power in the
right way; a title showing respect or honor. In
the Old Testament, LORD is capitalized, showing that He is special and that He rules "all
things and all people." Lord, with only the "L"
capitalized, is the title given to Jesus because
He was fully God, and fully human.

Genesis 2:7 And the *L* God formed man of the dust
Genesis 4:4 the *L* had respect unto Abel
Genesis 18:22 but Abraham stood yet before the *L*
Genesis 28:16 Surely the *L* is in this place
Exodus 3:7 *L* said, I have surely seen the affliction
Exodus 6:6 I am the *L*, and I will bring you out
Exodus 9:22 the *L* said unto Moses, Stretch forth
Exodus 20:5 For I the *L* thy God am a jealous God
Exodus 20:7 take the name of the *L* thy God in vain
Exodus 20:10 seventh day is the sabbath of the *L*
Exodus 20:11 in six days the *L* made heaven and earth
Exodus 24:7 All that the *L* hath said will we do
Exodus 40:34 glory of the *L* filled the tabernacle
Deuteronomy 5:9 for I the *L* thy God an a jealous God
Joshua 1:9 for the *L* thy God is with thee
1 Samuel 1:15 have poured out my soul before the *L*
1 Kings 17:2 the word of the *L* came unto him
Nehemiah 8:10 the joy of the *L* is your strength
Psalm 18:2 The *L* is my rock, and my fortress
Psalm 18:3 I will call upon the *L*, who is worthy
Psalm 18:6 In my distress I called upon the *L*
Psalm 23:1 The *L* is my shepherd; I shall not want
Psalm 25:4 Show me thy ways, O *L*
Psalm 27:1 The *L* is my light and my salvation
Psalm 27:14 Wait on the *L*: be of good courage
Psalm 33:12 is the nation whose God is the *L*
Psalm 37:3 Trust in the *L*, and do good
Psalm 55:22 Cast thy burden upon the *L*

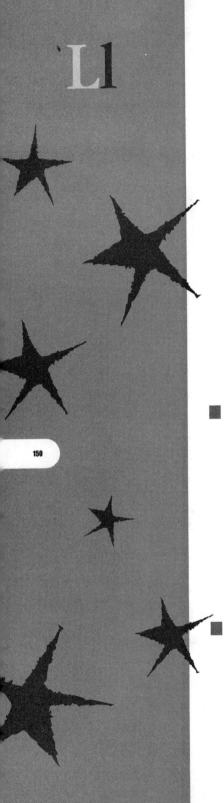

Ll

Psalm 86:11 Teach me thy way, O **L**
Psalm 105:1 O give thanks unto the **L**: call upon
Psalm 118:24 This is the day which the **L** hath made
Psalm 121:2 My help cometh from the **L**, which made
Psalm 136:1 O give thanks unto the **L**; for he is
Proverbs 1:7 fear of the **L** is the beginning of
Proverbs 3:5 Trust in the **L** with all thine heart
Isaiah 40:31 the **L** shall renew their strength
Jonah 1:1 Now the word of the **L** came unto Jonah
Matthew 1:20 the angel of the **L** appeared unto
Matthew 4:7 Thou shalt not tempt the **L** thy God
Matthew 4:10 Thou shalt worship the **L** thy God
Mark 1:3 Prepare ye the way of the **L**
Mark 12:29 The **L** our God is one **L**
Mark 12:30 thou shalt love the **L** thy God with
Luke 2:11 a Savior, which is Christ the **L**
Luke 4:8 Thou shalt worship the **L** thy God
Luke 4:12 Thou shalt not tempt the **L** thy God
Luke 4:18 The Spirit of the **L** is upon me
Luke 24:34 The **L** is risen indeed, and hath
John 9:38 And he said, **L**, I believe
John 20:25 said unto him, We have seen the **L**
John 21:7 saith unto Peter, It is the **L**

■ Lose (LOOZ)
To forget, give up, misplace, waste.

Matthew 10:39 He that findeth his life shall *l* it
Matthew 16:25 will save his life shall *l* it
Matthew 16:25 will *l* his life for my sake shall
Matthew 16:26 the whole world and *l* his own soul
Mark 8:35 whosoever will save his life shall *l* it
Mark 8:35 whosoever shall *l* his life for my sake
Mark 8:36 gain the whole world, and *l* his own soul
Luke 9:24 whosoever will save his life shall *l* it
Luke 9:24 whosoever will *l* his life for my sake
Luke 9:25 gain the whole world, and *l* himself
John 12:25 He that loveth his life shall *l* it

■ Lot (LAHT)
The name means "concealed." His father was
Haran, and Abraham was his uncle. Lot left Ur
of the Chaldees with his father, Haran, grandfa-
ther, Terah, and Abraham, and all their families.
They traveled to Haran, then Lot went with
Abraham to Canaan. After they arrived in
Canaan, Lot's herdsmen quarreled with
Abraham's herdsmen because there was not
enough grass or water to feed all their herds.
Abraham wanted peace in the family. He offered
Lot the choice of the land near the Jordan River

or the land in the hills. Lot chose the fertile land and settled near the city of Sodom.

Genesis 11:27 Nahor, and Haran; and Haran begat **L**
Genesis 12:4 and **L** went with him
Genesis 13:8 Abram said unto **L**, Let there be no
Genesis 13:11 **L** chose him all the plain of Jordan

Loud (LOWD)
Much noise, opposite of quiet or soft.

Psalm 98:4 make a **l** noise, and rejoice, and
Psalm 150:5 Praise him upon the **l** cymbals
Matthew 27:46 Jesus cried with a **l** voice, saying
Matthew 27:50 he had cried again with a **l** voice
Mark 15:34 ninth hour Jesus cried with a **l** voice
Mark 15:37 And Jesus cried with a **l** voice
Luke 17:15 and with a **l** voice glorified God
Luke 23:46 when Jesus had cried with a **l** voice
John 11:43 cried with a **l** voice, Lazarus, come

Love (LUV)
An emotion of a great and warm feeling; deep friendship; to like a great deal.

Leviticus 19:18 shalt **l** thy neighbor as thyself
Deuteronomy 6:5 thou shalt **l** the LORD thy God
Psalm 119:97 O how I **l** thy law
Ecclesiastes 3:8 A time to **l**, and a time to hate
Micah 6:8 do justly, and to **l** mercy, and to walk
Matthew 5:43 Thou shalt **l** thy neighbor, and
Matthew 5:44 I say unto you, **L** your enemies
Mark 12:30 thou shalt **l** the Lord thy God with
Mark 12:31 Thou shalt **l** thy neighbor as thyself
Luke 6:27 **L** your enemies, do good to them which
Luke 10:27 Thou shalt **l** the Lord thy God with
John 13:34 That ye **l** one another; as I have loved
John 13:34 loved you, that ye also **l** one another
John 14:15 If ye **l** me, keep my commandments
John 15:13 Greater **l** hath no man than this, that
1 John 4:7 let us **l** one another: for **l** is of God
1 John 4:8 loveth not knoweth not God; for God is **l**

Loved (LUVD)
Past tense of "love."

Genesis 25:28 And Isaac **l** Esau
Genesis 25:28 but Rebekah **l** Jacob
Mark 10:21 Jesus looked at him and **l** him (NIV)
John 3:16 For God so **l** the world, that he gave
John 3:19 and men **l** darkness rather than light
John 11:5 Now Jesus **l** Martha, and her sister, and
John 13:34 as I have **l** you, that ye also love one

151

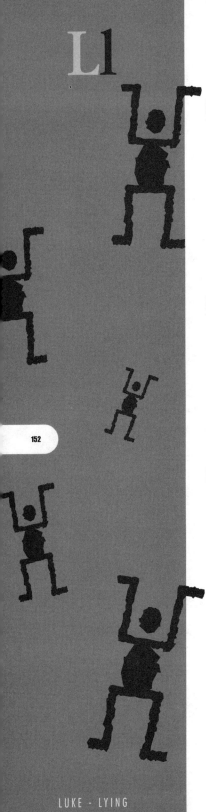

John 15:12 love one another, as I have *I* you
1 John 4:10 not that we *I* God, but that he *I* us
1 John 4:11 if God so *I* us, we ought to love one
1 John 4:19 We love him because he first *I* us

■ Luke (LEWK)
A Gentile and possibly a Greek doctor who was a good friend to Paul. He went on several of Paul's missionary trips. He wrote the Gospel book of Luke, and Acts, the only History book in the New Testament. Luke must have talked to a lot of people when he was preparing to write the Gospel book, Luke. He tells many stories about Jesus that are not included in the other three Gospel books.

Colossians 4:14 **L**, the beloved physician
2 Timothy 4:11 Only **L** is with me

■ Luke, Book of (LEWK)
The third book of the New Testament and the third in the division, Gospels. The author is Luke, the physician, who also wrote Acts. He was a Gentile and a friend of Paul. As a historian he knew how to ask questions to help him write a complete biography (life story) of Jesus. Many stories he wrote are found only in his Gospel. He wrote for both Gentile and Jewish Christians. He stressed that Jesus was the Son of God and came to save all people from their sins.

■ Lydia (LID ih uh)
A woman who lived in the city of Thyatira in Asia Minor. She sold cloth dyed purple which probably made her very rich. Only the wealthy people and those in high office could afford to buy it. After she became a Christian, she invited Paul and his companions to stay in her house and to use her house as a headquarters for their work in the area.

Acts 16:14 woman named **L**, a seller of purple
Acts 16:40 and entered into the house of **L**

■ Lying (LIGH eeng)
1. Not telling the truth.

Psalm 31:18 Let the *I* lips be put to silence
Psalm 119:163 I hate and abhor *I*: but thy law
Proverbs 12:19 a *I* tongue is but for a moment
Proverbs 12:22 The LORD detests *I* lips

2. In a position of being flat or stretched out.

Luke 2:12 swaddling clothes, *I* in a manger
Luke 2:16 Joseph, and the babe *I* in a manger

Lystra (LISS truh)

A city in south central Asia Minor (now in south central Turkey). Paul's first and second missionary journeys took him to Lystra (see map on page 341). Timothy may have lived in that city. Paul invited him to go with him when he left Lystra, possibly on his second missionary journey. Timothy's mother and grandmother were believers and may have been among the first Christians in Lystra.

Acts 14:8 In **L** there sat a man crippled in his (NIV)
Acts 14:21 had taught many, they returned to **L**
Acts 16:1 Then came he to Derbe and **L**
Acts 16:2 reported of by the brethren that were at **L**

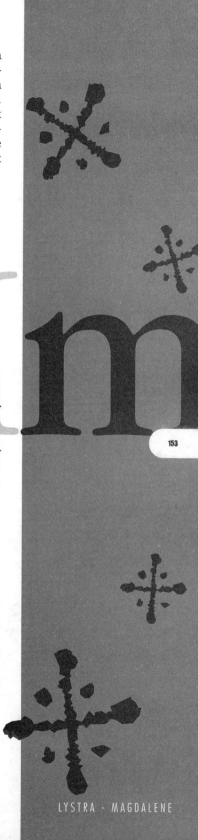

Macedonia (MASS uh DOH nih uh)

A country north of Achaia or Greece.(see map on page 341). During New Testament times, it was a Roman province. Paul preached in several of its major cities: Philippi, Beroea, and Thessalonica, and churches were begun in each city. Paul had a dream and saw a man of Macedonia calling him to come help. First and Second Thessalonians were written to the Christians at Thessalonica.

Acts 16:9 There stood a man of **M**, and prayed
Acts 16:9 saying, Come over into **M**, and help us
Acts 16:10 we got ready at once to leave for **M** (NIV)
1 Corinthians 16:5 when I shall pass through **M**
Philippians 4:15 when I departed from **M**, no church

Magdala (MAG duh luh)

The name might mean "tower." It is a city located on the west side of the Sea of Galilee (see map on page 340). A highway passed from Tiberius to the south through Magdala. Jesus healed a woman of demons who was from this city and was known as Mary Magdalene.

Matthew 15:39 and came into the coasts of **M**

Magdalene (MAG duh leen)

A person who lives in Magdala. A woman named Mary, from Magdala, had a demon and was healed by Jesus. She is referred to as Mary

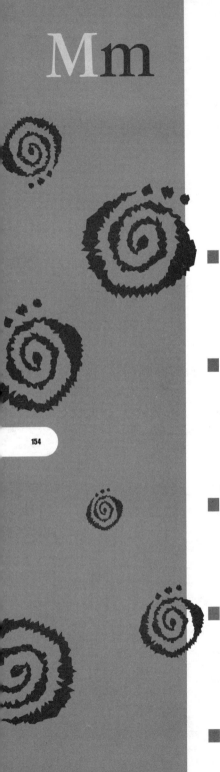

Mm

Magdalene in several Bible passages.

Matthew 27:56 Among which was Mary **M**
Matthew 27:61 And there was Mary **M**
Matthew 28:1 came Mary **M** and the other Mary
Mark 15:40 among whom was Mary **M**, and Mary
Mark 15:47 and Mary **M** and Mary the mother of
Mark 16:1 when the sabbath was past, Mary **M**
Mark 16:9 he appeared first to Mary **M**
Luke 8:2 Mary called **M**, out of whom went
Luke 24:10 It was Mary **M**, and Joanna, and
John 19:25 the wife of Cleophas, and Mary **M**
John 20:1 first day of the week cometh Mary **M**
John 20:18 Mary **M** came and told the disciples

Magnify (MAG nih figh)
To make great or important; to give much praise; to worship.

Psalm 34:3 O **m** the LORD with me, and let us
Psalm 69:30 and will **m** him with thanksgiving
Luke 1:46 Mary said, My soul doth **m** the Lord

Maid (MAYD)
A girl who is unmarried; a female servant.

Matthew 9:24 for the **m** is not dead, but sleepeth
Matthew 9:25 took her by the hand, and the **m** arose
Matthew 26:71 into the porch, another **m** saw him
Mark 14:69 And a **m** saw him again, and began
Luke 8:54 and called, saying, **M**, arise
Luke 22:56 But a certain **m** beheld him as he

Maidservant (MAYD suhr vint)
A slave who is female.

Exodus 20:10 thy manservant, nor thy **m**, nor thy
Exodus 20:17 nor his manservant, nor his **m**, nor
Deuteronomy 5:14 nor thy manservant, nor thy **m**
Deuteronomy 5:14 thy manservant and thy **m** may rest

Maimed (MAYMD)
Someone who has been hurt badly or caused to become lame; loss of a limb (arm or leg) or other injury to cause a person's looks to be changed extremely.

Matthew 15:30 those that were lame, blind, dumb, **m**
Matthew 15:31 the **m** to be whole, the lame to walk

Majesty (MADJ eh stee)
Relating to royalty. The power, respect and honor that a person of royalty displays.

Psalm 29:4 the voice of the LORD is full of **m**

Psalm 96:6 Honour and ***m*** are before him
Psalm 104:1 thou art clothed with honor and ***m***
Micah 5:4 in the ***m*** of the name of the LORD

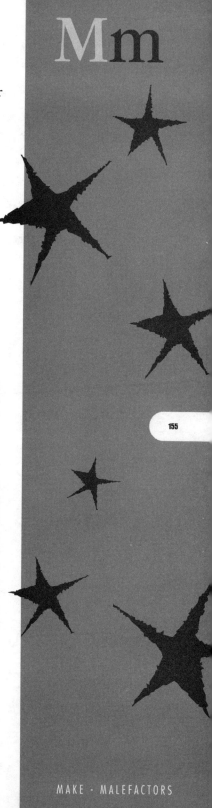

Mm

◼ Make (MAYK)
To build, create, or form; to cause to happen or come into being; to compel or order.

Genesis 1:26 Let us ***m*** man in our image
Genesis 6:16 A window shalt thou ***m*** to the ark
Genesis 27:4 ***m*** me savoury meat such as I love
Genesis 35:1 and ***m*** there an altar unto God
Exodus 20:4 shalt not ***m*** unto thee any graven image
Exodus 20:23 Ye shall not ***m*** with me gods of
Psalm 66:1 ***M*** a joyful noise unto God, all ye
Psalm 100:1 ***M*** a joyful noise unto the LORD, all
Matthew 4:19 and I will ***m*** you fishers of men
Mark 1:17 I will ***m*** you to become fishers of men
Mark 14:15 there ***m*** ready for us
Luke 9:14 ***M*** them sit down by fifties in a
Luke 19:5 Zaccheus ***m*** haste, and come down; for
Luke 22:12 upper room furnished: there ***m*** ready
John 8:32 and the truth shall ***m*** you free

◼ Maker (MAYK uhr)
One who causes something to come into being; a creator. God is our maker because He created everything around us on earth and in the heavens.

Psalm 95:6 let us kneel before the LORD our ***m***

◼ Malachi, Book of (MAL uh kigh)
The name means "my messenger" or "my angel." Nothing is known about Malachi except what Malachi 1:1 says about him. The book is the last book in the Old Testament and the twelfth book in the division, Minor Prophets. Malachi was written so that God's people would know He loved them, and they would show honor and respect to Him. He required them to be faithful in the way they lived, worshiped, and in the giving of their tithes and offerings. Malachi also warned them to repent or face God's judgment.

◼ Male (MAYL)
A boy, fellow, guy, man.

Genesis 1:27 ***m*** and female created he them
Genesis 5:2 ***M*** and female created he them

◼ Malefactors (MAL ih fak turs)
The word was translated into Latin from the Greek and means "robber" or "criminal." The

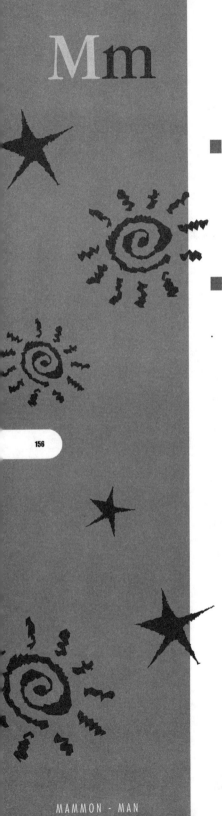

Mm

two criminals crucified with Jesus were referred to as "malefactors" in the King James Version of the Bible.

Luke 23:32 also two other, *m*, led with him
Luke 23:33 crucified him, and the *m*, one on the
Luke 23:39 one of the *m* which were hanged

◼ Mammon (MAM uhn)

A Greek word meaning "money," "riches," "property," "worldly goods," or "profit." Mammon can keep a person from serving God. Wealth or riches becomes a problem when it is more important to a person than God.

Matthew 6:24 Ye cannot serve God and *m*
Luke 16:13 Ye cannot serve God and *m*

◼ Man (MAN)

A male human being who has become an adult. He was formed in the image of God. The term can also refer to the whole race of humans.

Genesis 1:26 Let us make *m* in our image
Genesis 2:7 LORD God formed *m* of the dust of
Genesis 2:7 and *m* became a living soul
Genesis 25:27 Esau was a cunning hunter, a *m* of
Genesis 25:27 and Jacob was a plain *m*, dwelling
Ruth 1:2 the name of the *m* was Elimelech
1 Kings 17:24 I know that thou art a *m* of God
Psalm 1:1 Blessed is the *m* that walketh not
Psalm 84:12 blessed is the *m* that trusteth in thee
Psalm 112:1 Blessed is the *m* that feareth the LORD
Proverbs 1:5 A wise *m* will hear, and will
Proverbs 3:13 Happy is the *m* that findeth wisdom
Proverbs 16:25 way that seemeth right to a *m*
Proverbs 18:24 A *m* that hath friends must show
Matthew 4:4 *M* shall not live by bread alone
Matthew 6:24 No *m* can serve two masters
Matthew 17:22 The Son of *m* shall be betrayed
Mark 2:27 sabbath was made for *m*, and not *m* for
Mark 2:28 Son of *m* is Lord also of the sabbath
Mark 10:45 Son of *m* came not to be ministered unto
Mark 11:2 colt tied, whereon never *m* sat
Luke 4:4 That *m* shall not live by bread alone
Luke 9:23 If any *m* will come after me, let him deny
Luke 15:11 A certain *m* had two sons
Luke 19:10 For the Son of *m* is come to seek and to
John 3:3 Except a *m* be born again, he cannot see
John 15:13 Greater love hath no *m* than this
John 15:13 that a *m* lay down his life for his
1 Timothy 4:12 Let no *m* despise thy youth

Manger (MAYN jer)

A feeding box for animals. During Bible times, many mangers were made by making a hole in a rock or stone. Some were made by using bricks made from clay and straw or stones cut from limestone. They were usually rectangular in shape.

Luke 2:7 and laid him in a **m**
Luke 2:12 in swaddling clothes, lying in a **m**
Luke 2:16 and the babe lying in a **m**

Manna (MAN uh)

Whitish round flakes which were present each morning in the desert camp of the Israelites. After leaving Egypt, the Israelites had no way of growing food in the desert. God provided the manna for them. They were to collect a certain amount each morning, enough for each person for the day. If they collected more, to save for the next day, it rotted and stank. On the sixth day, they were to collect enough for two days, since there would be no work on the sabbath. God was showing them that He would provide for them but they had to trust Him. The people called the flakes "manna" which means "What is it?" The flakes could be boiled or ground like wheat and baked into cakes. The Israelites ate manna for forty years while they were in the wilderness.

Exodus 16:15 said to one another, It is **m**
Exodus 16:31 Israel called the name thereof **M**
Exodus 16:35 of Israel did eat **m** forty years
Exodus 16:35 did eat **m** until they came into
Joshua 5:12 **m** ceased on the morrow after they
Joshua 5:12 had the children of Israel **m** any more

Manner (MAN uhr)

1. Kind, type, or sort.

Matthew 4:23 and healing all **m** of sickness
Matthew 4:23 all **m** of disease among the people
Matthew 5:11 shall say all **m** of evil against you
Mark 4:41 What **m** of man is this, that even the
Luke 24:17 What **m** of communications are these

2. Method, practice, way.

Ruth 4:7 Now this was the **m** in former time
Matthew 6:9 After this **m** therefore pray ye
John 19:40 as the **m** of the Jews is to bury

Mm

Manger

157

Mm

Manservant (MAN sur vint)
A male slave.

Exodus 20:10 nor thy daughter, nor thy **m**, nor
Exodus 20:17 nor his **m**, nor his maidservant,

Mantle (MAN tuhl)
An outer garment that was loose and flowing much like a robe or cape. Elijah is known for his mantle which he gave to Elisha. This mantle carried with it the ability to prophesy for God and the power of God. These types of garments are still worn in the Middle East today.

1 Kings 19:13 he wrapped his face in his **m**
1 Kings 19:19 Elijah passed by him, and cast his **m**
2 Kings 2:8 Elijah took his **m**, and wrapped it
2 Kings 2:13 He took up also the **m** of Elijah
2 Kings 2:14 he took the **m** of Elijah that fell

Mark (MAHRK)
A relative of Barnabas. His Roman name was Marcus but he was called Mark. He also had a Jewish name, John. He was often referred to as John Mark. He began the first missionary journey with Paul but quit and returned to his home in Jerusalem. Later, he worked with Barnabas and became a dependable worker. He worked with Peter as well.

Acts 12:12 John, whose surname was **M**
Acts 12:25 with them John, whose surname was **M**
Acts 15:37 them John, whose surname was **M**
Acts 15:39 Barnabas took **M**, and sailed to Cyprus
2 Timothy 4:11 Take **M**, and bring him with thee

Mark, Book of (MAHRK)
The second book of the New Testament and the second in the division, Gospels. The author is John Mark, who worked with Peter and Paul. Mark showed Jesus as human, with the same emotions that humans show: sorrow, sadness, love, anger, understanding, and pity. The book stresses the things Jesus did rather than the words He spoke.

Martha (MAHR thuh)
The name means "lady [of the house]" or "mistress." She was the oldest sister of Mary and Lazarus, friends of Jesus, whose home was in Bethany. Martha worked hard to prepare food and entertain those who came to her house. Jesus reminded her that other things were more

important than the cooking and cleaning.

Luke 10:38 a certain woman named **M** received him
Luke 10:40 **M** was distracted by all the preparations (NIV)
Luke 10:41 said unto her, **M**, **M**, thou art careful
John 11:1 the town of Mary and her sister **M**
John 11:5 Jesus loved **M**, and her sister, and
John 12:2 made him a supper; and **M** served

Marvel (MAHR vuhl)
To wonder, be amazed, be surprised.

Mark 5:20 had done for him: and all men did **m**
John 3:7 **M** not that I said unto thee, Ye must
Acts 3:12 Ye men of Israel, why **m** ye at this

Marvelled (MAHR vuhld)
Past tense of "marvel."

Matthew 8:10 When Jesus heard it, he **m**, and
Matthew 8:27 But the men **m**, saying, What manner
Matthew 9:33 the dumb spake: and the multitudes **m**
Mark 12:17 And they **m** at him
Mark 15:5 answered nothing; so that Pilate **m**
Mark 15:44 And Pilate **m** if he were already dead
Luke 2:33 Joseph and his mother **m** at those things
Luke 20:26 and they **m** at his answer, and

Marvellous (MAHR vuhl us)
Also spelled "marvelous." Causing wonder, amazement, or surprise; wonderful, great.

Psalm 9:1 I will show forth all thy **m** works
Psalm 17:7 Show thy **m** lovingkindness
Psalm 98:1 for he hath done **m** things
Psalm 105:5 Remember his **m** words that he hath

Mary (MAY rih)
The name means "rebellious, bitter." Mary is the Greek form of the Hebrew name, Miriam. It was a common name during New Testament times. Three Mary's are important in the New Testament and they will be listed individually as follows.

1. Mary, the mother of Jesus was a young Jewish girl engaged to Joseph, a carpenter. The angel Gabriel told her that God had chosen her to become the mother of God's son. Just before time for the baby to be born, Mary and Joseph went to Bethlehem to pay their taxes, and the baby was born there, in a stable. They named him Jesus, just as Gabriel had told them to do. Later, the family moved to Nazareth, where

Mary

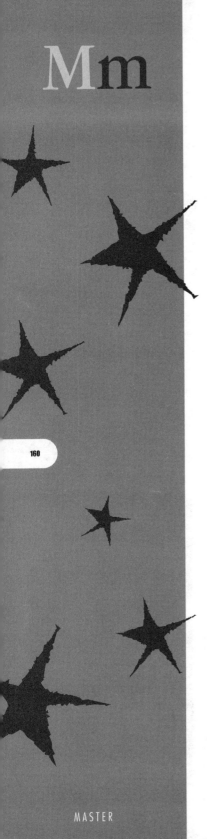

Mm

Jesus grew into a man. Mary probably had four more boys and two or three girls. Mary may have been a widow by the time Jesus started His work for God. She was present at the crucifixion and became one of His followers after He was resurrected.

Matthew 1:18 When as his mother **M** was espoused
Matthew 13:55 is not his mother called **M**
Mark 6:3 Is not this the carpenter, the son of **M**
Luke 1:27 and the virgin's name was **M**
Luke 1:30 the angel said unto her, Fear not, **M**
Luke 1:34 Then said **M** unto the angel, How shall
Luke 2:5 To be taxed with **M** his espoused wife
Luke 2:16 came with haste, and found **M**, and
Luke 2:19 But **M** kept all these things, and

2. Mary Magdalene was from Magdala, an important trade center of Galilee. Mary was healed of demons by Jesus, and became one of His faithful followers. Jesus appeared to her at the tomb after he was resurrected.

Matthew 27:56 which was **M** Magdalene, and **M** the
Matthew 27:61 And there was **M** Magdalene, and
Mark 15:40 among whom was **M** Magdalene, and
Mark 16:9 he appeared first to **M** Magdalene
Luke 8:2 **M** called Magdalene, out of whom went
Luke 24:10 It was **M** Magdalene, and Joanna
John 19:25 wife of Cleophas, and **M** Magdalene
John 20:1 cometh **M** Magdalene early, when it was
John 20:11 But **M** stood without at the sepulcher
John 20:16 Jesus saith unto her, **M**. She turned
John 20:18 **M** Magdalene came and told the

3. Mary was the sister of Lazarus and Martha, friends of Jesus, who lived at Bethany. She listened as Jesus taught and seemed to understand the coming death of Jesus. She anointed his feet with some expensive oil.

Luke 10:39 And she had a sister called **M**
Luke 10:42 **M** hath chosen that good part
John 11:1 Bethany, the town of **M** and her sister
John 11:19 Jews came to Martha and **M**, to comfort
John 11:45 many of the Jews which came to **M**
John 12:3 Then took **M** a pound of ointment of

Master (MAST uhr)
Leader, lord, ruler, teacher. Means teacher or rabbi when used to address Jesus.

Matthew 26:25 betrayed him, answered and said, **M**

Luke 5:5 **M**, we have toiled all the night, and
Luke 18:18 Good **M**, what shall I do to inherit
Luke 22:11 The **M** saith unto thee, Where is
John 13:13 Ye call me **M** and Lord: and ye
John 20:16 Rabboni; which is to say, **M**

Masters (MAST uhrz)
Plural of "master."

Matthew 6:24 No man can serve two **m**
Luke 16:13 No servant can serve two **m**

Matter (MAT uhr)
Affair, concern, problem.

Exodus 18:16 When they have a **m**, they come to
Proverbs 16:20 He that handleth a **m** wisely shall
Mark 1:45 and to blaze abroad the **m**
Acts 17:32 We will hear thee again of this **m**

Matthew (MATH yoo)
The name means "the gift of Yahweh." Matthew
was a tax collector and also known as Levi, the
son of Alpheus. Jesus called him because he
was trainable and knew how to keep good
records. He would be able to write about his
experiences with Jesus.

Matthew 9:9 he saw a man, named **M**, sitting at
Matthew 10:3 Thomas, and **M**, the publican
Mark 3:18 Bartholomew, and **M**, and Thomas
Luke 6:15 **M** and Thomas, James the son of
Acts 1:13 Thomas, Bartholomew, and **M**, James

Matthew, Book of (MATH yoo)
The first book of the New Testament as well as
the first book in the division, Gospels. The writer
was Matthew, the tax collector whom Jesus
chose as one of His disciples. He shows Jesus as
a teacher, the Messiah, the Son of God, and he
is the only New Testament writer to tell about
the visit of the Wise Men. He uses three chapters to write a detailed story of the Sermon on
the Mount. Matthew records that Pilate saw
Jesus as a king, making a sign to go on the top
of the cross which read, "THIS IS JESUS THE
KING OF THE JEWS." And the soldier at the foot
of the cross called him "the Son of God."

Measure (MEH zuhr)
A dry or liquid weight, a length, or an area of
land. In biblical times, these ways of measuring
were not always the same, depending on the
time or the place. Two examples of a dry mea-

161

Mm

sure are ephah (one-half bushel), and homer (5.16 bushels). A hin (one gallon) is an example of a liquid measure. The cubit (about 17.5 inches) is the main example of a length. Land was measured by how much a yoke of oxen could plow in one day, which was about an acre. The prophets, and Jesus, warned against using unjust measures, thereby cheating others.

Matthew 7:2 **m** you use, it will be measured to you (NIV)
Mark 4:24 the **m** you use, it will be measured to you (NIV)
Luke 6:38 A good **m**, pressed down, shaken together (NIV)
Luke 6:38 the **m** you use, it will be measured to you (NIV)

■ Meat (MEET)
The term is used two ways in the King James Version Bible. 1. To refer to solid food. 2. To refer to a meal. To "sit at meat" means to eat a meal. "To come to meat" means to come to the meal.

Matthew 6:25 Is not the life more than **m**
Matthew 25:35 was an hungered, and ye gave me **m**
Matthew 25:42 an hungered, and ye gave me no **m**
Luke 7:37 she knew that Jesus sat at **m**
Luke 12:23 life is more than **m**, and the body
Luke 24:41 said unto them, Have ye here any **m**
John 21:5 unto them, Children, have you any **m**

■ Medicine (MED ih suhn)
Very little information is given in the Bible about the types of medicines used in biblical times. The Romans, Greeks, and Egyptians had records of various medicines and prescriptions they were using. Many plants were used to obtain medicines. Also, blood, milk, ground-up bone, or shells from animals were used. Certain minerals were also in use. Olive oil, herbs, frankincense, myrrh, and wine were other types of medicines used to help treat diseases and ailments. Since the physicians of biblical times did not understand about viruses and bacteria, many illnesses were not treated properly, or they could not be treated at all. People would die, go blind, or have other problems that they had to be concerned about.

Proverbs 17:22 A merry heart doeth good like a **m**

■ Meditate (MED ih tayt)
To quietly think about something or to make plans. We develop our relationship with Christ when we meditate on His words in the Bible and how He wants us to live.

Psalm 1:2 in his law doth he **m** day and night
1 Timothy 4:15 **M** upon these things

■ Meditation (MED ih TAY shun)
Meditating or thinking about something.

Psalm 19:14 words of my mouth, and the **m** of my
Psalm 104:34 My **m** of him shall be sweet
Psalm 119:97 it is my **m** all the day

■ Meek (MEEK)
To be gentle, kind, patient. To have a spirit of discipline or control. To rely on God rather than self. Another word for meek is "humility."

Psalm 25:9 The **m** will he guide in judgment
Psalm 25:9 the **m** will he teach his way
Psalm 37:11 But the **m** shall inherit the earth
Matthew 5:5 Blessed are the **m**: for they shall
Matthew 11:29 for I am **m** and lowly in heart
Matthew 21:5 king cometh unto thee, **m**, and sitting

■ Member (MEM buhr)
A person in a group, such as a Christian, who is part of the church. Also, the various parts, such as the body. The eyes, mouth, brain, heart, hands, or feet, are part of the human body.

James 3:5 the tongue is a little **m**, and boasteth

■ Men (MEN)
Plural of "man."

Psalm 107:8 Oh that **m** would praise the LORD
Proverbs 10:14 Wise **m** lay up knowledge
Matthew 2:1 there came wise **m** from the east
Matthew 2:7 when he had privily called the wise **m**
Matthew 4:19 and I will make you fishers of **m**
Matthew 5:16 Let your light so shine before **m**
Matthew 6:14 if ye forgive **m** their trespasses
Matthew 6:15 if ye forgive not **m** their trespasses
Mark 1:17 will make you to become fishers of **m**
Mark 10:27 With **m** it is impossible, but not with
Luke 5:10 from henceforth thou shalt catch **m**
Luke 12:8 Whosoever shall confess me before **m**
Luke 18:27 impossible with **m** are possible with God
Luke 24:4 two **m** stood by them in shining garments
John 3:19 **m** loved darkness rather than light
John 12:32 will draw all **m** unto me

■ Mention (MEN shun)
To speak of, bring up.

Romans 1:9 I make **m** of you always in my prayers

Mm

Ephesians 1:16 making *m* of you in my prayers
1 Thessalonians 1:2 making *m* of you in our prayers
Philemon 4 making *m* of thee always in my prayers

Mephibosheth (meh FIB oh sheth)
The name means "shame destroyer" or "image breaker." A son of Jonathan who was crippled at the age of five. Later, wanting to do something for his friend, Jonathan, King David invited Mephibosheth to come live in the palace.

2 Samuel 4:4 And his name was *M*
2 Samuel 9:6 Now when *M*, the son of Jonathan
2 Samuel 9:10 but *M* thy master's son shall eat
2 Samuel 9:13 So *M* dwelt in Jerusalem

Mercies (MEHR cees)
Plural of "mercy."

Psalm 89:1 I will sing of the *m* of the LORD
Psalm 119:156 Great are thy tender *m*, O LORD
Romans 12:1 by the *m* of God, that ye present

Merciful (MEHR sih fuhl)
Forgiving.

Psalm 57:1 Be *m* unto me, O God, be *m*
Psalm 103:8 The LORD is *m* and gracious
Matthew 5:7 Blessed are the *m*: for they shall
Luke 6:36 Be ye therefore *m*, as your Father

Mercy (MEHR cee)
Feelings of caring, forgiveness, kindness, pity, love, tenderness, or a combination of any of these.

Psalm 23:6 *m* shall follow me all the days of my life
Psalm 30:10 Hear, O LORD, and have *m* upon me
Psalm 51:1 Have *m* upon me, O God
Psalm 100:5 LORD is good: his *m* is everlasting
Psalm 103:8 slow to anger, and plenteous in *m*
Psalm 136:1 for his *m* endureth for ever
Matthew 5:7 for they shall obtain *m*
Matthew 9:27 Thou Son of David, have *m* on us
Mark 10:48 Thou son of David, have *m* on me
Luke 18:38 Jesus, thou son of David, have *m* on me

Merry (MEH rih)
Cheerful, happy, joyful; festive.

Proverbs 15:13 A *m* heart maketh a cheerful countenance
Proverbs 17:22 A *m* heart doeth good like a medicine
Luke 15:23 and let us eat, and be *m*
Luke 15:24 and is found. And they began to be *m*

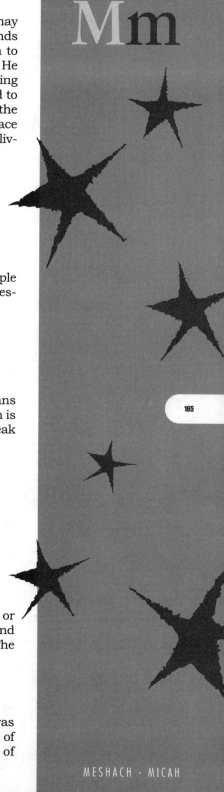

Meshach (MEE shak)

The name has an unknown meaning and may be Babylonian. He was one of Daniel's friends who had been captured in Judah and taken to Babylon. His Hebrew name was Mishael. He refused to eat the king's rich foods, preferring vegetables and water instead. He also refused to bow down to the king because he worshiped the true God, and was thrown into a fiery furnace with Shadrach and Abednego. But God delivered them from the fire.

Daniel 1:7 and to Mishael, of *M*
Daniel 2:49 he set Shadrach, *M*, and Abed-nego
Daniel 3:23 *M*, and Abed-nego, fell down bound into
Daniel 3:28 Blessed be the God of Shadrach, *M*, and
Daniel 3:30 the king promoted Shadrach, *M*, and

Messenger (MESS in jer)

One who is sent with a message. One example is the prophets whom God sent to tell His message to the Israelites.

Matthew 11:10 Behold, I send my *m* before thy face
Mark 1:2 Behold, I send my *m* before thy face
Luke 7:27 Behold, I send my *m* before thy face

Messiah (muh SIGH uh)

The Greek form of "Messias." The name means "Anointed One." The Hebrew word for Messiah is "Christ." Both words (Messiah and Christ) speak of the coming ruler or Savior. See "Christ."

John 1:41 saith unto him, We have found the *M*
John 4:25 know that *M* cometh, which is called Christ

Mete (MEET)

To measure.

Matthew 7:2 with what measure ye *m*, it shall be
Mark 4:24 with what measure ye *m*, it shall be
Luke 6:38 same measure that ye *m* withal it shall be

Methuselah (mih THOOZ uh luh)

The name may mean "man of the javelin" or "worshiper of Selah." His father was Enoch and Methuselah was the grandfather of Noah. The Bible states he lived 969 years.

Genesis 5:27 days of *M* were nine hundred sixty

Micah (MIGH kuh)

The name means "Who is like Yahweh?" He was a prophet of Judah and was from the town of Moresheth, twenty-five miles southwest of

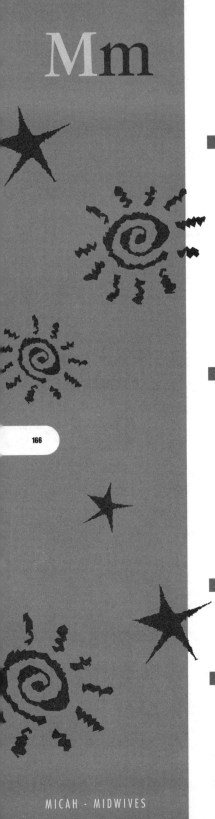

Mm

Jerusalem. He prophesied in Judah during the reigns of three kings of Judah. He told the people of Jerusalem that God would punish them for their wickedness. He also said that the Saviour would be born in Bethlehem.

Micah 1:1 came to **M** the Morasthite in the days of

Micah, Book of (MIGH kuh)
The book is the sixth book in the Old Testament division, Minor Prophets. The book tells about the ministry of Micah in Judah. The people were worshiping God but also worshiped other gods. Micah stressed their need to focus on God alone. Also, the rich people were causing great problems to the poor, cheating them out of what little they had, pushing them out of their homes, stealing their things, and taking their land. In spite of the judgment that was sure to come, Micah said that a remnant (a small group of people) would be able to return to Jerusalem. In Micah 5:2, he told about the ruler to come who would be born in Bethlehem.

Midian (MID ih uhn)
Personal and clan name that means "strife." An area in the desert of what is now northwestern Saudi Arabia. The people who lived in that area were Midianites, and were descended from Midian, one of the sons of Abraham. This is the area where Moses fled when he had to leave Egypt. He married a Midianite woman and took care of his father-in-law's sheep.

Exodus 2:15 and dwelt in the land of **M**
Exodus 2:16 Now the priest of **M** had seven daughters
Exodus 4:19 The LORD said unto Moses in **M**
Exodus 18:1 When Jethro, the priest of **M**

Midnight (MID night)
Twelve o'clock at night.

Exodus 11:4 About **m** I will go out into the midst of
Exodus 12:29 at **m** the LORD smote all the firstborn
Acts 16:25 And at **m** Paul and Silas prayed, and sang

Midwives (MID wighvz)
Plural for "midwife." A woman who helps a woman who is giving birth to a baby.

Exodus 1:15 king of Egypt spake to the Hebrew **m**
Exodus 1:17 But the **m** feared God, and did not as
Exodus 1:19 **m** said unto Pharaoh, Because the
Exodus 1:20 Therefore God dealt well with the **m**

Might (MIGHT)
1. Past tense of "may." Maybe possible, but not likely.

Psalm 119:11 that I ***m*** not sin against thee
Matthew 26:4 consulted that they ***m*** take Jesus
Mark 10:51 Lord, that I ***m*** receive my sight
Mark 11:18 and sought how they ***m*** destroy him
Luke 6:11 with another what they ***m*** do to Jesus
Luke 22:4 how he ***m*** betray him unto them
John 1:7 that all men through him ***m*** believe
John 3:17 that the world through him ***m*** be saved
John 5:40 not come to me, that ye ***m*** have life
John 10:10 I am come that they ***m*** have life

2. Power, strength, force.

Deuteronomy 6:5 all thy soul, and with all thy ***m***

Mighty (MIGH tee)
Having or showing much power or strength.

Exodus 10:19 The LORD turned a ***m*** strong west wind
Psalm 150:2 Praise him for his ***m*** acts
Acts 2:2 sound from heaven as of a rushing ***m*** wind

Milk (MILK)
A healthy whitish liquid obtained from animals and humans. By-products such as cheese and butter are made from the milk. The use of the term "milk" in the Old Testament often meant blessing or abundance.

Exodus 3:8 unto a land flowing with ***m*** and honey
Exodus 13:5 a land flowing with ***m*** and honey
Exodus 33:3 unto a land flowing with ***m*** and honey

Mind (MIGHND)
The part of a person that remembers things. Also, the part of a person that thinks over things, has understanding, cares, and listens carefully.

Matthew 22:37 all thy soul, and with all thy m
Mark 12:30 all thy soul, and with all thy m
Luke 10:27 all thy strength, and with all thy ***m***

Minister (MIHN ih stuhr)
One who helps or serves others, like a pastor or deacon; to help or serve.

Exodus 24:13 Moses rose up, and his ***m*** Joshua
Exodus 28:35 it shall be upon Aaron to ***m***

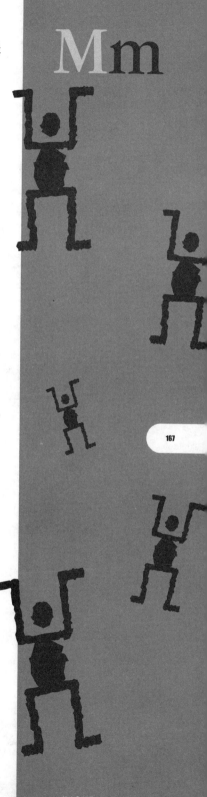

Mm

167

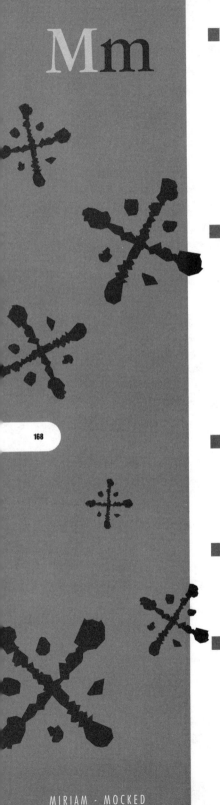

Mm

■ Miriam (MIHR ih uhm)

The name may mean "bitter," "God's gift," or "beloved." She was Moses' older sister. Her parents were Jochobed and Amram. She help save Moses from death when he was an infant. Miriam left Egypt with her brothers, Moses and Aaron, and rejoiced with the Israelites after they crossed the Red Sea on dry land.

Exodus 15:20 And ***M*** the prophetess, the sister of
Exodus 15:21 ***M*** answered them, Sing ye to the LORD
Numbers 12:1 ***M*** and Aaron spake against Moses
Numbers 12:10 ***M*** became leprous, white as snow

■ Moab (MOH ab)

The strip of land on the east side of the Dead Sea (see map on page 337). The area averages 3300 feet above sea level. The Arnon River, which runs east to west, almost divides the land in half. The river flows through a deep canyon into the Dead Sea. Lot's grandson was named Moab, and he settled in this area. His descendants were the Moabites. Ruth was from Moab. King David, Ruth's great grandson, sent his family to Moab for protection.

Ruth 1:1 went to sojourn in the country of ***M***
Ruth 1:6 she might return from the country of ***M***

■ Moabitess (MOH uh bight ess)

A woman or girl who lives in, or is from Moab. Ruth was a Moabitess.

Ruth 1:22 Naomi returned, and Ruth the ***M***
Ruth 2:2 Ruth the ***M*** said unto Naomi, Let me now go
Ruth 2:21 And Ruth the ***M*** said, He said unto me

■ Mock (MAHK)

To make fun of, to laugh at, to tease.

Proverbs 14:9 Fools make a ***m*** at sin
Matthew 20:19 deliver him to the Gentiles to ***m***
Mark 10:34 they shall ***m*** him, and shall scourge

■ Mocked (MAHKT)

Past tense of "mock."

Matthew 27:29 and ***m*** him, saying, "Hail, King of
Matthew 27:31 And after that they had ***m*** him
Mark 15:20 And when they had ***m*** him, they
Luke 22:63 the men that held Jesus ***m*** him
Luke 23:11 ***m*** him, and arrayed him in a
Luke 23:36 soldiers also ***m*** him, coming to him
Galatians 6:7 Be not deceived; God is not ***m***

Mocker (MAHK uhr)
One who makes fun of or laughs at another.

Proverbs 20:1 Wine is a *m*, strong drink is raging

Money (MUHN ee)
Gold, silver, or copper coins used to purchase goods. Also, paper money which is used in place of the coins. In Old Testament times, a system of weights was used to determine the value of goods or wages. During New Testament times, coins were in use.

Matthew 22:19 Show me the tribute *m*
Matthew 28:15 So they took the *m*, and did as they
Mark 14:11 were glad, and promised to give him *m*
John 2:14 doves, and the changers of *m* sitting
Acts 4:37 sold it, and brought the *m*, and laid it
1 Timothy 6:10 the love of *m* is the root of all evil

Moneychangers (MON ee chain jers)
Men who exchanged foreign money for the special coins that had to be used to pay the Temple tax. The moneychangers charged a fee for the exchange and often required a large fee. The moneychangers were Jews and were hated by other Jews because of their greed.

Matthew 21:12 and overthrew the tables of the m
Mark 11:15 and overthrew the tables of the m

Moon (MOON)
The light which God put in the night sky. The moon reflects light from the sun. As the moon orbits around the earth, the different phases control the tides and other things on earth.

Psalm 8:3 work of thy fingers, the *m* and the stars
Psalm 104:19 He appointed the *m* for seasons
Psalm 136:9 The *m* and stars to rule by night

Mordecai (MAWR duh kigh)
The name means "little man." He was an older cousin of Esther. He raised her after her parents died. After Esther became queen, a man named Haman was promoted in the king's court. All the people bowed to Haman, but Mordecai refused to bow to anyone because he was a Jew. Haman tried to destroy all the Jews. Much later, Mordecai became an official in the Persian court after he heard of the plot to kill all the Jews. He told Esther, the queen, about it. Because of her willingness to help, the Jews were saved.

Esther 2:5 a certain Jew, whose name was *M*

Mm

Moneychangers

Mm

Esther 2:11 *M* walked every day before the court
Esther 3:2 But *M* bowed not, nor did him reverence
Esther 3:5 when Haman saw that *M* bowed not
Esther 4:1 *M* rent his clothes, and put on sackcloth
Esther 10:3 For *M* the Jew was next unto King

■ Morning (MAWR neeng)
The time of day from just before dawn to twelve o'clock noon.

Genesis 1:5 evening and the *m* were the first day
Genesis 1:8 evening and the *m* were the second day
Genesis 1:13 evening and the *m* were the third day
Genesis 1:19 evening and the *m* were the fourth day
Genesis 1:23 evening and the *m* were the fifth day
Genesis 1:31 evening and the *m* were the sixth day
Psalm 30:5 but joy cometh in the *m*
Psalm 55:17 Evening, and *m*, and at noon, will I pray
Mark 16:2 early in the *m* the first day of the week
Luke 24:1 very early in the *m*, they came to the
John 21:4 But when the *m* was now come, Jesus stood

■ Moses (MOH ziss)
The name means "drawn out of the water." Moses was the leader who brought the Israelites out of Egyptian slavery and bondage. He was an Israelite born in Egypt, but he was raised by Pharaoh's daughter in the palace. He had an older sister, Miriam, and a brother, Aaron. Moses killed an Egyptian who was abusing an Hebrew slave. Then Moses fled to the land of Midian where he lived for 40 years before God called him to return to Egypt to free the Israelites. God gave Moses the Ten Commandments, as well as other laws for the people to obey. Moses led the people to the edge of the Promised Land, but he was not able to enter because he had disobeyed God. He is credited with writing the five books of Law: Genesis, Exodus, Leviticus, Numbers, and Deuteronomy.

Exodus 2:10 And she called his name *M*: and she
Exodus 2:15 But *M* fled from the face of Pharaoh
Exodus 3:1 Now *M* kept the flock of Jethro
Exodus 3:3 *M* said, I will now turn aside, and see
Exodus 3:6 *M* hid his face; for he was afraid
Exodus 4:19 LORD said unto *M* in Midian, Go, return
Exodus 10:12 LORD said unto *M*, Stretch out thine
Deuteronomy 34:5 *M* the servant of the LORD died there
Deuteronomy 34:7 *M* was an hundred and twenty years old
Joshua 1:1 after the death of *M* the servant of the

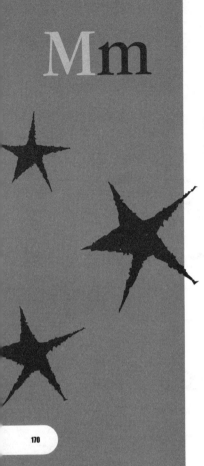

Moses

Most (MOHST)

The majority; the greatest. "Most" is often used as part of the name that describes God. Most, when referring to God, means divine, holy, or godly.

Genesis 14:20 blessed be the **m** high God, which
Psalm 9:2 praise to thy name, O thou **m** High
Psalm 47:2 How awesome is the LORD **M** High (NIV)
Mark 5:7 Jesus, thou Son of the **m** high God
Luke 8:28 Jesus, thou Son of God **m** high

Mother (MUTH uhr)

The female parent who cares for a child after she gives birth.

Exodus 20:12 Honor thy father and thy **m**
Leviticus 19:3 Each of you must respect his **m** and (NIV)
Deuteronomy 5:16 Honor thy father and thy **m**
Proverbs 1:8 and forsake not the law of thy **m**
Proverbs 6:20 and forsake not the law of thy **m**
Proverbs 15:20 a foolish man despiseth his **m**
Matthew 2:11 saw the young child with Mary his **m**
Luke 2:34 and said unto Mary his **m**
Luke 2:43 and Joseph and his **m** knew not of it
Luke 2:48 and his **m** said unto him, Son, why
John 2:1 and the **m** of Jesus was there
John 2:3 the **m** of Jesus saith unto him
John 2:5 His **m** saith unto the servants
John 6:42 of Joseph, whose father and **m** we know
Ephesians 6:2 Honor thy father and **m**

Mount (MOWNT)

A high hill. Also, mountain. Palestine and the land around it has many hills and mountains. Some are about 1630 feet above sea level while one mountain soars to 9,230 feet high. Mountains were important to help people defend themselves, to go as a place of safety, and especially to worship. Several places in the Bible tell that Jesus went up to a mountain to pray.

Exodus 18:5 where he encamped at the **m** of God
Exodus 34:4 and went up unto **m** Sinai
1 Kings 18:19 gather to me all Israel unto **m** Carmel
1 Kings 18:20 the prophets together unto **m** Carmel
1 Kings 19:8 forty nights unto Horeb the **m** of God
1 Kings 19:11 stand upon the **m** before the LORD
Matthew 24:3 And as he sat upon the **m** of Olives
Mark 14:26 they went out into the **m** of Olives
Luke 19:29 at the **m** called the **m** of Olives
John 8:1 Jesus went unto the **m** of Olives

171

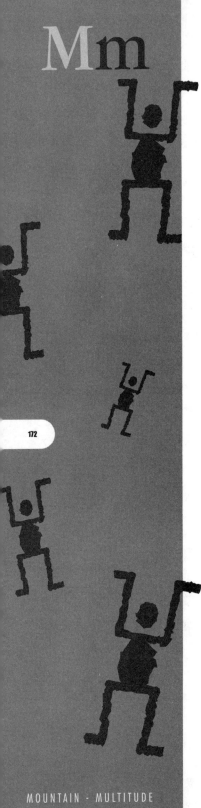

Mm

Mountain (MOWN tuhn)
A very high hill. See "Mount."

Matthew 14:23 he went up into a **m** apart to pray
Matthew 28:16 into Galilee, into a **m** where Jesus
Mark 6:46 he departed into a **m** to pray
John 6:3 And Jesus went up into a **m**

Mountains (MOWN tuhnz)
Plural for "mountain."

Genesis 7:20 and the **m** were covered
Genesis 8:4 upon the **m** of Ararat

Mourn (MAWRN)
To feel or show sorrow, pain, or grief, such as at the death of a loved one; to cry or weep.

Ecclesiastes 3:4 a time to **m**, and a time to dance
Matthew 5:4 blessed are they that **m**: for they

Mouth (MOWTH)
An opening. The part of the head used to eat food, drink liquids, and speak.

Psalm 19:14 Let the words of my **m**, and the
Psalm 49:3 My **m** shall speak of wisdom
Psalm 141:3 Set a guard over my **m**, O LORD (NIV)
Psalm 145:21 My **m** shall speak the praise of
Proverbs 18:7 A fool's **m** is his destruction
Proverbs 21:23 Whoso keepeth his **m** and his
Matthew 4:4 proceedeth out of the **m** of God
James 3:10 Out of the same **m** proceedeth blessing

Moved (MOOVD)
Past tense of "move." To inspire, or stir one's feelings; to shift or change.

Genesis 1:2 the spirit of God **m** upon the face of
Matthew 9:36 he was **m** with compassion on them
Matthew 14:14 and was **m** with compassion toward them
Mark 1:41 And Jesus, **m** with compassion, put forth
Mark 6:34 and was **m** with compassion toward them
Mark 15:11 the chief priests **m** the people, that he

Multitude (MUHL tih tood)
Many people or things; a great crowd.

Psalm 51:1 un*to the **m** of thy tender mercies
Matthew 13:36 Then Jesus sent the **m** away
Matthew 14:15 Send the **m** away, that they may
Matthew 15:32 I have compassion on the **m**
Matthew 20:29 from Jericho, a great **m** followed
Matthew 26:47 came, and with him a great **m**
Mark 3:7 and a great **m** from Galilee followed

172

Mark 8:2 I have compassion on the **m**
Mark 15:8 And the **m** crying aloud began to
Luke 3:7 Then he said to the **m** that came
Luke 5:6 they inclosed a great **m** of fishes
Luke 6:19 And the whole **m** sought to touch him
John 6:2 **m** followed him, because they saw

■ Murmured (MEHR mehrd)

Past tense of "murmur." To complain, grumble; speak with unhappiness; whisper or speak in a low voice.

Exodus 15:24 And the people **m** against Moses
Luke 5:30 and Pharisees **m** against his disciples
Luke 15:2 Pharisees and scribes **m**, saying, This
Luke 19:7 when they saw it, they all **m**, saying
John 6:41 The Jews then **m** against him

■ Must (MUHST)

A requirement.

Proverbs 18:24 man that hath friends **m** show
Matthew 16:21 how that he **m** go unto Jerusalem
Mark 9:12 son of man, that he **m** suffer many things
Luke 2:49 that I **m** be about my Father's business
Luke 4:43 I **m** preach the kingdom of God
Luke 9:22 The Son of man **m** suffer many things
John 3:7 I said unto thee, Ye **m** be born again
John 4:24 **m** worship him in spirit and in truth
John 20:9 that he **m** rise again from the dead

■ Mustard (MUHS tuhrd)

A fast growing plant whose seeds are spicy. It was once thought that its seeds were the smallest in the world. Because the plant grows fast, Jesus used this plant in a parable to tell that the kingdom of God would grow fast.

Matthew 17:20 have faith as a grain of **m** seed
Luke 17:6 If ye had faith as a grain of **m** seed

■ Myrrh (MUHR)

A gum (yellowish-brown resin) that comes from the stems and trunks of many plants. Myrrh has a pleasant odor and was used in perfumes, oils used for anointing, to deodorize clothing, and to embalm bodies after death. The Wise Men gave a gift of myrrh to Jesus when they found him.

Genesis 37:25 **m**, going to carry it down to Egypt
Matthew 2:11 gifts; gold, and frankincense, and **m**
Mark 15:23 wine mingled with **m**: but he received it not
John 19:39 brought a mixture of **m** and aloes

Myself (MIGH sehlf)
My own self; me.

Psalm 101:2 I will behave *m* wisely in a perfect way
Psalm 119:16 I will delight *m* in thy statutes
Luke 24:39 my hands and my feet, that it is *m*
John 14:3 I will come again, and receive you unto *m*

Naaman (NAY muhn)
The name means "pleasantness." A Syrian general who had leprosy. His wife's Hebrew maid told them about the prophet, Elisha, who had the ability to heal. After doing as Elisha directed, Naaman was healed of his leprosy. Then he claimed that he trusted in the God of Israel.

2 Kings 5:1 **N**, captain of the host of the king
2 Kings 5:9 So **N** came with his horses and
2 Kings 5:11 But **N** was wroth, and went away

Naboth (NAY bahth)
The name may mean "sprout." He owned a vineyard next to the palace of King Ahab. The king wanted the vineyard so he could grow vegetables but Naboth refused to sell it. The wife of Ahab, Jezebel, plotted to have Naboth killed, then she had Ahab go and claim the vineyard.

1 Kings 21:1 **N** the Jezreelite had a vineyard
1 Kings 21:2 And Ahab spake unto **N**, saying
1 Kings 21:9 set **N** on high among the people
1 Kings 21:13 **N** did blaspheme God and the king
1 Kings 21:15 Jezebel heard that **N** was stoned
1 Kings 21:16 When Ahab heard that **N** was dead

Nahum, Book of (NAY huhm)
The name means "comfort, encourage." This book is the seventh in the division, Minor Prophets, in the Old Testament. The message of Nahum foretold the destruction of Nineveh, the capital of Assyria. For over one hundred years, Israel and Judah had been paying heavily for Assyria to protect them. Nahum's message gave them hope that they would be delivered.

Naked (NAY kid)
Without any clothes; nude.

Genesis 2:25 And they were both *n*, the man
Genesis 3:7 and they knew that they were *n*
Genesis 3:10 I was afraid, because I was *n*
Genesis 3:11 Who told thee that thou was *n*
Matthew 25:36 *N*, and ye clothed me: I was
Matthew 25:38 or *n*, and clothed thee
Matthew 25:43 *n*, and ye clothed me not
Matthew 25:44 or a stranger, or *n*, or sick

■ Name (NAYM)

A person's reputation, fame, or standing; what a person is called.

Genesis 3:20 Adam called his wife's *n* Eve
Exodus 2:10 And she called his *n* Moses
Exodus 16:31 Israel called the *n* thereof Manna
Exodus 20:7 shalt not take the *n* of the LORD
Psalm 9:2 I will sing praise to thy *n*
Psalm 34:3 and let us exalt his *n* together
Psalm 96:8 the LORD the glory due unto his *n*
Proverbs 22:1 A good *n* is rather to be chosen
Ecclesiastes 7:1 A good *n* is better than precious
Isaiah 7:14 a son, and shall call his *n* Immanuel
Matthew 1:21 thou shalt call his *n* JESUS
Matthew 1:25 and he called his *n* JESUS
Matthew 6:9 art in heaven, Hallowed be thy *n*
Matthew 23:39 Blessed is he that cometh in the *n*
Luke 1:31 son, and shalt call his *n* JESUS
Luke 11:2 art in heaven, Hallowed be thy *n*
John 3:18 hath not believed in the *n* of the
John 14:13 Whatsoever ye shall ask in my *n*
Philippians 2:10 at the *n* of Jesus every knee

■ Named (NAYMD)

Past tense of "name."

Matthew 9:9 he saw a man, *n* Matthew, sitting
Mark 14:32 to a place which was *n* Gethsemane
Mark 15:7 there was one *n* Barabbas, which
Luke 5:27 and saw a publican, *n* Levi, sitting
Luke 6:14 Simon, (whom he also *n* Peter), and
Luke 10:38 a certain woman *n* Martha received
Luke 19:2 behold, there was a man *n* Zaccheus
John 3:1 man of the Pharisees, *n* Nicodemus

■ Naomi (nay OH mih)

The name means "my pleasantness." She was the wife of Elimelech, and they lived in Bethlehem of Judah. Elimelech took her and their two sons to Moab during a famine in Judah. While there, Elimelech died, the two sons married women from Moab, and then the

Nn

sons died. Naomi decided to return to Bethlehem and her two daughters-in-law, Ruth and Orpah, said they would go, too. Naomi encouraged them to stay with their own families. Orpah returned to her family, but Ruth insisted on going with Naomi. Ruth helped find food for herself and Naomi, and finally married a relative of Elimelech.

Ruth 1:2 and the name of his wife **N**
Ruth 1:20 Call me not **N**, call me Mara
Ruth 2:1 **N** had a kinsman of her husband's
Ruth 2:22 **N** said unto Ruth her daughter-in-law
Ruth 4:14 And the women said unto **N**

■ Napkin (NAP kuhn)
A small piece of cloth used as a table napkin or handkerchief. This cloth might be used to wipe sweat from the face and neck, cover the face of the dead, or wrap money in to be buried.

John 11:44 face was bound about with a **n**
John 20:7 the **n**, that was about his head

■ Nathan (NAY thuhn)
The name means "gift." He was a prophet during the time of King David. Sometimes he had to give a message to the king even when the king didn't want to hear it.

2 Samuel 7:2 the king said unto **N** the prophet
2 Samuel 7:4 the word of the LORD came unto **N**
2 Samuel 12:1 The LORD sent **N** unto David

■ Nathanael (nuh THAN ay uhl)
The name means "giver of God." He was from Cana of Galilee. Philip brought him to Jesus and he became one of the twelve disciples of Jesus. He may be the same person as Bartholomew.

John 1:45 Philip findeth **N**, and saith unto him
John 1:47 Jesus saw **N** coming to him, and
John 1:48 **N** saith unto him, Whence knowest
John 1:49 **N** answered and saith unto him

■ Nation (NAY shun)
A country; a government within a defined territory; a race of people.

Genesis 12:2 I will make of thee a great **n**
Psalm 33:12 Blessed is the **n** whose God is the LORD

■ Nations (NAY shuhnz)
Plural of "nation."

Genesis 17:4 thou shalt be a father of many **n**

Psalm 72:11 all **n** shall serve him
Psalm 72:17 all **n** shall call him blessed
Psalm 113:4 The LORD is exalted over all the **n** (NIV)
Matthew 28:19 Go ye therefore, and teach all **n**
Luke 24:47 be preached in his name among all **n**

Naughty (NAW tee)
Bad, bratty; acting in a way that is not right.

Proverbs 6:12 A **n** person, a wicked man, walketh
Proverbs 17:4 a liar giveth ear to a **n** tongue

Nazarene (NAZ uh reen)
A person born and raised in Nazareth; one who followed Jesus of Nazareth.

Matthew 2:23 He shall be called a **N**

Nazareth (NAZ uh reth)
The name means "branch." The town in Galilee located about 70 miles north of Jerusalem and about 15 miles west of the Sea of Galilee, in the hill country (see map on page 340). Mary and Joseph both lived in Nazareth, and Jesus grew up in Nazareth. At that time, it was a small village. It wasn't well known until Jesus began His ministry.

Matthew 2:23 came and dwelt in a city called **N**
Matthew 21:11 This is Jesus the prophet of **N** of
Mark 1:9 that Jesus came from **N** of Galilee
Mark 16:6 Ye seek Jesus of **N**, which was crucified
Luke 1:26 unto a city of Galilee, named **N**
Luke 24:19 said unto him, Concerning Jesus of **N**
John 19:19 JESUS OF **N** THE KING OF THE JEWS
Acts 3:6 In the name of Jesus Christ of **N**

Nebuchadnezzar (NEB yoo kad NEZ uhr)
The name means "Nabu protects." He was the king of Babylon who conquered Judah and led many Israelites into captivity in Babylon. It was Nebuchadnezzar who ordered Shadrach, Meshach, and Abednego into the fiery furnace.

2 Kings 24:1 **N** king of Babylon came up, and
Daniel 1:1 came **N** king of Babylon unto Jerusalem
Daniel 3:13 Then **N** in his rage and fury
Daniel 3:26 Then **N** came near to the mouth of
Daniel 3:28 **N** spake, and said, Blessed be the God

Nebuchadrezzar (NEB yoo kad DREZ uhr)
Another form of the name "Nebuchadnezzar," used in the book of Jeremiah. Nebuchadnezzar is used more often.

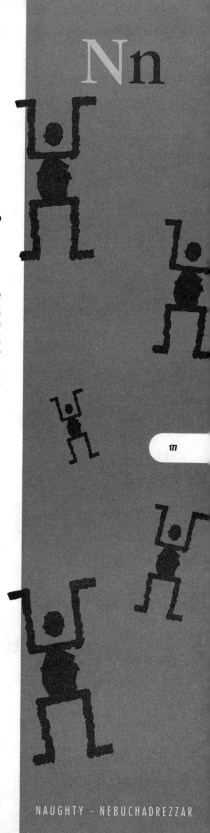

177

Nn

Jeremiah 21:2 for **N** of Babylon maketh war against
Jeremiah 52:29 year of **N** he carried away captives

◾ Necessity (nih SESS ih tee)
A basic need, a requirement.

Luke 23:17 of **n** he must release one unto them
2 Corinthians 9:7 give; not grudgingly, or of **n**:

◾ Need (NEED)
Require, want; lacking something that is necessary.

Matthew 3:14 I have **n** to be baptized of thee
Matthew 6:8 knoweth what things ye have **n** of
Matthew 9:12 They that be whole **n** not a physician
Matthew 21:3 The Lord hath **n** of them
Mark 2:17 that are whole have no **n** of the physician
Luke 5:31 They that are whole **n** not a physician
Luke 19:31 Because the Lord hath **n** of him
Luke 22:71 said, What **n** we any further witness

◾ Needful (NEED fuhl)
Necessary.

Luke 10:42 one thing is **n**: and Mary hath chosen

◾ Needy (NEED ee)
The very poor.

Psalm 72:12 he shall deliver the **n** when he crieth
Psalm 72:13 He shall spare the poor and **n**
Psalm 72:13 shall save the souls of the **n**

◾ Neglect (nih GLEKT)
Abandon, forget, overlook; to not give proper time or attention to.

1 Timothy 4:14 **N** not the gift that is in thee
Hebrews 2:3 we escape, if we **n** so great salvation

◾ Nehemiah (NEE huh MIGH uh)
The name means "Yah comforts or encourages." He was a Jew who was cupbearer to King Artaxerxes I of Persia. The cupbearer was the one who tasted all food and drink before the king ate any of it. The king gave Nehemiah permission to return to Jerusalem to help rebuild the walls around the city. He was a godly leader and hard worker. Because of his leadership, the wall was completed in fifty-two days.

Nehemiah 1:1 The words of **N** the son of

Nehemiah, Book of (NEE huh MIGH uh)

The book is the eleventh book in the division, History, in the Old Testament. The writer was probably Nehemiah, but could have been Ezra. The book tells about Nehemiah's return to Jerusalem and how he directed the rebuilding of the walls of the city. He knew how to encourage the workers, and they rebuilt the wall and made the city secure in only fifty-two days. The people asked Ezra to read the law of Moses. When Ezra finished reading, they celebrated the Feast of Tabernacles, a Jewish feast celebrating the ingathering of crops. They confessed their wrongs and worshiped God. They wanted to be obedient to Him and His laws.

Neighbor (NAY buhr)

Also spelled "neighbour." The person living next door or across the street; another human being. The Bible mentions in several places how we are to treat our neighbor. And Jesus said we are to love our neighbor as we love ourselves.

Exodus 20:16 not bear false witness against thy *n*
Leviticus 19:18 thou shalt love thy *n* as thyself
Proverbs 3:29 Do not plot harm against your *n* (NIV)
Matthew 5:43 Thou shalt love thy *n*, and hate thine
Matthew 19:19 Thou shalt love thy *n* as thyself
Mark 12:31 Thou shalt love thy *n* as thyself
Luke 10:27 and thy *n* as thyself
Luke 10:29 said unto Jesus, And who is my *n*
Luke 10:36 thinkest thou, was *n* unto him
Galatians 5:14 Thou shalt love thy *n* as thyself
Ephesians 4:25 speak every man truth with his *n*

Neighbors (NAY buhrz)

Plural of "neighbor."

Ruth 4:17 And the women her *n* gave it a name
Luke 15:6 he calleth together his friends and *n*
Luke 15:6 she calleth her friends and her *n*

Neither (NEE thur)

"Not the one and not the other."

Exodus 20:23 *n* shall ye make unto you gods of
Psalm 121:4 keepeth Israel shall *n* slumber nor sleep
Matthew 5:15 *N* do men light a candle, and put it
Matthew 6:15 men their trespasses, *n* will your Father
Mark 11:26 ye do not forgive, *n* will your Father
Luke 11:33 *n* under a bushel, but on a candlestick
John 14:27 heart be troubled, *n* let it be afraid

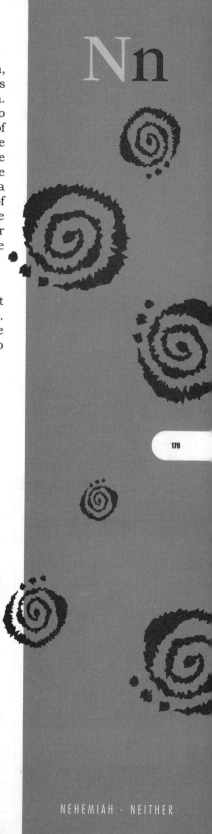

Nn

179

Nn

Never (NEH vuhr)
At no time, not ever.

Psalm 31:1 I put my trust; let me *n* be ashamed
Psalm 55:22 he will *n* let the righteous fall (NIV)
Psalm 119:93 I will *n* forget thy precepts
Mark 11:2 a colt tied, whereon *n* man sat
Luke 19:30 a colt tied, whereon yet *n* man sat
John 4:14 water that I shall give him shall *n* thirst
John 7:46 *N* man spake like this man
John 11:26 liveth and believeth in me shall *n* die
1 Corinthians 13:8 Love *n* fails (NIV)

Nevertheless (NEH vuhr thuh LESS)
Even so; however.

Matthew 26:39 *n* not as I will, but as thou wilt
Mark 14:36 *n* not what I will, but what thou wilt
Luke 5:5 *n* at thy word, I will let down the net
Luke 22:42 *n* not my will, but thine, be done

Nicodemus (NIK uh DEE muhs)
The name means "innocent of blood." He was a Pharisee, a member of the Jewish Sanhedrin or ruling council. He was also a teacher and had much knowledge about the Hebrew scriptures. He met Jesus at night to ask Him about eternal life. Jesus told him he needed to be born again. He may have been a secret follower of Jesus. He did speak out for Jesus and brought spices to help bury Jesus after He was crucified.

John 3:1 Pharisees, named *N*, a ruler of the Jews
John 3:4 *N* saith unto him, How can a man be born
John 3:9 *N* answered and said unto him, How can
John 7:50 *N* saith unto them (he that came to Jesus
John 19:39 And there came also *N*, which at the

Nigh (NIGH)
Near.

Psalm 34:18 The LORD is *n* unto them that
Psalm 145:18 The LORD is *n* unto all them that
Mark 2:4 could not come *n* unto him for the press
Luke 18:35 as he was come *n* unto Jericho
John 19:20 Jesus was crucified was *n* to the city
John 19:42 for the sepulcher was *n* at hand

Night (NIGHT)
Evening. The darkness between sunset and sunrise.

Genesis 1:5 Day, and the darkness he called *N*
Genesis 1:16 the lesser light to rule the *n*

Nicodemus

180

Psalm 1:2 his law doth he meditate day and **n**
Psalm 136:9 The moon and stars to rule by **n**
Matthew 26:34 this **n**, before the cock crow,
Luke 2:8 keeping watch over their flock by **n**
John 3:2 The same came to Jesus by **n**, and said
John 21:3 and that **n** they caught nothing

Nights (NIGHTS)
Plural of "night."

Genesis 7:12 upon the earth forty days and forty **n**
Genesis 24:18 in the mount forty days and forty **n**
1 Kings 19:8 of that meat forty days and forty **n**
Jonah 1:17 belly of the fish three days and three **n**
Matthew 4:2 had fasted forty days and forty **n**

Nine (NIGHN)
One less than ten.

Genesis 5:5 that Adam lived were **n** hundred and
Genesis 9:29 of Noah were **n** hundred and fifty
Matthew 18:12 leave the ninety and **n**, and
Luke 15:4 leave the ninety and **n** in the
Luke 17:17 ten cleansed? but where are the **n**

Nineveh (NIN uh vuh)
The greatest capital of Assyria, and the last, before the city was destroyed by Babylon in 612 B.C. The city lay on the left bank of the Tigris River (see map on page 339). The area is not a part of northern Iraq. It was to Nineveh that God sent Jonah to warn them of the judgment God would send if they didn't repent. The people did repent and the city was spared.

Jonah 1:2 Arise, go to **N**, that great city
Jonah 3:2 Arise, go unto **N**, that great city
Jonah 3:3 Now **N** was an exceeding great city
Jonah 3:5 So the people of **N** believed God

Ninth (NIGHNTH)
Number nine in a series. In biblical times, the people noted the position of the sun in the sky to mark the segments of a day. A day began in the early morning as the sun rose and ended at sunset. So, noon (when the sun was overhead) was the sixth hour. The ninth hour would be at three o'clock in the afternoon.

Matthew 27:45 over all the land unto the **n** hour
Matthew 27:46 About the **n** hour Jesus cried with
Mark 15:33 over the whole land until the **n** hour
Mark 15:34 And at the **n** hour Jesus cried with
Luke 23:44 over all the earth until the **n** hour

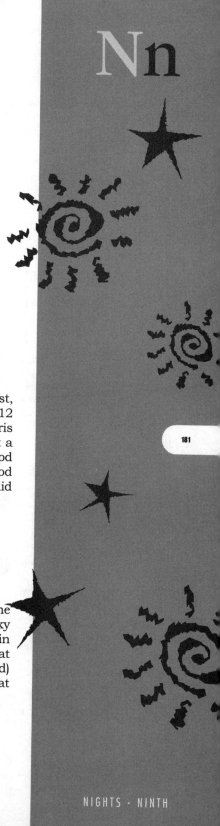

Nn

Noah

■ **Noah (NOH uh)**
The name is related to the word "rest." He was a "good and righteous man" and lived during a time of much evil doings by mankind. God directed him to build an ark with specific instructions on its size and how it was to be on the inside. Noah did as God said. Noah placed many animals in the ark, which God told him to do. Noah, his wife, his three sons and their wives, were the only people in the ark. Rain fell for "forty days and forty nights," flooding the entire earth. Noah and his family were in the ark for almost a year. Noah has been called the "only really good man of his times."

Genesis 6:8 **N** found grace in the eyes of the LORD
Genesis 6:9 **N** was a just man and perfect
Genesis 6:9 and **N** walked with God
Genesis 6:13 God said unto **N**, The end of all
Genesis 7:1 LORD said unto **N**, Come thou and all
Genesis 8:1 God remembered **N**, and every living
Genesis 8:20 And **N** builded an altar unto the LORD
Genesis 9:29 days of **N** were nine hundred and fifty

■ **Noise (NOYZ)**
A loud sound.

Psalm 66:1 Make a joyful **n** unto God, all ye
Psalm 100:1 Make a joyful **n** unto the LORD, all

■ **Noised (NOYZD)**
Past tense of "noise." To spread by telling; to make known.

Mark 2:1 it was **n** that he was in the house
Luke 1:65 these sayings were **n** abroad
Acts 2:6 this was **n** abroad, the multitude came

■ **Noon (NEWN)**
Twelve o'clock in the daytime.

1 Kings 18:26 of Baal from morning even until **n**
1 Kings 18:27 at **n**, that Elijah mocked them, and
Psalm 55:17 and morning, and at **n**, will I pray
Acts 22:6 was come nigh unto Damascus about **n**

■ **North (NORTH)**
Bible people determined directions by facing toward the sunrise (east). To the left was north, to the right was south, and behind was west, or where the sun set.

Genesis 28:14 the east, to the **n**, and to the south

Nothing (NUH thing)
None; not anything.

Matthew 17:20 and **n** shall be impossible unto you
Mark 15:5 But Jesus yet answered **n**
Luke 1:37 with God **n** shall be impossible

Numbers, Book of (NUHM buhrz)
The fourth book in the division, Law, in the Old Testament. Moses wrote this book, telling about the Israelites as they camped at Mount Sinai, wandered in the wilderness for forty years, and then stood in Moab east of the Jordan River ready to cross into the Promised Land. Moses had a census taken of the people (had them numbered), and this may be how the book got its name. Throughout this book, God is present in all that the Israelites were doing.

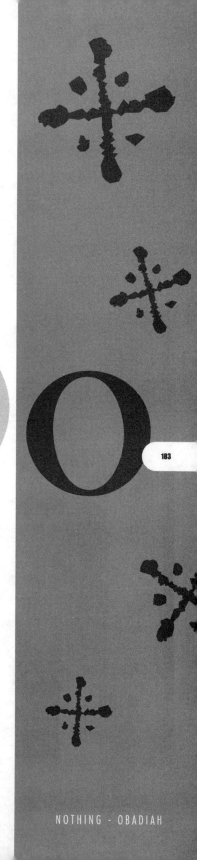

Oath (OHTH)
A promise, usually sworn with God's name. In biblical times, an oath was considered most serious. A person said he would do or not do something. Once a person gave an oath, he was required to fulfill it. An oath was like a legal document is for us today. A document is a written statement about a certain thing. Peter gave an oath when he denied Jesus the second time, but he also gave a curse with this oath. In this way, he was using an oath in a way that is not right.

Matthew 26:72 again he denied with an **o**, I

Obadiah (OH buh DIGH uh)
The name means "servant of Yahweh." Two of the many men with the name Obadiah are mentioned here.

1. The prophet whose book by his name is the shortest book of the Minor Prophets. Nothing is known about him.

Obadiah 1 The vision of **O**. Thus saith the LORD

2. This man was the governor of King Ahab's household. Although Ahab did not obey God, Obadiah was a faithful worshiper of the LORD. He saved one hundred of God's prophets from the terrible anger of Queen Jezebel.

Oo

1 Kings 18:3 Ahab called **O**, which was the
1 Kings 18:3 (Now **O** feared the LORD greatly

■ Obadiah, Book of (OH buh DIGH uh)
The fourth book in the division, Minor Prophets, in the Old Testament. Nothing is known about this prophet. He predicted judgement on the Edomites. Edom was the area south of the Dead Sea. These people were related to the Israelites, but they had not treated the Israelites very fairly. They had refused to help Judah and had even stolen things from Jerusalem. God vowed He would defeat them. Obadiah tried to show that God would care for His own.

■ Obed (OH bed)
The name means "serving." He was the son of Ruth and Boaz, and became the father of Jesse, and the grandfather of King David. Thus, Obed is an ancestor of Jesus.

Ruth 4:17 they called his name **O**
Ruth 4:21 Salmon begat Boaz, and Boaz begat **O**
Ruth 4:22 **O** begat Jesse, and Jesse begat David

■ Obedient (oh BEE dih uhnt)
Happy to obey; pleased to do what is right.

Exodus 24:7 hath said will we do, and be **o**

■ Obeisance (oh BEE uh sunce)
To bow one's face to the ground. This shows a willingness to obey and to show honor, respect, and worship.

Genesis 37:7 round about, and made **o** to my sheaf
Genesis 37:9 the eleven stars made **o** to me
Genesis 43:28 bowed down their heads, and made **o**

■ Obey (oh BAY)
To follow, mind, do as asked.

Matthew 8:27 even the winds and the sea **o** him
Mark 4:41 even the wind and the sea **o** him
Luke 8:25 winds and water, and they **o** him
Acts 5:29 we ought to **o** God rather than men
Ephesians 6:1 Children, **o** your parents in the Lord
Colossians 3:20 Children, **o** your parents in all things

■ Observe (ahb SURV)
To see or watch; mind or obey; celebrate, remember.

Exodus 12:17 ye shall **o** the feast of unleavened
Psalm 119:34 I shall **o** it with my whole heart
Matthew 28:20 Teaching them to **o** all things

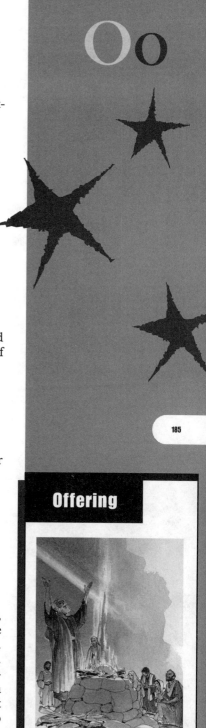

Obtain (ahb TAYN)
To buy, earn, get.

Matthew 5:7 merciful: for they shall *o* mercy

Offend (aw FEND)
To cause anger; to upset; to do something hurtful to another.

Matthew 18:6 whoso shall *o* one of these
Mark 9:42 whosoever shall *o* one of these

Offended (aw FEN did)
Past tense of "offend."

Proverbs 18:19 A brother *o* is harder to be won
Matthew 13:57 they were *o* in him. But Jesus said
Matthew 26:31 All ye shall be *o* because of me
Mark 6:3 And they were *o* at him
Mark 14:27 All ye shall be *o* because of me
Luke 7:23 whosoever shall not be *o* in me

Offer (AW fuhr)
To give or present a thing that could be received or turned down. To give something as a part of worship.

Psalm 50:14 *O* unto God thanksgiving
Luke 2:24 And to *o* a sacrifice according to
Luke 6:29 smiteth thee on the one cheek *o* also

Offering (AW fuhr eeng)
Something given as a part of worship; to offer something, such as a gift or money.

Genesis 4:3 fruit of the ground an *o* unto the LORD
Genesis 4:4 LORD had respect unto Abel and to his *o*
Genesis 4:5 unto Cain and to his *o* he had not respect
1 Kings 18:29 time of the *o* of the evening sacrifice
1 Kings 18:36 time of the *o* of the evening sacrifice
Luke 23:36 coming to him, and *o* him vinegar

Oil (OYL)
A greasy liquid obtained from plants, animals, or minerals. The main uses of oil are to grease something, as a fuel for motors, and as a food. During biblical times, most oil came from olives. Oil mixed with perfume was used as a cosmetic. Oil was used to prepare food, as a fuel in lamps, during the worship services, to anoint people for God's service, and as medicine to treat wounds.

1 Samuel 16:13 of *o*, and anointed him in the midst
1 Kings 17:12 and a little *o* in a cruse: and, behold

Offering

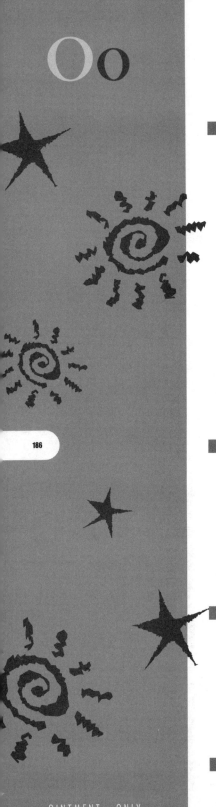

1 Kings 17:14 neither shall the cruse of *o* fail
1 Kings 17:16 neither did the cruse of *o* fail
Psalm 23:5 thou anointest my head with *o*
Luke 7:46 My head with *o* thou didst not anoint
Luke 10:34 wounds, pouring in *o* and wine

Ointment (OYNT mint)

A greasy medicine that is applied to the skin. In biblical times, ointments were used as cosmetics, medicines, and in worship services. Ointments were made from olive oil with perfume added. The ointment was stored in alabaster jars (see "Alabaster"). Some ointments were very costly, depending on what was added to the oil. Rubbing ointments on the skin helped protect the skin from the hot dry winds of the desert.

Matthew 26:7 alabaster box of very precious *o*
Matthew 26:9 this *o* might have been sold for
Mark 14:3 box of *o* of spikenard, very precious
Mark 14:4 Why was this waste of the *o* made
Luke 7:37 brought an alabaster box of *o*
Luke 7:46 woman hath anointed my feet with *o*
John 11:2 Mary, which anointed the Lord with *o*
John 12:3 took Mary a pound of *o* of spikenard
John 12:5 Why was not this *o* sold for three

Omer (OH muhr)

A measure used in biblical times that was slightly more than two quarts, or about two liters in today's metric measurements. This was the amount that God told Moses the people could collect each day when they gathered manna in the wilderness.

Exodus 16:16 an *o* for every man, according to
Exodus 16:32 Fill an *o* of it to be kept for your
Exodus 16:33 and put an *o* full of manna therein

Onesimus (oh NESS ih muhs)

The name may mean "profitable." He was a slave who had run away from his master, Philemon. Onesimus met Paul, learned about Jesus, and became a Christian. When he returned to his master, he took a letter from Paul, which is our book of Philemon in the New Testament.

Colossians 4:9 *O*, a faithful and beloved brother
Philemon 10 I beseech thee for my son *O*

Only (OWN lee)

Alone, mainly; better than the others.

Deuteronomy 8:3 man doth not live by bread **o**
Joshua 1:7 **O** be thou strong and very courageous
Psalm 62:2 He **o** is my rock and my salvation
Matthew 4:10 God, and him **o** shalt thou serve
Matthew 14:36 might **o** touch the hem of his garment
Mark 2:7 Who can forgive sins but God **o**
Mark 5:36 Be not afraid, **o** believe
Luke 4:8 God, and him **o** shalt thou serve
John 3:16 he gave his **o** begotten Son, that
John 3:18 in the name of the **o** begotten Son of God

■ Open (OH pin)
Not shut or closed; unlocked.

John 1:51 Hereafter ye shall see heaven **o**
Acts 16:27 seeing the prison doors **o**, he drew out
Revelation 3:20 any man hear my voice, and **o** the door

■ Opened (OH pind)
Past tense of "open."

Matthew 2:11 and when they had **o** their treasures
Matthew 7:7 Knock, and it shall be **o** unto you
Matthew 7:8 to him that knocketh, it shall be **o**
Mark 7:35 And straightway his ears were **o**
Luke 11:9 Knock, and it shall be **o** unto you
Luke 11:10 to him that knocketh it shall be **o**
Luke 24:31 their eyes were **o**, and they knew him

■ Opportunity (OP poor TU nih tee)
The right mixture of time, place and event; a chance or possibility.

Matthew 22:16 from that time he sought **o** to betray
Luke 22:6 promised, and sought **o** to betray him
Galatians 6:10 As we have therefore **o**, let us do

■ Oppressed (AW prehst)
Past tense of "oppress." To feel beaten down, used in an improper way, or weighted down with problems.

Isaiah 53:7 He was **o**, and he was afflicted

■ Ordained (awr DAYND)
Past tense of "ordain." To be ordained is to be set aside for a particular purpose for God; also, created.

Psalm 8:3 moon and the stars, which thou hast **o**
Mark 3:14 And he **o** twelve, that they should be
John 15:16 I have chosen you, and **o** you

■ Ordinance (AWR dih nins)
A law, command, or order given by God or His

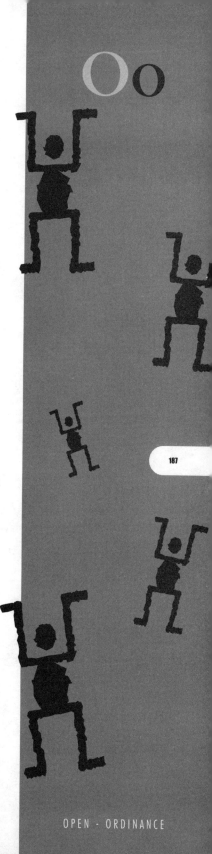

187

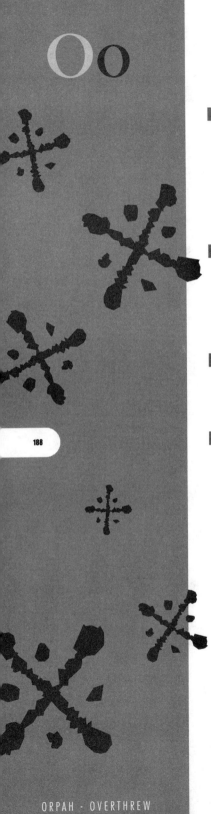

Oo

Son, Jesus, that his followers were to obey. Baptism and the Lord's Supper are two ordinances which Christians celebrate.

Exodus 12:43 This is the *o* of the passover

◼ Orpah (AWR puh)
The name may mean "neck," "girl with a full mane," or "rain cloud." She was one of Naomi's daughters-in-law from Moab and chose to stay with her family rather than go to a foreign country with Naomi.

Ruth 1:4 the name of the one was *O*
Ruth 1:14 and *O* kissed her mother-in-law

◼ Ought (AWT)
Should; anything.

Ruth 1:17 if *o* but death part thee and me
Mark 11:25 forgive, if ye have *o* against any
John 4:20 Jerusalem is the place where men *o* to
Acts 5:29 We *o* to obey God rather than men

◼ Overcome (oh vuhr KUM)
Gain the victory, win.

John 16:33 be of good cheer; I have *o* the world
Romans 12:21 Be not *o* of evil, but *o* evil with good

◼ Overthrew (oh vuhr THROO)
Past tense of "overthrow." To have been beaten, destroyed, or outnumbered.

Exodus 14:27 the LORD *o* the Egyptians in the midst
Matthew 21:12 and *o* the tables of the moneychangers
Mark 11:15 and *o* the tables of the moneychangers
John 2:15 out the changers' money, and *o* the tables

Pair (PAIR)

Two.

Luke 2:24 A **p** of turtledoves, or two young

Palace (PA luhs)

A place where the royal family, or the high priest lives; a grand house.

1 Kings 21:1 close to the **p** of Ahab king of (NIV)
Matthew 26:3 unto the **p** of the high priest, who
Matthew 26:58 afar off unto the high priest's **p**
Matthew 26:69 Now Peter sat without in the **p**
Mark 14:54 even unto the **p** of the high priest
Mark 14:66 as Peter was beneath in the **p**
John 18:15 and went with Jesus into the **p** of

Palestine (PAL uhs tighn)

The name comes from the name "Philistines." It is a strip of land between the Mediterranean Sea and just east of the Jordan River, from north of the Sea of Galilee to south of the Dead Sea (see map on page 340). Other biblical names for Palestine are "the Promised Land, Canaan, Israel, and Judah." Today the area is called the Holy Land. The land ranges in width from about 70 miles to 150 miles, and contains mountains, deserts, valleys, and seacoast.

(The only reference to Palestine in the King James Version of the Bible is Joel 3:4).

Palm (PAWLM)

1. A tree growing in the Jordan Valley whose fruit is the date. This tree is a tall tree with a tuft of feather-like leaves at the top. It has been grown for over 5,000 years. They grow best in areas where plenty of water can be found. The fruit of the date palm can be eaten fresh or made into cakes which are easy to carry. The palm branches were used to represent praise when Jesus rode into Jerusalem on the colt.

Exodus 15:27 water and threescore and ten **p** trees
John 12:13 Took branches of **p** trees, and went forth

2. The underside of the hand, from the wrist to the ends of the fingers.

John 18:22 struck Jesus with the **p** of his hand

Palm

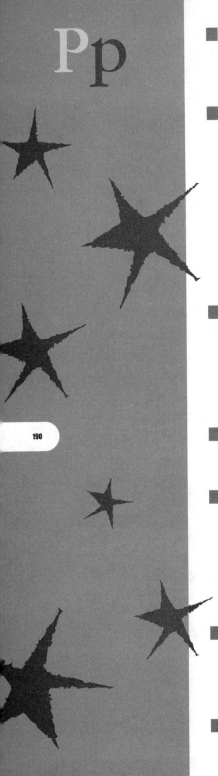

Pp

Palms (PAWLMZ)
Plural of "Palm (2)," the reference to the hand.

Matthew 26:67 smote him with the **p** of their hands
Mark 14:65 did strike him with the **p** of their hands

Palsy (PAWL zee)
The word for paralysis, a condition whereby a person has lost part or all of his ability to move or have feeling. Palsy might also refer to shaking that the person cannot control.

Matthew 8:6 servant lieth at home sick of the **p**
Matthew 9:2 brought to him a man sick of the **p**
Matthew 9:6 (then saith he to the sick of the **p**)
Mark 2:4 the bed wherein the sick of the **p** lay
Mark 2:5 he said unto the sick of the **p**
Luke 5:18 a bed a man which was taken with a **p**
Luke 5:24 (he said unto the sick of the **p**)

Parable (PAIR uh buhl)
A story that has two meanings; also a story that compares one thing with another. Jesus used the parables to teach his listeners things about daily life as well as things about heaven.

Mark 4:34 But without a **p** spake he not unto
Luke 15:3 he spake this **p** unto them, saying

Parables (PAIR uh buhlz)
Plural of "parable."

Mark 4:33 with many such **p** spake he the word

Paradise (PAIR uh dighz)
An old Persian word meaning "enclosure" or "wooded park." The word gradually came to mean the same as heaven because it was thought heaven was like the Garden of Eden. Paradise refers to a place where believers in God live forever.

Luke 23:43 Today thou shalt be with me in **p**

Pardon (PAR duhn)
To forgive a wrong; to cover or pass over a wrong.

Psalm 25:11 O LORD, **p** mine iniquity; for it is great
Isaiah 55:7 to our God, for he will abundantly **p**

Parents (PAIR uhnts)
Plural of "parent." A child's mother and father; the guardians who care for a child.

Luke 2:27 when the **p** brought in the child Jesus

Luke 2:41 Now his **p** went up to Jerusalem every year
Ephesians 6:1 Children, obey your **p** in the Lord
Colossians 3:20 Children, obey your **p** in all things

■ Part (PART)

Three definitions will be included with this word.
1. A piece or section of a thing.

Mark 4:38 he was in the hinder **p** of the ship
Luke 10:42 Mary hath chosen that good **p**
Acts 1:8 unto the uttermost **p** of the earth

2. To leave or go away from someone; to separate from.

Ruth 1:17 if ought but death **p** thee and me

3. To make more parts out of one.

Psalm 22:18 They **p** my garments among them
John 19:33 made four **p**, to every soldier a **p**

■ Parted (PAR tihd)
"Past tense of "Part, 3."

Matthew 27:35 crucified him, and **p** his garments
Mark 15:24 crucified him, they **p** his garments
Luke 23:34 And they **p** his raiment, and cast lots
John 19:24 They **p** my raiment among them

■ Pass (PASS)
Go by, leave, move away; to happen.

Genesis 7:10 And it came to **p** after seven days
Exodus 12:13 when I see the blood, I will **p** over
Matthew 24:35 Heaven and earth shall **p** away
Matthew 24:35 but my words will not **p** away
Matthew 26:39 be possible, let this cup **p** from me
Mark 4:35 Let us **p** over unto the other side
Mark 13:31 Heaven and earth shall **p** away
Mark 13:31 but my words shall not **p** away
Luke 2:1 And it came to **p** in those days
Luke 2:15 And it came to **p**, as the angels
Luke 2:15 see this thing which is come to **p**
Luke 21:33 Heaven and earth shall **p** away
Luke 21:33 but my words shall not **p** away

■ Passed (PAST)
Past tense of "pass."

Exodus 12:27 Passover, who **p** over the houses
Matthew 20:30 when they heard that Jesus **p** by
Mark 2:14 as he **p** by, he saw Levi the son of
Luke 10:31 saw him, he **p** by on the other side
Luke 10:32 looked on him, and **p** by on the other

191

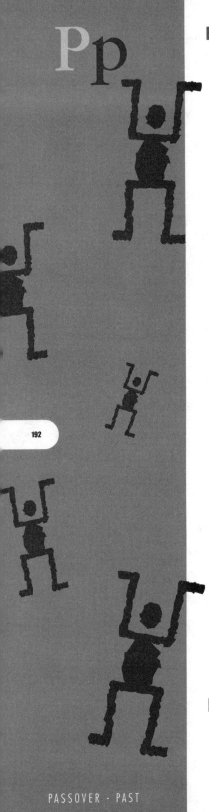

Pp

■ Passover (PASS oh vuhr)

One of the most important feasts the Hebrews celebrated. The event that began the Passover started in Egypt, just before Moses led the Israelites out of slavery. That night, each house was to have blood from a lamb painted on the doorpost. The lamb was to be roasted and eaten at the feast. No yeast was to be used in the bread because there would be no time for it to rise. At midnight, the death angel would pass over all of Egypt. Any house with the blood would be protected and the firstborn would be spared. Those who did not have the blood over the doorpost would have the firstborn child or animal die. This plague was the last of ten God sent to the Egyptians. Pharaoh then let the people go.

The feast has also been called "the Feast of Unleavened Bread," because no yeast, or leavening, was used in the bread. The Hebrew people were to observe this feast each spring to remind them that God brought them out of slavery in Egypt.

At the time of Jesus, the lamb was killed in the Temple. The family member took it home and roasted it whole. It was served with the unleavened bread, bitter herbs (to remind them of the slavery), fruits and nuts made into a paste (to remind them of the mortar used with the bricks), and wine.

When Jesus was crucified, He became our Passover lamb. His blood helped free us from the slavery of sin.

Exodus 12:11 eat it in haste: it is the LORD's **p**
Matthew 26:2 after two days is the feast of the **p**
Matthew 26:17 prepare for thee to eat the **p**
Matthew 26:18 I will keep the **p** at thy house
Mark 14:12 prepare that thou mayest eat the **p**
Mark 14:14 where I shall eat the **p** with my
Mark 14:16 and they made ready the **p**
Luke 22:8 Go and prepare us the **p**
Luke 22:11 where I shall eat the **p** with my
Luke 22:13 and they made ready the **p**
John 18:39 release unto you one at the **p**
John 19:14 And it was the preparation of the **p**

■ Past (PAST)

Refers to a time gone by; once.

1 Kings 18:29 it came to pass, when midday was **p**
Matthew 14:15 time is now **p**; send the multitude
Mark 16:1 And when the sabbath was **p**, Mary

Pastors (PAS tuhrz)
Plural of "pastor." A pastor is a man who is the leader of the church. Other words for pastor are "minister," "priest," or "shepherd." A shepherd cares for his sheep, takes them to good grass, and clean water. In the same way, a pastor is to lead the people of his church so that they get good Bible teaching and learn to live as God wants them to live.

Ephesians 4:11 and some, *p* and teachers

Pasture (PAS chur)
Open land where animals can graze (feed).

Psalm 95:7 and we are the people of his *p*
Psalm 100:3 his people, and the sheep of his *p*

Pastures (PAS churz)
Plural of "pasture."

Psalm 23:2 He maketh me to lie down in green *p*

Path (PATH)
A trail or track where one walks.

Psalm 119:105 lamp unto my feet, and a light unto my *p*

Paths (PATHZ)
Plural of "path."

Psalm 23:3 leadeth me in the *p* of righteousness
Psalm 25:4 O LORD; teach me thy *p*
Matthew 3:3 way of the Lord, make his *p* straight
Mark 1:3 way of the Lord, make his *p* straight
Luke 3:4 way of the Lord, make his *p* straight

Patience (PAY shunts)
The ability to stay calm (see "Patient").

Matthew 18:26 have *p* with me, and I will pay
Matthew 18:29 Have *p* with me, and I will pay

Patient (PAY shunt)
To act in a calm, quiet, or easy way.

Ecclesiastes 7:8 the *p* in spirit is better than

Patiently (PAY shunt lee)
Waiting with much patience.

Psalm 40:1 I waited *p* for the LORD; and he

Paul (PAWL)
His Jewish name was Saul. Paul was his official Roman name because he was born in a Roman city, thereby making him a Roman citizen. He

Paul

193

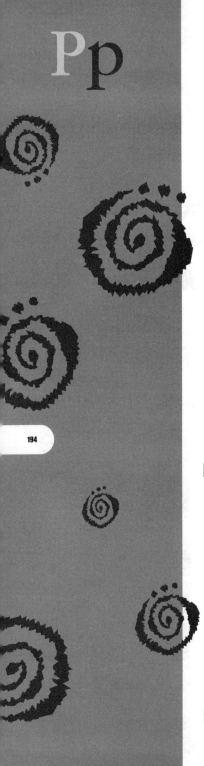

was a strict Pharisee. His family was wealthy and he had the best education available. He began to harass the Christian Jews, putting them in prison. On his way to Damascus one day, he saw the risen Christ in a vision, was blinded for three days, and began to preach about Jesus after he received his sight. He is probably the greatest Christian leader of all times. He made several missionary journeys, taking the good news to the lands along the Mediterranean Sea west of Palestine, even as far as Rome, in present-day Italy. Barnabas, Silas, and Luke were among those who went with Paul on his trips to share the good news of Jesus.

He wrote many letters, thirteen of which are included in the division of the New Testament called Pauline Epistles, or Paul's Letters. Most of the information about Paul is found in the book of Acts, written by Luke.

Acts 13:9 Then Saul (who is also called **P**)
Acts 14:11 when the people saw what **P** had done
Acts 15:35 **P** also and Barnabas continued in
Acts 16:25 And at midnight **P** and Silas prayed
Acts 17:2 And **P**, as his manner was, went in
Acts 17:22 **P** stood in the midst of Mars' hill
Acts 18:9 Then spake the Lord to **P** in the night
Acts 19:6 when **P** had laid his hands upon them
Acts 26:28 Then Agrippa said unto **P**, Almost thou

■ Peace (PEES)
Feeling of contentment and calm; freedom from struggles that can occur inside one's mind, or around him; to be quiet, say nothing.

Exodus 4:18 And Jethro said to Moses, Go in **p**
Psalm 29:11 the LORD will bless his people with **p**
Psalm 34:14 seek **p**, and pursue it
Ecclesiastes 3:8 a time of war, and a time of **p**
Isaiah 9:6 everlasting Father, the Prince of **P**
Matthew 20:31 because they should hold their **p**
Matthew 26:63 But Jesus held his **p**
Mark 4:39 and said unto the sea, **P**, be still
Luke 2:14 on earth **p**, good will toward men
John 14:27 **P** I leave with you, my **p** I give
John 20:26 stood in the midst, and said, **P**

■ Peaceable (PEES uh buhl)
Peaceful, gentle, easygoing.

Genesis 34:21 These men are **p** with us

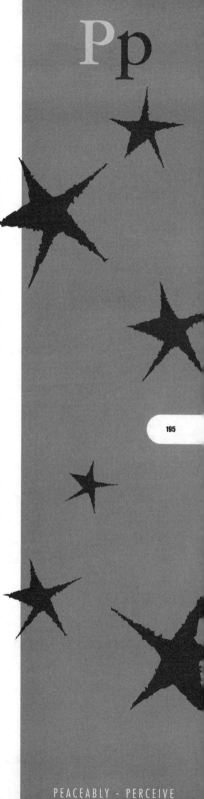

Pp

Peaceably (PEES uh blee)
(See "Peaceable").

Romans 12:18 live **p** with all men

Peacemakers (PEES may kurz)
Those who try everything to make peace or settle disagreements.

Matthew 5:9 Blessed are the **p**: for they shall

Penknife (PEN nighf)
Another name for a scribe's knife. The knife was a special tool which a scribe used to make the papyrus or parchment into the right size. This knife was also used on leather.

Jeremiah 36:23 cut it with the **p**, and cast it

Penny (PEN ee)
A metal coin, made of silver, that would pay a man's wages for one day. The name of this coin was "denarius." The coin was made in Rome. A Roman soldier received one denarius a day as his pay. This was also the same wage for any other worker in Palestine.

Matthew 22:19 And they brought unto him a **p**
Mark 12:15 bring me a **p**, that I may see it
Luke 20:24 Show me a **p**. Whose image and

195

Pentecost (PEN tih kawst)
A Jewish feast which came fifty days after Passover. Sometimes called the "Feast of Weeks" or the "Feast of Harvest." The first Pentecost occurred after the resurrection of Jesus. It was at this time that the Holy Spirit came upon the believers, or followers of Jesus.

Acts 2:1 When the day of **P** was fully come

People (PEE puhl)
Human beings. A group of persons representing a race (Jewish people), nation, or a tribe.

Exodus 5:1 Let my **p** go, that they may hold a feast
Matthew 1:21 he shall save his **p** from their sins
Matthew 27:25 Then answered all the **p**, and said
Mark 15:11 the chief priests moved the **p**
Mark 15:15 so Pilate, willing to content the **p**
Luke 2:10 great joy, which shall be to all **p**

Perceive (puhr SEEV)
To recognize, notice, sense, understand.

Luke 8:46 I **p** that virtue is gone out of me

Pp

John 4:19 Sir, I **p** that thou art a prophet
Acts 10:34 I **p** that God is no respecter of persons

■ Perceived (puhr SEEVD)
Past tense of "perceive."

1 Samuel 3:8 And Eli **p** that the LORD had called
Esther 4:1 When Mordecai **p** all that was done
Matthew 22:18 But Jesus **p** their wickedness
Mark 2:8 when Jesus **p** in his spirit that they
Luke 1:22 they *p* that he had seen a vision
Luke 20:23 But he **p** their craftiness, and said
John 6:15 Jesus therefore **p** that they would come
Acts 4:13 and **p** that they were unlearned and

■ Perfect (PUHR fikt)
Complete, excellent, blameless.

Genesis 6:9 Noah was a just man and **p** in his
Psalm 18:30 As for God, his way is **p**
Psalm 19:7 The law of the LORD is **p**
Matthew 5:48 Be ye therefore **p**, even as your
Matthew 5:48 Father which is in heaven is **p**

■ Perga (PUHR guh)
A very old city in Pamphylia, a Roman province (see map on page 341). The city was located a few miles from the Mediterranean Sea. This area is now southeastern Turkey. Paul, Barnabas, and Mark came to this city on the first missionary journey. Mark, a young man, left and returned to Jerusalem.

Acts 13:13 they came to **P** in Pamphylia
Acts 13:14 But when they departed from **P**
Acts 14:25 when they had preached the word in **P**

■ Perish (PEHR ish)
Die, be destroyed; to always be apart from God.

Esther 4:16 and if I **p**, I **p**
Psalm 1:6 the way of the ungodly shall **p**
Matthew 8:25 saying, Lord, save us: we **p**
Mark 4:38 Master, carest thou not that we **p**
Luke 8:24 Master, master, we **p**
Luke 13:3 ye repent, ye shall all likewise **p**
John 3:15 believeth in him should not **p**
John 3:16 believeth in him should not **p**

■ Persecute (PUHR sih kyoot)
To harass or pick on someone because they are different in some way; to cause suffering.

Matthew 5:11 when people insult you, **p** you and (NIV)

Matthew 5:44 which despitefully use you, and **p** you
John 5:16 And therefore did the Jews **p** Jesus
John 15:20 have persecuted me, they will **p** you
Romans 12:14 Bless them which **p** you: bless

◼ Persecuted (PUHR si kyoot id)
Past tense of "persecute."

Matthew 5:10 Blessed are they which are **p** for
John 15:20 If they have **p** me, they will also

◼ Persia (PUHR zhuh)
A large empire located in what is now Iran (see map on page 339). At different times in early history, the boundaries ranged from India to Libya in Africa, and to Macedonia, in Asia. The Jews had been carried off to Babylonia and then Persia conquered Babylonia. Cyrus became the king of Persia in 559 B.C. He allowed some of the Jewish people to return to Jerusalem to rebuild the wall and the Temple which the Babylonians destroyed.

2 Chronicles 36:22 first year of Cyrus king of **P**
2 Chronicles 36:22 stirred up the spirit of Cyrus king of **P**
Ezra 1:2 Thus saith Cyrus king of **P**, The LORD God

◼ Persons (PUHR suhnz)
Plural of "person." Human beings, people.

Luke 15:7 more than over ninety and nine just **p**
Acts 10:34 I perceive that God is no respecter of **p**

◼ Persuade (PUHR swayd)
To compel, sway, win over.

Matthew 28:14 we will **p** him, and secure you

◼ Persuaded (PUHR sway did)
Past tense of "persuade."

Romans 8:38 For I am **p**, that neither death, nor

◼ Peter (PEE tuhr)
The name is Greek and means "rock." He was a fisherman along with his brother, Andrew, who brought him to meet Jesus. Jesus changed his name from Simon to Peter because, it is thought, that Jesus could see that Peter could become a strong leader. Peter was one of the twelve disciples and is always listed first. He was one of the three disciples who were the closest to Jesus (James and John were the other two).

Peter was usually the one who spoke for the whole group and asked many questions of

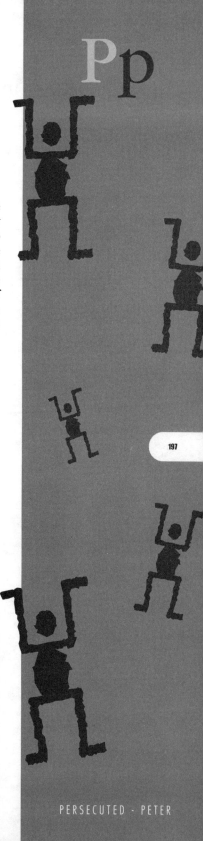

Pp

Jesus. He denied Jesus the night Jesus was arrested but later became a bold and fearless leader of the early church.

An early writer of Christian history reported that Peter was crucified with his head downward because he did not feel worthy to be crucified in the same way as Jesus was crucified.

Matthew 4:18 saw two brethren, Simon called **P**
Matthew 10:2 The first, Simon, who is called **P**
Matthew 16:16 Simon **P** answered and said, Thou art
Matthew 16:18 That thou art **P**, and upon this rock
Matthew 26:69 Now **P** sat without in the palace
Mark 3:16 And Simon he surnamed **P**
Mark 14:29 But **P** said unto him, Although all
Mark 14:54 And **P** followed him afar off
Luke 6:14 Simon (whom he also named **P**,) and
Luke 22:8 And he sent **P** and John, saying, Go
Luke 22:54 priest's house. And **P** followed afar
Luke 22:58 And **P** said, Man, I am not
John 18:27 **P** then denied again: and immediately
John 20:6 Then cometh Simon **P** following him
John 21:7 saith unto **P**, It is the Lord
John 21:7 Simon **P** heard that it was the Lord
Acts 3:6 **P** said, Silver and gold have I none
Acts 10:9 **P** went up upon the housetop to pray

■ **Peter, 1, 2, Books of (PEE tuhr)**
These two letters are the third and fourth books in the division, General Letters, in the New Testament. They were written by Peter, one of Jesus' disciples. The group of people to whom he wrote were the Christians (Jews and Gentiles) living in Asia Minor (now Turkey). In 1 Peter, he was encouraging them to not give up hope in God in spite of the persecution and suffering they were having. It was written about A.D. 64

In 2 Peter, he reminded the believers to be aware of false teachers who were trying to lead them into a sinful way of life. He encouraged them to live in a Christlike way. It was written about A.D. 68, probably just before he was killed in Rome.

■ **Pharaoh (FEHR oh)**
A title for the ancient kings of Egypt. The name means "great house." When a pharaoh became the new ruler, he was given five "great names." It was not fitting that these names be spoken except at certain times. Therefore, the title "pharaoh" came to be the way to address the

198

king. The pharaoh who ruled when Joseph was in Egypt invited all of Joseph's family to move to Egypt. Four hundred years later, a different pharaoh made slaves of the Israelites.

Exodus 1:11 They built for **P** treasure cities
Exodus 1:19 And the midwives said unto **P**
Exodus 1:22 **P** charged all his people, saying
Exodus 2:5 daughter of **P** came down to wash
Exodus 3:10 I will send thee unto **P**, that thou
Exodus 3:11 Who am I, that I should go unto **P**
Exodus 9:35 And the heart of **P** was hardened
Exodus 12:30 And **P** rose up in the night, he
Exodus 14:8 The LORD hardened the heart of **P**
Exodus 14:9 all the horses and chariots of **P**
Exodus 14:28 host of **P** that came into the sea

▋ Pharisee (FEHR uh see)
The name means "separated ones." This was a religious and political group of men who had a lot of authority and power. During Jesus' time, they felt they must be sure everyone kept the law. There were many rules and laws in the Old Testament but they had also invented many other unimportant laws. The Pharisees did not like the things Jesus was teaching and kept trying to find ways to get rid of Him.

Luke 7:39 when the **P** which had bidden him saw it
Luke 18:10 the one a **P**, and the other a publican
Luke 18:11 The **P** stood and prayed thus, God, I
Acts 5:34 Then stood up one in the council, a **P**
Acts 23:6 and brethren, I am a **P**, the son of a **P**

▋ Pharisees (FEHR uh seez)
Plural of "Pharisee."

Matthew 9:11 And when the **P** saw it, they said
Matthew 22:15 **P** went out and laid plans to trap him (NIV)
Matthew 27:62 priests and **P** came together unto Pilate
Luke 6:7 And the scribes and **P** watched him
Luke 19:39 some of the **P** from among the multitude
John 3:1 There was a man of the **P**, named Nicodemus,
John 18:3 officers from the chief priests and **P**

▋ Philemon, Book of (figh LEE muhn)
The name means "affectionate." The book is the thirteenth and last book of the division, Paul's Letters, in the New Testament. Paul and Philemon became good friends while Paul was working in Ephesus. Later, when Paul was in prison in Rome, Philemon's slave, Onesimus, came to see Paul. Onesimus was in trouble

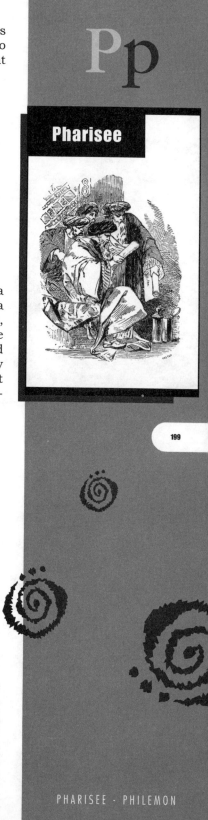

Pharisee

199

because he had robbed his owner and then ran away. Paul persuaded Onesimus to return to Philemon after Onesimus became a believer. He sent this beautiful letter with Onesimus to give to Philemon. He encouraged Philemon to forgive Onesimus and take him back like a brother and "as you would welcome me" (verse 17).

Philip (FIL ip)
1. The name means "fond of horses." He was one of the twelve disciples. He brought his brother Nathaniel to meet Jesus. He helped feed the many people who came to hear Jesus, and also brought others to Jesus. He lived in the town of Bethsaida, which is on the northeast side of the Sea of Galilee.

Matthew 10:3 **P** and Bartholomew; Thomas, and
Mark 3:18 Andrew, and **P**, and Bartholomew
Luke 6:14 James and John, **P** and Bartholomew
John 1:43 findeth **P**, and saith unto him
John 1:44 **P** was of Bethsaida, the city of
John 1:45 **P** findeth Nathaniel, and saith unto
John 1:46 **P** saith unto him, Come and see

2. He was selected as one of the seven men to serve as the first deacons in the early church. He later preached to the people in Samaria. Philip was led by the Holy Spirit to the road to Gaza where he met the Ethiopian eunuch who was reading a part of Isaiah. After telling the Ethiopian about Jesus, the man was baptized by Philip. The Spirit then took him to Azotus, several miles away.

Acts 6:5 and **P**, and Prochorus, and
Acts 8:26 angel of the Lord spake unto **P**
Acts 8:29 The Spirit said unto **P**, Go near
Acts 8:35 Then **P** opened his mouth, and began
Acts 8:37 **P** said, If thou believest with all
Acts 8:38 into the water, both **P** and the eunuch
Acts 8:39 Spirit of the Lord caught away **P**
Acts 8:40 But **P** was found at Azotus

Philippi (FIH lih pigh)
A Roman colony in the province of Macedonia (see map on page 341). Paul came to this city on his second missionary journey because of a vision of a man from Macedonia calling him to come. It was in Philippi where Paul preached to a group beside the river. There Lydia was converted along with many others. Paul was put into jail because he healed a slave girl from

demons. He later wrote a letter to the church at Philippi.

Acts 16:12 to **P**, which is the chief city of
Philippians 1:1 in Christ Jesus which are at **P**

■ Philippians, Book of (fih LIP ih uhnz)

The sixth book in the division, Paul's Letters, in the New Testament. Paul wrote this letter while he was in prison in Rome, about A.D. 61. Some friends from the church at Philippi took a message and a gift, possibly some money, to Paul to help him. He sent the letter back to the church by the friends who had come to see him. He thanked the church for the gift, told them what was happening to him, and assured them he wanted to come to the church at Philippi. He encouraged the believers to be Christlike in all they did.

■ Philistine (fih LISS teen)

A person who lived in the area of Philistia on the Mediterranean Sea, from Joppa to south of Gaza (see map on page 338).

1 Samuel 17:11 Israel heard those words of the **P**
1 Samuel 17:23 the **P** of Gath, Goliath by name
1 Samuel 17:42 the **P** looked about, and saw David
1 Samuel 17:49 and smote the **P** in his forehead

■ Philistines (fih LISS teenz)

Plural of "Philistine." They were a tribe who ruled cities along the coast of the Mediterranean Sea. Each of these cities were also considered states. During the time of the judges and while Kings Saul and David ruled Israel, the Philistines were enemies of Israel. After David defeated them, they never regained their former military strength. They made armor and weapons from bronze. From the iron they mined, they made iron chariots.

Genesis 26:1 unto Abimelech king of the **P**
Exodus 13:17 the way of the land of the **P**

■ Phrygia (FRIJ ih uh)

The name means "parched." An area in Asia Minor (now a part of southwest central Turkey (see map on page 341). Paul visited several cities in this area on his second missionary journey and started churches in some of the cities. The Galatian cities are included in this area.

Acts 16:6 when they had gone throughout **P**
Acts 18:23 over all the country of Galatia and **P**

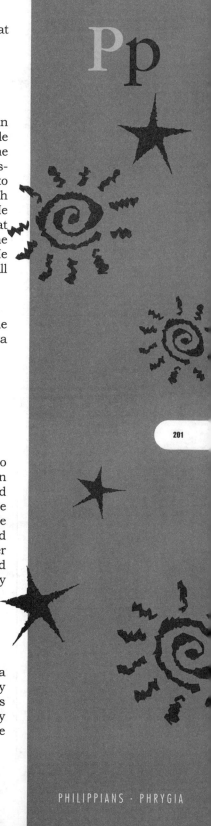

201

Pp

Pilate

■ **Physician (fih ZIH shun)**
A doctor of medicine.

Matthew 9:12 They that be whole need not a **p**
Mark 2:17 that are whole have no need of the **p**
Luke 5:31 They that are whole need not a **p**

■ **Piece (PEES)**
A part of a thing; one item.

Luke 15:8 if she lose one **p**, doth not light a
Luke 15:9 found the **p** which I had lost
Luke 24:42 they gave him a **p** of a broiled fish

■ **Pieces (PEE sihz)**
Plural of "piece." More than one piece. Can refer to coins.

Matthew 26:15 with him for thirty **p** of silver
Matthew 27:3 brought again the thirty **p** of silver
Matthew 27:5 he cast down the **p** of silver in the
Matthew 27:6 chief priests took the silver **p**
Luke 15:8 what woman having ten **p** of silver

■ **Pigeons (PIH juhns)**
Doves and turtledoves are smaller pigeons. Pigeons have "a stout body, short legs, and smooth feathers." Some of these pigeons are all white while others range in colors of gray, light brown or tan, to almost black. Many have touches of other colors on their breasts or wings. During Bible times, if a family or person could not afford to provide a lamb for their sacrifice, two turtledoves or pigeons could be offered instead. Mary, the mother of Jesus, gave two turtledoves for her sacrifice after the birth of Jesus.

Leviticus 12:8 bring two doves or two young **p** (NIV)
Luke 2:24 A pair of turtledoves, or two young **p**

■ **Pilate, Pontius (PIGH luht, PAHN shuhs)**
The Roman governor of Judea during and after the ministry of Jesus. He did not like the Jews and did many things to cause problems for them. However, he did listen to the accusations against Jesus brought by the Jewish ruling council. He could not find Jesus guilty of any crime, but he gave in to the demands of the priests and people that Jesus must die. Finally, the Romans replaced Pilate because of all the terrible things he had done.

Matthew 27:2 and delivered him to Pontius **P**
Matthew 27:58 He went to **P**, and begged the body

Matthew 27:58 **P** commanded the body to be delivered
Mark 15:1 carried him away, and delivered him to **P**
Mark 15:2 **P** asked him, Art thou the King of the Jews
Mark 15:15 **P**, willing to content the people, released
Mark 15:43 came, and went in boldly unto **P**, and
Mark 15:44 And **P** marveled if he were already dead
Luke 3:1 Pontius **P** being governor of Judea
Luke 23:1 of them arose, and led him unto **P**
Luke 23:20 **P** therefore, willing to release Jesus
Luke 23:52 man went unto **P**, and begged the body
John 18:31 **P** said unto them, Take ye him, and
John 19:1 **P** therefore took Jesus, and scourged him
John 19:19 **P** wrote a title, and put it on the cross
John 19:38 besought **P** that he might take away
John 19:38 the body of Jesus: and **P** gave him leave

Pit (PIHT)
A hole in the ground; a well, or cistern.

Genesis 37:24 took him, and cast him into a **p**
Genesis 37:24 **p** was empty, there was no water in it
Genesis 37:28 and lifted up Joseph out of the **p**
Genesis 37:29 And Reuben returned unto the **p**
Genesis 37:29 behold, Joseph was not in the **p**

Pitcher (PIT chur)
A container with a handle and spout, or molded lip from which liquid can be poured easily; a jug. During biblical times, pitchers varied in shape and size according to the need and the liquid to be placed in them.

Genesis 24:14 to whom I shall say, Let down thy **p**
Genesis 24:15 with her **p** upon her shoulder
Genesis 24:17 drink a little water of thy **p**
Genesis 24:18 she hasted, and let down her **p**
Mark 14:13 meet you a man bearing a **p** of water
Luke 22:10 man meet you, bearing a **p** of water

Pitieth (PIT ee uhth)
The old way of saying or writing "pities," the plural of "pity."

Psalm 103:13 Like a father **p** his children
Psalm 103:13 so the LORD **p** them that fear him

Pity (PIH tee)
A feeling of kindness, being sorry for, or understanding toward a person who is sad, hurting, suffering, or having problems.

Proverbs 19:17 He that hath **p** upon the poor

Jonah 4:10 the LORD, Thou has had **p** on the gourd
Matthew 18:33 even as I had **p** on thee

Place (PLAYC)
Area, location, room, spot.

Exodus 3:5 the **p** whereon thou standest is holy
Psalm 24:3 who shall stand in his holy **p**
Psalm 32:7 Thou art my hiding **p**
Matthew 26:36 with them unto a **p** called Gethsemane
Matthew 27:33 were come unto a **p** called Golgotha
Matthew 28:6 Come see the **p** where the Lord lay
Mark 15:22 they bring him unto the **p** of Golgotha
Mark 16:6 behold the **p** where they laid him
Luke 23:33 come to the **p** which is called Calvary
John 14:2 I go to prepare a **p** for you
John 18:2 which betrayed him, knew the **p**
John 19:41 Now in the **p** where he was crucified
John 20:7 but wrapped together in a **p** by itself

Plague (PLAYG)
Widespread illness or destruction that could result in death. The ten plagues God sent upon Egypt were meant to punish the Egyptians and to show that He (God) alone had absolute power. He wanted Pharaoh to free the Israelites from their slavery and he used the plagues to do it. Most of the plagues God sent to the Egyptians were "events of nature" that could have happened in Egypt.

Exodus 11:1 will I bring one **p** more upon Pharaoh
Exodus 12:13 pass over you, and the **p** shall not be
Mark 5:29 that she was healed of that **p**
Mark 5:34 go in peace, and be whole of thy **p**

Plant (PLANT)
Living thing, such as grass, tree, flower, weed; to place seeds or small plants in the ground to grow.

Genesis 2:5 And every **p** of the field before it
Ecclesiastes 3:2 A time to **p**, and a time to pluck

Planted (PLANT id)
Past tense of "plant."

Genesis 2:8 LORD God **p** a garden eastward in Eden
Psalm 1:3 shall be like a tree **p** by the rivers

Platted (PLAH tihd)
Past tense of "plat." To braid, as the hair; weave.

Matthew 27:29 when they had **p** a crown of thorns
Mark 15:17 and **p** a crown of thorns, and put it
John 19:2 the soldiers **p** a crown of thorns

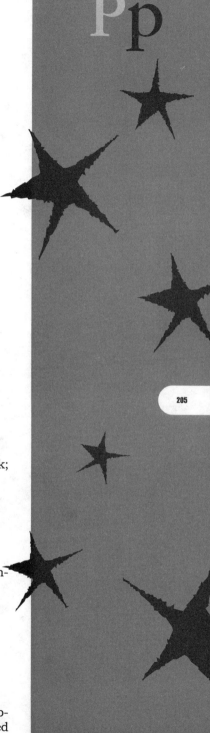

Pp

Pleasant (PLEH zuhnt)
Agreeable, friendly, nice, charming.

Genesis 2:9 every tree that is *p* to the sight
Psalm 133:1 how good and how *p* it is for brethren

Please (PLEEZ)
To delight, to give pleasure, make happy.

Proverbs 16:7 when a man's ways *p* the LORD
John 8:29 I do always those things that *p* him
Hebrews 11:6 without faith it is impossible to *p* him

Pleased (PLEEZD)
Past tense of "please."

Matthew 3:17 my beloved Son, in whom I am well *p*
Mark 1:11 my beloved Son, in whom I am well *p*
Luke 3:22 my beloved Son; in thee I am well *p*

Pleasure (PLEH zhuhr)
A feeling of inner joy, happiness, feeling good.

Psalm 147:11 LORD taketh *p* in them that fear him
Luke 12:32 it is your Father's good *p* to give you

Plenteous (PLEN tih uhs)
More than enough; a great amount.

Genesis 41:34 land of Egypt in the seven *p* years
Genesis 41:47 in the seven *p* years the earth brought
Psalm 103:8 slow to anger, and *p* in mercy
Matthew 9:37 The harvest truly is *p*, but the

Pluck (PLUK)
To grab and remove quickly; to snatch; pick; harvest.

Ecclesiastes 3:2 time to *p* up that which is planted
Matthew 12:1 began to *p* the ears of corn, and to eat
Mark 2:23 began, as they went, to *p* the ears of corn

Ponder (PAHN duhr)
To think about something very carefully; to consider.

Proverbs 4:26 *P* the path of thy feet, and let all

Pondered (PAHN duhrd)
Past tense of "ponder."

Luke 2:19 Mary kept all these things, and *p* them

Pool (PUEL)
A small body of water, varying in depth. In biblical times, a pool was a container that collected rain water. Most pools were carved from stone.

Pp

The water was used to irrigate gardens or for drinking.

John 5:2 at Jerusalem by the sheep market a **p**
John 5:4 went down at a certain season into the **p**
John 5:7 water is troubled, to put me into the **p**
John 9:7 unto him, Go, wash in the **p** of Siloam

Poor (PAWHR)
1. Needy; not rich; not having enough.

Psalm 41:1 Blessed is he that considereth the **p**
Matthew 5:3 Blessed are the **p** in spirit
Matthew 19:21 that thou hast, and give to the **p**
Matthew 26:11 For ye have the **p** with you always
Mark 14:7 For ye have the **p** with you always
Luke 19:8 half of my goods I give to the **p**
Luke 21:2 saw also a certain **p** widow casting in
Luke 21:3 **p** widow hath cast in more than they
John 12:8 For the **p** always ye have with you

2. Lean, skinny; sick.

Genesis 41:19 **p** and very ill favored and

Possess (puh ZESS)
1. To enter in and take control of.

Joshua 1:11 go in to **p** the land, which the LORD

2. To have or own.

Luke 18:12 I give tithes of all that I **p**

Possessed (puh ZEST)
Past tense of "possess." In biblical times, it referred to a person being under the power of demons or devils.

Matthew 4:24 and those which were **p** with devils
Matthew 8:28 there met him two **p** with devils
Matthew 9:32 to him a dumb man **p** with a devil
Mark 1:32 and them that were **p** with devils
Mark 5:15 and see him that was **p** with the devil
Luke 8:36 he that was **p** of the devils was healed

Possessions (puh ZEH shuhnz)
Plural of "possession." The things one calls his own.

Matthew 19:22 away sorrowful: for he had great **p**
Mark 10:22 went away grieved: for he had great **p**
Acts 2:45 and sold their **p** and goods, and

Possible (PAHS ih buhl)
Likely; could happen.

206

Matthew 19:26 but with God all things are ***p***
Matthew 26:39 O my Father, if it be ***p***, let this cup
Mark 9:23 all things are ***p*** to him that believeth
Mark 10:27 for with God all things are ***p***
Mark 14:35 if it were ***p***, the hour might pass from
Mark 14:36 Father, all things are ***p*** unto thee
Luke 18:27 impossible with men are ***p*** with God

Potiphar (PAHT ih fuhr)

The name means "belonging to the sun." He was a captain of the guard under Pharaoh, king of Egypt. Potiphar bought Joseph from the Midianite traders who had brought him to Egypt. Potiphar saw that Joseph had great abilities and made him the manager of his whole house. The wife of Potiphar tried to get Joseph to be unfaithful but he refused. She falsely accused Joseph, and Potiphar had him put in prison.

Genesis 37:36 sold him into Egypt under ***P***, an officer
Genesis 39:1 ***P***, an officer of Pharaoh, captain of the

Pottage (PAHT idj)

A spicy soup made thick with vegetables and lentils. It was this kind of soup which Jacob gave Esau in exchange for the birthright.

Genesis 25:30 I pray thee, with that same red ***p***
Genesis 25:34 gave Esau bread and ***p*** of lentils

Potter's Field (PAHT uhrz FEELD)

Belonging to the potter. A potter is one who makes pottery from clay. The potter's field was a piece of land outside of Jerusalem which had been used as a cemetery for many years. After Judas betrayed Jesus, he returned the money to the priests. They could not put it back into the treasury because it had caused bloodshed (Jesus'). They bought the old cemetery with the money so they could bury strangers in it.

Matthew 27:7 bought with them the ***p*** field
Matthew 27:10 and gave them for the ***p*** field

Pour (PAWHR)

To spill, to let flow, to empty.

Exodus 4:9 water of the river, and ***p*** it upon the
1 Kings 18:33 barrels with water, and pour it on
Malachi 3:10 of heaven, and ***p*** you out a blessing

Poured (PAWHRD)

Past tense of "pour."

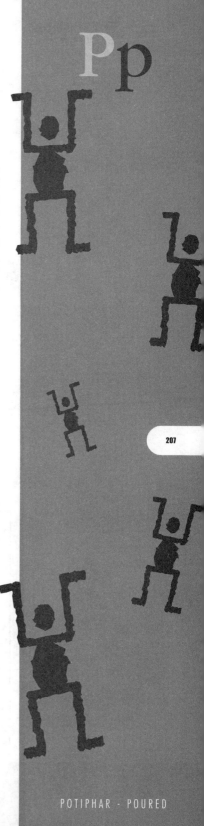

207

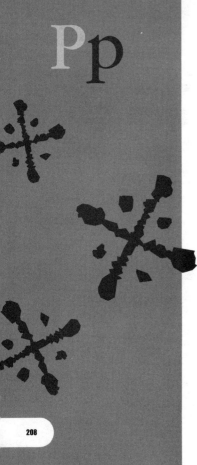

Pp

1 Samuel 1:15 have **p** out my soul before the LORD
Matthew 26:7 and **p** it on his head, as he sat
Matthew 26:12 that she hath **p** this ointment on
Mark 14:3 brake the box, and **p** it on his head
John 2:15 and **p** out the changers' money, and

■ Power (POW uhr)
Authority, force, control, strength; "the ability to act." We see God's power as we read the Bible and the stories of how He worked in the lives of Bible people. We see His power in nature, as well as in the lives of people today. When Jesus performed miracles, forgave people their sins, and treated the poor and unlovable in a lovable manner, He showed God's power too.

Proverbs 3:27 when it is in the **p** of thine hand to
Matthew 6:13 thine is the kingdom, and the **p**, and
Matthew 9:6 Son of man hath **p** on earth to forgive
Matthew 28:18 All **p** is given unto me in heaven and
Luke 5:24 Son of man hath **p** upon earth to forgive
John 10:18 **p** to lay it down, and I have **p** to take
Acts 1:8 But ye shall receive **p**, after that the
Acts 6:8 And Stephen, full of faith and **p**, did

■ Praise (PRAYZ)
To glorify, honor, especially through worship to God. Praise has been translated from the Latin, meaning "value" or "price." When a person praises God, he is expressing that God has worth. We praise God in many ways: with our mouths, singing, giving offerings and tithes, having the right attitude, in worship, and obeying His laws.

Psalm 7:17 I will **p** the LORD according to his
Psalm 9:2 I will sing **p** to thy name
Psalm 33:2 **P** the LORD with harp: sing unto him
Psalm 100:4 thanksgiving, and into his courts with **p**
Luke 18:43 when they saw it, gave **p** unto God
Luke 19:37 disciples began to rejoice and **p** God

■ Praised (PRAYZD)
Past tense of "praise."

Psalm 18:3 upon the LORD, who is worthy to be **p**
Psalm 96:4 LORD is great, and greatly to be **p**

■ Praises (PRAY zez)
Plural of "praise."

Psalm 47:6 Sing **p** to God, sing **p**: sing **p** unto
Acts 16:25 Paul and Silas prayed, and sang **p**

Praise

Praising (PRAY zeeng)

The act of giving praise. See "Praise."

Luke 2:20 glorifying and **p** God for all the
Luke 24:53 in the temple, **p** and blessing God
Acts 3:8 walking, and leaping, and **p** God

Pray (PRAY)

1. To ask or beg.

Exodus 5:3 let us go, we **p** thee, three days'
Ruth 2:7 I **p** you, let me glean and gather
1 Kings 17:10 Fetch me, I **p** thee, a little water
1 Kings 17:11 Bring me, I **p** thee, a morsel of
1 Kings 17:21 O LORD my God, I **p** thee, let

2. To speak to God in an act of worship and
thanksgiving, and ask Him for what is needed.

Psalm 55:17 and morning, and at noon will I **p**
Matthew 5:44 **p** for them which despitefully use you
Matthew 6:6 **p** to thy Father which is in secret
Matthew 6:9 After this manner therefore **p** thee
Matthew 26:36 Sit ye here, while I go and **p**
Matthew 26:41 Watch and **p**, that ye enter not into
Mark 14:32 Sit ye here, while I shall **p**
Mark 14:38 Watch ye and **p**, lest ye enter into
Luke 11:2 When ye **p**, say, Our Father which art
1 Thessalonians 5:17 **P** without ceasing

Prayed (PRAYD)

Past tense of "pray."

Matthew 26:39 fell on his face, and **p**, saying
Mark 1:35 into a solitary place, and there **p**
Mark 14:35 and fell on the ground, and **p**
Acts 4:31 when they had **p**, the place was shaken

Prayer (PRAIR)

Listening to God, as well as speaking to Him. In
the Old Testament, we read of prayers being
offered to God for protection, salvation from enemies, forgiveness, for healing, and for strength.
In the New Testament, especially in the four
Gospels, Jesus taught the people how to pray to
God. He also showed how important prayer was
because He often went away from the disciples to
pray. And, He told the disciples to keep on asking
for what they needed, not ask for it just one time.
God wanted them to ask for what they needed.

Matthew 21:13 house shall be called the house of **p**
Matthew 21:22 whatsoever ye shall ask in **p**
Luke 6:12 and continued all night in **p** to God

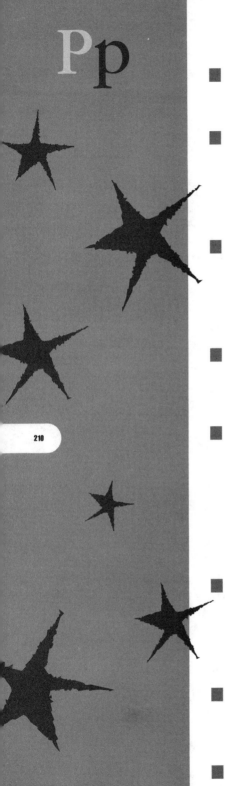

Luke 19:46 My house is the house of **p**
James 5:16 The **p** of a righteous man is powerful (NIV)

◼ Prayest (PRAY ist)
Old way of saying or writing "you do pray."

Matthew 6:6 when thou **p**, enter into thy closet

◼ Praying (PRAY eeng)
The act of saying a prayer. See "Pray."

1 Samuel 1:12 as she continued **p** before the LORD
Luke 3:21 And as he was **p**, heaven was opened (NIV)
Luke 11:1 day Jesus was in **p** in a certain place (NIV)
Acts 11:5 I was in the city of Joppa **p**

◼ Preach (PREECH)
To teach, counsel, advise; to tell the good news about God and His kingdom.

Matthew 4:17 From that time Jesus began to **p**
Mark 16:15 and **p** the gospel to every creature
Romans 10:15 how shall they **p**, except they be

◼ Precious (PREH shuhs)
A thing that is costly, dear, loved, or valuable.

Matthew 26:7 alabaster box of very **p** ointment
Mark 14:3 box of ointment of spikenard very **p**

◼ Prepare (pree PAIR)
To make arrangements, get ready.

1 Kings 18:44 **P** thy chariot, and get thee down
Isaiah 40:3 **P** ye the way of the LORD
Matthew 3:3 **P** ye the way of the Lord
Mark 1:3 **P** ye the way of the Lord
Luke 3:4 **P** ye the way of the Lord
Luke 22:8 Go and **p** us the passover, that
John 14:2 I go to **p** a place for you

◼ Prepared (pree PAIRD)
Past tense of "prepare."

Jonah 1:17 LORD had **p** a great fish to swallow
Mark 14:15 a large upper room furnished and **p**
Luke 23:56 returned, and **p** spices and ointments
Luke 24:1 bringing the spices which they had **p**

◼ Preparest (pree PAIR ist)
The old way of saying or writing "you do prepare."

Psalm 23:5 Thou **p** a table before me in the

◼ Presence (PREH zens)
In attendance, existence, being near by.

Exodus 33:14 My **p** shall go with thee, and I
Psalm 23:5 a table before me in the **p** of mine
Psalm 51:11 Cast me not away from thy **p**
Psalm 100:2 come before his **p** with singing
Jonah 1:3 unto Tarshish from the **p** of the LORD
Luke 15:10 joy in the **p** of the angels of God

Present (PREHZ uhnt)
adj In attendance, nearby.

Psalm 46:1 a very **p** help in trouble

Present (pree ZENT)
vb To show, offer, give.

Exodus 34:2 **p** thyself there to me in the top of
Luke 2:22 to Jerusalem, to **p** him to the Lord

Presented (pree ZEN tid)
Past tense of "present, vb."

Genesis 46:29 his father, to Goshen, and **p** himself
Matthew 2:11 they **p** unto him gifts; gold, and

Preserve (pree ZURV)
To care for, keep, or save.

Genesis 45:5 God did send me before you to **p** life
Genesis 45:7 God sent me before you to **p** you
Luke 17:33 shall lose his life shall **p** it

Press (PREHS)
A great number of people gathered together; a crowd.

Mark 2:4 could not come nigh unto him for the **p**
Luke 8:19 and could not come at him for the **p**
Luke 19:3 and could not for the **p**, because he

Pretense (PREE tins)
Being a show-off; making untrue statements just to impress someone.

Matthew 23:14 and for a **p** make long prayer

Pride (PRIGHD)
Thinking one is more important or better than others; trusting in oneself. Pride gives glory to self rather than to God, and this is sin. Pride causes a person to look down on others.

Proverbs 11:2 When **p** cometh, then cometh shame
Proverbs 16:18 **P** goeth before destruction, and an
Proverbs 29:23 A man's **p** shall bring him low

Priest (PREEST)
A person who speaks to God on behalf of others.

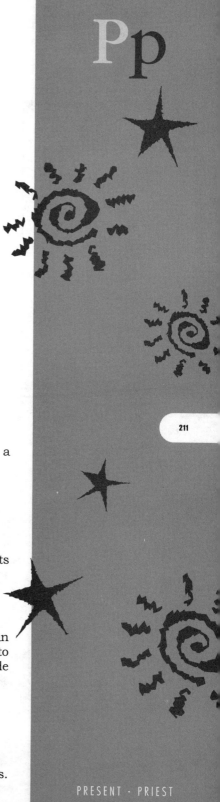

211

Pp

Priest

The high priest, or chief priest as he was also called, led the people in worship in the tabernacle, and later in the Temple. The high priest was the only one who could enter the holy of holies (the innermost part of the tabernacle or Temple), and he went in only once a year. Other duties or responsibilities of the priests were to prepare and offer sacrifices for the people, lead prayers, and meet with God.

God gave specific instructions to Moses that the priests were to determine when a skin disease was healed sufficiently. Then the person could be declared clean and he could participate in worship. These instructions are given in Leviticus 13.

Matthew 8:4 go thy way, show thyself to the **p**
Matthew 26:3 unto the palace of the high **p**
Mark 1:44 go thy way, show thyself to the **p**
Mark 14:53 they led Jesus away to the high **p**
Luke 5:14 but go, and show thyself to the **p**
Luke 10:31 came down a certain **p** that way
John 18:13 to Caiaphas, which was the high **p**

Priests (PREESTS)
Plural of "priest."

Matthew 2:4 when he had gathered all the chief **p**
Matthew 26:3 Then assembled together the chief **p**
Matthew 26:14 Judas Iscariot, went unto the chief **p**
Matthew 26:59 Now the chief **p**, and elders, and all
Matthew 27:3 thirty pieces of silver to the chief **p**
Mark 11:18 chief **p** heard it, and sought how they
Mark 15:1 chief **p** held a consultation with the
Mark 15:10 the chief **p** had delivered him for envy
Mark 15:11 But the chief **p** moved the people, that
Luke 17:14 unto them, Go show yourselves unto the **p**
John 19:15 The chief **p** answered, We have no king
John 19:21 said the chief **p** of the Jews to Pilate

Prince (PRIHNS)
The son of a nobleman; of royalty, high office. When Jesus refers to the "prince of this world," He is speaking of Satan.

Exodus 2:14 Who made thee a **p** and a judge over us
Isaiah 9:6 everlasting Father, the **P** of Peace

Print (PRINT)
A mark made by using pressure.

John 20:25 see in his hands the **p** of the nails
John 20:25 put my finger into the **p** of the nails

Priscilla (prih SIL uh)
The wife of Aquila. They moved to Corinth when

212

the emperor of Rome forced all Jews to leave Rome. They became Christians and were some of Paul's helpers. They also helped and encouraged Apollos, a preacher of the gospel.

Acts 18:2 lately come from Italy, with his wife **P**
Acts 18:18 unto Syria, and with him **P** and Aquila
Acts 18:26 whom when Aquila and **P** had heard, they took

Prison (PRIH zuhn)
A cell or jail where wrongdoers are kept. In Old Testament times, a prison could have been an underground cellar or well, or a small house or room near the palace.

Genesis 39:20 took him, and put him into the **p**
Matthew 4:12 heard that John was cast into **p**
Matthew 25:36 I was in **p**, and ye came unto me
Matthew 25:39 when saw we thee sick, or in **p**
Mark 1:14 after that John was put in **p**
Luke 3:20 that he shut up John in **p**
John 3:24 For John was not yet cast into **p**

Prisoner (PRIH zuhn uhr)
One who has been put into prison. Usually someone who had committed a crime, or who had done something worth putting him into prison for. John the Baptist, Paul, Peter, and Silas are a few Bible people who were jailed, mostly for offending the rulers by teaching the truth.

Matthew 27:15 release unto the people a **p**
Matthew 27:16 then a notable **p**, called Barabbas
Mark 15:6 he released unto them one **p**

Privately (PRIGH vuht lee)
Secretly; quietly.

Mark 6:32 into a desert place by ship **p**
Luke 9:10 and went aside **p** into a desert place

Proclaim (proh KLAYM)
To announce or report publicly.

Exodus 33:19 I will **p** the name of the LORD
1 Kings 21:9 **P** a fast, and set Naboth on high

Profane (proh FAYN)
To treat with great disrespect, especially God or things relating to God. To treat holy things in an unholy way.

Leviticus 19:12 neither shalt thou **p** the name of

Pp

Profit (PRAH fiht)
To benefit or gain from something.

Genesis 25:32 what **p** shall this birthright do
Mark 8:36 what shall it **p** a man, if he shall

Profitable (PRAH fit uh buhl)
That which causes a profit.

2 Timothy 3:16 is **p** for doctrine, for reproof, for

Profited (PRAH fih tid)
Past tense of "profit."

Matthew 16:26 For what is a man **p**, if he shall

Promise (PRAH miss)
A vow one makes to do, or not do, a thing. God promised to send a Redeemer or Savior into the world and that promise was fulfilled in Jesus, His only Son.

2 Chronicles 1:9 let thy **p** unto David my father be
Luke 24:49 I send the **p** of my Father upon you
Acts 1:4 but wait for the **p** of the Father
Ephesians 6:2 which is the first commandment with **p**

Promised (PRAH mist)
Past tense of "promise."

Luke 22:6 he **p**, and sought opportunity to betray

Prophesy (PRAH fi sigh)
Foretell; tell what God has spoken.

Matthew 26:68 saying, **P** unto us, thou Christ
Mark 14:65 **P**: and the servants did strike him
Luke 22:64 **P**, who is it that smote thee

Prophet (PRAHF it)
A person who speaks for God, especially when he says the exact words God has spoken to him. Prophets were not always popular because they said what the people needed to hear but the people didn't always want to hear it.

1 Kings 18:36 Elijah the **p** came near, and said
Jeremiah 36:26 Jeremiah the **p**: but the LORD hid
Matthew 1:22 spoken of the Lord by the **p**
Matthew 21:4 fulfilled which was spoken by the **p**
Mark 6:4 A **p** is not without honor, but in his
Luke 4:24 No **p** is accepted in his own country

Prophetess (PRAHF it iss)
A woman prophet. Only five women are listed in the Bible as prophetesses: Miriam, Deborah,

Huldah, Noadiah (a false prophetess), and Anna.

Exodus 15:20 And Miriam the *p*, the sister of
2 Kings 22:14 went unto Huldah the *p*, the wife of
Luke 2:36 And there was one Anna, a *p*

Prophets (PRAHF itz)
Plural of "prophet."

1 Kings 18:25 Elijah said unto the *p* of Baal
Matthew 2:23 fulfilled which was spoken by the *p*
Matthew 22:40 commandments hang all the law and the *p*
Mark 1:2 it is written in the *p*, Behold, I send my
Luke 24:27 And beginning at Moses and all the *p*, he

Propitiation (pro PISH ee ay shuhn)
The act of Jesus' death on the cross which provides forgiveness of our sins. This allows us to have a right relationship with God. Otherwise, our sins would keep us from God.

1 John 2:2 And he is the *p* for our sins: and not
1 John 4:10 sent his Son to be the *p* for our sins

Prosper (PRAHS puhr)
Do well, succeed, earn money.

Joshua 1:7 mayest *p* whithersoever thou goest
Psalm 1:3 whatsoever he doeth shall *p*

Prove (PROOV)
To test something.

Psalm 26:2 Examine me, O LORD, and *p* me
Romans 12:2 ye may *p* what is that good, and
Galatians 6:4 But let every man *p* his own work

Proverbs, Book of (PRAHV uhrbz)
The third book in the division, Poetry and Wisdom, in the Old Testament. It is a collection of sayings and truths that are to guide the reader to make wise choices, live a pure life, and to be able to get along with others. Solomon wrote many of the sayings but several other people wrote them, too. They were written over many hundreds of years and collected into books. It is thought that Jewish school boys used Proverbs as a schoolbook.

Provoke (proh VOHK)
To cause someone to feel anger or hurt feelings

1 Kings 16:33 Ahab did more to *p* the LORD God of
Ephesians 6:4 fathers, *p* not your children to wrath
Colossians 3:21 Fathers, *p* not your children to anger

215

Pp

■ Prudent (PROO dent)
Careful in what one does or the choices he makes; wise.

Proverbs 12:16 a **p** man overlooks an insult (NIV)
Proverbs 12:23 A **p** man keeps his knowledge to (NIV)

■ Psalms (SAHLMZ)
The second book in the division, Poetry and Wisdom, in the Old Testament. It is the longest book in the Bible with 150 chapters. Chapter 119 is the longest chapter with 176 verses. Psalms is found in the middle of the Bible. It is often called the songbook of the Bible. King David wrote many of the Psalms but other men wrote them, too. Some types of psalms are the thanksgiving or praise psalms, hymns, or psalms of lament (or crying out to God). Many hymns, songs, and choruses we sing today are taken from Psalms. The word "Psalms" includes all the 150 hymns. A "Psalm" refers to one hymn.

■ Psaltery (SAWL tuh re)
A musical instrument that is almost like the zither or dulcimer used today. Harp is another word for psaltery.

Psalm 33:2 sing unto him with the **p** and
Psalm 71:22 I will also praise thee with the **p**
Psalm 150:3 praise him with the **p** and harp

■ Publican (PUHB lih kuhn)
A tax collector for the Roman government. Most publicans were hated because they not only collected the money required by the government but demanded much more. The extra money was theirs to keep. Zacchaeus and Matthew were publicans in Jesus' day.

Matthew 10:3 Thomas, and Matthew the **p**; James the
Luke 5:27 went forth, and saw a **p**, named Levi

■ Publicans (PUHB lih kunz)
Plural of "publican."

Matthew 9:11 Why eateth your Master with **p** and
Mark 2:16 Pharisees saw him eat with **p** and sinners
Mark 2:16 he eateth and drinketh with **p** and sinners
Luke 3:12 Then came also **p** to be baptized, and said
Luke 5:30 Why do ye eat and drink with **p** and sinners
Luke 19:2 Zacchaeus, which was the chief among the **p**

Punishment (PUHN ish mint)
That which one receives for wrong actions or for a crime.

Genesis 4:13 My **p** is greater than I can bear
Matthew 25:46 shall go away into everlasting **p**

Pure (PYOOR)
Perfect, spotless, clean; free from anything that might pollute; sinless.

Psalm 19:8 the commandment of the LORD is **p**
Psalm 24:4 He that hath clean hands, and a **p** heart
Proverbs 30:5 Every word of God is **p**
Matthew 5:8 Blessed are the **p** in heart

Purple (PER puhl)
A color obtained by mixing red and blue. Fine, specially weaved linen, was dyed this color. It was worn by kings and people in high offices. The person who wore purple was usually very rich. During the trial of Jesus, a purple robe was placed on Him as the soldiers mocked him. Lydia, a woman living in Philippi, sold purple cloth.

Mark 15:17 And they clothed him in **p**, and
Mark 15:20 mocked him, they took off the **p**
John 19:2 and they put on him a **p** robe
John 19:5 the crown of thorns, and the **p** robe
Acts 16:14 woman named Lydia, a seller of **p**

Purpose (PER puhs)
Reason, plan.

Ruth 2:16 also some of the handfuls of **p** for her
Ecclesiastes 3:1 time to every **p** under the heaven
Matthew 26:8 saying, To what **p** is this waste
Romans 8:28 are the called according to his **p**

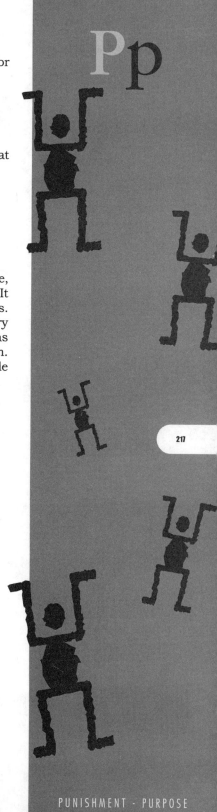

Pp

Quails (KWAYLZ)
Small spotted brown birds that migrate in large flocks. These birds wintered in Africa and then passed over the area in the Sinai desert where the Israelites camped. When the birds would stop to rest, they could be caught easily because they were tired. God provided these birds for the Israelites for forty years during their wilderness wandering.

Exodus 16:13 the *q* came up, and covered the camp

Quarrel (KWAH ruhl)
Argue, disagree, have words.

Colossians 3:13 if any man have a *q* against any

Quarter (KWOR tur)
Area, territory, district.

Mark 1:45 and they came to him from every *q*

Quench (KWINCH)
Drown, put out.

1 Thessalonians 5:19 **Q** not the Spirit

Quirinius (kwih RIN ih uhs)
Latin or Roman name for Cyrenius. He was the governor of Syria at the time Jesus was born. See Cyrenius.

Luke 2:2 took place while **Q** was governor of Syria (NIV)

Rabbi (RAB igh)
The word means "my master," a title of respect usually given to a teacher, or one with high office. Luke is the only Gospel writer who does not use the term "rabbi" in any of his writing. The disciples called Jesus "Rabbi" because He was their teacher, but they also knew Him as their Lord.

Mark 14:45 Judas said, "**R**!" and kissed him (NIV)
John 1:38 They said unto him, **R** (which is to say
John 1:49 **R**, thou art the Son of God
John 3:2 by night, and said unto him, **R**
John 6:25 said unto him, **R**, when camest thou

Rabboni (ra BOH nigh)
A different way to spell "Rabbi."

John 20:16 unto him, **R**, which is to say, Master

Rachel (RAY chul)
The name means "ewe." She was the daughter of Laban, and he was the brother of Rebekah, wife of Isaac. Rachel married Jacob and had two sons, Joseph and Benjamin. Jacob loved Rachel and was tricked into marrying her older sister, Leah, before he could marry her. For many years, Rachel had no children. Then she had Joseph and Benjamin, but she died when Benjamin was born.

Genesis 29:6 **R** his daughter cometh with the sheep
Genesis 29:9 **R** came with her father's sheep
Genesis 29:18 And Jacob loved **R**; and said, I
Genesis 35:19 And **R** died, and was buried in the

Raiment (RAY mint)
Clothing.

Matthew 6:25 more than meat, and the body than **r**
Matthew 28:3 and his **r** white as snow
Luke 23:34 And they parted his **r**, and cast lots

Rain (RAYN)
Mist or water that falls to earth from clouds in the sky. The moisture is necessary for plants to grow and to provide fresh water for humans and animals.

Genesis 2:5 LORD God had not caused it to **r**
Genesis 7:4 to **r** upon the earth forty days and
Genesis 7:12 **r** was upon the earth forty days and

Rachel

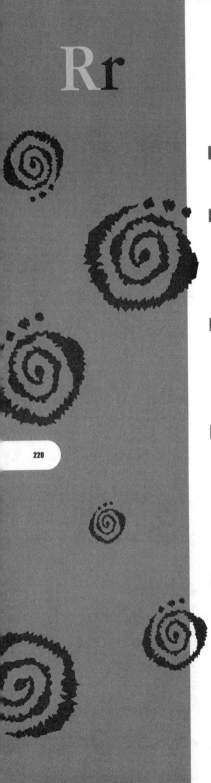

Rr

1 Kings 18:1 and I will send **r** upon the earth
1 Kings 18:41 there is a sound of abundance of **r**
1 Kings 18:45 and wind, and there was a great **r**
Matthew 5:45 sendeth **r** on the just and on the
Matthew 7:25 the **r** descended, and the floods came
Matthew 7:27 And the **r** descended, and the floods

Raise (RAYZ)
To elevate, lift up.

John 2:19 and in three days I will **r** it up

Raised (RAYZD)
Past tense of "raise."

Matthew 16:21 and be **r** again the third day
Matthew 17:23 the third day he shall be **r** again
John 12:1 whom Jesus had **r** from the dead (NIV)
John 12:9 Lazarus also, whom he had **r** from the

Ram (RAM)
A male goat or sheep used often in the animal sacrifices that God ordered the Israelites to perform.

Genesis 22:13 behind him a **r** caught in a thicket
Genesis 22:13 Abraham went and took the **r**, and

Rameses (RAM uh seez)
The capital city of Egypt and the location of the royal palace. As slaves, the Israelites helped build Rameses, one of the cities where food and goods were stored for Pharaoh Rameses II. Several Pharaohs not mentioned in the Bible used Rameses as part of their names.

Genesis 47:11 best of the land, in the land of **R**
Exodus 12:37 children of Israel journeyed from **R**

Ran (RAN)
Past tense of "run." To go fast, hurry, race; flow.

1 Kings 18:35 And the water **r** round about the
1 Kings 18:46 **r** before Ahab to the entrance of Jezreel
Matthew 27:48 one of them **r**, and took a sponge
Mark 5:6 saw Jesus afar off, he **r** and worshiped him
Luke 15:20 father saw him, and had compassion, and **r**
Luke 19:4 he **r** before, and climbed up into a sycamore
Luke 24:12 Then arose Peter, and **r** unto the sepulchre
John 20:4 So they **r** both together: and the other

Ransom (RAN suhm)
Buy back; the price paid for a thing. Jesus gave his life so He could pay for the sins of everyone who will trust in Him.

Matthew 20:28 to give his life a **r** for many
Mark 10:45 to give his life a **r** for many

■ **Rather (RATH uhr)**
Instead; in place of.

Mark 15:11 that he should **r** release Barabbas
Luke 12:31 But **r** seek ye the kingdom of God
John 3:19 and men loved darkness **r** than light
Acts 5:29 We ought to obey God **r** than men

■ **Ravens (RAY venz)**
Black birds of the crow family. The raven is a scavenger, a bird that eats from rotted or decayed material. Ravens were declared unclean birds by God. Yet, it was a raven that Noah first sent from the ark after the waters began to go down. And, ravens were sent to Elijah to provide the food he needed.

1 Kings 17:4 I have commanded the **r** to feed thee
1 Kings 17:6 **r** brought him bread and meat in (NIV)
Luke 12:24 Consider the **r**. for they neither sow

■ **Reach (REECH)**
Stretch out; touch.

John 20:27 saith he to Thomas, **R** hither thy finger
John 20:27 and **r** hither thy hand, and thrust it

■ **Ready (RED ee)**
Fit, prepared, willing.

Genesis 46:29 Joseph had his chariot made **r** (NIV)
Psalm 86:5 thou LORD, art good, and **r** to forgive
Matthew 26:19 and they made **r** the passover
Mark 14:15 and prepared: there make **r** for us
Mark 14:16 and they made **r** the passover
Mark 14:38 The spirit truly is **r,** but the flesh
Luke 22:12 upper room furnished: there make **r**
Luke 22:13 and they made **r** the passover

■ **Reap (REEP)**
To harvest. To cut grain by hand, using a scythe, a cutting tool with a curved blade attached to a long handle. It is in the shape of an "L."

Leviticus 19:9 when ye **r** the harvest of your land
Leviticus 19:9 thou shalt not wholly **r** the corners
Psalm 126:5 They that sow in tears shall **r** in joy
Matthew 6:26 they sow not, neither do they **r**

■ **Reapers (REEP uhrz)**
Plural for "reaper." A reaper is one who cuts and

Reap

221

Rr

gathers in the harvest

Ruth 2:3 and gleaned in the field after the **r**

◼ **Reason (REE zuhn)**
1. To think.

Mark 2:8 perceived in his Spirit that they so **r**
Luke 5:21 scribes and Pharisees began to **r**
Luke 5:22 said unto them, What **r** ye in your hearts

2. Because; the cause of.

John 6:18 the sea arose by **r** of a great wind

◼ **Rebekah (reh BEK uh)**
The name means "cow." Her brother was Laban, her husband was Isaac, and she had two sons, Esau and Jacob. Rebekah was a beautiful woman and helped the servant of Abraham water his camels. Abraham's servant had gone to the land of Laban to search for a wife for Isaac, the son of Abraham and Sarah. The servant asked God for a sign to show him the woman who was to become Isaac's wife. Later, after she had married Isaac and they had the twin boys, Rebekah favored Jacob while Isaac favored Esau. Rebekah encouraged Jacob to cheat Esau out of the blessing that Isaac would give before he died. After he received the blessing, he had to flee for his life to get away from Esau. She probably died before Jacob returned to the land of Canaan twenty years later.

Genesis 24:29 And **R** had a brother, and his name
Genesis 24:45 **R** came forth with her pitcher on
Genesis 25:28 but **R** loved Jacob
Genesis 27:5 **R** heard when Isaac spake to Esau
Genesis 27:6 **R** spake unto Jacob her son
Genesis 27:42 of Esau her elder son were told to **R**

◼ **Rebuke (ree BYUK)**
Blame, find fault, accuse; show strong dislike.

Proverbs 9:8 **r** a wise man, and he will love thee
Matthew 16:22 Peter took him, and began to **r** him
Mark 8:32 And Peter took him, and began to **r** him
Luke 19:39 said unto him, Master, **r** thy disciples

◼ **Rebuked (ree BYUKT)**
Past tense of "rebuke."

Matthew 8:26 he arose, and **r** the wind, and
Mark 4:39 And he arose, and **r** the wind, and

Luke 8:24 Then he arose, and **r** the wind and
Luke 23:40 But the other answering **r** him

■ **Receipt (ree SEET)**
A bill or ticket showing money had been paid.

Matthew 9:9 named Matthew, sitting at the **r** of custom
Mark 2:14 sitting at the **r** of custom, and said unto
Luke 5:27 named Levi, sitting at the **r** of custom

■ **Receive (ree SEEV)**
To accept, get, take in.

Proverbs 19:20 Hear counsel, and **r** instruction
Matthew 18:5 shall **r** one such little child in
Matthew 21::22 ask in prayer, believing, ye shall **r**
Mark 2:2 that there was no room to **r** them
Mark 9:37 whosoever shall **r** one of such children
Mark 10:51 Lord, that I might **r** my sight
Luke 9:48 Whosoever shall **r** this child in my
Luke 18:41 Lord, that I may **r** my sight
Luke 18:42 **R** thy sight: thy faith hath saved
Acts 1:8 But ye shall **r** power, after that the
Acts 20:35 more blessed to give than to **r**

■ **Received (ree SEEVD)**
Past tense of "receive."

Matthew 10:8 freely ye have **r**, freely give
Mark 10:52 immediately he **r** his sight, and
Luke 10:38 Martha **r** him into her house
Luke 15:27 because he hath **r** him safe and
Luke 18:43 And immediately he **r** his sight
Acts 2:41 gladly **r** his word were baptized

■ **Receiveth (ree SEEV ith)**
Old way of writing or saying "receives."

Matthew 7:8 For everyone that asketh **r**
Matthew 18:5 a little child in my name **r** me
Mark 9:37 such children in my name, **r** me
Luke 9:48 this child in my name **r** me
Luke 9:48 shall receive me **r** him that sent me
Luke 11:10 For everyone that asketh **r**

■ **Record (REK uhrd)**
A report; to see or watch, witness.

John 1:32 And John bare **r**, saying, I saw the
John 1:34 and bare **r** that this is the Son of God
John 12:17 and raised him from the dead, bare **r**
John 19:35 that saw it bare **r**, and his **r** is true

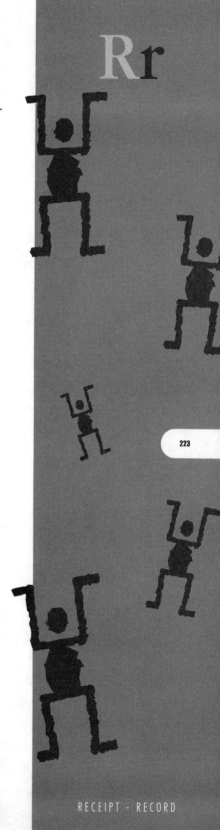

Rr

223

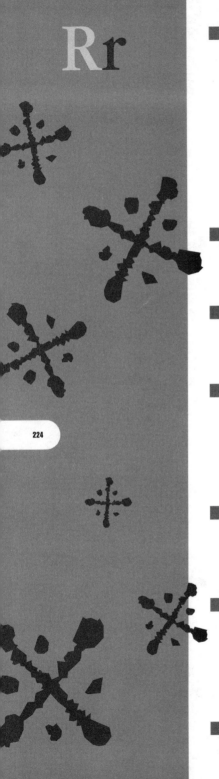

Rr

Red (RED)
1. The color called "red."

Genesis 25:25 the first came out **r** all over
Genesis 25:30 with that same **r** pottage; for I am

2. The name of the sea in Egypt over which the Israelites crossed on dry ground when they left Egyptian slavery. The Red Sea is also known as the "Reed Sea." (see map on page 337).

Exodus 10:19 locusts, and cast them into the **R** sea
Exodus 13:18 way of the wilderness of the **R** sea
Exodus 15:4 captains also are drowned in the **R** sea

Redeem (ree DEEM)
To purchase, buy, pay off a debt; to save.

Exodus 6:6 I will **r** you with a stretched out
Ruth 4:4 If thou wilt **r** it, **r** it

Redeemed (ree DEEMD)
Past tense of "redeem."

Luke 1:68 he hath visited and **r** his people
Luke 24:21 he which should have **r** Israel

Redeemer (ree DEEM uhr)
One who buys back. Jesus Christ became the redeemer for all people when He gave His life on the cross. The sacrifice of His life was the required payment for our sins

Job 19:25 For I know that my **r** liveth
Psalm 19:14 O LORD, my strength, and my **r**

Redemption (ree DEMP shun)
Paying the price so freedom can be given. Jesus gave us freedom from sin when He paid the price (His life on the cross).

Luke 2:38 them that looked for **r** in Jerusalem

Reed (REED)
A plant with a slender stalk that grows in shallow water.

Matthew 27:30 took the **r**, and smote him on the
Matthew 27:48 put it on a **r**, and gave him to
Mark 15:19 smote him on the head with a **r**
Mark 15:36 full of vinegar, and put it on a **r**

Refuge (REF yooj)
A place of hiding or protection; safety.

Psalm 46:1 God is our **r** and strength

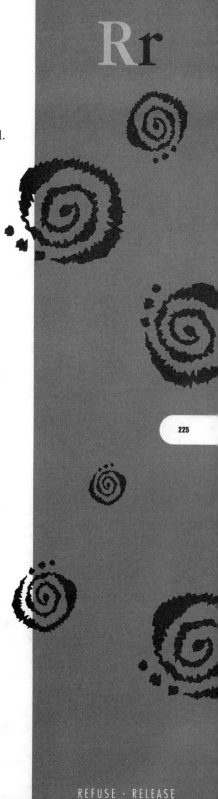

Refuse (ree FYOOZ)
To forbid, not allow; to prevent.

Exodus 8:2 And if thou **r** to let them go
Exodus 10:4 if thou **r** to let my people go
Proverbs 8:33 and be wise, and **r** it not

Region (REE juhn)
An area whose borders are not clearly defined.

Matthew 3:5 and all the **r** round about Jerusalem
Mark 1:28 fame spread abroad throughout all the **r**
Mark 6:55 They ran throughout that whole **r** (NIV)
Luke 4:14 a fame of him through all the **r**
Luke 7:17 and throughout all the **r** round about

Reign (RAYN)
To govern, lead, or rule as a king.

Exodus 15:18 The LORD shall **r** for ever and ever
Psalm 146:10 The LORD shall **r** forever
Luke 1:33 he shall **r** over the house of Jacob

Rejected (ree JEK tid)
Past tense of "reject."

1 Samuel 8:7 not **r** thee, but they have **r** me
Isaiah 53:3 He is despised and **r** of men
Mark 8:31 must suffer many things, and be **r**
Luke 9:22 be **r** of the elders and chief priests

Rejoice (ree JOYS)
Be happy, full of joy, celebrate.

Psalm 118:24 we will **r** and be glad in it
Proverbs 24:17 **R** not when thine enemy falleth
Romans 12:15 **R** with them that do **r**
Philippians 4:4 **R** in the Lord always
Philippians 4:4 and again I say, **R**

Rejoiced (ree JOYST)
Past tense of "rejoice."

Matthew 2:10 saw the star, they **r** with exceeding
Luke 1:47 my spirit hath **r** in God my Savior
Luke 13:17 the people **r** for all the glorious things

Rejoiceth (ree JOY seth)
Old way of writing or saying "rejoices."

Matthew 18:13 he **r** more of that sheep, than of the

Release (ree LEES)
To let go, free.

Matthew 27:15 custom at the Feast to **r** a prisoner (NIV)

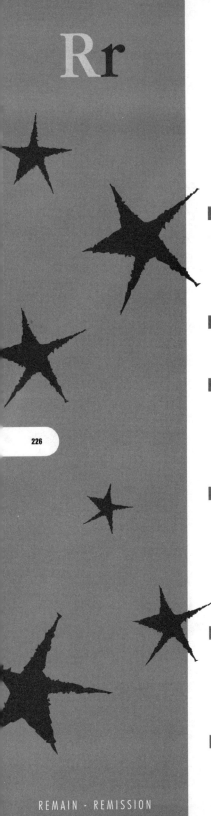

Rr

Matthew 27:17 me to **r** to you: Barabbas, or Jesus (NIV)
Mark 15:9 that I **r** unto you the King of the Jews
Mark 15:11 should rather **r** Barabbas unto them
Luke 23:16 will therefore chastise him, and **r** him
Luke 23:17 of necessity, he must **r** one
Luke 23:18 Away with this man, and **r** unto us Barabbas
Luke 23:20 Pilate therefore, willing to **r** Jesus
John 18:39 custom, that I should **r** unto you one
John 18:39 I **r** unto you the King of the Jews
John 19:12 Pilate sought to **r** him, but the Jews cried

■ Remain (ree MAYN)
To stay, linger, wait.

Exodus 12:10 let nothing of it **r** until the morning
1 Kings 18:22 even I only, **r** a prophet of the LORD
John 6:12 Gather up the fragments that **r**
John 19:31 bodies should not **r** upon the cross

■ Remained (ree MAYND)
Past tense of "remain."

Matthew 14:20 fragments that **r** twelve baskets full

■ Remember (ree MEM buhr)
To not forget; think of again; recall.

Exodus 20:8 **R** the sabbath day, to keep it holy
Ecclesiastes 12:1 **R** now thy Creator in the days of
Luke 23:42 **r** me when thou comest into thy kingdom
Luke 24:6 **r** how he spake unto you when he was yet

■ Remembered (ree MEM buhrd)
Past tense of "remember."

Genesis 8:1 God **r** Noah, and every living thing
Exodus 2:24 God **r** his covenant with Abraham
Matthew 26:75 Peter **r** the words of Jesus, which
Luke 22:61 And Peter **r** the word of the Lord
Luke 24:8 And they **r** his words
John 12:16 then **r** they these things that were

■ Remembrance (ree MEM bruns)
To have remembered.

Luke 22:19 do this in **r** of me
1 Corinthians 11:24 this do in **r** of me
1 Corinthians 11:25 as oft as ye drink it, in **r** of me
Philippians 1:3 I thank my God upon every **r** of you

■ Remission (ree MISS shun)
Forgiveness, pardon.

Matthew 26:28 which is shed for the **r** of sins

Mark 1:4 baptism of repentance for the *r* of sins
Acts 2:38 name of Jesus Christ for the *r* of sins

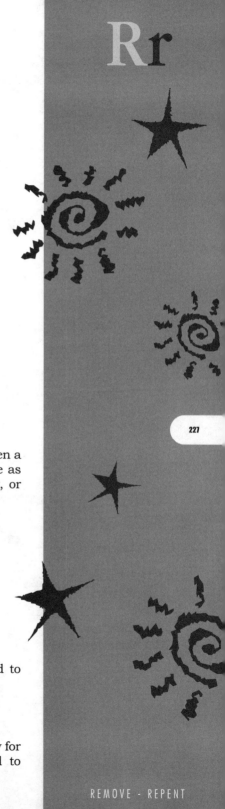

■ Remove (ree MOOV)
To take away.

Luke 22:42 if thou be willing, *r* this cup from me

■ Removed (ree MOOVD)
Past tense of "remove."

Psalm 103:12 so far hath he *r* our transgressions

■ Rend (REND)
To rip, split, tear.

Ecclesiastes 3:7 A time to *r*, and a time to sew
John 19:24 Let us not *r* it, but cast lots for it

■ Render (REHN duhr)
To repay, or give back.

Matthew 22:21 **R** therefore unto Caesar the things
Mark 12:17 **R** to Caesar the things that are Caesar's
Luke 20:25 **R** therefore unto Caesar the things

■ Renew (ree NYOO)
To make anew, to make fresh.

Psalm 51:10 and *r* a right spirit within me

■ Rent (WRINT)
Past tense of "rend." During Bible times, when a person rent his or her clothing, it was done as an act of great sorrow, sadness, mourning, or grief.

Genesis 37:29 not in the pit; and he *r* his clothes
1 Kings 19:11 great and strong wind *r* the mountains
Matthew 26:65 Then the high priest *r* his clothes
Matthew 27:51 the veil of the temple was *r* in twain
Matthew 27:51 the earth did quake, and the rocks *r*
Mark 14:63 Then the high priest *r* his clothes
Mark 15:38 veil of the temple was *r* in twain
Luke 23:45 and the veil of the temple was *r*

■ Repay (ree PAY)
Pay back or return something that is owed to another person.

Luke 10:35 when I come again, I will *r* thee

■ Repent (ree PENT)
To feel sorrow about something. To feel sorry for the wrong things a person has done and to

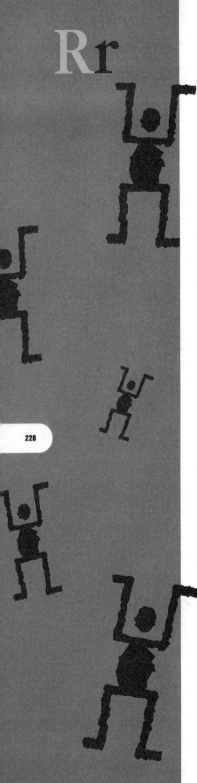

Rr

decide to do what is right. To let God be a part of one's life.

Matthew 4:17 Jesus began to preach, and to say, **R**
Mark 1:15 kingdom of God is at hand: **r** ye, and
Mark 6:12 and preached that men should **r**
Luke 13:3 except ye **r**, ye shall all likewise perish

■ Repentance (ree PEN tunce)
The act of repenting.

Matthew 9:13 to call the righteous, but sinners to **r**
Mark 2:17 call the righteous, but sinners to **r**
Luke 5:32 call the righteous, but sinners to **r**

■ Repented (ree PEN tid)
Past tense for "repent."

Genesis 6:6 it **r** the LORD that he had made man
Matthew 27:3 saw that he was condemned, **r** himself

■ Repenteth (ree PEN tith)
The old way of writing or saying "repents."

Genesis 6:7 for it **r** me that I have made them
Luke 15:7 in heaven over one sinner that **r**
Luke 15:10 angels of God over one sinner that **r**

■ Repetitions (reh pih TIH shunz)
The act of saying something over again.

Matthew 6:7 when ye pray, use not vain **r**

■ Replenish (ree PLIN ish)
Refill, renew.

Genesis 1:28 and multiply, and **r** the earth
Genesis 9:1 and multiply, and **r** the earth

■ Request (ree KWEST)
Appeal to, or ask for something.

Esther 5:3 what is thy **r**? It shall be even
Esther 5:7 and said, My petition and my **r** is
Esther 7:2 what is thy **r**, and it shall be performed

■ Resist (ree ZIST)
To fight, oppose, or stop; stand up against.

Matthew 5:39 I tell you, Do not **r** an evil person (NIV)
James 4:7 **R** the devil, and he will flee from you

■ Resisteth (ree ZIST eth)
The old way of writing or saying "resists."

James 4:6 God **r** the proud, but giveth grace to
1 Peter 5:5 God **r** the proud, and giveth grace to

Respect (ree SPEKT)
To have high regard for; approval; favor.

Genesis 4:4 the LORD had *r* unto Abel and to
Genesis 4:5 Cain and to his offering he had not *r*

Respecter (ree SPEK tuhr)
One who shows partiality or favoritism. God does not show favoritism, so we are not to show favoritism, either.

Acts 10:34 I perceive that God is no *r* of persons

Rest (WREST)
1. Pause, sleep, be quiet. Jesus encouraged us to have the rest He offers. The only way we can have it is to trust in Him. His rest is not so much the physical kind, but the spiritual kind.

Genesis 8:9 the dove found no *r* for the sole of
Psalm 37:7 **R** in the LORD, and wait patiently
Matthew 11:28 heavy laden, and I will give you *r*
Matthew 11:29 ye shall find *r* unto your souls
Matthew 26:45 Sleep on now, and take your *r*
Mark 6:31 apart into a desert place, and *r* awhile
Mark 14:41 Sleep on now, and take your *r*

2. That which is left over; the remainder.

Matthew 27:49 The *r* said, Let be, let us see

Restore (ree STOR)
To fix, mend, make new again; return.

Psalm 51:12 **R** unto me the joy of thy salvation
Luke 19:8 false accusation, I *r* him fourfold

Restored (ree STORD)
Past tense of "restore."

Matthew 12:13 stretched it forth, and it was *r* whole
Mark 3:5 stretched it out: and his hand was *r*
Mark 8:25 he was *r*, and saw every man clearly
Luke 6:10 and his hand was *r* whole as the other

Restoreth (ree STOR ith)
Old way of writing or saying "restores."

Psalm 23:3 He *r* my soul: he leadeth me in the paths

Resurrection (re zu REK shun)
Receiving life again after one has died. Jesus was resurrected after His death on the cross. That made it possible for every one who believes and trusts in His name to have life after death. This life is called eternal life.

Resurrection

Rr

Matthew 27:53 came out of the graves after his **r**
John 11:25 Jesus said unto her, I am the **r**, and

◼ Return (ree TERN)
Give back, go back.

Exodus 4:19 Go, **r** into Egypt: for all the men are
Ruth 1:16 or to **r** from following after thee
Matthew 2:12 that they should not **r** unto Herod
Luke 8:39 **R** to thine own house, and show
Luke 17:18 Was no one found to **r** and give praise (NIV)

◼ Returned (ree TERND)
Past tense of "return."

Luke 23:56 they **r**, and prepared spices and ointments
Luke 24:9 **r** from the sepulcher, and told all these
Luke 24:33 rose up the same hour, and **r** to Jerusalem
Luke 24:52 worshiped him, and **r** to Jerusalem

◼ Reuben (RHOO ben)
The name means "see, a son." The oldest son of
Jacob and Leah. His other brothers wanted to
kill Joseph but Reuben talked them into putting
him into a pit. He planned to return later and
release Joseph. His descendants were one of the
twelve tribes of Israel.

Genesis 37:22 **R** said unto them, Shed no blood
Genesis 37:29 **R** returned unto the pit; and, behold
Genesis 42:22 **R** answered them, saying, Spake I
Genesis 42:37 **R** spake unto his father, saying

◼ Reuel (RHOO el)
The name means "friend of God." He was the
father-in-law of Moses, and was also known as
Jethro. His daughter, Zipporah, married Moses.

Exodus 2:18 when they came to **R** their father

◼ Revealed (ree VEELD)
Past tense of "reveal." Tell, show.

1 Samuel 3:21 the LORD **r** himself to Samuel
Daniel 2:19 Then was the secret **r** unto Daniel
Luke 2:26 it was **r** unto him by the Holy Ghost

◼ Revelation, Book of (REV uh LAY shuhn)
The only book listed in the New Testament divi-
sion of Prophecy. It is the last book in the Bible.
The writer is John the apostle, the son of
Zebedee. He wrote it while he was in exile on the
island of Patmos, a small island in the Aegean
Sea governed by Rome. Political prisoners were

230

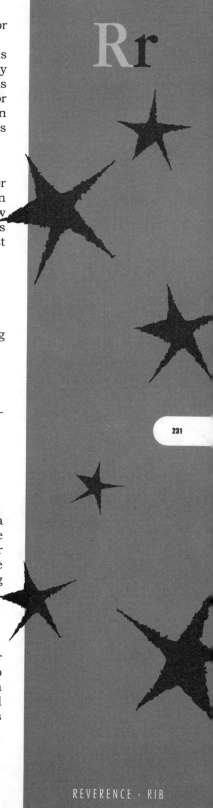

kept there. John was probably arrested for preaching about Jesus.

The book of Revelation tells about various visions John had in which God revealed many things about the end of time and how Jesus would finally conquer sin. It is a book of hope for the Christian who faithfully obeys God. John used many symbols, or images, to tell of his visions.

Reverence (REV uhr ins)
Love, honor, or respect shown to a person or object. Persons to whom reverence is to be given are parents and God. We are expected to show reverence in "God's sanctuary" and to the laws He has given us. We show reverence to Christ when we obey Him.

Leviticus 19:30 Keep my sabbaths, and **r** my sanctuary
Esther 3:2 Mordecai bowed not, nor did him **r**

Revile (ree VIGHL)
To insult or put down a person by yelling unkind words or calling bad names.

Matthew 5:11 Blessed are ye, when men shall **r** you

Reward (ree WAHRD)
Something that is given for good or bad behavior or actions.

Matthew 5:12 for great is your **r** in heaven
Matthew 6:4 in secret himself shall **r** thee openly
Luke 23:41 we receive the due **r** of our deeds

Rhoda (ROH duh)
The name means "rose." She may have been a servant for Mary, the mother of John Mark. She answered Peter's knock at the door when Peter was led from prison by an angel. In her surprise and shock at seeing Peter, she left him standing at the door while she ran to tell the others.

Acts 12:13 a servant girl named **R** came to answer (NIV)

Rib (RIB)
One of the many curved bones in the upper body or chest area. These bones are attached to the spine and are flexible, or movable, to aid in breathing. The ribs protect the lungs, heart, and other vital body organs. God used one of Adam's ribs to form Eve.

Genesis 2:22 And the **r**, which the LORD God had

Rr

Ribs (RIBZ)
Plural for "rib."

Genesis 2:21 and he took one of his **r**, and

Rich (RICH)
Wealthy, having a lot of money or possessions.

Genesis 13:2 Abram was very **r** in cattle, in silver
Matthew 19:23 a **r** man shall hardly enter into the
Matthew 19:24 for a **r** man to enter into the kingdom
Matthew 27:57 there came a **r** man of Arimathea
Mark 10:25 for a **r** man to enter into the kingdom
Luke 18:25 for a **r** man to enter into the kingdom
Luke 21:1 saw the **r** men casting their gifts into

Riches (RICH iz)
Possessions and money that makes one wealthy.

Mark 10:23 How hardly shall they that have **r**
Mark 10:24 trust in **r** to enter into the kingdom

Rider (RIGH duhr)
One who rides. In the Bible, it refers to one riding on the back of an animal.

Exodus 15:1 horse and his **r** hath he thrown into
Exodus 15:21 horse and his **r** hath he thrown into

Riding (RIGH ding)
The act of moving about while on the back of an animal.

Zechariah 9:9 **r** on a donkey, on a colt, the foal (NIV)

Right (RIGHT)
1. Opposite of the left.

Exodus 14:22 a wall unto them; on their **r** hand
Matthew 5:39 smite thee on thy **r** cheek, turn
Luke 22:50 high priest, and cut off his **r** ear
Luke 23:33 one on the **r** hand, and the other on
John 18:10 servant, and cut off his **r** ear

2. Good, honest, moral.

Deuteronomy 6:18 do that which is **r** and good
Psalm 19:8 The statutes of the LORD are **r**
Psalm 51:10 and renew a **r** spirit within me
Proverbs 14:12 way which seemeth **r** unto a man
Proverbs 16:25 way that seemeth **r** to a man

Righteous (RIGH chus)
Moral, honest, and right in what one does. Only through Christ can a person be made right so that he can have a close friendship with God.

Matthew 9:13 not come to call the *r*, but sinners
Mark 2:17 came not to call the *r*, but sinners
Luke 5:32 I came not to call the *r*, but sinners
Luke 23:47 certainly this was a *r* man
Romans 3:10 There is none *r*, no not one

■ Righteousness (RIGH chus niss)
Right living by the rules God has given. Living and acting so that what we do matches or is equal to the laws and purposes God has given.

Psalm 23:3 he leadeth me in the paths of *r*
Matthew 5:6 which do hunger and thirst after *r*
Matthew 6:33 first the kingdom of God, and his *r*
Romans 10:10 with the heart man believeth unto *r*

■ Rise (RIGHZ)
1. To stand; to get up; ascend.

Exodus 8:20 **R** up early in the morning, and stand
Matthew 5:45 maketh his sun to *r* on the evil
Matthew 26:46 **R**, let us be going: behold
Luke 22:46 Why sleep ye? **R** and pray
John 5:8 **R**, take up thy bed, and walk
Acts 3:6 name of Jesus Christ of Nazareth, *r* up

2. To return from death.

Matthew 20:19 and the third day he shall *r* again
Matthew 27:63 After three days, I will *r* again
Mark 8:31 killed, and after three days *r* again
Mark 10:34 the third day he shall *r* again
Luke 18:33 and the third day he shall *r* again
Luke 24:7 be crucified, and the third day *r* again

■ Risen (RIZEN)
Has gotten up, ascended, returned from death.

Matthew 26:32 But after I am *r* again, I will
Matthew 27:64 and say unto the people, He is *r*
Matthew 28:6 He is not here: for he is *r*, as he
Matthew 28:7 tell his disciples that he is *r*
Mark 16:6 crucified: he is *r*, he is not here
Mark 16:9 when Jesus was *r* early the first day
Luke 24:6 He is not here, but is *r*. remember
Luke 24:34 saying, The Lord is *r* indeed, and
John 21:14 after that he was *r* from the dead

■ River (RIH vuhr)
A natural waterway or stream.

Genesis 2:10 a *r* went out of Eden to water
Exodus 2:5 came down to wash herself at the *r*
Mark 1:5 baptized him in the *r* of Jordan

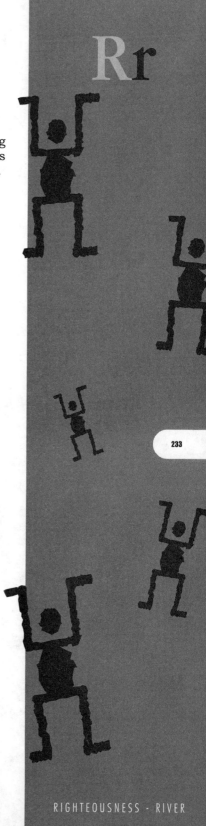

R r

233

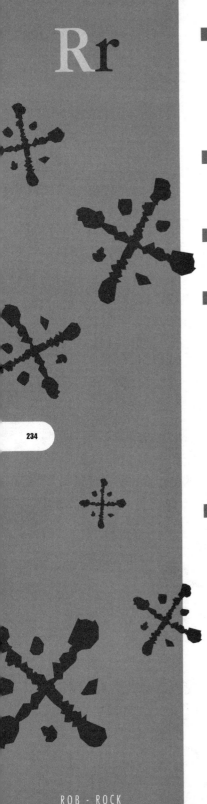

Rr

Rob (RAHB)
To take another person's belongings using force, or by cheating, with no thought of returning it; to steal.

Leviticus 19:13 not defraud thy neighbor, neither **r** him
Proverbs 22:22 **R** not the poor, because he is poor
Malachi 3:8 Will a man **r** God? Yet ye have robbed

Robbed (RAHBD)
Past tense of "rob."

Malachi 3:8 Yet ye have **r** me. But ye say
Malachi 3:8 Wherein have we **r** thee? In tithes

Robber (RAHB buhr)
One who robs or steals.

John 18:40 but Barabbas. Now Barabbas was a **r**

Robe (ROWB)
A coat; an outer garment, usually long, and loose. In Bible times, the robe was used to cover a person at night. Kings and the rich wore robes of purple and blue, and were often made in different styles. In many places in the Bible, a robe is also called "a mantle."

Matthew 27:28 and put on him a scarlet **r**
Matthew 27:31 they took the **r** off from him
Luke 15:22 Bring forth the best **r**, and put it
Luke 23:11 arrayed him in a gorgeous **r**, and sent
John 19:2 they put on him a purple **r**
John 19:5 crown of thorns, and the purple **r**

Rock (RAHK)
A huge stone which did not change and which could not be moved. Biblical people would sometimes go to a rocky place to find safety. God has sometimes been described as a rock because He does not change, He is strong and unmoving, and He provides protection for His people. The faith that Peter had in seeing Jesus as "Christ, the Son of the living God," is probably what Jesus meant when He said, "Upon this rock I will build my church" (Matthew 16:18).

Exodus 17:6 smite the **r**, and there shall come water
Exodus 33:21 and thou shalt stand upon a **r**
Exodus 33:22 I will put thee in a cleft of the **r**
Deuteronomy 32:4 He is the **R**, his work is perfect
Psalm 18:2 The LORD is my **R**, and my fortress
Psalm 61:2 lead me to the **r** that is higher than
Psalm 62:2 He only is my **r** and my salvation

Matthew 7:24 man, which built his house upon a **r**
Matthew 7:25 for it was founded upon a **r**
Matthew 16:18 upon this **r** I will build my church
Matthew 27:60 tomb, which he had hewn out in the **r**
Mark 15:46 sepulcher which was hewn out of a **r**
Luke 6:48 and laid the foundation on a **r**

Rod (RAHD)
A bar, pole, or long stick. Another word used in the Bible is the word "staff." In biblical times, a rod had many purposes and was made from a strong wood or some type of metal. A rod could be used to defend oneself or one's property, as a walking stick, to punish someone, or to measure things.

Exodus 4:2 in thine hand? And he said, A **r**
Exodus 7:10 Aaron cast down his **r** before Pharaoh
Exodus 14:16 But lift thou up thy **r**, and stretch out
Psalm 23:4 thy **r** and thy staff they comfort me

Roll (ROWL)
Turn over.

Mark 16:3 Who shall **r** us away the stone from

Rolled (ROWLD)
Past tense of "roll."

Matthew 27:60 he **r** a great stone to the door
Matthew 28:2 and **r** back the stone from the door
Mark 15:46 and **r** a stone unto the door
Mark 16:4 saw that the stone was **r** away
Luke 24:2 they found the stone **r** away

Roman (ROH muhn)
Someone who was born in Rome or who lived there.

Acts 22:26 heed what thou doest: for this man is a **R**

Romans, Book of (ROH muhnz)
The first book in the division, Paul's Letters, in the New Testament. Paul, the writer of Romans, had longed to go to Rome and talk to the Christians there. This letter was telling them of his coming visit, but he also asked them to pray for him as he went to Jerusalem. He had an offering from Gentile Christians in Macedonia to give to the Christians in Jerusalem. Some distrust had been present at one time about the Gentile believers. He also explained to the Roman believers about God's righteousness and the rules by which God expects believers to live.

235

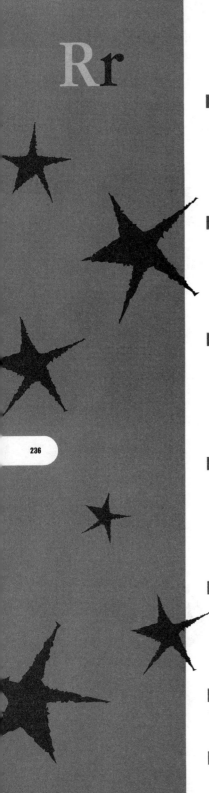

Rr

He stressed that a person could be saved only by Jesus Christ, that he couldn't do it himself by living a good life.

■ Rome (ROHM)
The capital of the Roman empire, located in Italy on the Tiber River (see map on page 341). It was a large city during the time of Paul. Emperors who had ruled the Roman Empire had made it a beautiful and great city.

Acts 23:11 so must thou bear witness also at *R*

■ Roof (REWF)
The top part of a building, either flat or with a slope.

Matthew 8:8 that thou shouldest come under my *r*
Mark 2:4 they uncovered the *r* where he was
Luke 7:6 that thou shouldest enter under my *r*

■ Room (REWM)
An area or part of a building; space.

Mark 2:2 there was no *r* to receive them
Mark 14:15 show you a large upper *r* furnished
Luke 2:7 there was no *r* for them in the inn
Luke 22:12 a large upper *r* furnished
Acts 1:13 they went up into an upper *r*

■ Rose (ROWZ)
Past tense of "rise."

Genesis 4:8 Cain *r* up against Abel his brother
Exodus 12:30 And Pharaoh *r* up in the night
Luke 5:28 he left all, *r* up, and followed him
Luke 22:45 And when he *r* up from prayer
Luke 24:33 And they *r* up the same hour

■ Rubies (ROO bees)
Plural for "ruby." A deep red mineral. When cut and polished, it is quite beautiful. It is called a "precious stone" because it is beautiful and somewhat rare.

Proverbs 8:11 For wisdom is better than *r*

■ Ruin (ROO in)
Downfall; great loss.

Luke 6:49 and the *r* of that house was great

■ Rule (REWL)
To control or govern.

Genesis 1:16 the greater light to *r* the day

Genesis 1:16 the lesser light to **r** the night
Matthew 2:6 Governor, that shall **r** my people

◼ Ruler (REWL uhr)
One who rules or governs.

Genesis 41:43 made him **r** over all the land of Egypt
Matthew 9:18 behold, there came a certain **r**
Mark 5:35 came from the **r** of the synagogue's house
Luke 13:14 the **r** of the synagogue answered
Luke 18:18 And a certain **r** asked him, saying
John 3:1 Nicodemus, a **r** of the Jews

◼ Rulers (REWL uhrz)
Plural of "ruler."

Mark 5:22 cometh one of the **r** of the synagogue
Luke 23:13 chief priests and the **r** and the people
Luke 23:35 And the **r** also with them derided him
Luke 24:20 chief priests and our **r** delivered him
John 12:42 among the chief **r** also many believed

◼ Ruth (ROOTH or REWTH)
A young woman from Moab who married one of the sons of Naomi and Elimelech. A famine in Judah around Bethlehem caused Naomi's family to move to Moab. While there, Elimelech died. The sons married Moabite women and then the two sons died, leaving Naomi, Ruth, and Orpah widows. Ruth went to Bethlehem with Naomi and lived in her home. She worked in the fields of Boaz, a kinsman of Naomi's. Later, Ruth married Boaz. Their son, Obed, was an ancestor of King David, and of Jesus.

Ruth 1:4 the name of the other **R**
Ruth 1:16 And **R** said, Entreat me not to leave
Ruth 2:2 **R** the Moabitess said unto Naomi
Ruth 4:10 Moreover **R** the Moabitess, the wife of

◼ Ruth, Book of (ROOTH or REWTH)
The third book in the division, History, in the Old Testament. The writer is not known. It is called an historical short story and shows that God loves all people, and could even use a foreigner (Ruth) in His plan for the salvation of the world.

Ruth

237

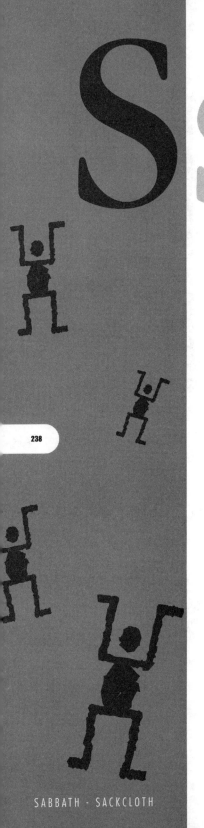

Sabbath (SAB uhth)

The word means to "cease" or "desist." The Sabbath is the seventh day of the week. It was on the seventh day that God rested from His work of creation. Throughout the Bible, the Sabbath means the seventh day of the week, or Saturday. Sabbath was from Friday at sundown until Saturday at sundown. It was on this day that the Israelites met together to worship God, and they rested from their work. After Jesus was resurrected, His believers met together on Sunday, the first day of the week. This became their holy day, their day to worship Jesus Christ the Savior, the Son of God.

Exodus 16:23 a day of rest, a holy **s** to the LORD (NIV)
Exodus 16:25 for today is a **s** unto the LORD
Exodus 20:8 Remember the **s** day, to keep it holy
Leviticus 23:3 the seventh day is the **s** of rest
Deuteronomy 5:12 Keep the **s** day to sanctify it
Matthew 12:8 Son of man is Lord even of the **s**
Matthew 28:1 the end of the **s**, as it began to dawn
Mark 2:27 The **s** was made for man,
Mark 2:27 and not man for the **s**
Mark 15:42 that is, the day before the **s**
Mark 16:1 when the **s** was past, Mary Magdalene
Luke 6:5 Son of man is Lord also of the **s**
Luke 23:54 and the **s** was about to begin (NIV)
Luke 23:56 they rested on the **s** in obedience (NIV)
John 19:31 not remain upon the cross on the **s**
John 19:31 (for that **s** day was an high day,)
Acts 1:12 from Jerusalem about a **s** day's journey
Acts 13:14 into the synagogue on the **s** day

Sackcloth (SAK kloth)

Rough clothing made from goat or camel hair. It was worn to show that a person was suffering because of a death, sorrow, some kind of trouble, or shame over wrong choices made. The garment could have been loose fitting, like a sack, or wrapped around the waist to cover the hips and thighs.

Genesis 37:34 and put **s** upon his loins and mourned
Esther 4:1 and put on **s** with ashes
Jonah 3:5 proclaimed a fast, and put on **s**

Ss

Sack's (SAX)
Possessive of "sack."

Genesis 42:27 behold, it was in his **s** mouth
Genesis 44:1 put every man's money in his **s** mouth
Genesis 44:2 in the **s** mouth of the youngest

Sacks (SAX)
Plural of "sack." A large bag or pouch. In biblical times, grain was carried in sacks.

Genesis 42:25 fill their **s** with corn, and to
Genesis 43:21 we opened our **s**, and, behold
Genesis 44:1 Fill the men's **s** with food

Sacrifice (SAC rih fighs)
A type of offering to God. During Old Testament times, a sacrifice was offered as an act of being obedient to God, to ask for forgiveness, or to express worship. Different and specific animals were to be used for the sacrifices. The poor could offer pigeons or turtledoves.

In New Testament times, the Hebrew people still offered sacrifices, but they stopped doing so after the Temple was destroyed in 70 A.D. The death of Jesus made the sacrifices of animals no longer necessary. The believer in Jesus was to offer a worthy "spiritual sacrifice." In this type of sacrifice, the Christian made a pledge or promise to God to obey His laws and to live like Christ.

Genesis 31:54 Then Jacob offered **s** upon the mount
Exodus 8:8 that they may do **s** unto the LORD
1 Samuel 1:21 offer unto the LORD the yearly **s**
1 Samuel 16:2 I am come to **s** to the LORD
1 Samuel 16:3 and call Jesse to the **s**
1 Kings 18:29 of the offering of the evening **s**
1 Kings 18:38 the LORD fell and burned up the **s** (NIV)
Jonah 1:16 offered a **s** unto the LORD, and
Jonah 2:9 But I will **s** unto thee with the voice
Luke 2:24 to offer a **s** according to that which

Sacrifices (SAK rih figh ses)
Plural of "sacrifice."

Genesis 46:1 offered **s** unto the God of his father

Sad (SAD)
Unhappy, full of sorrow, down.

Genesis 40:6 and, behold, they were **s**
Mark 10:22 he was **s** at that saying, and went
Luke 24:17 to another, as ye walk, and are **s**

Ss

240

■ Sadducees (SAD joo seez)
The name means "righteous ones." A religious group of Jewish men who believed that the five books of Law were the only true Scripture. They did not believe in angels, certainly did not agree with the Pharisees, and did not believe that there is life after death. They were against all the things Jesus did. Some of those belonging to the Sadducees were the high priests and wealthy rulers.

Matthew 16:1 The Pharisees also with the **S** came
Matthew 22:34 heard that he had put the **S** to silence

■ Safely (SAYF lee)
Out of danger, secure.

Mark 14:44 take him, and lead him away **s**
Acts 16:23 charging the jailer to keep them **s**

■ Sailed (SAYLD)
Past tense of "sail." To travel by boat, with the wind moving the boat by means of large sheets of canvas attached to upright poles.

Luke 8:23 But as they **s**, he fell asleep
Acts 13:4 and **s** from there to Cyprus (NIV)

■ Saints (SAYNTS)
A name given to the people of God. In the Old Testament, a saint was one who worshiped God. In the New Testament, a saint was anyone who had "accepted Jesus as Lord and Savior."

Psalm 31:23 O love the LORD, all ye his **s**
Psalm 34:9 O fear the LORD, ye his **s**
Matthew 27:52 bodies of the **s** which slept arose

■ Sake (SAYK)
Benefit, cause, interest.

Genesis 18:29 I will not do it for forty's **s**
Matthew 5:10 persecuted for righteousness' **s**
Matthew 5:11 evil against you falsely, for my **s**
Matthew 16:25 loseth his life for my **s** shall find it
Mark 8:35 shall lose his life for my **s** and
Luke 9:24 whosoever will lose his life for my **s**
John 13:38 Wilt thou lay down thy life for my **s**

■ Sakes (SAYKS)
Plural of "sake."

John 11:15 glad for your **s** that I was not there

■ Salome (suh LOH mih)
The name means "pacific." Her sons were James

and John, two of the disciples of Jesus. She was the wife of Zebedee. Salome became a follower of Jesus and was one of the women who helped prepare Jesus' body to be buried.

Mark 15:40 of James the less and of Joses, and **S**
Mark 16:1 Mary the mother of James, and **S**

■ Salt (SAWLT)
A compound used to season foods, as well as to preserve meats and fish. Jesus compared the disciples' lives to salt. If they lived as God led them and obeyed His commandments, they would make a difference in the world. Because salt makes things taste better, a Christian is to bring out the best in others. Otherwise, a Christian is not worth anything.

Genesis 19:26 and she became a pillar of **s**
Matthew 5:13 Ye are the **s** of the earth
Matthew 5:13 But if the **s** loses its saltiness (NIV)
Mark 9:50 **S** is good: but if the **s** have lost
Luke 14:34 **S** is good: but if the **s** have lost

■ Salutation (sal yoo TAY shun)
A word or act of greeting.

Luke 1:29 what manner of **s** this should be

■ Salute (sah LOOT)
To address, greet, show honor or respect.

Mark 15:18 began to **s** him, Hail, King of the Jews

■ Salvation (sal VAY shun)
To rescue a person from death or anything that might hurt or destroy a person. Spiritually, it means to free a person from the punishment and the hold of sin on a person's life. This is done through the life, death, and resurrection of Jesus Christ.

Exodus 14:13 stand still, and see the **s** of the LORD
Psalm 27:1 The LORD is my light and my **s**
Psalm 51:12 Restore unto me the joy of thy **s**
Luke 3:6 all mankind will see God's **s** (NIV)
Luke 19:9 This day is **s** come to this house

■ Samaria (suh MEHR ih uh)
The name means "mountain of watching." The name of a mountain, a city which was built on the mountain, and a region surrounding the mountain. Samaria is about 42 miles north of Jerusalem and about 25 miles east of the Mediterranean Sea (see map on page 340).

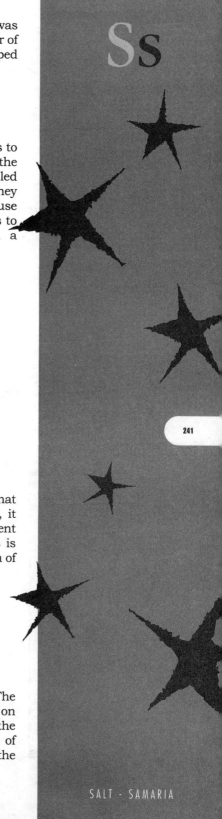

241

Ss

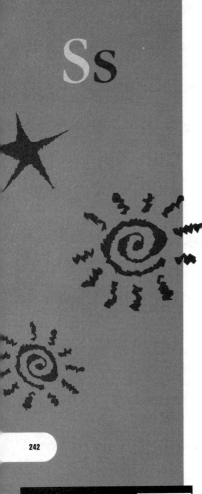

Samaria was the capital city of the region of Samaria. King Ahab's palace was in Samaria. In New Testament times, Samaria lay between Galilee to the north, and Judah to the south. Jews had lived in Samaria from the time Joshua led the Israelites into the land. Over the years, they had married other people who were not Jews. Jews in Galilee and Judah had bad feelings toward the Samaritans and would not go through the land. Instead, they would cross the Jordan River twice to avoid walking through the area.

Luke 17:11 he passed through the midst of **S** and
John 4:4 and he must needs go through **S**
John 4:7 cometh a woman of **S** to draw water
Acts 1:8 and in all Judea, and in **S**, and unto

◼ Samaritan (suh MEHR ih tuhn)
A person who lived in Samaria. Also referred to a race of people when the Jews married non-Jews. The Samaritans also worshiped as the Jews worshiped. (See "Samaria.")

Luke 10:33 But a certain **S**, as he journeyed
Luke 17:16 giving him thanks: and he was a **S**

◼ Samaritans (suh MEHR ih tuhnz)
Plural of "Samaritan."

John 4:9 the Jews have no dealings with the **S**
John 4:39 And many of the **S** of that city believed

◼ Samuel (SAM yoo uhl)
The name means "The name is God," "God is exalted," or "son of God." Hannah, the mother of Samuel, prayed to God for a son, and she gave (or offered) him to God even before he was born. Samuel grew up in the sanctuary in Shiloh, helping Eli, the priest, and learning from him about God. Samuel was the last judge of Israel, warning the Israelite people to worship God only. When he was old, the people asked for a king. God told Samuel whom to anoint and Saul became the first king of Israel. He also anointed David, who would follow Saul as king. Samuel was honest and fair in all his work.

1 Samuel 1:20 she bare a son, and called his name **S**
1 Samuel 2:18 **S** ministered before the LORD
1 Samuel 2:21 the child **S** grew before the LORD
1 Samuel 3:4 the LORD called **S**: and he answered
1 Samuel 3:9 Eli said to **S**, Go, lie down: and
1 Samuel 3:16 Then Eli called **S**, and said, **S** my son

Samuel

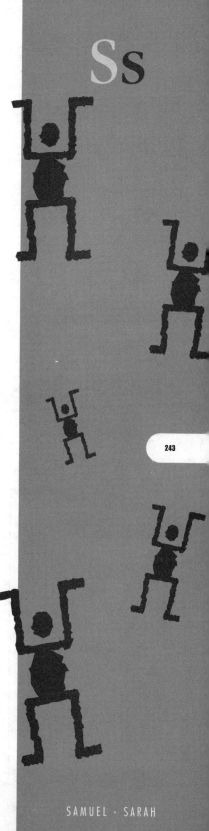

Samuel, 1, 2, Books of (SAM yoo uhl)
Samuel 1 and 2 are the fourth and fifth books in the division, History, in the Old Testament. First Samuel tells about King Saul and Samuel up to the time of their deaths and about David when he was secretly anointed king. However, he did not become king until Saul died. Second Samuel tells the events of David's life while he was king. It is not known who wrote the books. The main idea in both books is that when one obeys God, good things will come to him but when he does not obey God, bad things can happen. God can still use a person who disobeys Him if that person will ask God to forgive him of his wrongdoing.

Sanctified (SANK tih fighd)
Past tense of "sanctify."

Genesis 2:3 God blessed the seventh day, and **s** it
1 Samuel 16:5 and he **s** Jesse and his sons, and
John 17:19 they also might be **s** through the truth

Sanctify (SANK tih figh)
To set apart, to make holy, to use for God. A Christian is set apart once he accepts Jesus as his Lord and Savior. This allows him to come before God.

1 Samuel 16:5 **s** yourselves, and come with me to the
John 17:19 for their sakes I **s** myself, that they

Sand (SAND)
A fine gravel made up of small grains.

Genesis 22:17 as the **s** which is upon the sea shore
Matthew 7:26 man which built his house upon the **s**

Sang (SANG)
Past tense of "sing." To make music with the voice. Not the same as speaking.

Exodus 15:1 Then **s** Moses and the children of
Judges 5:1 Then **s** Deborah and Barak the son
Acts 16:25 Paul and Silas prayed, and **s** praises

Sank (SANK)
Past tense of "sink." To drop, fall, or move downward.

Exodus 15:5 they **s** into the bottom as a stone
Exodus 15:10 they **s** as lead in the mighty waters

Sarah (SEHR uh)
A different form of the Hebrew name "Sarai."

Ss

243

Ss

Genesis 17:15 not call her name Sarai, but **S**
Genesis 17:17 shall **S**, that is ninety years old
Genesis 17:19 **S** thy wife shall bear thee a son
Genesis 23:1 And **S** was an hundred and seven and

■ Sarai (SEHR igh (eye))

The name means "Princess." She was the wife of Abram (Abraham) and also his half sister. Her name was later changed to Sarah. She was a beautiful woman, even as she grew older. She had no children for a long time. God told Abraham she would have a son in her old age and this son would begin a great tribe. She laughed at the idea for she was about ninety years old. She did have a son a year later and named him Isaac. She died at 127 years of age.

Genesis 12:5 Abram took **S** his wife, and Lot his

■ Satan (SAY tuhn)

The word means "adversary." An adversary (ADD vuhr sair ee) is an enemy, or an attacker. Satan is another name for the devil. Satan opposes all that God is and His purposes for mankind.

Job 1:6 And **S** came also among them
Matthew 4:10 Get thee hence, **S**, for it is written
Matthew 16:23 unto Peter, Get thee behind me, **S**
Mark 8:33 Peter, saying, Get thee behind me, **S**
Luke 4:8 said unto him, Get thee behind me, **S**
Luke 22:3 Then entered **S** into Judas surnamed

■ Saul (SAWL)

The name means "asked for."

1. The first king of Israel. He was tall and handsome, chosen by God, anointed secretly by Samuel. He was a good leader. However, he disobeyed God and God rejected him. He had periods of torment by an evil spirit. David's playing on his lyre (or harp) helped calm Saul.

1 Samuel 9:2 he had a son, whose name was **S**
1 Samuel 9:17 when Samuel saw **S**, the LORD said

2. Saul was Hebrew for Paul. Saul caused many problems for the early believers in Jesus. He had them jailed when he could find them. After he met Jesus on the road to Damascus, his name was changed to Paul and he began preaching about Jesus. He was one of the greatest leaders of the early church. He preached all over Asia Minor as well as in Rome.

Saul

Acts 7:58 a young man's feet, whose name was **S**
Acts 8:1 **S** was there, giving approval to his death (NIV)
Acts 8:3 As for **S**, he made havoc of the church
Acts 9:4 saying unto him, **S**, **S**, why persecutest
Acts 9:22 **S** increased the more in strength

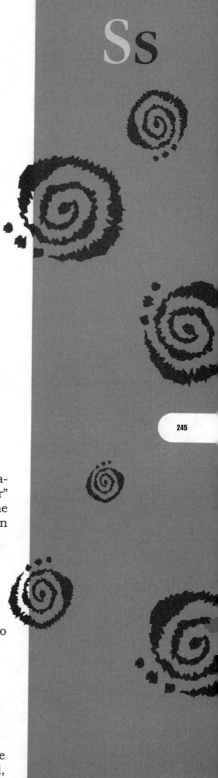

Save (SAYV)

To rescue a person from danger.

Psalm 55:16 upon God; and the LORD shall **s** me
Matthew 1:21 shall **s** his people from their sins
Matthew 8:25 and awoke him, saying, Lord, **s** us
Matthew 14:30 he cried, saying, Lord, **s** me
Matthew 16:25 shall **s** his life shall lose it
Matthew 18:11 Son of man is come to **s** that
Mark 8:35 will **s** his live shall lose it
Mark 15:30 **S** thyself, and come down from the
Luke 9:24 will **s** his live shall lose it
Luke 19:10 seek and to **s** that which was lost
Luke 23:37 be the king of the Jews, **s** thyself

Saved (SAYVD)

Past tense of "save."

Exodus 14:30 the LORD **s** Israel that day
Matthew 24:13 unto the end, the same shall be **s**
John 3:17 that the world through him might be **s**
Acts 2:21 call on the name of the Lord shall be **s**
Acts 16:30 Sirs, what must I do to be **s**
Acts 16:31 Lord Jesus Christ, and thou shalt be **s**

Savior (SAY vih'awr)

The one who saves, or delivers, or brings salvation. The Old Testament reference to "Savior" usually means God. In the New Testament, the reference is mainly to Jesus but can also mean God.

Luke 1:47 my spirit hath rejoiced in God my **S**
Luke 2:11 a **S**, which is Christ the Lord
John 4:42 the Christ, the **S** of the world

Savoury (SAY vor ee)

Same as "savory." Something that is pleasant to the taste or smell; juicy; tasty.

Genesis 27:4 make me **s** meat, such as I love
Genesis 27:9 I will make them **s** meat for thy
Genesis 27:14 mother made **s** meat, such as
Genesis 27:17 gave the **s** meat and the bread

Scarlet (SKAR lit)

Another word for "crimson." A bright red dye made from certain insects; fine cloth, dyed red,

worn by the wealthy or by rulers.

Exodus 25:4 blue, and purple, and **s**, and fine linen
Matthew 27:28 and put on him a **s** robe

Scorn (SKORN)
Mock, tease; dislike combined with anger or disgust. Sometimes expressed in laughter so as to make fun of.

Matthew 9:24 And they laughed him to **s**
Mark 5:40 And they laughed him to **s**
Luke 8:53 And they laughed him to **s**

Scourge (SKURJ)
A whip made of several cords onto which were tied sharp pieces of bone or metal. Also, a harsh, awful type of punishment or beating. The person would receive 39 blows or hits. Those receiving this punishment often died because of it.

Matthew 20:19 to mock, and to **s**, and to crucify him
Mark 10:34 they shall mock him, and shall **s** him
Luke 18:33 shall **s** him, and put him to death
John 2:15 he had made a **s** of small cords

Scribe (SKRIHB)
An official trained to write letters and make a record of important happenings and decisions. Some scribes copied God's written word, or taught it. In the New Testament times , a scribe usually taught Jewish laws, or was an authority of the law.

Jeremiah 36:10 Gemariah the son of Shaphan the **s**
Jeremiah 36:32 roll, and gave it to Baruch the **s**
Mark 12:32 the **s** said unto him, Well, Master

Scribes (SKRIHBZ)
Plural of "scribe."

Matthew 16:21 elders and chief priests and **s**
Matthew 21:15 the chief priests and **s** saw the
Matthew 26:57 where the **s** and the elders were
Matthew 27:41 mocking him, with the **s** and elders
Mark 8:31 the chief priests, and **s**, and be killed
Mark 15:31 with the **s**, He saved others; himself
Luke 6:7 the **s** and Pharisees watched him
Luke 23:10 **s** stood and vehemently accused him

Scripture (SKRIP chur)
The word means "a writing." The term generally refers to the Bible, a divine book, inspired by God. Can also refer to a Bible verse or passage.

246

Mark 15:28 And the **s** was fulfilled, which saith
Luke 4:21 This day is this **s** fulfilled
John 13:18 but that the **s** may be fulfilled
John 20:9 as yet they knew not the **s**
2 Timothy 3:16 All **S** is God-breathed and is useful (NIV)

◼ Scriptures (SKRIP churz)
Plural of "scripture."

Matthew 26:54 how then shall the **s** be fulfilled
Luke 24:27 in all the **s** the things concerning
Luke 24:32 and while he opened to us the **s**

◼ Sea (CEE)
A large body of water, usually surrounded by land, and smaller than an ocean.

Genesis 1:26 dominion over the fish of the **s**,
Exodus 14:16 stretch out thine hand over the **s**
Exodus 14:22 the midst of the **s** upon dry ground
Exodus 14:29 upon dry land in the midst of the **s**
Matthew 8:24 there arose a great tempest in the **s**
Matthew 8:26 and rebuked the winds and the **s**
Matthew 8:27 even the winds and the **s** obey him
Matthew 14:26 disciples saw him walking on the **s**
Mark 1:16 his brother casting a net into the **s**
Mark 6:48 cometh unto them, walking on the **s**
Mark 6:49 they saw him walking upon the **s**
John 6:1 which is the **s** of Tiberias
John 6:18 **s** arose by reason of a great wind
John 6:19 they see Jesus walking on the **s**
John 21:1 to the disciples at the **s** of Tiberias

◼ Sea (of Galilee) (CEE uhv GAL ih lee)
The name means "circle." The sea is thirteen miles long and eight miles wide. It is 700 feet lower than the Mediterranean Sea. It is almost completely surrounded by hills and mountains. The mountains help create sudden violent storms on the Sea of Galilee (see map on page 340).

The Old Testament name for this body of water was "Chinnereth" (KIN uh reth). Another name used in New Testament times was "lake of Gennesaret."

Since this was a freshwater lake, fed by the Jordan River, fishing was one of the main ways to earn a living.

Matthew 4:18 Jesus, walking by the **s** of Galilee
Matthew 15:29 came nigh unto the **s** of Galilee
Mark 1:16 Now as he walked by the **s** of Galilee
Mark 7:31 he came unto the **s** of Galilee
John 6:1 Jesus went over the **s** of Galilee

Sea of Galilee

Ss

Seam (CEEM)
The place where two edges of fabric are sewn together.

John 19:23 now the coat was without **s**

Search (SURCH)
To look for, hunt, or try to find something.

Psalm 139:23 **S** me, O God, and know my heart
Matthew 2:8 Go and **s** diligently for the young child

Season (CEE zun)
A period of time; a cycle.

Psalm 1:3 that bringeth forth his fruit in his **s**
Proverbs 15:23 word fitly spoken in due **s**, how good
Ecclesiastes 3:1 To every thing there is a **s**
Luke 4:13 he departed from him for a **s**
John 5:4 an angel went down at a certain **s**

Seasoned (CEE zund)
Past tense of "season," meaning to add flavoring to.

Luke 14:34 lost his savor, wherewith shall it be **s**

Seasons (CEE zunz)
Plural for "season," a period of time.

Genesis 1:14 let them be for signs, and for **s**
Psalm 104:19 He appointed the moon for **s**

Second (SEH kund)
Following the first.

Genesis 1:8 evening and the morning were the **s** day
1 Kings 18:34 And he said, Do it the **s** time
1 Kings 18:34 And they did it the **s** time
Jonah 3:1 of the LORD came to Jonah the **s** time
Matthew 22:39 **s** is like unto it, Thou shalt love
Mark 14:72 And the **s** time the cock crew
John 21:16 saith to him again the **s** time, Simon

Secret (CEE krut)
Hidden, private, unknown.

Matthew 6:6 pray to thy Father which is in **s**
Matthew 6:6 thy Father which seeth in **s** shall

Secretly (CEE krut lee)
An adverb of "secret."

John 11:28 and called Mary her sister **s**, saying
John 19:38 **s** for fear of the Jews, besought Pilate

Sedition (seh DIH shun)
To strongly oppose or go against the government

248

or local authority. Barabbas was charged with sedition, as well as murder.

Luke 23:19 for a certain **s** made in the city
Luke 23:25 for **s** and murder was cast into
Acts 24:5 a mover of **s** among all the Jews

Seed (CEED)
1. The beginning of a plant that is encased so that it is protected; a pit.

Genesis 1:11 bring forth grass, the herb yielding **s**
Genesis 1:11 fruit after his kind, whose **s** is in
Exodus 16:31 Manna: and it was like coriander **s**
Matthew 17:20 faith as a grain of mustard **s**
Luke 17:6 had faith as a grain of mustard **s**

2. A person's descendant, or child.

Genesis 26:4 I will make thy **s** to multiply
John 7:42 Christ cometh of the **s** of David

Seek (CEEK)
To look for or search for; to try to find.

Matthew 6:33 But **s** ye first the kingdom of God
Matthew 7:7 **s**, and ye shall find; knock, and
Matthew 28:5 Fear not ye: for I know that ye **s** Jesus
Luke 11:9 **s**, and ye shall find; knock, and it
Luke 12:31 But rather **s** ye the kingdom of God
Luke 19:10 Son of man is come to **s** and to save
Acts 10:19 unto him, Behold, three men **s** thee

Seekest (CEEK ist)
The old way of writing or saying "seeks."

Genesis 37:15 asked him, saying, What **s** thou?
John 20:15 Woman, why weepest thou? Whom **s** thou

Seemeth (CEEM ith)
The old way of writing or saying "seems."

Proverbs 14:12 is a way that **s** right unto a man
Proverbs 16:25 is a way that **s** right unto a man

Sell (CELL)
To trade for money or something of value.

Genesis 25:31 said, **S** me this day thy birthright
Matthew 19:21 go and **s** that thou hast, and give to
Mark 10:21 **s** whatsoever thou hast, and give to the
Luke 12:33 **S** your possessions, and give to the poor (NIV)
Luke 18:22 **s** all that thou hast, and distribute

Seller (CELL uhr)
One who sells things. See "Sell."

Acts 16:14 woman named Lydia, a **s** of purple

Ss

Send (CIND)
To cause to go.

Exodus 3:10 and I will **s** thee unto Pharaoh
1 Kings 18:1 and I will **s** rain upon the earth
Isaiah 6:8 Whom shall I **s**, and who will go for
Isaiah 6:8 Then said I, Here am I; **s** me
Matthew 9:38 he will **s** forth laborors into his
Mark 1:2 I **s** my messenger before thy face
Luke 10:2 that he would **s** forth laborors
John 20:21 Father hath sent me, even so **s** I you
Acts 10:5 **s** men to Joppa, and call for one Simon
Acts 10:22 from God by an holy angel to **s** for thee

Sendeth (CIND ith)
The old way of writing or saying "sends."

1 Kings 17:14 until the day that the LORD **s** rain
Matthew 5:45 and **s** rain on the just and on the
Mark 11:1 he **s** forth two of his disciples
Mark 14:13 And he **s** forth two of his disciples

Sent (SENT)
Past tense of "send."

Genesis 8:7 And he **s** forth a raven, which went
Genesis 8:8 Also he **s** forth a dove from him
Genesis 45:7 God **s** me before you to preserve you
Matthew 2:8 And he **s** them to Bethlehem, and said
Matthew 21:1 of Olives, then **s** Jesus two disciples
Luke 23:11 gorgeous robe, and **s** him again to Pilate
John 1:6 There was a man **s** from God, whose
John 3:17 For God **s** not his Son into the world
John 20:21 my Father hath **s** me, even so send I you
1 John 4:14 the Father **s** the Son to be the Savior

Sentence (SEN tins)
A judgment, ruling, or opinion.

Luke 23:24 And Pilate gave **s** that it should be

Separate (SEP uh rayt)
To pull or keep apart.

Genesis 13:9 **s** thyself, I pray thee, from me
Acts 13:2 **S** me Barnabas and Saul for the work
Romans 8:35 Who shall **s** us from the love of Christ

Sepulcher (SEP uhl kuhr)
A grave or tomb, often carved out of the rock inside a cave. A body would be placed on a carved slab or ledge. Once the body had decayed, the bones would be moved to a hole

Sepulcher

250

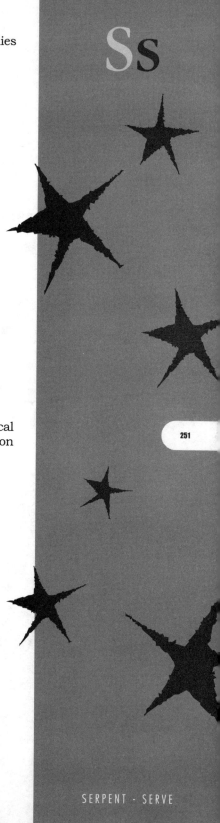

further back in the cave. Often many bodies would be buried in the same cave.

Matthew 27:60 a great stone to the door of the **s**
Matthew 27:64 Command therefore that the **s** be made
Matthew 27:66 made the **s** sure, sealing the stone
Matthew 28:1 and the other Mary to see the **s**
Mark 15:46 laid him in a **s** which was hewn out of a
Mark 15:46 rolled a stone unto the door of the **s**
Mark 16:2 came unto the **s** at the rising of the sun
Mark 16:5 And entering into the **s**, they saw a
Luke 23:53 laid it in a **s** that was hewn in stone
Luke 24:1 they came unto the **s**, bringing spices
Luke 24:2 found the stone rolled away from the **s**
John 19:41 and in the garden a new **s**
John 20:1 unto the **s**, and seeth the stone taken
John 20:4 outrun Peter, and came first to the **s**
John 20:11 Mary stood without at the **s** weeping

Serpent (SUR pent)

A snake, usually a large and poisonous one.

Genesis 3:1 Now the **s** was more crafty than any of (NIV)
Genesis 3:13 The woman said, The **s** deceived me (NIV)
Genesis 3:14 And the LORD God said unto the **s**

Servant (SUR vent)

A helper, one who is paid to help. In biblical times, a servant was owned by another person and may not have received any wages.

Joshua 1:2 Moses my **s** is dead; now therefore arise
1 Kings 18:43 And he said to his **s**, Go up now
Matthew 8:6 my **s** lieth at home sick of the palsy
Matthew 26:51 and struck a **s** of the high priest's
Luke 16:13 No **s** can serve two masters
John 18:10 and smote the high priest's s, and

Serve (SURV)

To lend a hand or wait on; to obey.

Genesis 29:18 I will **s** thee seven years for Rachel
Exodus 8:1 Let my people go, that they may **s** me
Exodus 20:5 not bow down thyself to them, nor **s** them
Deuteronomy 10:12 to **s** the LORD thy God with all thy
Matthew 4:10 Lord thy God, and him only shalt thou **s**
Matthew 6:24 No man can **s** two masters
Matthew 6:24 Ye cannot **s** God and mammon
Luke 4:8 thy God, and him only shalt thou **s**
Luke 16:13 No servant can **s** two masters
Luke 16:13 Ye cannot **s** God and mammon
John 12:26 If any man **s** me, let him follow me

Ss

Seventh (SEV inth)
The next number after the sixth in a series.

Genesis 2:2 And on the **s** day God ended his work
Genesis 2:3 And God blessed the **s** day
Exodus 20:10 But the **s** day is the sabbath of the
Exodus 20:11 and rested the **s** day
John 4:52 Yesterday at the **s** hour the fever left

Sew (SOH)
To fasten with needle and thread; to stitch.

Ecclesiastes 3:7 A time to rend, and a time to **s**

Shadow (SHAD oh)
The darkness that an object or person casts in the direction opposite light; a deep darkness.

Psalm 23:4 through the valley of the **s** of death
Jonah 4:5 booth, and sat under it in the **s**
Jonah 4:6 that it might be a **s** over his head

Shadrach (SHAD rak)
A Babylonian name that means "circuit of the sun." His Hebrew name was Hananiah. He was one of Daniel's three friends who were taken from Israel into exile to Babylon. The three friends of Daniel had refused to worship an image King Nebuchadnezzar had made. So the king had them thrown into a fiery furnace. The LORD God delivered them and the king recognized God's greatness. He promoted the three friends to a high place of honor in his kingdom.

Daniel 1:7 and to Hananiah, of **S**
Daniel 3:16 **S**, Meshach, and Abed-nego, answered
Daniel 3:23 **S**, Meshach, and Abed-nego, fell down
Daniel 3:28 Blessed be the God of **S**, Meshach
Daniel 3:30 Then the king promoted **S**, Meshach

Shaphan (SHAY fan)
The name means "coney." He was a scribe as well as an official during the reign of King Josiah in Judah. He took the book of the law to King Josiah after it was found in the Temple. The Temple was being cleaned up and repaired. He also was a friend and helper to Jeremiah, the prophet.

2 Kings 22:8 priest said unto **S** the scribe
2 Kings 22:8 Hilkiah gave the book to **S**
2 Kings 22:10 And **S** the scribe showed the king
2 Kings 22:10 and **S** read it before the king
Jeremiah 36:10 Gemariah the son of **S** the scribe

Sheaf (SHEEF)
A bundle or bunch of stalks of grain tied together, or piled separately from other piles.

Genesis 37:7 my **s** arose, and also stood upright
Genesis 37:7 and made obeisance to my **s**

Sheaves (SHEEVZ)
Plural of "sheaf."

Genesis 37:7 we were binding **s** in the field
Genesis 37:7 behold, your **s** stood round about
Ruth 2:7 gather after the reapers among the **s**
Ruth 2:15 Let her glean even among the **s**

Shechem (SHEK uhm)
The name means "should, back." This city became the capital of Israel, the Northern Kingdom, after the kingdom of Israel split into the Northern Kingdom and the Southern Kingdom. It is about 40 miles north of Jerusalem. When Abraham came into Canaan, his first stop was in Shechem. The city was built on the slope of Mount Ebal. Across the valley lies Mount Gerazim.

Genesis 37:12 to feed their father's flock in **S**
Genesis 37:13 not thy brethren feed the flock in **S**
Genesis 37:14 the vale of Hebron, and he came to **S**

Shed (SHED)
To drop, pour forth, flow.

Genesis 37:22 **S** no blood, but cast him into this
Matthew 26:28 which is **s** for many for the remission
Mark 14:24 of the new testament, which is **s** for many
Luke 22:20 testament in my blood, which is **s** for you

Sheep (SHEEP)
Small animals, tamed for the purpose of obtaining their wool for clothing and other uses, and the meat for food. Sheep need a leader and the shepherd is that leader. Throughout the Bible, people have been compared to sheep because people also need a leader. Jesus is the Good Shepherd because He leads His people in the right way. But people must follow Him, just as the sheep must follow their shepherd.

Genesis 4:2 And Abel was a keeper of **s**
Genesis 29:9 Rachel came with her father's **s**
Isaiah 53:6 All we like **s** have gone astray
Matthew 18:12 if a man have an hundred **s**, and
Matthew 18:13 he rejoiceth more of that **s**, than of

Ss

253

Sheep

Ss

Shepherd

Luke 15:4 What man of you, having an hundred **s**
Luke 15:6 I have found my **s** which was lost
John 21:16 He saith unto him, Feed my **s**
John 21:17 Jesus saith unto him, Feed my **s**

■ Shepherd (SHEP urd)
One who keeps or watches sheep. Some of the responsibilities of a shepherd were to lead the sheep to good pastures, to find still (not running) water, and to protect them from wild animals. A shepherd might keep the sheep on the hillside at night or in a sheepfold, like a corral. God and Jesus Christ have been called a shepherd. Their "sheep" are the true believers in Jesus.

Psalm 23:1 The LORD is my **s**; I shall not want
Mark 6:34 they were as sheep not having a **s**
John 10:11 I am the good **s**: the good **s** giveth
John 10:14 I am the good **s**, and know my sheep

■ Shepherds (SHEP urds)
Plural for "shepherd."

Genesis 46:32 And the men are **s**, for their trade
Genesis 47:3 said unto Pharaoh, Thy servants are **s**
Luke 2:8 in the same country **s** abiding in the field
Luke 2:15 the **s** said one to another, Let us go even
Luke 2:18 the things which were told them by the **s**
Luke 2:20 the **s** returned, glorifying and praising

■ Shiloh (SHIGH low)
The name may mean "tranquil, secure." It lies about 30 miles north of Jerusalem (see map on page 338). It became an important center of worship after Joshua led the Israelites into Canaan. For many years, the tabernacle was located in Shiloh, as well as the ark of the covenant. The young Samuel helped Eli in the tabernacle at Shiloh. The ruins of this city lie in what is now Jordan.

Joshua 18:1 of Israel assembled together at **S**
1 Samuel 3:21 the LORD appeared again in **S**
1 Samuel 3:21 LORD revealed himself to Samuel in **S**

■ Shine (SHIGN)
To gleam; give off light.

Numbers 6:25 The LORD make his face **s** upon thee
Matthew 5:16 Let your light so **s** before men, that

■ Ship (SHIP)
A large boat that travels on water. During biblical times, ships were moved across the water by

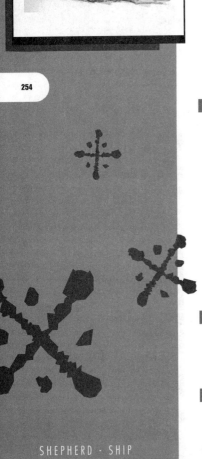

254

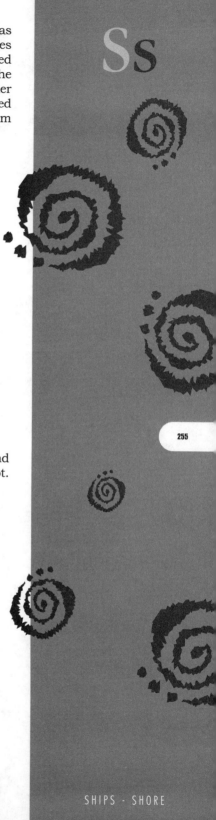

many men using oars in a rhythmic pattern, as well as large canvas sheets, called sails. Besides carrying people, they carried goods to be traded or sold at the ports where they docked. The boats used on the Sea of Galilee were smaller and more suitable for fishing but still needed oars and probably a single sail to move them across the water.

Matthew 4:21 in a **s** with Zebedee their father
Matthew 4:22 they immediately left the **s** and
Matthew 14:22 get into a **s**, and go before him to
Matthew 14:24 the **s** was now in the midst of the sea
Matthew 14:32 were come into the **s**, the wind ceased
Matthew 14:33 that were in the **s** came and worshiped
Mark 1:20 left their father Zebedee in the **s**
Mark 6:32 And they departed into a desert place by **s**
Mark 6:47 the **s** was in the midst of the sea, and
Luke 5:3 and taught the people out of the **s**
John 21:6 Cast the net on the right side of the **s**

Ships (SHIPS)
Plural of "ship."

Mark 4:36 were also with him other little **s**
Luke 5:2 And saw two **s** standing by the lake
Luke 5:3 And he entered into one of the **s**
Luke 5:7 they came, and filled both the **s**

Shoe (SHOO)
Footwear, usually with a stiff sole and heel, and softer upper part; something to wear on the foot. In biblical times it usually meant "sandal."

Joshua 5:15 Loose thy **s** from off thy foot
Ruth 4:7 a man plucked off his **s**, and gave it
Ruth 4:8 So he drew off his **s**

Shoes (SHOOZ)
Plural of "shoe."

Exodus 3:5 put off thy **s** from off thy feet
Matthew 3:11 whose **s** I am not worthy to bear
Mark 1:7 the latchet of whose **s** I am not worthy
Luke 3:16 the latchet of whose **s** I am not worthy

Shore (SHORE)
The beach of the coast of any body of water.

Genesis 22:17 as the sand which is upon the sea **s**
Exodus 14:30 saw the Egyptians dead upon the sea **s**
Mark 6:53 land of Gennesaret, and drew to the **s**
John 21:4 morning was now come, Jesus stood on the **s**

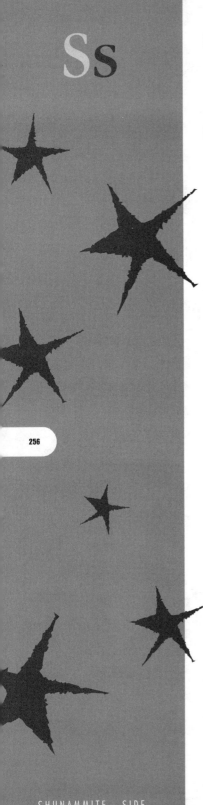

Ss

Shunammite (SHOO nuh might)
A person who lived in Shunem.

2 Kings 4:12 to Gehazi his servant, Call this **S**
2 Kings 4:25 Behold, yonder is that **S**
2 Kings 4:36 called Gehazi, and said, Call this **S**

Shunem (SHOO nem)
The meaning of the name is not certain. This was a town located southeast of Mount Carmel a few miles north of the town of Jezreel. It had been occupied at different times in biblical history by Egypt, and was captured by Joshua. Elisha, the prophet, spent much time in the home of a couple who lived in Shunem.

2 Kings 4:8 Elisha passed to **S**, where was a great woman

Shushan (SHOO shan)
A Persian name that may mean "lily" or "lotus." The city is in what is now southwestern Iran. It was an ancient Persian capital of the nation, Elam. Modern Bible translations call the city "Susa." It was a very rich city because of the trade routes that passed through it. Esther was queen in Shushan.

Nehemiah 1:1 as I was in **S** the palace
Esther 1:2 kingdom, which was in **S** the palace
Daniel 8:2 that I was at **S** in the palace

Shut (SHUHT)
To close or make secure.

Genesis 7:16 and the LORD **s** him in
Matthew 6:6 when thou hast **s** thy door, pray to
John 20:19 doors were **s** where the disciples were
John 20:26 then came Jesus, the doors being **s**

Sick (SIK)
Ill, not well, unhealthy.

Matthew 9:12 healthy who need a doctor, but the **s** (NIV)
Mark 1:30 Simon's wife's mother lay **s** of a fever
Mark 2:5 faith, he said unto the **s** of the palsy
Mark 2:17 the healthy who need a doctor, but the (NIV)
John 11:1 a certain man was **s**, named Lazarus

Side (SIGHD)
1. Border or edge; to the right or to the left.

Matthew 13:1 out of the house, and sat by the sea **s**
Matthew 20:30 two blind men sitting by the way **s**
Mark 10:46 sat by the highway **s** begging
John 19:34 the soldiers with a spear pierced his **s**

John 20:20 he showed unto them his hands and his **s**
John 20:27 thy hand, and thrust it into my **s**: and be
John 21:6 Cast the net on the right **s** of the ship

2. Away from or beyond.

Mark 4:35 Let us pass over to the other **s**
Luke 10:31 saw him, he passed by on the other **s**
Luke 10:32 and passed by on the other **s**

Sight (SIGHT)
Vision, the ability to see, eyesight.

Psalm 19:14 my heart be acceptable in thy **s**, O LORD
Matthew 20:34 and immediately their eyes received **s**
Mark 10:51 Lord, that I might receive my **s**
Mark 10:52 And immediately he received his **s**
Luke 18:41 he said, Lord, that I may receive my **s**
Luke 18:42 Jesus said unto him, Receive thy **s**
Luke 18:43 And immediately he received his **s**
Acts 1:9 and a cloud received him out of their **s**

Sign (SIGHN)
A clue or hint about something that is special.

Isaiah 7:14 the LORD himself shall give you a **s**
Matthew 26:48 he that betrayed him gave them a **s**
Luke 2:12 And this shall be a **s** unto you; Ye shall

Signs (SIGHNZ)
Plural of "sign."

Genesis 1:14 let them be for **s**, and for seasons
John 20:30 And many other **s** truly did Jesus in

Silver (SIL vuhr)
A precious metal with a white color that shines brilliantly when polished. It does not rust. In early biblical times it was rare and therefore, quite valuable. It has been used for eating utensils, money, and, of course, jewelry.

Matthew 26:15 they counted out for him thirty **s** coins (NIV)
Matthew 27:3 brought again the thirty pieces of **s**
Matthew 27:6 the chief priests took the **s** pieces
Acts 3:6 Then Peter said, **S** and gold have I none

Simeon (SIM ih uhn)
The name means "hearing." A very religious Jew who faithfully worshiped God. He lived in Jerusalem at the time Jesus was born. He spent his time in the Temple. God had promised him he would not die until he could see the Christ. As Mary and Joseph entered the Temple with

257

Jesus, Simeon recognized the baby as the Christ. He told the parents the plan God had for their baby.

Luke 2:25 a man in Jerusalem, whose name was **S**
Luke 2:34 And **S** blessed them, and said unto Mary

■ Simon (SIGH muhn)
The name means "flat nosed" and is of Greek origin. Two men named Simon are important to us.

1. The brother of Andrew and a disciple of Jesus. This Simon was a fisherman on the Sea of Galilee. Jesus later changed his name to Peter, which means "rock."

Matthew 4:18 saw two brothers, **S** called Peter, and
Mark 1:16 he saw **S** and Andrew his brother casting a
Mark 1:29 entered into the house of **S** and Andrew
Mark 3:16 And **S** he surnamed Peter
Luke 5:8 When **S** Peter saw it, he fell down at Jesus'
Luke 6:14 **S** (whom he also named Peter,) and Andrew
John 6:8 Andrew, **S** Peter's brother, saith unto him
John 18:15 And **S** Peter followed Jesus, and so did
John 18:25 And **S** Peter stood and warmed himself
John 20:2 she runneth, and cometh to **S** Peter
John 21:11 **S** Peter climbed aboard and dragged (NIV)

2. A man from Cyrene, a place in Northern Africa, who was pulled out of the crowd and told to carry Jesus' cross the rest of the way to Golgotha.

Matthew 27:32 they found a man of Cyrene, **S** by name
Mark 15:21 And they compel one **S** a Cyrenian, who
Luke 23:26 they laid hold upon one **S**, a Cyrenian

■ Sin (SIN)
Actions, attitudes, words, or thoughts that keep a person separated from God. God knows what is best for us. That is why He gave us the laws and guidelines to follow. When we disobey those laws, we are disobeying God. And this keeps us separated from Him.

Psalm 4:4 Stand in awe, and **s** not
Psalm 119:11 that I might not **s** against thee
John 1:29 which taketh away the **s** of the world
Romans 6:23 For the wages of **s** is death
Ephesians 4:26 In your anger do not **s**: Do not let (NIV)

■ Sinai (SIGH nigh)
The name may mean "shining." An area east of Egypt and part of Arabia (see map on page 337).

It was in this peninsula where God led Moses and the Israelites as they left Egypt on their way to Canaan. Located in the Sinai peninsula is a mountain called Mount Sinai. It was on this mountain where God gave the Ten Commandments to Moses. This peninsula, which is shaped like an arrowhead, now belongs to the United Arab Republic.

Exodus 19:2 and were come to the desert of **S**
Exodus 19:20 the LORD came down upon Mount **S**

Sing (SEENG)
To give honor or praise to someone or something; to make "musical sounds with the voice."

Exodus 15:1 I will **s** unto the LORD, for he hath
Psalm 9:2 I will **s** praise to thy name
Psalm 95:1 O come, let us **s** unto the LORD

Sinned (SIND)
Past tense of "sin."

Exodus 10:16 I have **s** against the LORD your God
Psalm 41:4 heal my soul; for I have **s** against thee
Matthew 27:4 I have **s** in that I have betrayed the
Luke 15:18 Father, I have **s** against heaven, and
Luke 15:21 Father, I have **s** against heaven, and in
Romans 3:23 For all have **s**, and come short of the

Sinner (SIN uhr)
One who sins.

Luke 15:7 joy shall be in heaven over one **s** that
Luke 15:10 angels of God over one **s** that repenteth
Luke 19:7 to be a guest with a man that is a **s**

Sinners (SIN uhrz)
Plural of "sinner."

Psalm 51:13 and s shall be converted unto thee
Matthew 9:11 eateth your Master with publicans and **s**
Matthew 9:13 call the righteous, but **s** to repentance
Matthew 26:45 is betrayed into the hands of **s**
Mark 2:16 Pharisees saw him eat with publicans and **s**
Mark 14:41 of man is betrayed into the hands of **s**
Luke 5:30 eat and drink with publicans and **s**
Romans 5:8 while we were yet **s**, Christ died for us

Sins (SINZ)
Plural of "sin."

Isaiah 1:18 though your **s** be as scarlet, they
Matthew 1:21 he shall save his people from their **s**
Mark 2:7 who can forgive **s** but God only

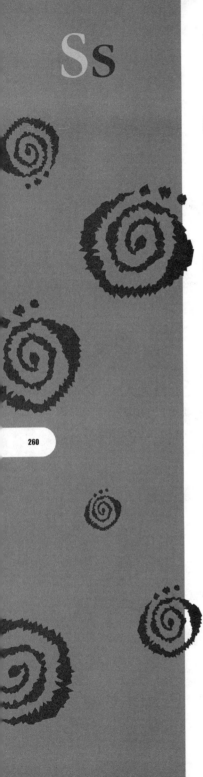

Ss

Mark 2:9 sick of the palsy, Thy **s** be forgiven
Luke 5:20 Man, thy **s** are forgiven thee
Luke 5:21 Who can forgive **s**, but God alone
1 John 1:9 If we confess our **s**, he is faithful
1 John 1:9 and just to forgive us our **s**, and

■ Six (SIKS)
One more than five.

Exodus 16:26 **S** days shall ye gather it; but on
Exodus 20:9 **S** days shalt though labor, and do all
Exodus 20:11 For in **s** days the LORD made heaven
Ruth 3:15 he measured **s** measures of barley
Luke 13:14 There are **s** days in which men ought
John 12:1 **S** days before the Passover, Jesus arrived (NIV)

■ Sixth (SIKSTH)
Following the fifth in a series.

Genesis 1:31 evening and the morning were the **s** day
Exodus 16:22 on the **s** day they gathered twice as much
Matthew 27:45 Now from the **s** hour there was darkness
Mark 15:33 **s** hour was come, there was darkness
Luke 1:26 in the **s** month the angel Gabriel was sent
Luke 23:44 about the **s** hour, and there was a darkness
John 4:6 and it was about the **s** hour
John 19:14 of the passover, and about the **s** hour
Acts 10:9 upon the housetop to pray about the **s** hour

■ Skull (SKUHL)
The bones that make up the head and face. The brain is located inside the skull. The jaw is attached to the sides of the skull.

Matthew 27:33 Golgotha, that is to say, a place of a **s**
Mark 15:22 being interpreted, The place of a **s**
John 19:17 forth into place called the place of a **s**

■ Sleep (SLEEP)
To take a nap; rest.

Genesis 2:21 God caused a deep **s** to fall upon Adam
Matthew 26:45 **S** on now, and take your rest
Mark 14:41 **S** on now, and take your rest
Luke 22:46 Why **s** ye? Rise and pray, lest ye enter
John 11:11 that I may awake him out of **s**

■ Sleepeth (SLEEP ith)
The old way of saying or writing "sleeps."

1 Kings 18:27 peradventure he **s**, and must be awakened
Matthew **9:24** for the maid is not dead, but **s**
Mark 5:39 the damsel is not dead, but **s**
Luke 8:52 Weep not; she is not dead, but **s**

John 11:11 saith unto them, Our friend Lazarus **s**

Ss

Slow (SLOW)
Not fast, unhurried.

Psalm 103:8 **s** to anger, and plenteous in mercy
Psalm 145:8 **s** to anger, and of great mercy

Slumber (SLUM buhr)
To rest or sleep; slumber.

Psalm 121:3 he who watches over you will not **s** (NIV)

Small (SMAWL)
Little, tiny.

Exodus 16:14 lay a **s** round thing, as **s** as the
1 Kings 19:12 and after the fire a still **s** voice
Mark 8:7 they had a few **s** fishes: and he blessed
John 2:15 he had made a scourge of **s** cords
John 6:9 five barley loaves, and two **s** fishes

Smite (SMIGHT)
To hit or strike hard.

Exodus 3:20 and **s** Egypt with all my wonders
Exodus 12:12 and will **s** all the firstborn in the land
Matthew 5:39 shall **s** thee on thy right cheek

Smiteth (SMIGHT ith)
The old way of writing or saying "smites."

Luke 6:29 him that **s** thee on the one cheek offer

Smote (SMOHT)
Past tense of "smite."

Exodus 9:25 hail **s** throughout all the land
Matthew 26:51 the high priest's, and **s** off his ear
Matthew 26:67 **s** him with the palms of their hands
Matthew 27:30 took the reed, and **s** him on the head
Mark 14:47 and **s** a servant of the high priest, and
Mark 15:19 And they **s** him on the head with a reed
Luke 22:50 one of them **s** the servant of the high
Luke 22:63 men that held Jesus mocked him, and **s** him
John 18:10 and **s** the high priest's servant, and
John 19:3 and they **s** him with their hands

Snow (SNOH)
Ice crystals which are white, light, and drift to the ground. After a snowfall, everything is covered in white and looks quite beautiful. In the Bible, snow represents a whiteness, or cleanness.

Numbers 12:10 Miriam became leprous, white as **s**

Ss

Psalm 51:7 and I shall be whiter than **s**
Isaiah 1:18 they shall be white as **s**
Matthew 28:3 and his raiment white as **s**

■ **Sodom (SAHD uhm)**
A city located near the south end of the Dead Sea during the days of Abraham. The people who lived in Sodom were very wicked. Gomorrah, another city not far away, was also very wicked. God sent an angel to Sodom to lead Abraham's nephew, Lot, and his family to safety. Then God destroyed both cities by sending fire and brimstone from the sky. Brimstone is a form of sulfur.

Genesis 14:12 Abram's brother's son, who dwelt in **S**
Genesis 19:24 LORD rained upon **S** and upon Gomorrah

■ **Soft (SAWFT)**
Calm, gentle, kind, forgiving.

Proverbs 15:1 A **s** answer turneth away wrath

■ **Sojourn (SOH juhrn)**
To reside for a short time in another place.

Genesis 12:10 went down to Egypt to **s** there
Ruth 1:1 went to **s** in the country of Moab

■ **Sold (SOLD)**
Past tense of "sell."

Genesis 25:33 and he **s** his birthright unto Jacob
Genesis 37:28 and **s** Joseph to the Ishmaelites for
Genesis 37:36 Midianites **s** him into Egypt unto
Genesis 45:4 your brother, whom ye **s** into Egypt
Matthew 21:12 cast out all them that **s** and bought
Matthew 26:9 ointment might have been **s** for much
Mark 11:15 cast out them that **s** and bought
Mark 14:5 it might have been **s** for more than
Luke 19:45 began to cast out them that **s** therein
John 2:16 And he said unto them that **s** doves

■ **Soldiers (SOHL jerz)**
Plural of "soldier." A soldier was a man who had received training to be a warrior and fighter to help defend the country.

Matthew 27:27 Then the **s** of the governor took Jesus
Matthew 28:12 they gave large money unto the **s**
Mark 15:16 the **s** led him away into the hall
Luke 23:36 And the **s** also mocked him, coming to him
John 19:2 the **s** platted a crown of thorns, and
John 19:23 **s**, when they had crucified Jesus, took
John 19:34 the **s** with a spear pierced his side

262

Solomon (SAHL uh muhn)

The name means "his peace" or "(God) is peace." One of David's sons and the third king of Israel before the nation was divided. He reigned for forty years. He wrote thousands of proverbs and many songs. Solomon built the Temple for which his father had collected the lumber and other things to put in it. When he became king, Solomon asked God for wisdom to lead the nation. God granted him wisdom and much wealth. He was a wise king but he often acted in unwise ways, like making his people work hard and forcing them to pay heavy taxes.

1 Kings 1:46 And also **S** sitteth on the throne of the
1 Kings 3:5 the LORD appeared to **S** in a dream by night
Matthew 6:29 even **S** in all his glory was not arrayed
Luke 12:27 **S** in all his glory was not arrayed like

Son (SUHN)

A male child; a boy; a lad.

Genesis 11:31 Terah took Abram his **s**, and Lot the
Genesis 27:1 he called Esau his eldest **s**, and said
Genesis 27:20 Isaac said unto his, How is it that
Genesis 43:29 his brother Benjamin, his mother's **s**
Genesis 45:28 Joseph my **s** is yet alive: I will go
Ruth 4:17 There is a **s** born to Naomi
1 Samuel 3:6 I called not, my **s**; lie down again
1 Kings 17:17 **s** of the woman, the mistress of the
1 Kings 17:23 and Elijah said, See, thy **s** liveth
Isaiah 7:14 a **s**, and shall call his name Immanuel
Isaiah 9:6 a child is born, unto us a **s** is given
Matthew 1:21 she shall bring forth a **s**, and thou
Matthew 26:45 **S** of man is betrayed into the hands
Matthew 28:19 name of the Father, and of the **S**
Mark 1:11 Thou art my beloved **S**, in whom I am
Mark 2:28 **S** of man is Lord also of the sabbath
Mark 10:45 **S** of man came not to be ministered
Mark 14:41 **S** of man is betrayed into the hands
Mark 15:39 Truly this man was the **S** of God
Luke 2:7 she brought forth her firstborn **s**
Luke 3:22 Thou art my beloved **S**; in thee I am
Luke 6:5 **S** of man is Lord also of the sabbath
John 3:16 that he gave his only begotten **S**
John 3:17 God sent not his **S** into the world to
John 3:18 the name of the only begotten **S** of God

Son of Man (SUHN uv man)

Jesus' description of Himself. The expression occurs 84 times in the Gospels. All but one of these occurrences were used by Jesus to refer to Himself. The expression is used in the Old

Solomon's Temple

Testament to refer to human beings. Ezekiel, the prophet, called himself "son of man" to emphasize his humanity. In Daniel, "son of man" refers to one who comes on the clouds of heaven and is granted authority over all people and is given a kingdom that will never end.

Ezekiel 2:1 he said unto me, **S**, stand
Daniel 7:13 one like the **S** came with the clouds
Matthew 24:30 the **S** coming in the clouds
Mark 2:10 the **S** hath power on earth
Mark 2:28 **S** is Lord . . . of the sabbath
Mark 8:31 **S** must suffer many things
Mark 14:62 **S** sitting on the right hand

Song (SAWNG)
Music made by singing; a tune, a melody; a hymn.

Exodus 15:1 Moses and the Israelites sang this **s** (NIV)
Psalm 28:7 and with my **s** will I praise him
Psalm 68:30 I will praise the name of God with a **s**
Psalm 96:1 O sing unto the LORD a new **s**

Song of Solomon, Book of (SAWNG uhv SAHL uh muhn)
The fifth book in the division, Poetry and Wisdom, in the Old Testament. It is a collection of love songs by a husband to his wife, and the wife to her husband. The book possibly shows the importance God placed on the friendship between husband and wife.

Sons (SUHNS)
Plural for "son."

Genesis 7:7 Noah went in, and his **s**, and his
Ruth 1:1 of Moab, he, and his wife, and his two **s**
Matthew 26:37 Peter, and the two **s** of Zebedee
Mark 3:17 which is, The **s** of thunder
Luke 15:11 And he said, A certain man had two **s**
John 21:2 the **s** of Zebedee, and two other of his

Sop (SAHP)
A bit of bread that one dipped in wine or other liquid. Bread that could be dipped in stew or gravy. When a host dipped a piece of bread into the liquid, and then handed it to a guest, it was a way of honoring the guest. Jesus handed Judas a sop, to encourage him to change his mind about betraying Jesus. Even today in the Middle East, the lands of the Bible, a host will honor his guest by dipping the bread in the liquid and handing it to him.

John 13:26 had dipped the **s**, he gave it to Judas
John 13:27 after the **s** Satan entered into him
John 13:30 having received the **s** went immediately

■ Sore (SORE)
It means "very, greatly," very much, very great.

Genesis 41:56 famine waxed **s** in the land of Egypt
Genesis 41:57 the famine was so **s** in all lands
Exodus 14:10 after them; and they were **s** afraid
Matthew 21:15 son of David; they were **s** displeased
Luke 2:9 round about them: and they were **s** afraid

■ Sorrow (SAHR row)
Pain, sadness, suffering; trouble, usually because something loved is lost or has died. Often feelings of shame or worry are a part of the sorrow a person feels.

Luke 22:45 found them asleep, exhausted from **s** (NIV)

■ Sought (SAWT)
Past tense of "seek."

Matthew 2:20 which **s** the young child's life
Matthew 26:16 he **s** opportunity to betray him
Mark 14:1 scribes **s** how they might take him
Mark 14:11 he **s** how he might conveniently betray
Luke 2:44 they **s** him among their kinsfolk
Luke 2:49 said unto them, How is it that ye **s** me
Luke 22:2 priests and scribes **s** how they might kill
Luke 22:6 he promised, and **s** opportunity to betray
John 19:12 Pilate **s** to release him: but the Jews

■ Soul (SOWL)
The total person: all that makes him what he is; his spirit.

Genesis 2:7 and man became a living **s**
Deuteronomy 6:5 thine heart, and with all thy **s**
1 Kings 17:21 let this child's **s** come into him
1 Kings 17:22 the **s** of the child came into him
Psalm 23:3 He restoreth my **s**: he leadeth me in
Matthew 16:26 the whole world, and lose his own **s**
Matthew 16:26 a man give in exchange for his **s**
Matthew 22:37 all thy heart, and with all thy **s**
Matthew 26:38 My **s** is exceeding sorrowful, even
Mark 8:36 the whole world, and lose his own **s**
Mark 8:37 a man give in exchange for his **s**
Mark 12:30 all thy heart, and with all thy **s**
Mark 14:34 My **s** is exceeding sorrowful unto death
Luke 1:46 My **s** doth magnify the Lord
Luke 10:27 all thy heart, and with all thy **s**

Ss

Ss

Souls (SOWLZ)
Plural of "soul."

Proverbs 11:30 he that winneth **s** is wise
Matthew 11:29 ye shall find rest unto your **s**
Acts 2:41 added unto them about three thousand **s**

Sow (SOH)
To plant, or throw seed about so it will grow.

Psalm 126:5 They that **s** in tears shall reap in joy
Matthew 6:26 fowls of the air: for they **s** not
Luke 12:24 ravens: for they neither **s** nor reap

Soweth (SOH ith)
The old way of writing or saying "sows."

Galatians 6:7 whatsoever a man **s**, that shall he
Galatians 6:8 he that **s** to his flesh shall reap
Galatians 6:8 he that **s** to the Spirit shall of

Sparrows (SPAIR ohz)
Small brownish birds of the finch family. These birds were considered "clean" by God and could be eaten as food, usually by the poor. Jesus used the sparrow as an example to show that a person had more worth than a sparrow.

Matthew 10:29 Are not two **s** sold for a farthing
Matthew 10:31 ye are of more value than many **s**
Luke 12:6 Are not five **s** sold for two farthings
Luke 12:7 ye are of more value than many **s**

Speak (SPEEK)
To say words; talk; voice ideas or thoughts.

Exodus 4:14 I know that he can **s** well
Exodus 5:23 I came to Pharaoh to **s** in thy name
Matthew 8:8 but **s** the word only, and my servant
Matthew 15:31 saw the dumb to **s**, the maimed to be
Mark 2:7 Why doth this man thus **s** blasphemies
Mark 7:37 the deaf to hear, and the dumb to **s**
Mark 14:71 I know not this man of whom ye **s**
Luke 7:15 he that was dead sat up, and began to **s**
John 4:26 saith unto her, I that **s** unto thee am he
Acts 2:4 to **s** with other tongues, as the Spirit
Acts 2:6 man heard them **s** in his own language
Acts 2:11 **s** in our tongues the wonderful works of God

Spear (SPEER)
A weapon made with a long handle and a sharp, narrow blade. This weapon was carried by soldiers, or others, and was either thrown or used to jab the enemy.

Sparrows

John 19:34 the soldiers with a *s* pierced his side

Speech (SPEECH)

Words that are spoken; talk.

Exodus 4:10 I am slow of *s*, and of a slow tongue
Matthew 26:73 one of them; for thy *s* betrayeth thee
Colossians 4:6 Let your *s* be always with grace

Spices (SPIGH sez)

Sweet-smelling products made from vegetables for cosmetics, incense, special oils used in worship, perfumes, and to prepare for burial of the dead. They were very costly and anyone who owned the spices valued them.

Mark 16:1 and Salome, had bought sweet *s*, that they
Luke 23:56 returned, and prepared *s* and ointments
Luke 24:1 unto the sepulchrer, bringing the *s*
John 19:40 wound it in linen clothes with the *s*

Spikenard (SPIK nahrd)

A very costly and sweet-smelling spice that was used to make perfume. It is made from a plant grown in India.

Mark 14:3 box of ointment of *s* very precious
John 12:3 pound of ointment of *s*, very costly

Spirit (SPIRH it)

The Hebrew and Greek words used in the Bible for Spirit translate to mean "wind," "breath," or "spirit," depending on how the word is used. Both God and human beings are spirit. Many references in the Bible to the Spirit mean the Holy Spirit. Spirit is also the heart, mind, soul, strength, and life of a human being.

The Spirit of God can be seen wherever one looks. The Holy Spirit was sent by Jesus when he left earth to return to heaven. The Holy Spirit is in each person who believes in and accepts Jesus as Savior. The Spirit guides and helps the believer to do right.

In biblical times, people believed there were spirits that did not have bodies. That is why the disciples were frightened when they saw Jesus walk on the water of the Sea of Galilee.

Genesis 1:2 the *S* of God moved upon the face of the
Genesis 41:8 in the morning that his *s* was troubled
1 Samuel 1:15 I am a woman of a sorrowful *s*
Psalm 31:5 Into thine hand I commit my *s*
Psalm 51:10 and renew a right *s* within me

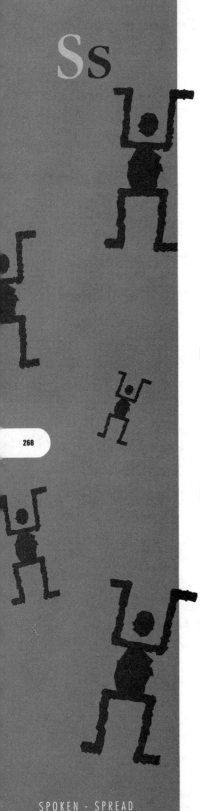

Ss

Psalm 51:11 take not thy holy **s** from me
Matthew 3:16 and he saw the **S** of God descending
Matthew 4:1 Then Jesus was led by the **S** into the (NIV)
Matthew 5:3 Blessed are the poor in **s**
Matthew 14:26 they were troubled, saying, It is a **s**
Mark 1:10 and the **S** like a dove descending upon him
Mark 1:12 immediately the **S** driveth him into the
Mark 6:49 they supposed it had been a **s**, and cried
Mark 14:38 The **s** is willing, but the body is weak (NIV)
Luke 1:80 the child grew and became strong in **s**
Luke 4:1 was led by the **S** into the wilderness
Luke 23:46 Father, into thy hands I commend my **s**
Luke 24:37 and supposed that they had seen a **s**
Luke 24:39 for a **s** hath not flesh and bones
John 3:5 Except a man be born of water and of the **S**
John 4:23 shall worship the Father in **s** and in truth
John 4:24 God is a **S**: and they that worship him must
Ephesians 4:30 And grieve not the holy **S** of God
1 Thessalonians 5:19 Quench not the **S**

■ Spoken (SPOH kin)
Past participle of "speak."

Exodus 10:29 Thou hast **s** well, I will see thy face
Exodus 19:8 All that the LORD hath **s** we will do
Proverbs 15:23 a word **s** in due season, how good is it
Matthew 1:22 which was **s** of the Lord by the prophet
Matthew 26:65 saying, He hath **s** blasphemy
Matthew 27:35 fulfilled which was **s** by the prophet

■ Sponge (SPUNJ)
The skeleton of certain sea animals that is able
to hold water. A sponge was used when one took
a bath. The only time a sponge is mentioned in
the Bible is at the crucifixion of Jesus.

Matthew 27:48 one of them ran, and took a **s**, and
Mark 15:36 filled a **s** full of vinegar, and put it
John 19:29 filled a **s** with vinegar, and put it

■ Spread (SPREHD)
1. To tell something to another person (example:
to spread the word).

Matthew 9:31 they were departed, **s** abroad his fame
Mark 1:28 And immediately his fame **s** abroad
Mark 6:14 Herod heard of him; (for his name was **s**
2. To lay a thing down so as to cover, such as a
cloth over a table.

Mark 11:8 And many **s** their garments in the way
Luke 19:36 he went, they **s** their clothes in the way

268

SPOKEN - SPREAD

Staff (STAF)
A long, straight stick one used to lean on when walking, to defend oneself, to punish another, or to measure a thing.

Exodus 12:11 shoes on your feet, and your **s** in your
1 Samuel 17:7 the **s** of his spear was like a weaver's
1 Samuel 17:40 And he took his **s** in his hand, and
Psalm 23:4 thy rod and thy **s** they comfort me

Stalk (STAWLK)
The stem of a plant.

Genesis 41:5 seven ears of corn came upon one **s**
Genesis 41:22 seven ears came up in one **s**

Stand (STAND)
To rise to one's feet; remain on one's feet.

Genesis 24:13 I **s** here by the well of water
Exodus 8:20 in the morning, and **s** before Pharaoh
Exodus 14:13 Fear ye not, **s** still, and see the
1 Kings 17:1 God of Israel liveth, before whom I **s**
1 Kings 18:15 LORD of hosts liveth, before whom I **s**
1 Kings 19:11 and **s** upon the mount before the LORD
Psalm 4:4 **S** in awe, and sin not: commune with your
Mark 11:25 when ye **s** praying, forgive, if ye have
Luke 6:8 Rise up, and **s** forth in the midst
Revelation 3:20 Behold, I **s** at the door, and knock

Standing (STAND eeng)
The act of being on one's feet in an upright position (see "Stand").

Luke 5:2 And saw two ships **s** by the lake
John 19:26 saw his mother, and the disciple **s** by
John 20:14 saw Jesus **s**, and knew not that it was Jesus

Star (STAHR)
An object in the sky that gives off light, that can be seen at night, and which does not move in the sky. A star appears to be a tiny light in the night sky.

Matthew 2:2 for we have seen his **s** in the east
Matthew 2:7 them diligently what time the **s** appeared
Matthew 2:9 the **s**, which they saw in the east, went
Matthew 2:10 when they saw the **s**, they rejoiced

Stars (STAHRZ)
Plural of "star."

Genesis 1:16 rule the night: he made the **s** also
Psalm 8:3 the moon and the **s**, which thou hast

Ss

Staff

269

Ss

Stature (STACH uhr)
The height of a person, either of his physical body or his manner of acting his age, or of being grown up for his age.

Matthew 6:27 can add one cubit unto his **s**
Luke 2:52 Jesus increased in wisdom and **s**
Luke 12:25 can add to his **s** one cubit
Luke 19:3 because he was little of **s**

Statutes (STACH oots)
Plural of "statute." A statute is a law or command.

Psalm 19:8 The **s** of the LORD are right
Psalm 119:12 O LORD: teach me thy **s**
Psalm 119:16 I will delight myself in thy **s**

Steal (STEEL)
To rob or take something that belongs to someone else, intending to keep it for yourself.

Exodus 20:15 Thou shalt not **s**
Matthew 6:19 where thieves break through and **s**
Matthew 6:20 thieves do not break through nor **s**
Ephesians 4:28 Let him that stole **s** no more

Stephen (STEE vuhn)
The name means "crown." A leader in the Jerusalem church and one of seven men chosen to become the first deacons. He spoke boldly about Jesus, and the Jewish religious leaders had him stoned to death. Saul of Tarsus heard Stephen speak and held the cloaks of those who stoned him.

Acts 6:5 chose **S**, a man full of faith and of the
Acts 6:8 **S**, full of faith and power, did great
Acts 7:59 And they stoned **S**, calling upon God

Sticketh (STIK ith)
The old way of writing or saying "sticks." This is the meaning whereby something clings to another thing, or to join or stay close by.

Proverbs 18:24 friend that **s** closer than a brother

Sticks (STIKS)
Short branches or twigs of trees or bushes; narrow pieces of wood.
1 Kings 17:10 widow woman was there gathering **s**
1 Kings 17:12 behold, I am gathering two **s**

Still (STIHL)
Quiet; free from sound or motion; calm.

Exodus 14:13 Fear ye not, stand **s**, and see the
Psalm 23:2 he leadeth me beside the **s** waters
Psalm 46:10 Be **s**, and know that I am God
Matthew 20:32 Jesus stood **s**, and called them, and
Mark 4:39 said unto the sea, Peace, be **s**. And the
Mark 10:49 Jesus stood **s**, and commanded him to
Acts 8:38 he commanded the chariot to stand **s**

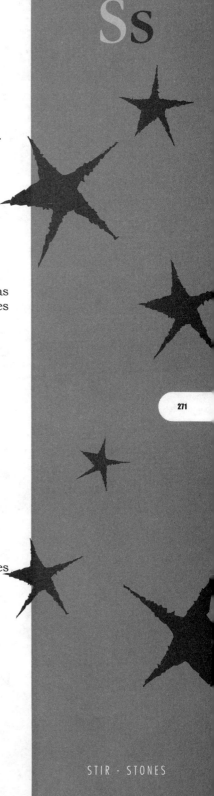

Stir (STUHR)
To excite; cause one to be upset; cause a fuss.

Proverbs 15:1 but grievous words **s** up anger
Acts 12:18 there was no small **s** among the soldiers

Stole (STOHL)
Past tense of "steal."

Matthew 28:13 came by night, and **s** him away
Ephesians 4:28 Let him that **s** steal no more

Stone (STOWN)
A pebble or a rock. The area of Palestine has been labeled a "stony country" because stones of every size are everywhere.

Exodus 15:5 they sank into the bottom as a **s**
1 Samuel 17:49 hand in his bag, and took thence a **s**
1 Samuel 17:49 the **s** sunk into his forehead
1 Samuel 17:50 the Philistine with a sling and a **s**
Matthew 27:60 he rolled a great **s** to the door
Matthew 27:66 made the sepulcher sure, sealing the **s**
Matthew 28:2 and rolled back the **s** from the door
Mark 15:46 and rolled a **s** unto the door
Mark 16:3 Who shall roll us away the **s**
Mark 16:4 saw that the **s** was rolled away
Luke 23:53 in a sepulchre that was hewn in **s**
Luke 24:2 they found the **s** rolled away from the
John 20:1 and seeth the **s** taken away from the

Stoned (STOWND)
Past tense of "stone," meaning to throw stones at a person.

Acts 7:59 And they **s** Stephen, calling upon God
Acts 14:19 **s** Paul and dragged him outside the (NIV)

Stones (STOWNZ)
Plural for "stone."

Genesis 28:11 and he took of the **s** of that place
Joshua 4:8 took up twelve **s** out of the midst of
1 Samuel 17:40 chose him five smooth **s** out of the
1 Kings 18:31 And Elijah took twelve **s**
1 Kings 18:32 with the **s** he built an altar

271

Ss

1 Kings 18:38 the wood, and the **s**, and the dust
Ecclesiastes 3:5 A time to cast away **s**
Ecclesiastes 3:5 a time to gather **s** together
Matthew 4:3 command that these **s** be made bread
Luke 19:40 the **s** would immediately cry out

■ Stood (STOOD)
Past tense of "stand."

Genesis 18:2 looked, and, lo, three men **s** by him
Genesis 41:46 he **s** before Pharaoh king of Egypt
Exodus 15:8 the floods **s** upright as an heap
Matthew 2:9 came and **s** over where the young child was
Matthew 27:11 And Jesus **s** before the governor
Luke 19:8 Zacchaeus **s**, and said unto the Lord
Luke 24:4 two men **s** by them in shining garments
Luke 24:36 Jesus himself **s** in the midst of them
John 18:5 Judas also, who betrayed him, **s** with them
John 18:16 But Peter **s** at the door without
John 18:18 And the servants and officers **s** there
John 18:18 and Peter **s** with them, and warmed himself
John 20:11 But Mary **s** without at the sepulcher
John 20:26 doors being shut, and **s** in the midst

■ Stoop (STEWP)
To bend over, or to bend down.

Mark 1:7 shoes I am not worthy to **s** down and unloose

■ Stooped (STEWPT)
Past tense of "stoop."

John 20:11 as she wept, she **s** down, and looked

■ Stooping (STEWP eeng)
In the act of a stoop.

Luke 24:12 **s** down, he beheld the linen clothes
John 20:5 he **s** down, and looking in, saw the

■ Storehouse (STORE hows)
A building designed to store goods. In earliest biblical times, a storehouse was built of stone in which to place crops that had just been harvested. This type of building discouraged bugs, rats, or other pests from destroying the crops.

Malachi 3:10 Bring ye all the tithes into the **s**

■ Storm (STORM)
A heavy rain or thunderstorm, often with strong winds.

Mark 4:37 there arose a great **s** of wind
Luke 8:23 came down a **s** of wind on the lake

Straight (STRAYT)
Not crooked.

Matthew 3:3 way of the Lord, make his paths *s*
Mark 1:3 way of the Lord, make his paths *s*
Luke 3:4 way of the Lord, make his paths *s*
Luke 13:13 immediately she was made *s*
John 1:23 Make *s* the way of the Lord

Straightway (STRAYT way)
Suddenly, immediately, without delay.

Matthew 3:16 baptized, went up *s* out of the water
Matthew 4:20 And they *s* left their nets, and
Matthew 14:22 And *s* Jesus constrained his disciples
Matthew 14:27 But *s* Jesus spake unto them, saying
Matthew 27:48 *s* one of them ran, and took a sponge
Mark 1:10 And *s* coming up out of the water
Mark 1:18 And *s* they forsook their nets, and
Mark 6:54 out of the ship, *s* they knew him

Strait (STRAYT)
A narrow passageway; road; street.

Matthew 7:13 Enter ye in at the *s* gate
Matthew 7:14 Because *s* is the gate, and narrow is
Luke 13:24 Strive to enter in at the *s* gate

Strange (STRAYNJ)
Unusual; not ordinary; odd; a thing of wonder.

Luke 5:26 saying, We have seen *s* things today

Stranger (STRAYN juhr)
One who is in a place that is not his home; an outsider.

Exodus 20:10 nor thy *s* that is within thy gates
Ruth 2:10 knowledge of me, seeing I am a *s*
Matthew 25:35 I was a *s*, and ye took me in
Matthew 25:38 When saw we thee a *s*, and took
Matthew 25:43 I was a *s*, and ye took me not in
Matthew 25:44 an hungered, or athirst, or a *s*
Luke 17:18 to give glory to God, save this *s*
Luke 24:18 Art thou only a *s* in Jerusalem

Strangers (STRAYN juhrz)
Plural of "stranger."

Matthew 27:7 the potter's field, to bury *s* in
Hebrews 13:2 Do not forget to entertain *s* (NIV)

Strawed (STRAWD)
Past tense for "straw," meaning to spread or scatter.

Exodus 32:20 to powder, and *s* it upon the water

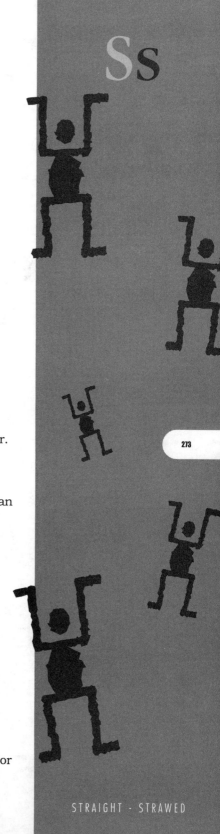

Ss

273

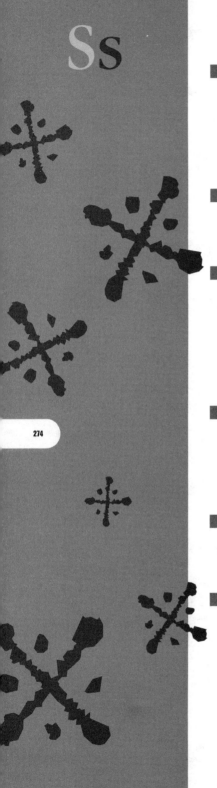

Ss

Matthew 21:8 from the trees, and **s** them in the way
Mark 11:8 off the trees, and **s** them in the way

◼ Strength (STRENKTH)
To be strong; have power or might; energy.

1 Kings 19:8 went in the **s** of that meat forty days
Psalm 27:1 the LORD is the **s** of my life
Psalm 46:1 God is our refuge and **s**, a very present
Mark 12:30 all thy mind, and with all thy **s**
Luke 10:27 all thy soul, and with all thy **s**

◼ Strengtheneth (STRENGTH ihn ith)
The old way of writing or saying "strengthens," plural of "strengthen."

Philippians 4:13 all things through Christ which **s**

◼ Stretch (STRECH)
To reach out, extend.

Exodus 3:20 I will **s** out my hand, and smite Egypt
Exodus 8:5 **S** forth thine hand with thy rod
Exodus 14:26 **S** out thine hand over the sea
Matthew 12:13 he to the man, **S** forth thine hand
Mark 3:5 saith unto the man, **S** forth thine hand
Luke 6:10 said unto the man, **S** forth thine hand

◼ Stretched (STRECHT)
Past tense of "stretch."

Exodus 14:21 Moses **s** out his hand over the sea
Matthew 12:13 he **s** it forth; and it was restored
Mark 3:5 he **s** it out: and his hand was restored
Luke 22:53 in the temple, ye **s** forth no hands

◼ Strife (STRIGHF)
A fight; an unhappy disagreement; an argument.

Genesis 13:7 there was a **s** between the herdmen of
Genesis 13:8 Let there be no **s**, I pray thee

◼ Strike (STRIGHK)
1. To hit or slap.

Mark 14:65 servants did **s** him with the palms

2. As they were preparing to leave Egypt, the Hebrew people were ordered by God to take the blood from the lamb they killed and put it on the sides and across the tops of the door frames of their houses. They would eat the lamb as they stood at the table. The King James Version of the Bible uses the term, "strike," which means to "put it on," much like one would put paint on the doorframe.

274

Exodus 12:7 the blood, and **s** it on the two side posts
Exodus 12:22 **s** the lintel and the two side posts

Stripes (STRIGHPS)
Plural for "stripe." The stripes referred to in the Bible passages have to do with a swelling or cut in the skin due to a severe beating.

Isaiah 53:5 and with his **s** we are healed
Acts 16:23 when they had laid many **s** upon them
Acts 16:33 same hour of the night, and washed their **s**

Strong (STRAWNG)
Mighty, powerful, severe; muscle power; measurement of one's character.

Exodus 10:19 the LORD turned a mighty **s** west wind
Exodus 14:21 the sea to go back by a **s** east wind
1 Kings 19:11 a great and **s** wind rent the mountains
Psalm 24:8 The LORD **s** and mighty, the LORD mighty
Luke 1:80 And the child grew, and waxed **s** in spirit
Luke 2:40 And the child grew, and waxed **s** in spirit
Ephesians 6:10 be **s** in the Lord, and in the power

Study (STUHD ee)
To explore so as to gain knowledge and learning.

2 Timothy 2:15 **S** to show thyself approved unto God

Submit (suhb MITT)
To obey, or yield to another, especially to those in authority. When we submit ourselves to God, we do so out of love, honor, and respect toward God and all that He is.

James 4:7 **S** yourselves therefore to God

Substance (SUHB stuhns)
Property; riches; those things which one owns; security.

Luke 15:13 there wasted his **s** with riotous living
Hebrews 11:1 Now faith is the **s** of things hoped for

Suddenly (SUHD ehn lee)
Quick, surprising, or unexpected; occurring with no warning.

Luke 2:13 And **s** there was with the angel a
Acts 2:2 And **s** there came a sound from heaven
Acts 9:3 and **s** there shined round about him a

Suffer (SUHF uhr)
1. To experience or endure pain.

Mark 8:31 The Son of man must **s** many things, and

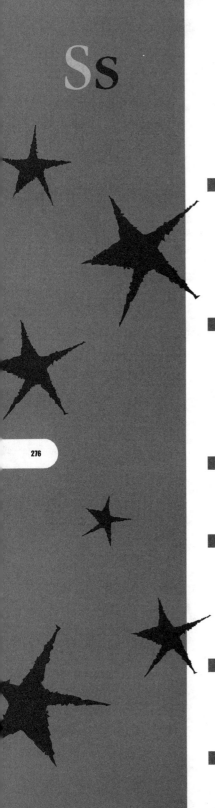

Ss

Luke 9:22 Son of man must **s** many things, and he
Luke 22:15 eat this passover with you before I **s**

2. Permit, allow.

Matthew 3:15 said unto him, **S** it to be so now
Matthew 19:14 **S** little children, and forbid them not
Mark 10:14 **S** the little children to come unto me
Luke 18:16 **S** little children to come unto me

Suffered (SUHF uhrd)
Past tense of "suffer, 1 and 2."

Matthew 3:15 Then he **s** him
Matthew 27:19 **s** many things this day in a dream
Mark 5:19 Howbeit Jesus **s** him not, but saith unto
Luke 8:51 he **s** no man to go in save Peter, and
Luke 24:26 Ought not Christ to have **s** these things
1 Peter 3:18 Christ also hath once **s** for sins

Sun (SUHN)
The bright light in our solar system around which Earth and other planets orbit.

Genesis 37:9 the **s** and the moon and the eleven
Matthew 5:45 he maketh his **s** to rise on the evil
Mark 16:2 into the sepulcher at the rising of the **s**
Luke 23:45 the **s** was darkened, and the veil of the
Ephesians 4:26 let not the **s** go down upon your wrath

Sung (SUHNG)
Past tense of "sing."

Matthew 26:30 when they had **s** an hymn, they went
Mark 14:26 they had **s** an hymn, they went out

Supper (SUHP uhr)
A meal, especially in the evening if the dinner meal is served at or about noon.

Luke 22:20 Likewise also the cup after **s**, saying
John 12:2 There they made him a **s**, and Martha
John 13:2 **s** being ended, the devil having now put
John 13:4 He riseth from **s**, and laid aside his

Supposed (SUH pozd)
Past tense of "suppose." A possible thought or the guessing of a thing to be true.

Mark 6:49 they **s** it had been a spirit, and cried
Luke 24:37 and **s** that they had seen a spirit

Surely (SHUHR lee)
Beyond question; absolutely; no doubt about it.

Psalm 23:6 **S** goodness and mercy shall follow me

Matthew 26:73 to Peter, **s** thou also art one of them
Mark 14:70 to Peter, **s** thou art one of them

Surety (SHUHR ih tee)

1. A person who promises he will be responsible for another person's payment of a debt if that person does not pay. He will make sure that a person returns safely and he will protect property or money which the person has trusted him to protect. When Joseph demanded that they bring Benjamin the next time they came for grain, Judah offered to become a "surety" for Benjamin to make sure that Benjamin was brought back to Jacob.

Genesis 43:9 I will be a **s** for him
Genesis 44:32 thy servant became a **s** for the lad

2. A certainty; to be sure.

Acts 12:11 Now I know of a **s**, that the Lord hath

Surnamed (SUHR naymd)

Past tense of "surname." A surname is a family or last name.

Mark 3:16 And Simon he **s** Peter
Mark 3:17 he **s** them Boanerges, which is
Luke 22:3 entered Satan into Judas **s** Iscariot
Acts 4:36 Joses, who by the apostles was **s** Barnabas

Sustain (suhs TAYN)

Support, provide one's needs; give relief to.

1 Kings 17:9 a widow woman there to **s** thee
Psalm 55:22 upon the LORD, and he shall **s** thee

Swaddling (SWAHD leeng)

Long, narrow strips of linen cloth used to wrap babies after they were first born. This helped to prevent the infant from moving but also may have made the babies feel more secure and warm.

Luke 2:7 and wrapped him in **s** clothes, and laid him
Luke 2:12 shall find the babe wrapped in **s** clothes

Swear (SWAIR)

To vow; give one's word; to make a promise and give an oath to keep the promise. Also means to curse or cuss, or use God's name in an unholy way. Peter cursed when he was identified as a follower of Jesus and then he gave an oath.

Matthew 26:74 began he to curse and to **s**, saying,
Mark 5:7 **S** to God that you won't torture me   (NIV)
Mark 14:71 he began to curse and to **s**, saying, I

Ss

Sweat (SWEHT)
Moisture or wetness that the body gives off during very warm weather or when a person works hard. This moisture has a saltiness to it.

Genesis 3:19 In the **s** of thy face shalt thou eat
Luke 22:44 his **s** was as it were great drops of blood

Sweet (SWEET)
Pleasant to the taste or smell.

Genesis 8:21 And the LORD smelled a **s** savor
Exodus 15:25 the waters, the waters were made **s**
Mark 16:1 and Salome, had brought **s** spices

Swine (SWIGHN)
Pig or pigs; hog or hogs. Swine were considered unclean, and the Israelites were forbidden to eat them or to be around them.

Matthew 8:30 an herd of many **s** feeding
Matthew 8:32 the whole herd of **s** ran violently
Mark 5:12 Send us into the **s**, that we may
Mark 5:13 spirits went out, and entered into the **s**
Luke 8:32 was there an herd of many **s** feeding
Luke 8:33 out of the man, and entered into the **s**
Luke 15:15 he sent him into his fields to feed **s**
Luke 15:16 with the husks that the **s** did eat

Sword (SAWRD)
A weapon with a long sharp blade used for defense in battle or war.

Judges 7:18 say, The **s** of the LORD, and of Gideon
Judges 7:20 cried, The **s** of the LORD, and of Gideon
Matthew 26:51 drew his **s**, and struck a servant of
Matthew 26:52 Put up again thy **s** into his place
Mark 14:47 them that stood by drew a **s**, and smote
Luke 22:49 Lord, shall we smite with the **s**
John 18:10 Simon Peter having a **s** drew it
John 18:11 Put up thy **s** into the sheath

Sycamore (SIK uh mawhr)
A tree grown in Asia Minor and Egypt for its fig-mulberry type of fruit. The branches spread wide and low, providing shade and ease of climbing. Its wood was used by poor people.

Luke 19:4 and climbed up into a **s** tree to see him

Synagogue (SIN uh gahg)
The building in which Jews gathered to worship and study. The synagogue probably began sometime after the Temple in Jerusalem was

destroyed in 587 B.C. A synagogue could be started if there were at least ten Jewish men who lived there. Women and children had to sit apart from the men. The service included prayers, the reading of Old Testament Scripture, reciting Deuteronomy 6:4-9 (called the Shema), a sermon, and a closing prayer.

Matthew 12:9 he went into their **s**
Matthew 13:54 he taught them in their **s**
Mark 5:22 one of the rulers of the **s**
Luke 4:16 he went into the **s** on the sabbath
John 18:20 I ever taught in the **s**, and in the
Acts 17:1 Thessalonica, where was a **s** of the Jews
Acts 18:4 he reasoned in the **s** every sabbath

■ Synagogues (SIN uh gahgz)
Plural for "synagogue."

Matthew 4:23 about all Galilee, teaching in their **s**
Matthew 9:35 and villages, teaching in their **s**
Mark 1:39 he preached in their **s** throughout all
Luke 4:15 he taught in their **s**, being glorified
Luke 4:44 And he preached in the **s** of Galilee
Luke 13:10 teaching in one of the **s** on the sabbath
Acts 9:2 letters to Damascus to the **s**
Acts 9:20 straightway he preached Christ in the **s**
Acts 13:5 they preached the word of God in the **s**

■ Syria (SIHR ih uh)
A nation north of Canaan (Israel and Judah) with its western border on the Mediterranean Sea and the eastern border at the Euphrates River (see map on page 341). Its capital was Damascus. At some times during biblical history, the Syrians fought the Hebrews, and at other times they were friends.

2 Kings 6:8 king of **S** warred against Israel
Matthew 4:24 his fame went throughout all **S**
Luke 2:2 when Cyrenius was governor of **S**

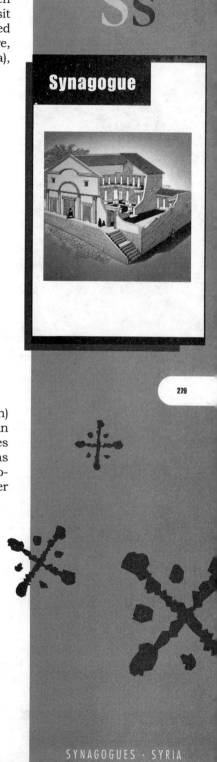

Synagogue

Tabernacle (TAB uhr NAK uhl)

The name may mean "tent, temporary dwelling place." A special tent considered sacred. Here the Hebrews worshiped God while they were in the desert after leaving Egypt, and after entering the Promised Land. Various references to the tent in the Bible include "the tent of meeting," "the tabernacle of the congregation," and "tent of witness."

The tabernacle was built so it could be moved about as the Israelites wandered in the wilderness. The people knew God was present in the tabernacle because the cloud remained on the tabernacle. Whenever Moses came near, the cloud filled the tabernacle so Moses could not go inside. But God spoke through the cloud to Moses.

Exodus 40:2 first month shalt thou set up the *t*
Exodus 40:21 And he brought the ark into the *t*
Exodus 40:38 cloud of the LORD was upon the *t* by day

Tabitha (TAB ih thuh)

The name means "gazelle" and is Aramaic. It means the same in the Greek as Dorcas. She was a faithful follower of Jesus. See "Dorcas."

Acts 9:36 at Joppa a certain disciple named *T*
Acts 9:40 said *T*, arise. And she opened her eyes

Table (TAY buhl)

A piece of furniture with a flat top on legs. In biblical times it could mean a piece of leather placed on the ground where food was set, a stone tablet, or a writing tablet. The last two would have a flat surface on which to write. Early tables had short legs so that a person sat on the ground, or reclined on a rug beside it. In New Testament times, the guests reclined on low couches while eating. They would prop up their heads with one hand while eating with the other.

Psalm 23:5 Thou preparest a *t* before me in the
John 12:2 them that sat at the *t* with him
John 13:28 Now no man at the *t* knew for what

Talebearer (TAYL bair uhr)

One who tattles, tells a secret, betrays another in any way, or tells on another; a gossip.

Proverbs 11:13 A *t* revealeth secrets

Tabernacle

280

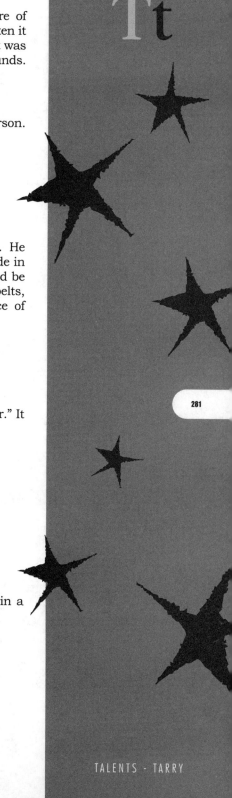

Talents (TAL ins)
Plural for "talent." A talent was a measure of weight used in the Old Testament times. Often it varied from one culture to the next. A talent was equal to 3,000 shekels or a weight of 75 pounds.

Matthew 18:24 which owed him ten thousand **t**

Talked (TAWLKT)
Past tense of "talk." To speak to another person.

Genesis 4:8 And Cain **t** with Abel his brother
Exodus 33:9 and the LORD **t** with Moses
Mark 6:50 immediately he **t** with them, and saith
Luke 24:32 while he **t** with us by the way, and
John 4:27 and marveled that he **t** with the woman

Tanner (TAN uhr)
One who prepared animal hides for use. He would remove the animal hair, soak the hide in a certain liquid mixture, and the hide would be changed into leather. Leather was used as belts, shoes, or other pieces of clothing. A piece of leather might also be used for a table.

Acts 9:43 many days in Joppa with one Simon a **t**
Acts 10:6 He lodgeth with one Simon a **t**
Acts 10:32 house of one Simon a **t** by the seaside

Tare (TAIR)
An old form of "tore," the past tense of "tear." It means to rip or pull apart.

Mark 9:20 straightway the spirit **t** him
Luke 9:42 the devil threw him down, and **t** him

Tarried (TAIR eed)
Past tense of "tarry."

Luke 2:43 the child Jesus **t** behind in Jerusalem
John 3:22 and there he **t** with them, and baptized
Acts 9:43 he **t** many days in Joppa with one Simon

Tarry (TAIR ee)
To remain, wait, or stay awhile; to not be in a hurry to leave.

2 Kings 2:2 And Elijah said unto Elisha, **T** here
2 Kings 2:4 Elijah said unto him, Elisha, **t** here
2 Kings 2:6 Elijah said unto him, **T**, I pray thee
Matthew 26:38 **t** ye here, and watch with me
Mark 14:34 **t** ye here, and watch
Luke 24:29 And he went in to **t** with them
Luke 24:49 but **t** ye in the city of Jerusalem
John 4:40 besought him that he would **t** with them

Tt

Tarshish (TAHR shish)
Exact location is unknown but may have been a city on the southern tip of Spain. When Jonah ran from God's call, he wanted to get as far away as possible. This trading post was wealthy, in that it traded in precious metals with seaport cities on the eastern Mediterranean shores.

Jonah 1:3 But Jonah rose up to flee unto **T**
Jonah 1:3 and he found a ship going to **T**
Jonah 1:3 unto **T** from the presence of the LORD
Jonah 4:2 Therefore I fled before unto **T**

Tarsus (TAHR suhs)
The ancient capital of Cilicia, a province of Rome, now located in southern Turkey (see map on page 341). This city was built on a river that drained into the Mediterranean Sea about ten miles away. Paul the apostle was born here. Tarsus was well known as a center for learning, especially in literature and philosophy. It was also known for the goat's-hair tents which were made there.

Acts 9:11 house of Judas, for one called Saul, of **T**
Acts 9:30 down to Caesarea, and sent him forth to **T**
Acts 11:25 departed Barnabas to **T**, for to seek Saul
Acts 21:39 Paul said, I am a man which am a Jew of **T**

Task (TASK)
A job; work.

Exodus 5:14 not fulfilled your **t** in making brick
Exodus 5:19 aught from your bricks of your daily **t**

Taskmasters (TASK mass tuhrz)
Plural of "taskmaster." One who is a boss or overseer of slaves who often mistreats those who work under him. The Hebrew slaves were forced by unfair taskmasters to complete difficult jobs for Pharaoh.

Exodus 1:11 they did set over them **t** to afflict them
Exodus 3:7 have heard their cry by reason of their **t**
Exodus 5:10 And the **t** of the people went out, and
Exodus 5:13 And the **t** hasted them, saying, Fulfil

Taste (TAYST)
Flavor.

Exodus 16:31 **t** of it was like wafers made with honey
Number 11:8 **t** of it was as the **t** of fresh oil

Tasted (TAYST ihd)
Past tense of "taste."

Matthew 27:34 he had *t* thereof, he would not drink
John 2:9 had *t* the water that was made wine

Taught (TAWT)
Past tense of "teach."

Matthew 5:2 he opened his mouth, and *t* them
Matthew 7:29 he *t* them as one having authority
Matthew 13:54 he *t* them in their synagogue
Mark 1:21 he entered into the synagogue, and *t*
Mark 1:22 he *t* them as one that had authority
Mark 9:31 For he *t* his disciples, and said
Luke 4:15 And he *t* in their synagogues, being
Luke 4:31 Galilee, and *t* them on the sabbath days
Luke 5:3 sat down, and *t* the people out of the ship
Luke 19:47 And he *t* daily in the temple
John 18:20 I ever *t* in the synagogue, and in the

Taxed (TAXT)
Past tense of "tax." Taxes were payment to rulers. In early Old Testament times, the taxes paid by the Israelites were to go to upkeep of the tabernacle and to pay the priests. Later, rulers who had conquered Israel and Judah forced them to pay taxes when the people had to register themselves, and sometimes their possessions. The Romans had such a tax as well as many others at the time Jesus was born. That is why Joseph and Mary had to go to Bethlehem: to register themselves so the Roman government could get the taxes.

Luke 2:1 that all the world should be *t*
Luke 2:3 And all went to be *t*, every one into his
Luke 2:5 To be *t* with Mary his espoused wife

Taxing (TAX eeng)
The act of being taxed.

Luke 2:2 (And this *t* was first made when Cyrenius

Teach (TEECH)
To educate or train; show how to do something.

Exodus 4:12 and *t* thee what thou shalt say
Deuteronomy 6:7 *t* them diligently unto thy children
Psalm 51:13 Then will I *t* transgressors thy way
Psalm 86:11 *T* me thy way, O LORD
Matthew 28:19 Go ye therefore, and *t* all nations
Mark 6:2 he began to *t* in the synagogue

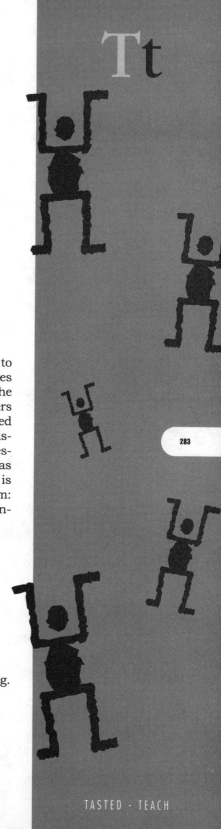

replaced appropriately.

283

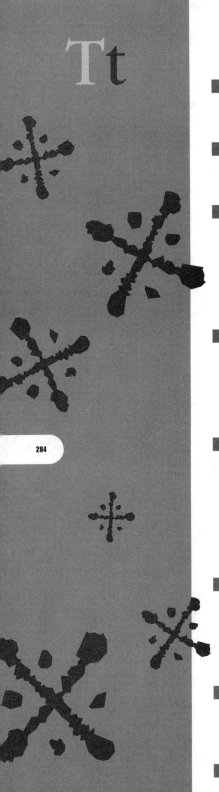

Tt

Luke 11:1 Lord, *t* us to pray, as John also
John 14:26 he shall *t* you all things, and bring

■ Teacher (TEE chur)
One who teaches; an educator, guide.

John 3:2 we know thou art a *t* come from God

■ Teachers (TEE churz)
Plural of "teacher."

Ephesians 4:11 evangelists; and some, pastors and *t*

■ Teaching (TEE cheeng)
The act of being a teacher; sharing knowledge.

Matthew 26:55 I sat daily with you *t* in the temple
Matthew 28:20 *T* them to observe all things
Mark 6:6 he went round about the villages, *t*
Mark 14:49 I was daily with you in the temple *t*
Luke 13:10 And he was *t* in one of the synagogues

■ Tears (TIHRZ)
Plural of "tear." Moisture that comes from the
eyes when one is sad, or happy.

Psalm 126:5 They that sow in *t* shall reap in joy
Luke 7:38 weeping, and began to wash his feet with *t*
Luke 7:44 she hath washed my feet with *t*

■ Tell (TELL)
To share, announce, give a report.

Genesis 29:15 *t* me, what shall thy wages be
Matthew 8:4 Jesus saith unto him, See thou *t* no man
Mark 5:19 Go home to thy friends, and *t* them how
Mark 7:36 charged them that they should *t* no man
Luke 22:34 I *t* thee, Peter, the cock shall not crow
John 20:15 *t* me where thou hast laid him, and I will

■ Tempest (TEM pust)
A wild storm with high winds, possibly hail, and
rain.

Jonah 1:4 and there was a mighty *t* in the sea
Jonah 1:12 for my sake this great *t* is upon you
Matthew 8:24 there arose a great *t* in the sea

■ Tempestuous (tem PEHS chew uhs)
Very wild, violent, raging, stormy.

Jonah 1:11 the sea wrought, and was *t*
Jonah 1:13 the sea wrought, and was *t* against them

■ Temple (TEM puhl)
A house or place of worship. The first Jewish

Temple was built in 957 B.C. by King Solomon in Jerusalem. The purpose of the Temple was to show God's people that the LORD God was among them. It may have taken seven years to complete all the work. Fine cedar and olive woods, bronze, and gold were some of the materials used in its construction. Beautiful carvings and other special work helped to make the Temple a great and magnificent building. It stood for over 350 years before it was destroyed by the Babylonians.

Later, Zerubbabel, a Jew who had been a captive in Babylonia, was allowed to return to Jerusalem as governor. He directed the rebuilding of the Temple in 516 B.C. Jews worshiped in this building until about 20 B.C. King Herod tore down this Temple and built a larger, more magnificent Temple. Herod's Temple was destroyed in A.D. 70, just as Jesus had said it would be.

Temple

Matthew 4:5 and setteth him on a pinnacle of the *t*
Matthew 21:12 And Jesus went into the *t* of God
Matthew 21:12 all them that sold and bought in the *t*
Matthew 26:55 I sat daily with you teaching in the *t*
Matthew 27:5 Cast down the pieces of silver in the *t*
Matthew 27:51 curtain of the *t* was torn in two from (NIV)
Mark 11:15 Jesus went into the *t*, and began to cast
Mark 11:15 out them that bought and sold in the *t*
Mark 14:49 I was daily with you in the *t* teaching
Mark 15:38 curtain of the *t* was torn in two from (NIV)
Luke 2:27 And he came by the Spirit into the *t*
Luke 2:37 departed not from the *t*, but served God
Luke 2:46 after three days they found him in the *t*
Luke 4:9 and set him on a pinnacle of the *t*
Luke 19:42 And he taught daily in the *t*
Luke 22:53 When I was daily with you in the *t*
Luke 23:45 the curtain of the *t* was torn in two (NIV)
John 2:15 he drove them all out of the *t*
John 8:2 morning he came again into the *t*
John 18:20 taught in the synagogue, and in the *t*

Tempt (TEMPT)
To give someone a good reason to do something that is wrong.

Deuteronomy 6:16 Ye shall not *t* the LORD your God
Matthew 4:7 Thou shalt not *t* the LORD your God
Matthew 22:18 Why *t* ye me, ye hypocrites
Mark 12:15 Why *t* ye me? bring me a penny
Luke 4:12 Thou shalt not *t* the Lord thy God
Luke 20:23 said unto them, Why *t* ye me

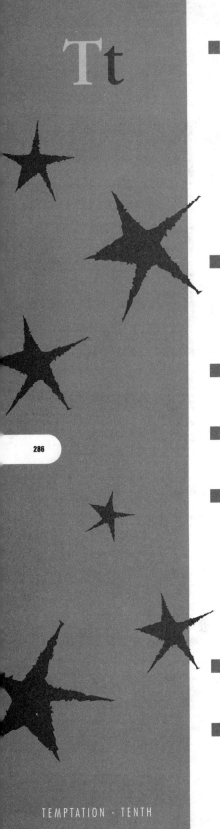

Tt

■ Temptation (tem TAY shun)
To cause or lead someone to do wrong; to want to make a wrong choice. It is not wrong to be tempted, but it is wrong to make the choice to do that which is not right.

Matthew 6:13 And lead us not into *t*, but deliver us
Matthew 26:41 pray, that ye enter not into *t*
Mark 14:38 pray, lest ye enter into *t*
Luke 11:4 And lead us not into *t*, but deliver us
Luke 22:40 Pray that ye enter not into *t*
Luke 22:46 rise and pray, lest ye enter into *t*
1 Corinthians 10:13 hath no *t* taken you but such
1 Corinthians 10:13 will with the *t* also make a way

■ Tempted (TEM tid)
Past tense of "tempt."

Exodus 17:7 because they *t* the LORD, saying
Matthew 4:1 into the wilderness to be *t* of the devil
Mark 1:13 in the wilderness forty days, *t* of Satan
Luke 4:2 Being forty days *t* of the devil

■ Tempter (TEM tuhr)
One who tempts.

Matthew 4:3 And when the *t* came to him, he said

■ Tempting (TEM teeng)
The act of being tempted.

Matthew 22:35 a lawyer, asked him a question, *t* him

■ Ten (TEN)
A number that follows nine.

Genesis 18:32 Peradventure *t* shall be found there
Genesis 42:3 Joseph's *t* brethren went down to buy corn
Ruth 1:4 and they dwelled there about *t* years
Ruth 4:2 And he took *t* men of the elders of the city
Matthew 18:24 which owed him *t* thousand talents
Luke 15:8 what woman having *t* pieces of silver
Luke 17:12 there met him *t* men that were lepers
Luke 17:17 said, Were there not *t* cleansed

■ Tenderhearted (ten duhr HAR tihd)
Caring, kind; have loving feelings toward others.

Ephesians 4:32 and be ye kind one to another, *t*

■ Tenth (TENTH)
The next after the ninth in a series.

Genesis 8:5 decreased continually until the *t* month
Genesis 28:22 I will surely give the *t* unto thee
John 1:39 that day: for it was about the *t* hour

Tentmakers (TINT may kurz)

Plural of "tentmaker." Those who made tents. Tents were usually made by weaving goat's hair. As the sun faded the hair, the tents appeared to be striped. Paul, Aquila, and Priscilla were tentmakers.

Acts 18:3 for by their occupation they were *t*

Terah (TEE ruh or TEHR uh)

The name meant "ibex" or "turning" or "wandering." He was the father of Abram, Nahor, and Haran. He moved his family from Ur of the Chaldees to Haran, following the Euphrates River so they could water and feed their flocks and herds of animals. He was 205 years old when he died in Haran.

Genesis 11:27 Now these are the generations of *T*
Genesis 11:27 *T* begat Abram, Nahor, and Haran
Genesis 11:31 *T* took Abram his son, and Lot his
Genesis 11:32 And the days of *T* were two hundred

Testament (TESS tuh muhnt)

An agreement between God and man. Also the two main parts of the Bible, the Old Testament, and the New Testament.

Matthew 26:28 For this is my blood of the new *t*
Mark 14:24 This is my blood of the new *t*
Luke 22:20 This cup is the new *t* in my blood
Testified (TEHS tih fighd) Past tense of "testify."
John 4:39 which *t*, He told me all that ever I did
John 4:44 Jesus himself *t*, that a prophet hath no
John 13:21 he was troubled in spirit, and *t*, and

Testified (TESS tuh fighd)

Past tense of "testify."

John 4:39 which *t*, He told me all that I ever did
John 4:44 Jesus himself *t*, that a prophet hath no
John 13:21 he was troubled in spirit, and *t*, and

Testify (TESS tuh figh)

To tell something as true; to be an eye witness to something.

John 3:11 we do know, and *t* that we have seen
Acts 2:40 with many other words did he *t*
1 John 4:14 and do *t* that the Father sent the Son

Testimonies (TESS tuh mow neez)

Plural of "testimony."

Psalm 119:2 Blessed are they that keep his *t*

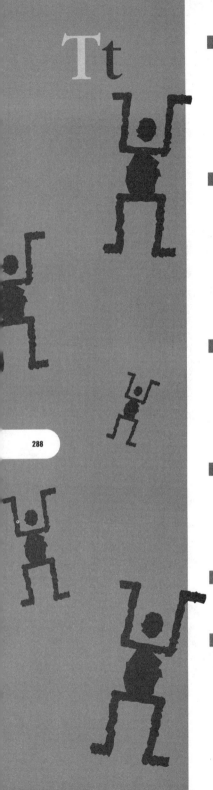

Testimony (TESS tuh mow nee)

An oral or written statement by a witness. In the Old Testament, testimony referred to God's laws or the Ten Commandments. In the New Testament, it usually refers to a person who tells others about Jesus.

Psalm 19:7 the *t* of the LORD is sure, making wise
John 21:24 and we know that his *t* is true

Tetrarch (TET rahrk)

One who ruled a territory of Rome. The title represented the size of the territory and how much authority the ruler had. Herod the Great was the tetrarch in Galilee during the time of Jesus, but Pontius Pilate, the governor, had more authority than Herod did.

Matthew 14:1 Herod the *t* heard of the fame of Jesus
Luke 3:1 And Herod being *t* of Galilee
Luke 3:1 and his brother Philip *t* of Iturea

Thaddeus (THAD ih uhs)

The name may mean "gift of God." He was one of the twelve disciples and was also known as Lebbaeus or Jude, the one who wrote the Bible book of Jude in the New Testament.

Matthew 10:3 and Lebbeus, whose surname was *T*
Mark 3:18 and James the son of Alpheus, and *T*

Thank (THANK)

To recognize, bless, praise; show respect to, and appreciation for.

Daniel 2:23 I *t* thee, and praise thee, O thou God
John 11:41 Father, I *t* thee, that thou hast heard
Philippians 1:3 I *t* my God upon every remembrance

Thankful (THANK fuhl)

Grateful, a feeling of appreciation.

Psalm 100:4 be *t* unto him, and bless his name

Thanks (THANX)

Plural of "thank." Showing that one is grateful.

1 Chronicles 16:34 O give *t* unto the LORD; for he
Psalm 105:1 O give *t* unto the LORD; call upon his
Matthew 15:36 loaves and the fishes, and gave *t*
Matthew 26:27 And he took the cup, and gave *t*
Mark 8:6 he took the seven loaves, and gave *t*
Mark 14:23 when he had given *t*, he gave it to them
Luke 2:38 And she coming that instant gave *t*
Luke 22:17 And he took the cup, and gave *t*

Luke 22:19 And he took the bread, and gave *t*
John 6:11 when he had given *t*, he distributed
1 Thessalonians 5:18 In everything give *t*

■ **Thanksgiving (thanks GIH veeng)**
Showing gratefulness, especially to God; giving thanks. An important part of worship in Old Testament worship services and by New Testament Christians, and Christians of today

Psalm 100:4 Enter into his gates with *t*, and into
Philippians 4:6 with *t* let your requests be made

■ **Themselves (them SELVZ)**
They alone; "their own selves."

Genesis 3:7 fig leaves together, and made *t* aprons
Exodus 5:7 let them go and gather straw for *t*
1 Kings 18:23 let them choose one bullock for *t*
1 Kings 18:28 they cried aloud, and cut *t* after
Matthew 9:3 certain of the scribes said within *t*
Matthew 14:15 go to the villages and buy *t* some (NIV)
Mark 6:36 may go into the villages, and by *t* bread
Luke 22:23 And they began to inquire among *t*
Luke 24:12 beheld the linen clothes laid by *t*
John 18:18 they warmed *t*: and Peter stood with them
John 19:24 They said therefore among *t*, Let us not

■ **Thenceforth (THENS forth)**
"From that time on."

Matthew 5:13 it is *t* good for nothing, but to
John 19:12 from *t* Pilate sought to release him

■ **Therefore (THAIR fore)**
So, thus; "for that reason."

Genesis 3:23 *T* the LORD God sent him forth from
Matthew 6:9 After this manner *t* pray ye: Our
Matthew 7:12 *T* all things whatsoever ye would that
Matthew 22:21 Render *t* unto Caesar the things which
Matthew 28:19 Go ye *t*, and teach all nations
Luke 20:25 Render *t* unto Caesar the things which
Luke 23:20 Pilate *t*, willing to release Jesus
John 5:18 *T* the Jews sought the more to kill him
John 19:1 Pilate *t* took Jesus, and scourged him
John 19:31 Jews *t*, because it was the preparation
John 19:38 He came *t*, and took the body of Jesus

■ **Thessalonians (THESS uh LOH nih uhnz)**
People who lived in or were from Thessalonica.

1 Thessalonians 1:1 unto the church of the *T* which is

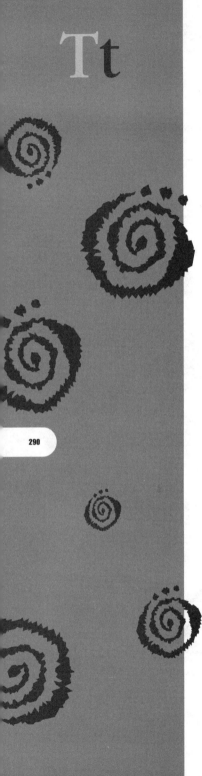

T t

Thessalonians, 1, 2, Books of (THESS uh LOH nih uhnz)

The eighth and ninth books of the division, Paul's Letters, in the New Testament. Paul wrote these letters to the believers in Thessalonica in about A.D. 50. It is believed that they are the earliest writings by the New Testament writers. After Paul started the church there, jealous Jews ran him out of town. Paul didn't have time to teach them how to live the Christian life. The first letter was to encourage the believers, tell them how thankful he was for their faithfulness, and he answered some questions they had concerning when Jesus returned. In the second letter, he tries to answer other questions about Christ's return. Some of the believers had stopped work and were depending on others to support them. He told them to get back to work. He also gave some guidelines for living as a Christian.

Thessalonica (THESS uh loh NIGH kuh)

The capital city of Macedonia. The present day city, Thessaloniki, lies over the ruins of the ancient city. It is now a part of northern Greece (see map on page 341). Thessalonica was a harbor city as well as having many businesses. Paul visited this city, began a church there, and later wrote two letters to the church. Those letters are part of our New Testament (see "Thessalonians, 1, 2, Books of").

Acts 17:1 they came to *T*, where was a synagogue
Acts 17:11 These were now more noble than those in *T*
Acts 17:13 when the Jews of *T* had knowledge that

Thicket (THIK iht)

Bushes or trees that are clumped together tightly in a small space.

Genesis 22:13 behind him a ram caught in a *t* by

Thief (THEEF)

A person who robs or steals; a burglar.

Matthew 26:55 come out as against a *t* with swords
Mark 14:48 ye come out, as against a *t*, with swords
Luke 22:52 come out, as against a *t*, with swords

Thieves (THEEVS)

Plural of "thief."

Matthew 6:19 and where *t* break through and steal
Matthew 6:20 and where *t* do not break through nor

Matthew 21:13 but ye have made it a den of *t*
Matthew 27:38 were there two *t* crucified with him
Mark 11:17 but ye have made it a den of *t*
Mark 15:27 And with him they crucify two *t*
Luke 10:30 Jerusalem to Jericho, and fell among *t*
Luke 19:46 but ye have made it a den of *t*

■ Think (THEENK)

To believe; have an idea; guess; reason out a thing.

Matthew 6:7 for they *t* that they shall be heard
Matthew 18:12 How *t* ye? If a man have an hundred
Matthew 26:66 What *t* ye? They answered and said
Mark 14:64 Ye have heard the blasphemy: what *t* ye
John 11:56 What *t* ye, that he will not come to the

■ Third (THURD)

Follows the second in a series.

Genesis 1:13 evening and the morning were the *t* day
1 Kings 18:1 the LORD came to Elijah in the *t* year
1 Kings 18:34 And he said, Do it the *t* time
Matthew 17:23 and the *t* day he shall be raised
Matthew 26:44 prayed the *t* time, saying the same
Mark 9:31 he shall rise the *t* day
Mark 14:41 And he cometh the *t* time, and saith
Luke 18:33 and the *t* day he shall rise again
Luke 23:22 And he said to them the *t* time
Acts 2:15 seeing it is but the *t* hour of the day

■ Thirst (THURST)

The dry feeling in the throat that tells a person he needs to take in, or drink, liquids.

Matthew 5:6 do hunger and *t* after righteousness
John 19:28 scripture might be fulfilled, saith, I *t*
Romans 12:20 if he *t*, give him drink: for in so

■ Thirsty (THUR stee)

Needing to drink liquids.

Matthew 25:35 I was *t*, and ye gave me drink
Matthew 25:37 fed thee? Or *t*, and gave thee drink
Matthew 25:42 I was *t*, and ye gave me no drink

■ Thomas (TAHM uhs)

The name means "a twin." One of the twelve disciples of Jesus. He was also called Didymus, which also means "a twin." He went with Jesus to Judea even though there was a risk of death. However, after Jesus' resurrection, Thomas had a hard time believing that Jesus was alive. When he saw Jesus, the nail prints, and the

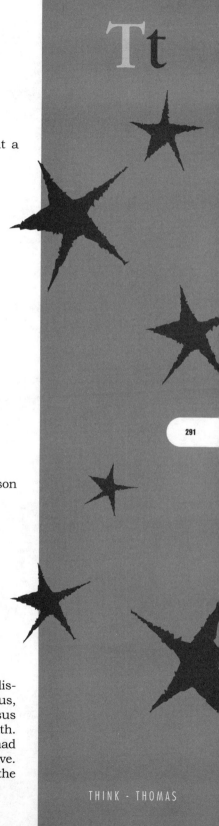

291

scar on His side, he no longer doubted.

Matthew 10:3 **T**, and Matthew the publican
Mark 3:18 Matthew, and **T**, and James the son of
Luke 6:15 Matthew, and **T**, James the son of
John 20:24 But **T**, one of the twelve, called
John 20:26 and **T** with them: then came Jesus
John 20:28 And **T** answered and said unto him

■ Thorns (THORNS)
A bushy plant with sharp spikes, like needles. Some thorns are short, like those on roses, while other plants have longer and more narrow thorns.

Matthew 27:29 when they had platted a crown of **t**
Mark 15:17 platted a crown of **t**, and put it about
John 19:2 And the soldiers platted a crown of **t**
John 19:5 came Jesus forth, wearing the crown of **t**

■ Thought (THOT)
Past tense of "think."

1 Samuel 1:13 therefore Eli **t** she had been drunken
Esther 6:6 Now Haman **t** in his heart, To whom would
Matthew 1:20 But while he **t** on these things
Luke 19:11 they **t** that the kingdom of God should
Acts 10:19 While Peter **t** on the vision, the Spirit

■ Thoughts (THAWTS)
Plural of the noun "thought." That which one thinks; ideas.

Psalm 94:11 The LORD knoweth the **t** of man
Psalm 139:23 try me, and know my **t**
Isaiah 55:7 and the unrighteous man his **t**
Isaiah 55:8 For my **t** are not your **t**, neither are
Isaiah 55:9 than your ways, and my **t** than your **t**
Matthew 9:4 And Jesus knowing their **t** said
Luke 5:22 But when Jesus perceived their **t**, he
Luke 6:8 But he knew their **t**, and said to the man

■ Thousand (THOW sund)
A large number; "ten times one hundred."

Psalm 90:4 For a **t** years in thy sight are but
Matthew 16:9 remember the five loaves of the five **t**
Matthew 16:10 Neither the seven loaves of the four **t**
Matthew 18:24 which owed him ten **t** talents
Mark 6:44 eat of the loaves were about five **t** men
Mark 8:9 they that had eaten were about four **t**
Mark 8:19 I brake the five loaves among five **t**
Mark 8:20 And when the seven among four **t**
John 6:10 men sat down, in number about five **t**

Acts 2:41 added unto them about three *t* souls

Threshingfloor (THRESH eeng flore)
A large flat rock, or an area of ground that has been beaten and smoothed. A threshingfloor was often located at the edge of the town so the wind could blow away the husks of the grain as the farmer tossed it into the air. The grain was heavier and would fall back to the ground.

Ruth 3:2 he winnoweth barley tonight in the *t*

Thrice (THRIS)
"Three times."

Matthew 26:34 the cock crow, thou shalt deny me *t*
Matthew 26:75 the cock crow, thou shalt deny me *t*
Mark 14:30 cock crow twice, thou shalt deny me *t*
Mark 14:72 cock crow twice, thou shalt deny me *t*
Luke 22:34 thou shalt *t* deny that thou knowest me
Luke 22:61 the cock crow, thou shalt deny me *t*
John 13:38 not crow, till thou hast denied me *t*

Throng (THRWNG)
To pack many people together in a group or crowd so that they press against one another.

Mark 3:9 the multitude, lest they should *t* him
Luke 8:45 Master, the multitude *t* thee and press

Thronged (THRWNGD)
Past tense of "throng."

Mark 5:24 much people followed him, and *t* him
Luke 8:42 But as he went the people *t* him

Through (THREW)
Among, between; by way of.

Exodus 12:12 I will pass *t* the land of Egypt this
Matthew 6:19 and where thieves break *t* and steal
Matthew 6:20 where thieves do not break *t* nor steal
Matthew 19:24 a camel to go *t* the eye of a needle
Luke 4:14 fame of him *t* all the region round about
Luke 5:19 let him down *t* the tiling with his couch
Luke 13:22 went *t* the cities and villages, teaching
Luke 18:25 easier for a camel to go *t* a needle's eye
Luke 19:1 Jesus entered and passed *t* Jericho
John 3:17 that the world *t* him might be saved
John 4:4 And he must needs go *t* Samaria
John 20:31 believing ye might have life *t* his name

Throughout (THREW owt)
Everywhere.

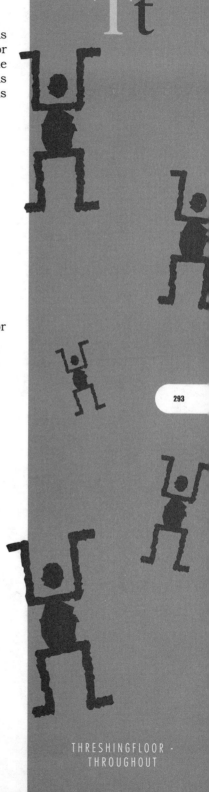

293

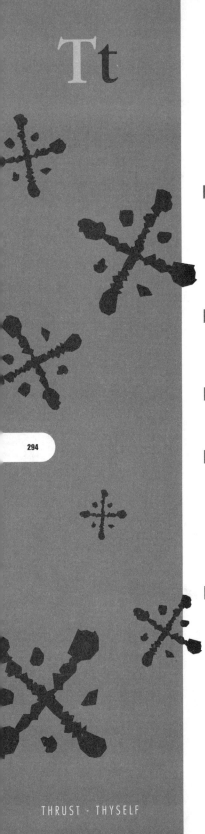

Genesis 41:29 great plenty *t* all the land of Egypt
Genesis 41:46 and went *t* all the land of Egypt
Exodus 11:6 be a great cry *t* all the land of Egypt
Matthew 4:24 And his fame went *t* all Syria
Mark 1:28 his fame spread *t* all the region
Mark 1:39 preached in their synagogues *t* all Galilee
Mark 14:9 gospel shall be preached *t* the whole world
Luke 4:25 when great famine was *t* all the land
John 19:23 was without seam, woven from the top *t*

■ Thrust (THRUST)
Push or shove; drive out with force.

Exodus 11:1 he shall surely *t* you out hence
Exodus 12:39 because they were *t* out of Egypt
Luke 4:29 rose up, and *t* him out of the city
John 20:25 *t* my hand into this side, I will not
John 20:27 *t* it into my side: and be not faithless

■ Thunder (THUN duhr)
Boom, roar, rumble.

Exodus 9:23 and the LORD sent *t* and hail
Mark 3:17 Boanerges, which is, The sons of *t*

■ Thundered (THUN duhrd)
Past tense of "thunder."

John 12:29 stood by, and heard it, said that it *t*

■ Thyatira (THIGH uh TIGH ruh)
A prosperous city located in what is now western Turkey (see map on page 341). The hometown of Lydia, a woman who sold fine purple cloth. She was one of the first people to become a Christian there after Paul preached about Jesus. A church grew from those first believers.

Acts 16:14 a seller of purple, of the city of *T*

■ Thyself (thigh SELF)
The old way of writing or saying "yourself."

Exodus 20:5 Thou shalt not bow down *t* to them
Leviticus 19:18 thou shalt love thy neighbour as *t*
Deuteronomy 5:9 shalt not bow down *t* unto them
Psalm 37:4 Delight *t* also in the LORD
Matthew 4:6 If thou be the Son of God, cast *t* down
Matthew 8:4 go thy way, show *t* to the priest
Matthew 19:19 Thou shalt love thy neighbour as *t*
Matthew 22:39 Thou shalt love thy neighbour as *t*
Mark 1:44 go thy way, show *t* to the priest
Mark 12:31 Thou shalt love thy neighbour as *t*
Mark 15:30 Save *t*, and come down from the cross

Luke 5:14 but go, and show **t** to the priest
Luke 10:27 all thy mind; and thy neighbour as **t**
Luke 23:39 If thou be Christ, save **t** and us
2 Timothy 2:15 Study to show **t** approved unto God

■ Tiberias (tigh BIHR ih uhs)

A city located on the west side of the Sea of Galilee (see map on page 340). Also, another name for the Sea of Galilee.

John 6:1 sea of Galilee, which is the sea of **T**
John 6:23 some boats from **T** landed near the place (NIV)
John 21:1 again to the disciples at the sea of **T**

■ Tiberius (tigh BIHR ih uhs)

The Roman emperor from the time Jesus was a young adult until after His resurrection.

Luke 3:1 in the fifteenth year of the reign of **T**

■ Tidings (TIGH deengs)

News.

Luke 2:10 I bring you good **t** of great joy

■ Tied (TIGHD)

Past tense of "tie." To use rope or cord in such a way as to keep an animal from wandering away.

Matthew 21:2 ye shall find and ass **t**, and a colt
Mark 11:2 shall find a colt **t**, whereon never man sat
Mark 11:4 and found the colt **t** by the door
Luke 19:30 at your entering ye shall find a colt **t**

■ Time (TIGHM)

A period, hour, day, season; moment.

Exodus 9:18 tomorrow about this **t** I will cause
Ruth 4:7 Now this was the manner in former **t**
1 Kings 18:34 Do it the second **t**
1 Kings 18:34 Do it the third **t**
1 Kings 18:44 it came to pass at the seventh **t**
Ecclesiastes 3:1 and a **t** to every purpose under the
Matthew 2:7 them diligently what **t** the star appeared
Matthew 4:17 From that **t** Jesus began to preach
Matthew 26:16 that **t** he sought opportunity to betray
Matthew 26:42 He went away again the second **t**
Matthew 26:44 prayed the third **t**, saying the same
Mark 14:41 he cometh the third **t**, and saith unto them
Mark 14:72 And the second **t** the cock crew
Luke 21:37 in the day **t** he was teaching in the temple
Luke 23:22 And he said unto them the third **t**

■ Times (TIGHMZ)

Plural for "time."

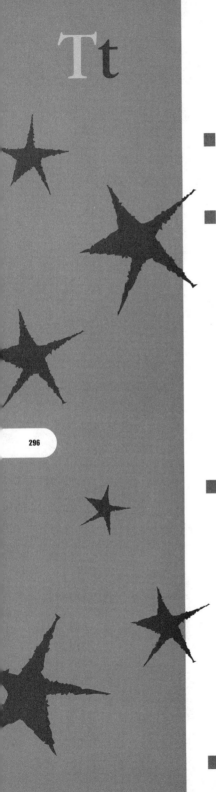

Genesis 27:36 He has deceived me these two *t* (NIV)
Psalm 34:1 I will bless the LORD at all *t*
Proverbs 17:17 A friend loveth at all *t*
Matthew 18:21 and I forgive him? Till seven *t*
Matthew 18:22 not seven *t*, but seventy-seven *t* (NIV)

■ **Timotheus (tih MOH thih uhs)**
Another way to write "Timothy." It means the same as "Timothy."

Acts 16:1 a certain disciple was there, named *T*

■ **Timothy (TIM uh thih)**
The name means "honoring God." Timothy is also written as "Timotheus." His home was in Lystra. His mother, Eunice, was Jewish and his father was a Greek. His grandmother, Lois, may have lived in his home. They are given credit for Timothy knowing about God. He probably met Paul on Paul's first missionary journey. Later, Timothy went with Paul and was a great help to him. He became a pastor and pastored churches while Paul was away. Paul often referred to Timothy as "my own son in the faith." Paul wrote two letters to Timothy, and they are included in the Bible

2 Corinthians 1:1 and *T* our brother, unto the church
1 Timothy 1:2 Unto *T*, my own son in the faith
2 Timothy 1:2 To *T*, my dearly beloved son

■ **Timothy, 1, 2, Books of (TIM uh thih)**
The tenth and eleventh books in the division, Paul's Letters, in the New Testament. The letters were written by Paul to his dear young friend, Timothy, who was pastor at the church in Ephesus. First Timothy was written shortly after Paul was released from the Roman prison. He was instructing Timothy on how pastors and church leaders are to behave. He gave advice on how to teach so the believers would not be turned away by false teaching.
Second Timothy was the last letter written by Paul while he was once again in a Roman prison. He was to go on trial because of his faith. He sent encouragement and advice on how to serve Christ. Paul asked Timothy to visit him before winter. Paul knew he would die very soon, and he was ready to meet Jesus.

■ **Tishbite (TISH bight)**
One who lived in Tishbe, a small village whose

actual location is unknown. Elijah was from that village.

1 Kings 17:1 And Elijah the *T*, who was of the
1 Kings 21:17 word of the LORD came to Elijah the *T*

Tithe (TIGHTH)

One tenth of a person's money or possessions. When a person gives one tenth of his money or possessions to God, he is giving a tithe. To tithe is one way a person can obey God, and it is also a part of his worship of God.

Leviticus 27:30 And all the *t* of the land
Leviticus 27:32 And concerning the *t* of the herd
Deuteronomy 14:22 Thou shalt truly *t* all the increase

Tithes (TIGHTHZ)

Plural of "tithe."

Genesis 14:20 and he gave him *t* of all
Malachi 3:8 Wherein have we robbed thee? In *t* and
Malachi 3:10 Bring ye all the *t* into the storehouse
Luke 18:12 I give *t* of all that I possess

Tittle (TIT uhl)

A small dot or accent mark placed over a word so as to set apart one word from another.

Matthew 5:18 one jot or one *t* shall in no wise pass
Luke 16:17 to pass, than one *t* of the law to fail

Titus (TIGH tuhs)

The twelfth book in the division, Paul's Letters, in the New Testament. Titus was a Gentile Christian who worked with Paul. Titus remained in Crete after he and Paul had visited there. Paul asked him to help with the church in Crete. Paul went on to Greece. The letter was written to encourage Titus to remain true to his teachings about Christ as he worked in the church at Crete. He also warned Titus about those who said they were believers but who had not accepted Christ as their Savior.

Together (too GETH uhr)

As one; side by side; as a group; at the same time.

Exodus 19:8 And all the people answered *t*
Psalm 34:3 and let us exalt his name *t*
Matthew 18:20 where two or three are gathered *t*
Matthew 27:62 priests and Pharisees came *t* unto Pilate
Mark 6:30 apostles gathered themselves *t* unto Jesus

297

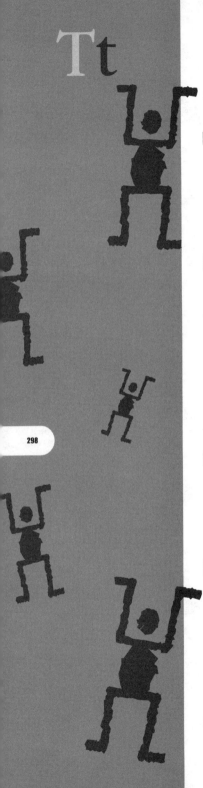

Luke 15:6 he calleth *t* his friends and neighbors
Luke 15:13 the younger son got *t* all he had (NIV)
Luke 24:15 while they communed *t* and reasoned
John 20:4 they ran both *t*: and the other disciple
John 20:7 but wrapped *t* in a place by itself
John 21:2 There *t* Simon Peter, and Thomas

■ Token (TOW kun)
A sign or a signal.

Genesis 9:12 God said, This is the *t* of the covenant
Genesis 9:13 shall be for a *t* of a covenant between
Genesis 9:17 unto Noah, This is the *t* of the covenant
Exodus 3:12 and this shall be a *t* unto thee, that I
Mark 14:44 he that betrayed him had given them a *t*

■ Tomb (TOOM)
A grave; a place to bury someone when they died. In later biblical times, tombs were often carved out of a large rock and included a ledge on which to place a body. The tomb would be sealed by rolling a heavy stone in a groove to seal the door of the tomb. The tomb in which Jesus' body was laid had been carved out of a rock in a garden not far from the site of the crucifixion.

Matthew 27:60 And laid it in his own new *t*
Mark 6:29 took up his corpse, and laid it in a *t*

■ Tombs (TOOMZ)
Plural of "tomb."

Matthew 8:28 possessed with devils, coming out of the *t*
Mark 5:2 there met him out of the *t* a man with an
Mark 5:3 Who had his dwelling among the *t*
Mark 5:5 he was in the mountains, and in the *t*

■ Tongue (TUNG)
The organ of the mouth that helps a person taste and swallow food. It also helps a person pronounce words.

Exodus 4:10 I am slow of speech, and of a slow *t*
Proverbs 15:2 The *t* of the wise useth knowledge
Mark 7:33 and he spit, and touched his *t*
Mark 7:35 and the string of his *t* was loosed
James 3:8 But the *t* can no man tame

■ Tongues (TUNGZ)
Plural of "tongue." Also, often means languages.

Acts 2:3 They saw what seemed to be *t* of fire (NIV)
Acts 2:4 and began to speak with other *t*

Torment (TAWR mint)
Misery; suffering. To cause one to have pain, either of body or mind.

Matthew 8:29 art thou come hither to *t* us
Mark 5:7 I adjure thee by God, that thou *t* me not
Luke 8:28 I beseech thee, *t* me not

Tormented (TAWR min tid)
Past tense of "torment."

Matthew 8:6 at home sick of the palsy, grievously *t*

Touch (TUCH)
To feel, handle, to hold.

Matthew 9:21 If I may but *t* his garment
Matthew 14:36 might only *t* the hem of his garment
Mark 3:10 they pressed upon him for to *t* him
Mark 5:28 If I may but *t* his clothes, I shall be
Mark 6:56 they might *t* if it were but the border
Luke 6:19 the whole multitude sought to *t* him
Luke 18:15 bringing babies to Jesus to have him *t* (NIV)
John 20:17 Jesus saith unto her, *T* me not

Touched (TUCHD)
Past tense of "touch."

Matthew 8:3 Jesus put forth his hand, and *t* him
Matthew 8:15 he *t* her hand, and the fever left
Matthew 9:20 and *t* the hem of his garment
Matthew 14:36 as many as *t* him were made whole
Mark 5:27 came in the press behind, and *t* his garment
Mark 5:30 and said, Who *t* my clothes
Mark 6:56 as many as *t* him were made whole
Luke 8:44 came behind him, and *t* the border of his
Luke 8:45 and Jesus said, Who *t* me
Luke 8:46 Jesus said, Somebody hath *t* me
Luke 22:51 And he *t* his ear, and healed him

Toward (too WAHRD)
To, "in the direction of."

Genesis 18:2 and bowed himself *t* the ground
Exodus 9:22 Stretch forth thine hand *t* heaven
1 Kings 18:43 Go up now, look *t* the sea
Esther 8:4 king held out the golden scepter *t* Esther
Matthew 14:14 and was moved with compassion *t* them
Mark 6:34 was moved with compassion *t* them, because
Luke 2:14 on earth peace, good will *t* men
Luke 24:29 Abide with us: for it is *t* evening
John 6:17 and went over the sea *t* Capernaum

Tt

Towel (TAUW uhl)
Cloth used to dry the body or wipe dishes.

John 13:4 and wrapped a **t** around his waist (NIV)
John 13:5 drying them with the **t** that was wrapped (NIV)

Transgressors (trans GREHS uhrz)
Plural of "transgressor." Those who disobey God; and who purposely do the wrong things when the right thing is known.

Psalm 51:13 Then will I teach **t** thy ways
Mark 15:28 And he was numbered with the **t**
Luke 22:37 And was numbered with the **t** (NIV)

Treasure (TREH zhuhr)
Something that has value or is very dear.

Matthew 6:21 For where your **t** is, there will your
Luke 12:34 For where your **t** is, there will your
Acts 8:27 who had the charge of all her **t**

Treasures (TREH zhuhrz)
Plural of "treasure."

Matthew 2:11 and when they had opened their **t**
Matthew 6:19 Lay not up for yourselves **t** upon earth
Matthew 6:20 But lay up for yourselves **t** in heaven

Tree (TREE)
A woody plant with a tall main trunk or stem whose branches begin a few feet from the ground. Most trees live for a long time. Some shed their leaves each fall and grow new ones in the spring. Others have green leaves or needles year round (called "evergreen" trees). Some trees produce fruit that can be eaten, like apples, oranges, while others produce nuts, or other edible foods.

Genesis 1:11 and the fruit **t** yielding fruit
Genesis 1:12 and the **t** yielding fruit, whose seed
Genesis 1:29 and every **t** that has fruit with seed (NIV)
Genesis 2:16 every **t** of the garden thou mayest
Genesis 2:17 But of the **t** of knowledge of good and
Genesis 3:6 woman saw that the **t** was good for food
Genesis 3:6 a **t** to be desired to make one wise
Exodus 15:25 and the LORD showed him a **t**
1 Kings 19:4 and came, and sat down under a juniper **t**
1 Kings 19:5 as he lay and slept under a juniper **t**
Luke 19:4 and climbed up into a sycamore **t** to see him
John 1:48 when thou was under the fig **t**, I saw thee
John 1:50 I saw thee under the fig **t**, believest thou

Trembled (TREHM buhld)
Past tense of "tremble." To shake, shiver; have great fear.

Exodus 19:16 the people that was in the camp *t*
Mark 16:8 for they *t*, and were amazed

Trembling (TREHM bleeng)
In the act of shaking or shivering.

Mark 5:33 But the woman fearing and *t*, knowing
Luke 8:47 she came *t*, and falling down before him
Acts 9:6 And he *t* and astonished said, Lord, what

Trench (TRENCH)
A channel or ditch.

1 Kings 18:32 and he made a *t* around the altar
1 Kings 18:35 and he filled the *t* also with water
1 Kings 18:38 licked up the water that was in the *t*

Trespasses (TRESS pass ihz)
Plural of "trespass." Sins; breaking God's laws; ignoring the rights of other humans.

Matthew 6:14 For if ye forgive men their *t*
Matthew 6:15 neither will your Father forgive your *t*
Mark 11:25 which is in heaven may forgive you your *t*
Mark 11:26 Father which is in heaven forgive your *t*

Tribute (TRIB yoot)
A tax that people were forced to pay to a government that had conquered them. Often the taxes required were too great for the defeated nations to pay.

Matthew 22:17 Is it lawful to give *t* unto Caesar
Matthew 22:19 Show me the *t* money. And they brought
Luke 20:22 Is it lawful for us to give *t* unto Caesar
Luke 23:2 and forbidding to give *t* to Caesar

Troas (TROH az)
A large seaport built on the Aegean Sea (see map on page 341). It was named after the ancient city of Troy. As a Roman colony, it was an important city for those traveling from Asia Minor to Macedonia. Paul visited this city on his second and third missionary journeys.

Acts 16:8 passing by Mysia came down to *T*
Acts 16:11 From *T* we put out to sea and sailed (NIV)

Trouble (TRUH buhl)
Bother, worry.

Psalm 46:1 and strength, a very present help in *t*

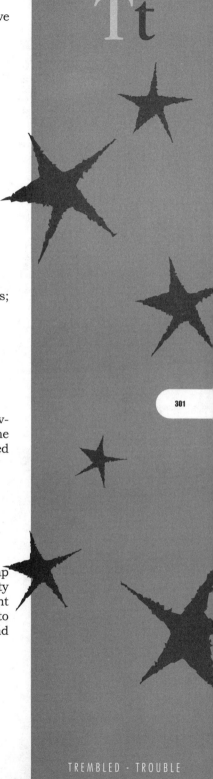

Tt

301

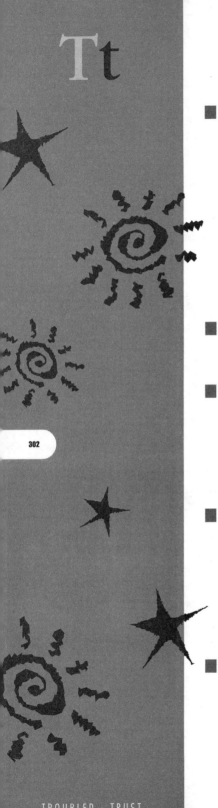

Matthew 26:10 he said unto them, Why *t* ye the woman
Mark 14:6 Jesus said, Let her alone; why *t* ye her
Luke 7:6 saying unto him, Lord, *t* not thyself
Luke 8:49 Thy daughter is dead; *t* not the Master

■ Troubled (TRUH buhld)
Past tense of "trouble."

Matthew 2:3 he was *t*, and all Jerusalem with him
Matthew 14:26 him walking on the sea, they were *t*
Mark 6:50 For they all say him, and were *t*
Luke 1:29 when she saw him, she was *t* at his saying
Luke 24:38 he said unto them, Why are ye *t*
John 5:4 certain season into the pool, and *t* the water
John 5:7 when the water is *t*, to put me into the pool
John 11:33 he groaned in the spirit, and was *t*
John 13:21 Jesus had thus said, he was *t* in spirit
John 14:1 Let not your heart be *t*: ye believe in
John 14:27 Let not your heart be *t*, neither let it

■ Troublest (TRUH buhl ist)
Old way of writing or saying "Do you trouble?"

Mark 5:35 Why *t* thou the Master any further

■ True (TROO)
Exact; faithful; honest; real; right.

Psalm 119:160 Thy word is *t* from the beginning
Matthew 22:16 Master, we know that thou art *t*
Mark 12:14 Master, we know that thou art *t*
John 19:35 saw it bare record, and his record is *t*
John 19:35 that he saith *t*, that ye might believe

■ Truly (TROO lee)
Truthfully, honestly, actually.

Matthew 9:37 The harvest *t* is plenteous, but the
Matthew 27:54 *T* this was the Son of God
Mark 14:38 The spirit *t* is ready, but the flesh is
Mark 15:39 *T* this man was the Son of God
Luke 10:2 The harvest *t* is great, but the
Luke 20:21 but teachest the way of God *t*
John 4:18 not thy husband: in that saidst thou *t*

■ Trust (TRUHST)
Belief, faith, hope; depend on.

Psalm 20:7 Some *t* in chariots, and some in horses
Psalm 37:3 *T* in the LORD, and do good
Psalm 56:3 What time I am afraid, I will *t* in thee
Proverbs 3:5 *T* in the LORD with all thine heart
Mark 10:24 how hard it is for them that *t* in riches

Trusted (TRUHS tid)
Past tense of "trust."

Matthew 27:43 He *t* in God; let him deliver him
Luke 24:21 But we *t* that it had been he which

Truth (TROOTH)
Fact, honesty, actual.

1 Kings 17:24 the word of the LORD in thy mouth is *t*
Psalm 25:5 Lead me in thy *t*, and teach me
Psalm 145:18 to all that call upon him in *t*
Matthew 14:33 Of a *t* thou art the Son of God
Matthew 22:16 and teaches the way of God in *t*
Mark 5:33 before him, and told him all the *t*
Mark 12:14 but teachest the way of God in *t*
Luke 21:3 And he said, Of a *t* I say unto you
Luke 22:59 Of a *t*, this fellow also was with him
John 4:24 must worship him in spirit and in *t*
John 14:6 I am the way, the *t*, and the life
Ephesians 4:25 speak every man *t* with his neighbor
2 Timothy 2:15 who correctly handles the word of *t* (NIV)

Turn (TEHRN)
Change position or direction.

Exodus 3:3 Moses said, I will now *t* aside, and see
Ruth 1:11 Naomi said, *T* again, my daughters: why
Jonah 3:9 Who can tell if God will *t* and repent
Jonah 3:9 and *t* away from his fierce anger
Matthew 5:39 right cheek, *t* to him the other also

Turtledoves (TUHR tuhl duhvz)
Plural of "turtledove." A dove or pigeon. Poor people used the dove for their sacrifices because the birds did not cost very much.

Luke 2:24 A pair of *t*, or two young pigeons

Turtles (TUHR tuhlz)
Another way of saying, "turtledoves."

Leviticus 12:8 bring two *t*, or two young pigeons

Twain (TWAYN)
Two; both.

Matthew 5:41 compel thee to go a mile, go with him *t*
Matthew 27:51 veil of the temple was rent in *t* from
Mark 15:38 veil of the temple was rent in *t* from the top

Twelve (TWELV)
The number following eleven.

Genesis 42:13 they said, Thy servants are *t* brethren
Matthew 9:20 diseased with an issue of blood *t* years

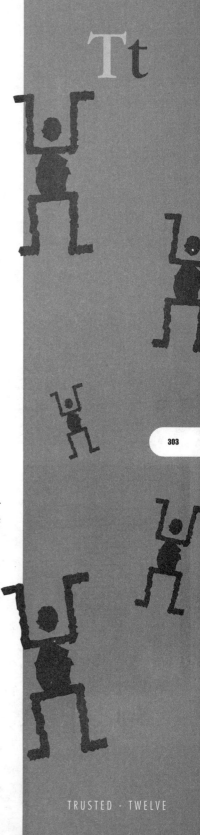

Tt

303

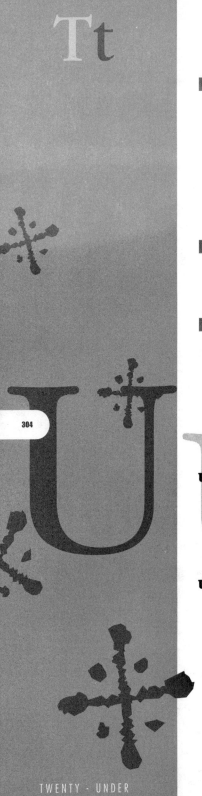

Tt

Matthew 10:2 Now the names of the **t** apostles are these
Matthew 26:14 Then one of the **t**, called Judas Iscariot
Matthew 26:20 even was come, he sat down with the **t**
Mark 3:14 he ordained **t**, that they should be with him
Mark 6:43 And they took up **t** baskets full of the
Mark 14:10 Judas Iscariot, one of the **t**, went unto
Mark 14:17 in the evening he cometh with the **t**
Mark 14:43 yet spake, cometh Judas, one of the **t**
Luke 2:42 and when he was **t** years old, they went
Luke 9:17 fragments that remained to them **t** baskets
Luke 22:47 he that was called Judas, one of the **t**
John 6:13 and filled **t** baskets with the fragments
John 6:71 that should betray him, being one of the **t**
John 20:24 But Thomas, one of the **t**, called Didymus

Twenty (TWEHN tee)
One number more than nineteen.

Genesis 37:28 to the Ishmaelites for **t** pieces of silver
John 6:19 had rowed about five and **t** or thirty furlongs

Twice (TWIGHS)
"Two times."

Mark 14:30 before the cock crow **t**, thou shalt deny
Mark 14:72 Before the cock crow **t**, thou shalt deny

Unbelief (UHN bee leef)
No faith or trust; doubt; does not believe. In the Bible, unbelief often refers to those who are not Christians.

Matthew 17:20 Jesus said unto them, Because of your **u**
Mark 9:24 Lord, I believe; help thou mine **u**

Under (UHN duhr)
Below, beneath, not on top.

Genesis 1:7 divided the waters which were **u** the
Genesis 1:9 waters **u** the heavens be gathered together
Exodus 6:6 I will bring you out from **u** the burdens
Exodus 20:4 or that is in the water **u** the earth
1 Kings 18:23 lay it on the wood, and put no fire **u**
1 Kings 18:25 name of your gods, but put no fire **u**
1 Kings 19:4 came and sat down **u** a juniper tree
1 Kings 19:5 as he lay and slept **u** a juniper tree
Matthew 2:16 from two years old and **u**, according to
Matthew 5:15 light a candle, and put it **u** a bushel

Mark 4:21 Is a candle brought to be put ***u*** a bushel
Luke 8:16 with a vessel, or putteth it ***u*** a bed
John 1:48 when thou wast ***u*** the fig tree, I saw thee
John 1:50 I saw thee ***u*** the fig tree, believest thou

■ Understand (uhn duhr STAND)
To believe, figure out, know.

Mark 14:68 I know not, neither ***u*** I what thou sayest
Luke 24:45 that they might ***u*** the scriptures

■ Understanding (uhn duhr STAN deeng)
The ability to believe, figure out, or know.

Proverbs 3:5 and lean not unto thine own ***u***
Luke 2:47 heard him were astonished at his ***u***
Luke 24:45 Then opened he their ***u***, that they

■ Understood (uhn duhr STUHD)
Past tense of "understand."

Genesis 42:23 And they knew not that Joseph ***u*** them

■ Ungodly (uhn GAHD lee)
Evil, sinful, wrong, being disobedient to God.

Psalm 1:1 walketh not in the counsel of the ***u***
Romans 5:6 in due time Christ died for the ***u***

■ Unjust (uhn JUHST)
Not fair, right, or true; wrong.

Matthew 5:45 sendeth rain on the just and on the ***u***

305

■ Unknown (uhn NOWN)
Not known or understood; not identified.

Acts 17:23 altar with this inscription, TO THE ***U*** GOD

■ Unleavened (uhn LEV uhnd)
Bread or foods made without yeast. Yeast or other leavenings cause a reaction when mixed with fluids making the dough of the bread to rise. The Israelites were commanded by God not to use leavening in their bread as they were preparing to leave Egypt. During Passover celebrations, they were also instructed not to use the leavenings, so they would be reminded how God brought them and their ancestors out of Egyptian slavery.

Exodus 12:8 roast with fire, and ***u*** bread; and with
Exodus 12:15 Seven day shall ye eat ***u*** bread
Exodus 12:17 shall observe the feast of ***u*** bread
Matthew 26:17 first day of the feast of ***u*** bread
Mark 14:1 feast of the passover, and of ***u*** bread

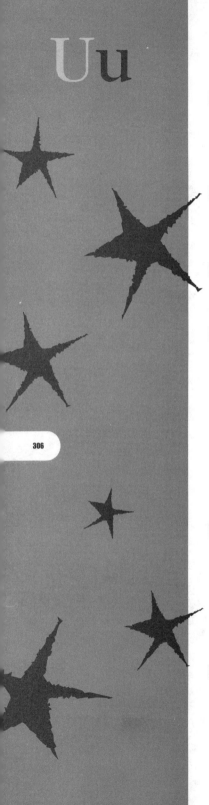

Uu

Mark 14:12 And the first day of **u** bread, when they
Luke 22:1 Now the feast of **u** bread drew nigh
Luke 22:7 Then came the day of **u** bread, when

■ Unloose (uhn LEWS)
To let go, untie.

Mark 1:7 shoes I am not worthy to stoop down and **u**
Luke 3:16 whose shoes I am not worthy to **u**
John 1:27 whose shoe's latchet I am not worthy to **u**

■ Unrighteous (uhn RIGH chus)
Doing that which is not right; not being acceptable to God.

Isaiah 55:7 his way, and the **u** man his thoughts

■ Uphold (uhp HOLD)
To hold up; to support; to stand by.

Psalm 51:12 **u** me with thy free spirit

■ Upper (UHP uhr)
Over, above. The upper room referred to in
Mark, Luke, and Acts, was a large room, probably on the second floor of the house. It was here
that the Passover was kept by Jesus and His
disciples just before His arrest, trial, and crucifixion. It may have been in the home of Mary,
John Mark's mother.

Exodus 12:7 and on the **u** door post of the houses
Mark 14:15 a large **u** room furnished and prepared
Luke 22:12 show you a large **u** room furnished
Acts 1:13 they went up into an **u** room

■ Upright (UHP right)
1. To stand up straight.

Genesis 37:7 my sheaf arose, and also stood **u**
Exodus 15:8 the floods stood **u** as in a heap
Acts 14:10 with a loud voice, Stand **u** on thy feet

2. Fair, honest, moral in all one says or does.

Proverbs 15:8 but the prayer of the **u** is his delight

■ Ur (UHR)
The name means "fire oven." An ancient city of
Babylonia which was located several miles south
and east of the city of Babylon (see map on page
336). Abraham and his father, Terah, began
their journey from Ur to the land God would
show them. The city was built beside the
Euphrates River and was prosperous because of
the harbor.

Genesis 11:31 they went forth with them from **U**
Genesis 15:7 LORD that brought thee out of **U** of the

Use (YEWZ)
1. "Make use of;" treat with kindness.

1 Peter 4:9 **U** hospitality one to another

2. To abuse, misuse, or take advantage of.

Matthew 5:44 pray for them which despitefully **u** you
Luke 6:28 pray for them which despitefully **u** you

Utter (UHT uhr)
To voice; say with words; speak.

Proverbs 14:5 but a false witness will **u** lies

Uttermost (UHT uhr mowst)
Farthest out; as far as one can go.

Acts 1:8 and unto the **u** most part of the earth

Vain (VAYN)
Empty, meaningless, useless; of no worth.

Exodus 20:7 take the name of the LORD thy God in **v**
Exodus 20:7 him guiltless that taketh his name in **v**
Deuteronomy 5:11 the name of the LORD thy God in **v**
Deuteronomy 5:11 guiltless that taketh his name in **v**

Valley (VAL ee)
A hollow or low space between hills or mountains.
Some valleys are narrow, and others are wide.

Genesis 26:17 pitched his tent in the **v** of Gerar
Genesis 26:19 And Isaac's servants digged in the **v**
Psalm 23:4 walk through the **v** of the shadow of death

Value (VAL yoo)
The price, or worth, of something.

Matthew 10:31 ye are of more **v** than many sparrows
Luke 12:7 ye are of more **v** than many sparrows

Vehement (VEE he mint)
Strong, hot (with great emotion); violent, or great
force.

Jonah 4:8 God prepared a **v** east wind

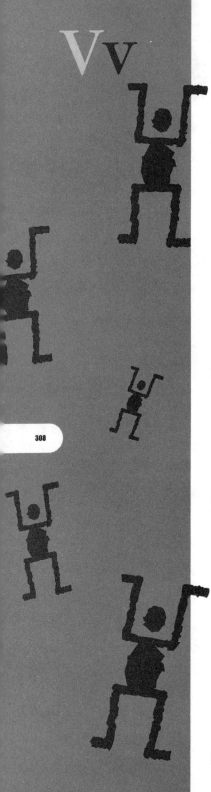

Vehemently (VEE heh mint lee)
See "Vehement."

Mark 14:31 But he spake the more *v*, If I should
Luke 6:48 the stream beat *v* upon that house
Luke 6:49 against which the stream did beat *v*
Luke 23:10 and scribes stood and *v* accused him

Veil (VAYL)
A covering or curtain made from cloth, much like a screen. A special cloth that separated the holy place in the Temple from the holy of holies, the most inner part. The only person who could go behind the veil was the high priest and only on a special day, the Day of Atonement. As Jesus died on the cross, the veil was torn from the top to the bottom to show that God, not man, had torn it. This did away with the wall that had separated man from God.

Matthew 27:51 the *v* of the temple was rent in twain
Mark 15:38 the *v* of the temple was rent in twain
Luke 23:45 the *v* of the temple was rent in the midst

Venison (VIN ih suhn)
Deer meat or meat from other wild game.

Genesis 25:28 because he did eat of his *v*
Genesis 27:5 Esau went to the field to hunt for *v*
Genesis 27:19 I pray thee, sit and eat of my *v*
Genesis 27:25 and I will eat of my son's *v*
Genesis 27:31 my father arise, and eat of his son's *v*

Verily (VEIR ih lee)
Truly; certainly; for a fact.

Matthew 8:10 *V* I say unto you, I have not found
Matthew 17:20 for *v* I say unto you, If ye have faith
Matthew 19:23 *V* I say unto you, That a rich man
Matthew 25:45 *V* I say unto you, Inasmuch as ye did
Matthew 26:21 *V* I say unto you, that one of you
Mark 12:43 *V* I say unto you, That this poor widow
Mark 14:9 *V* I say unto you, Wheresoever this gospel
Mark 14:18 *V* I say unto you, One of you which eateth
Mark 14:30 *V* I say unto thee, That this day, even in
Luke 4:24 *V* I say unto you, No prophet is accepted
Luke 23:43 *V* I say unto thee, Today shalt thou be
John 3:3 *V*, *v*, I say unto thee, Except a man be born
John 13:21 *V*, *v*, I say unto you, that one of you shall
John 13:38 *V*, *v*, I say unto thee, The cock shall not

Very (VEIR ee)
Exact, great; extremely.

Matthew 17:18 the child was cured from that **v** hour
Matthew 21:8 a **v** great multitude spread their garments
Matthew 26:7 and alabaster box of **v** precious ointment
Matthew 26:37 and began to be sorrowful and **v** heavy
Mark 14:3 box of ointment of spikenard **v** precious
Mark 14:33 to be sore amazed, and to be **v** heavy
Mark 16:2 **v** early in the morning, the first day
Luke 24:1 **v** early in the morning, they came unto the
John 12:3 pound of ointment of spikenard, **v** costly

Vessel (VEHS uhl)
Cup, bowl, or other container.

2 Kings 4:6 said unto her son, Bring me yet a **v**
2 Kings 4:6 he said unto her, There is not a **v** more
John 19:29 there was set a **v** full of vinegar
Acts 11:5 certain **v** descend, as it had been a great

Vessels (VEHS uhlz)
Plural of "vessel."

2 Kings 4:3 Go, borrow thee **v** abroad of all thy
2 Kings 4:3 all thy neighbors, even empty **v**
2 Kings 4:4 shalt pour out into all those **v**
2 Kings 4:6 **v** were full, that she said unto her son

Victuals (VIT uhls)
Plural of "victual." This is food or a supply of food.

Matthew 14:15 into the villages, and buy themselves **v**
Luke 9:12 country round about, and lodge, and get **v**

Village (VILL idj)
A small town or community. In biblical times, villages had no walls like the larger cities.

Matthew 21:2 Go into the **v** over against you, and
Mark 11:2 Go your way into the **v** over against you
Luke 17:12 And as he entered into a certain **v**
Luke 19:30 Go ye into the **v** over against you
Luke 24:28 And they drew nigh unto the **v**

Villages (VILL ih juhs)
Plural of "village."

Matthew 9:35 Jesus went about all the cities and **v**
Matthew 14:15 that they may go into the **v**, and buy
Mark 6:6 he went round about the **v**, teaching
Mark 6:36 into the **v**, and buy themselves some bread
Mark 6:56 he entered, into **v**, or cities, or country
Luke 13:22 he went through the cities and **v**

Vine (VIGHN)
A plant that creeps and clings to a surface as it

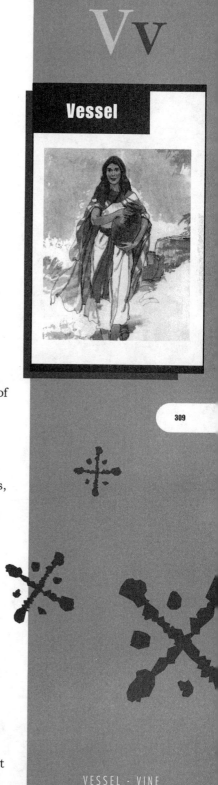

Vessel

Vv

grows. In the Bible, a vine almost always means a grapevine.

Matthew 26:29 not drink of this fruit of the **v** (NIV)
Mark 14:25 will drink no more of the fruit of the **v**
Luke 22:18 not drink of the fruit of the **v**

▪ Vinegar (VIN ih guhr)
Means "that which is soured." Vinegar could be made from fruits or grains. Usually it was made from grape wine that had spoiled. Some uses for vinegar included dipping bread in it for a tasty bite; adding drugs to it to give to criminals hanging on crosses so their pain would be eased; using vinegar to season food. Jesus was offered a vinegar mixture while he was on the cross but he refused it. Later he was offered vinegar which he drank just before He died.

Matthew 27:34 gave him **v** to drink mingled with gall
Matthew 27:48 took a sponge, and filled it with **v**
Mark 15:36 one ran and filled a sponge full of **v**
Luke 23:36 coming to him, and offering him **v**
John 19:29 there was set a vessel full of **v**
John 19:29 they filled a sponge with **v**, and
John 19:30 When Jesus therefore had received the **v**

▪ Vineyard (VIN yerd)
A field enclosed by a wall where grapevines were grown. The grapes were used to make wine, dried for raisins, or eaten from the vines. A man owning a vineyard often did not have to perform military duties. Most vineyards were passed down in a family rather than selling them. A man was to leave some grapes on the vines for widows and the poor to glean for their needs.

Leviticus 19:10 Thou shalt not glean thy **v**
1 Kings 21:1 Naboth the Jezreelite had a **v**
1 Kings 21:2 Ahab said to Naboth, Give me thy **v**
1 Kings 21:15 Ahab, Arise, take possession of the **v**
1 Kings 21:18 behold, he is in the **v** of Naboth

▪ Virgin (VUHR jihn)
A girl or woman "who has never had sexual relations."

Isaiah 7:14 a **v** shall conceive, and bear a son
Matthew 1:23 Behold, a **v** shall be with child
Luke 1:27 **v** espoused to a man whose name was Joseph

▪ Virtue (VUHR chew)
Character, goodness, morality, purity. In the Bible, it means power when referring to Jesus.

310

Mark 5:30 knowing in himself that **v** had gone out
Luke 6:19 went **v** out of him, and healed them all
Luke 8:46 I perceive that **v** is gone out of me

▌ Vision (VIH zhuhn)

Dream; image. When spoken of in the Bible, the way God used to give a special message to a person.

Genesis 15:1 word of the LORD came to Abram in a **v**
1 Samuel 3:15 And Samuel feared to show Eli the **v**
Daniel 2:19 secret revealed unto Daniel in a night **v**
Luke 1:22 that he had seen a **v** in the temple
Luke 24:23 that they had also seen a **v** of angels
Acts 9:10 to him said the Lord in a **v**, Ananias
Acts 10:3 About three in the afternoon he had a **v** (NIV)

▌ Visited (VIZ ih tihd)

Past tense of "visit." Went to see someone either as a friend, or to help.

Matthew 25:36 I was sick, and ye **v** me
Matthew 25:43 in prison, and ye **v** me not

▌ Voice (VOYS)

The sound one makes when speaking or singing.

Genesis 3:8 they heard the **v** of the LORD God
Genesis 3:10 heard thy **v** in the garden, and I was
Genesis 27:13 only obey my **v**, and go fetch me them
Genesis 27:38 And Esau lifted up his **v**, and wept
1 Kings 17:22 And the LORD heard the **v** of Elijah
1 Kings 18:26 O Baal, hear us. But there was no **v**
1 Kings 19:12 and after a fire a still small **v**
Matthew 3:3 The **v** of one crying in the wilderness
Matthew 3:17 lo a **v** from heaven, saying, This is my
Matthew 27:46 ninth hour Jesus cried with a loud **v**
Matthew 27:50 when he had cried again with a loud **v**
Mark 1:3 The **v** of one crying in the wilderness
Mark 1:11 there came a **v** from heaven, saying, Thou
Mark 15:34 ninth hour Jesus cried with a loud **v**
Mark 15:37 And Jesus cried with a loud **v**
Luke 3:4 The **v** of one crying in the wilderness
Luke 3:22 and a **v** came from heaven, which said
Luke 23:46 when Jesus had cried with a loud **v**
John 1:23 am the **v** of one crying in the wilderness
Acts 9:4 heard a **v** saying unto him, Saul, Saul
Revelation 3:20 if any man hear my **v**, and open the

▌ Vow (VOW)

A serious promise or commitment usually made to God. In the Bible, a vow often had certain

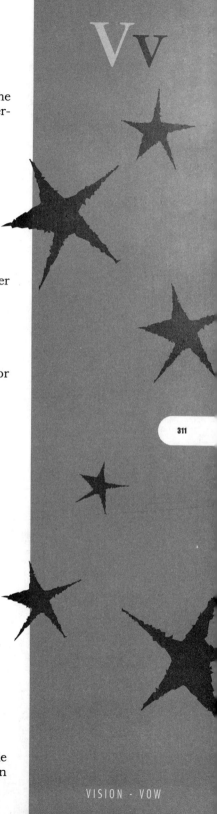

conditions. "If..." (a specific thing is said) "then..." (a certain thing would happen). Read 2 Chronicles 7:14 to find one of the many examples.

Genesis 28:20 And Jacob vowed a **v**, saying, If God

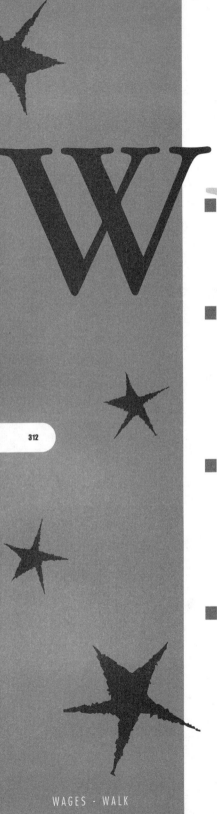

Wages (WAY jihs)
Money or goods one receives for the work he has done. Also, reward. In the Bible, wages can be the punishment one receives for the sins he has done.

Genesis 29:15 tell me, what shall thy **w** be
Romans 6:23 **w** of sin is death; but the gift of God

Wait (WAYT)
Pause, remain, stay; expect. In the Bible, we are encouraged to wait expectantly for God to act. He will bring us whatever we need when we are patient.

Psalm 27:14 **W** on the LORD: be of good courage
Psalm 27:14 **w**, I say, on the LORD
Isaiah 40:31 they that **w** upon the LORD shall renew
Mark 3:9 ship should **w** on him because of the multitude

Waited (WAY tid)
Past tense of "wait." Can also mean to serve food or help one another in some way.

2 Kings 5:2 little maid; and she **w** on Naaman's wife
Psalm 40:1 I **w** patiently for the LORD
Luke 1:21 the people **w** for Zacharias, and marveled
Luke 23:51 who also himself **w** for the kingdom of God
Acts 10:24 And Cornelius **w** for them, and had called

Walk (WAWK)
To move at a pace slower than running. In the Bible, it refers to the way a person lives or how he acts.

Psalm 23:4 Yea, though I **w** through the valley of the
Matthew 9:5 or to say, Arise, and **w**
Mark 2:9 or to say, Arise, take up thy bed, and **w**
Luke 5:23 or to say, Rise up and **w**
Luke 24:17 have one to another, as ye **w**, and are sad
John 5:8 Rise, take up thy bed, and **w**
Acts 3:6 of Jesus Christ of Nazareth rise up and **w**

Walked (WAWKD)
Past tense of "walk."

Matthew 14:29 he **w** on the water, to go to Jesus
Mark 1:16 Now as he **w** by the sea of Galilee
Mark 5:42 And straightway the damsel arose, and **w**
Mark 16:12 as they **w**, and went into the country
John 5:9 made whole, and took up his bed, and **w**
Acts 3:8 And he leaping up stood, and **w**, and

Walketh (WAW kith)
Old way of writing or saying "walks."

Psalm 1:1 Blessed is the man that **w** not in the

Walking (WAW keeng)
The act of moving at a slower pace than a run.

Genesis 3:8 LORD God **w** in the garden in the cool of
Matthew 4:18 Jesus, **w** by the sea of Galilee, saw
Matthew 14:25 Jesus went unto them, **w** on the sea
Matthew 14:26 the disciples saw him **w** on the sea
Mark 6:48 he cometh unto them, **w** upon the sea
Mark 6:49 But when they saw him **w** upon the sea
John 6:19 they see Jesus **w** on the sea, and

Wall (WAWL)
The part of a building that stands upright from the ground. In the Bible, a wall often surrounded a city or house for protection. Bricks made from clay mixed with reed or straw were hardened in the sun and stacked one atop the other until the wall was the right height.

Exodus 14:22 and the waters were a **w** unto them
Exodus 14:29 and the waters were a **w** unto them
Joshua 6:5 and the **w** of the city shall fall down
Joshua 6:20 great shout, that the **w** fell down flat
Acts 9:25 and let him down by the **w** in a basket

Want (WAHNT)
Hunger; need, require; lack.

Psalm 23:1 The LORD is my shepherd; I shall not **w**
Mark 12:44 she of her **w** did cast in all that she had
Luke 15:14 in that land; and he began to be in **w**

Warmed (WAHRMD)
Past tense of "warm." To heat or give off heat; to feel heat from a fire; to be wearing enough clothing.

Mark 14:54 sat with the servants, and **w** himself at
John 18:18 Peter stood with them, and **w** himself
John 18:25 And Simon Peter stood and **w** himself

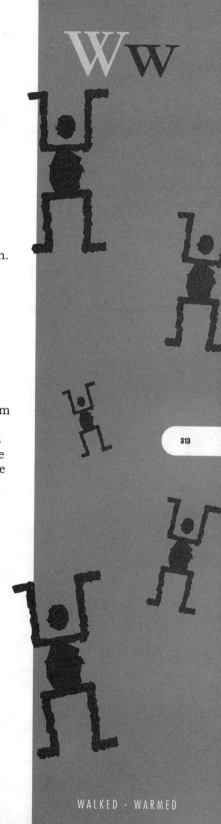

313

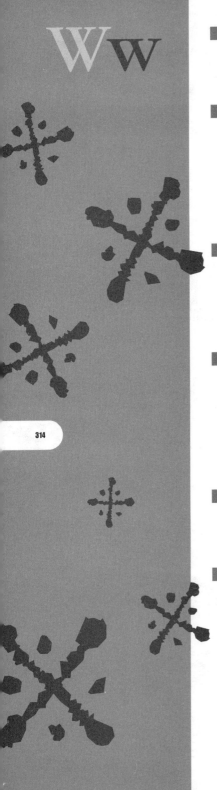

Ww

Warned (WAHRND)
Past tense of "warn." To advise, alert, or notify.

Matthew 2:12 being **w** of God in a dream that they
Matthew 2:22 being **w** of God in a dream, he turned

Wash (WAHSH)
To take a bath, clean one's clothing, or use water to make something clean.

Genesis 18:4 **w** your feet, and rest yourselves
Exodus 2:5 daughter of Pharaoh came down to **w** herself
Luke 7:38 and began to **w** his feet with tears
John 9:11 Go to the pool of Siloam, and **w**: and I
John 13:5 and began to **w** the disciples' feet

Washed (WAHSHT)
Past tense of "wash."

Matthew 27:24 and **w** his hands before the multitude
Luke 7:44 but she hath **w** my feet with tears
John 9:15 He put clay upon mine eyes, and I **w**
John 13:12 So after he had **w** their feet, and

Waste (WAYST)
To spend or use something in a careless way; to ruin or bring to ruin. In the Bible, waste can mean a place of drought, a place that is deserted or lonely, or empty of signs of life.

1 Kings 17:14 The barrel of meal shall not **w**
Matthew 26:8 saying, To what purpose is this **w**
Mark 14:4 Why was this **w** of the ointment made

Wasted (WAY stihd)
Past tense of "waste."

1 Kings 17:16 And the barrel of meal **w** not
Luke 15:13 and there **w** his substance with riotous

Watch (WACH)
To guard; stay awake; be on the lookout. In the Bible, a watch was also a designated time period when a person stayed awake to guard something. The Romans had divided the night into four watches: (1) 6:00P.M.–9:00P.M.; (2) 9:00P.M.–Midnight; (3) Midnight–3:00A.M.; (4) 3:00A.M.–6:00A.M. The Jews had only three watches during the night: (1) Sunset–10:00P.M.; (2) 10:00P.M.–2:00A.M.; (3) 2:00A.M.–Sunrise.

Matthew 14:25 in the fourth **w** of the night Jesus
Matthew 26:38 tarry ye here, and **w** with me
Matthew 26:40 could ye not **w** with me one hour
Matthew 26:41 **W** and pray, that ye enter not into

314

Matthew 27:65 Pilate said unto them, Ye have a **w**. go
Mark 6:48 about the fourth **w** of the night he cometh
Mark 14:34 sorrowful unto death: tarry ye here, and **w**
Mark 14:37 couldest not thou **w** one hour
Mark 14:38 **W** ye and pray, lest ye enter into
Luke 2:8 Keeping **w** over their flock by night

■ Watched (WACHT)
Past tense of "watch."

Matthew 27:36 And sitting down they **w** him there
Mark 3:2 And they **w** him, whether he would heal
Luke 6:7 And the scribes and Pharisees **w** him
Luke 20:20 they **w** him, and sent forth spies

■ Water (WAH tuhr)
Liquid that falls as rain, forming streams, rivers, lakes, oceans. Without water, plants would not grow, and animals and humans would die.

Genesis 2:10 river went out of Eden to **w** the garden
Exodus 2:10 Because I drew him out of the **w**
Exodus 15:27 to Elim, where were twelve wells of **w**
1 Kings 17:10 Fetch me, I pray thee, a little **w**
1 Kings 18:33 Fill four barrels with **w**, and pour
1 Kings 18:35 the **w** ran round about the altar
1 Kings 18:35 and he filled the trench also with **w**
1 Kings 18:38 licked up the **w** that was in the trench
1 Kings 19:6 and a cruse of **w** at his head
Matthew 3:16 went up straightway out of the **w**
Matthew 14:28 bid me come unto thee on the **w**
Matthew 14:29 he walked on the **w**, to go to Jesus
Mark 1:10 straightway coming up out of the **w**, he
Mark 14:13 meet you a man bearing a pitcher of **w**
Luke 8:24 rebuked the wind and the raging of the **w**
Luke 8:25 the winds and the **w**, and they obey him
Luke 22:10 man meet you, bearing a pitcher of **w**
John 2:7 unto them, fill the waterpots with **w**
John 3:5 a man be born of **w** and of the Spirit
John 4:7 cometh a woman of Samaria to draw **w**
John 5:3 waiting for the moving of the **w**
John 5:4 season into the pool, and troubled the **w**
John 5:7 I have no man, when the **w** is troubled, to
John 19:34 bringing a sudden flow of blood and **w** (NIV)

■ Waters (WAH tuhrz)
Plural of "water."

Genesis 1:2 of God moved upon the face of the **w**
Genesis 1:9 Let the **w** under the heaven be gathered
Genesis 1:10 together of the **w** called he Seas

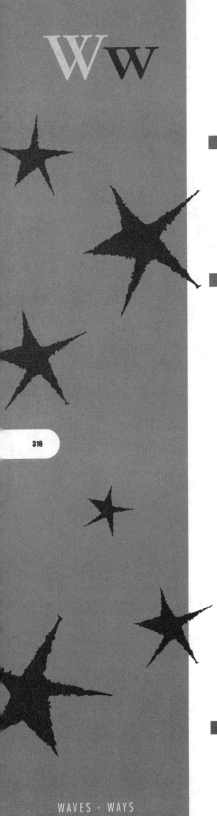

Ww

Genesis 7:18 And the **w** prevailed, and were increased
Genesis 7:18 the ark went upon the face of the **w**
Genesis 8:11 Noah knew that the **w** were abated
Exodus 14:21 the sea dry land, and the **w** were divided
Exodus 14:22 **w** were a wall unto them on their right
Psalm 23:2 he leadeth me beside the still **w**

Waves (WAYVZ)
Plural of "wave." A ripple. The motion or movement upon water by the wind that creates a ridge. The stronger the wind, the larger the waves.

Matthew 8:24 that the ship was covered with the **w**
Matthew 14:24 midst of the sea, tossed with **w**
Mark 4:37 and the **w** beat into the ship, so that

Way (WAY)
Direction, course; path, road, or route.

Ruth 1:12 Turn again, my daughters, go your **w**
Psalm 18:30 As for God, his **w** is perfect
Psalm 37:5 Commit thy **w** unto the LORD
Proverbs 14:12 There is a **w** which seemeth right
Matthew 2:12 departed into their own country another **w**
Matthew 3:3 Prepare ye the **w** of the Lord
Matthew 7:13 wide is the gate, and broad is the **w**
Matthew 7:14 strait is the gate, and narrow is the **w**
Matthew 8:4 go thy **w**, show thyself to the priest
Matthew 20:30 two blind men sitting by the **w** side
Matthew 21:8 multitude spread their garments in the **w**
Matthew 21:8 from the trees and strewed them in the **w**
Mark 1:3 Prepare ye the **w** of the Lord
Mark 1:44 but go thy **w**, show thyself to the priest
Mark 11:2 Go your **w** into the village over against
Mark 11:4 And they went their **w**, and found the colt
Mark 11:8 many spread their garments in the **w**
Mark 16:7 But go your **w**, tell his disciples and
Luke 3:4 Prepare ye the **w** of the Lord
Luke 15:20 when he was yet a great **w** off
Luke 18:35 blind man sat by the **w** side begging
Luke 19:4 to see him: for he was to pass that **w**
Luke 19:36 they spread their clothes in the **w**
Luke 24:32 while he talked with us by the **w**
John 1:23 Make straight the **w** of the Lord
John 14:6 Jesus saith unto him, I am the **w**

Ways (WAYZ)
Plural of "way."

Psalm 51:13 will I teach transgressors thy **w**
Matthew 8:33 went their **w** into the city, and told

Luke 1:76 the face of the Lord to prepare his **w**
John 11:46 some of them went their **w** to the Pharisees

■ Weak (WEEK)
Helpless, powerless, not enough strength.

Matthew 26:41 indeed is willing, but the flesh is **w**
Mark 14:38 spirit truly is ready, but the flesh is **w**

■ Weaned (WEEND)
Past tense of "wean." To cause a young child or animal to eat food other than the milk from its mother.

Genesis 21:8 And the child grew, and was **w**
Genesis 21:8 feast the same day that Isaac was **w**
1 Samuel 1:22 I will not go up until the child is **w**
1 Samuel 1:24 And when she had **w** him, she took him

■ Weary (WEER ee)
Bored, sick, tired, usually from one's work or other activities.

Galatians 6:9 And let us not be **w** in well doing

■ Week (WEEK)
Seven days in a row, from Sunday to Saturday. The five or six days children are in school or the time period a person works. The Jews considered that a week was seven days in a row that ended with a Sabbath.

Matthew 28:1 dawn toward the first day of the **w**
Mark 16:2 in the morning the first day of the **w**
Mark 16:9 was risen early the first day of the **w**
Luke 24:1 upon the first day of the **w**, very early
John 20:1 the first day of the **w** cometh Mary
John 20:19 evening, being the first day of the **w**

■ Weepest (WEE pist)
The old way of writing or saying "do you weep?" To weep is to cry or sob, shed tears.

1 Samuel 1:8 husband said to her, Hannah, why **w** thou
John 20:13 they say unto her, Woman, why **w** thou
John 20:15 Jesus saith unto her, Woman, why **w** thou

■ Weeping (WEE ping)
The act of crying.

Psalm 30:5 **w** may endure for a night, but joy cometh
Luke 7:38 stood at his feet behind him **w**
John 11:33 When Jesus therefore saw her **w**
John 20:11 Mary stood without at the sepulcher **w**

Ww

Well

Well (WEHL)

1. A hole dug into the earth to reach water, or to collect rain water as it falls. A spring. In Bible times, wells were very important because it hardly ever rained in Palestine. The water was used by people, and for their animals.

Exodus 2:15 of Midian: and he sat down by a **w**
John 4:6 Now Jacob's **w** was there. Jesus therefore
John 4:11 nothing to draw with, and the **w** is deep

2. Acceptable, favorable, satisfactory.

Exodus 4:14 I know that he can speak **w**
Matthew 3:17 my beloved son, in whom I am **w** pleased
Mark 1:11 beloved son, in whom I am **w** pleased
Luke 3:22 my beloved Son; in thee I am **w** pleased
Galatians 6:9 And let us not be weary in **w** doing

Wept (WEPT)
Past tense for "weep."

Genesis 27:38 And Esau lifted up his voice, and **w**
Genesis 45:2 And he **w** aloud: and the Egyptians
Genesis 45:14 his brother Benjamin's neck, and **w**
Genesis 45:14 and Benjamin **w** upon his neck
Exodus 2:6 and, behold, the child **w**
Ruth 1:9 and they lifted up their voice, and **w**
Matthew 26:75 And he went out, and **w** bitterly
Luke 22:62 And Peter went out, and **w** bitterly
John 11:35 Jesus **w**
John 20:11 and as she **w**, she stooped down

West (WEST)
The direction in which the sun sets. Opposite of East.

Psalm 103:12 As far as the east is from the **w**

Whales (HWAYLZ)
Plural of "whale." A large sea animal that is warm-blooded and feeds its young with its own milk. Whales must come to the surface of the sea every so often to breathe air. In the Bible, a whale could have meant an ancient sea monster or dragon. Jonah called it "a great fish."

Genesis 1:21 And God created great **w**

Whatsoever (hwaht sow EV uhr)
Whatever; anything; "no matter what."

Matthew 7:12 **w** ye would that men should do to you
Matthew 21:22 **w** ye shall ask in prayer, believing
Matthew 28:20 observe all things **w** I have commanded

Mark 10:21 sell **w** thou hast, and give to the poor
Galatians 6:7 **w** a man soweth, that shall he also reap

Where (HWAIR)
In what place or direction.

Exodus 5:11 Go ye, get you straw **w** ye can find it
Exodus 15:27 Elim, **w** were twelve wells of water
Matthew 6:19 treasures upon earth, **w** moth and
Matthew 6:19 and **w** thieves break through and steal
Matthew 6:20 in heaven, **w** neither moth nor rust
Matthew 6:20 **w** thieves do not break through nor
Matthew 6:21 For **w** your treasure is, there will
Matthew 28:6 Come, see the place **w** the Lord lay
Mark 2:4 they uncovered the roof **w** he was
Mark 14:12 **W** wilt thou that we go and prepare
Mark 16:6 behold the place **w** they laid him
John 12:1 came to Bethany, **w** Lazarus was
John 18:1 over the brook Cedron, **w** was a garden
John 19:18 **W** they crucified him, and two other
John 19:20 the place **w** Jesus was crucified was
John 20:13 I know not **w** they have laid him

While (HWIGHL)
As, at the same time; "a period of time."

Genesis 8:22 **W** the earth remaineth, seedtime and
1 Kings 17:7 after a **w**, that the brook dried up
1 Kings 18:45 in the mean **w**, that the heaven was black
Matthew 26:47 And **w** he yet spake, lo, Judas, one of
Mark 14:32 his disciples, sit ye here, **w** I shall pray
Mark 14:43 **w** he yet spake, cometh Judas, one of the
Luke 2:6 And so it was, that, **w** they were there
Luke 22:47 And **w** he yet spake, behold a multitude
Luke 22:58 after a little **w** another saw him, and
Luke 22:60 immediately, **w** he yet spake, the cock crew
Luke 24:15 **w** they communed together and reasoned

Whirlwind (HWURL wind)
A violent wind that moves in circles, like a spiral. They occur anytime cool winds meet hot winds. These types of storms often occur near the Mediterranean Sea. It was a wind like this that took Elijah to heaven.

2 Kings 2:1 take up Elijah into heaven by a **w**
2 Kings 2:11 Elijah went up by a **w** into heaven

White (HWIGHT)
An absence of color; opposite of black. The color of new snow.

Exodus 16:31 and it was like coriander seed, **w**

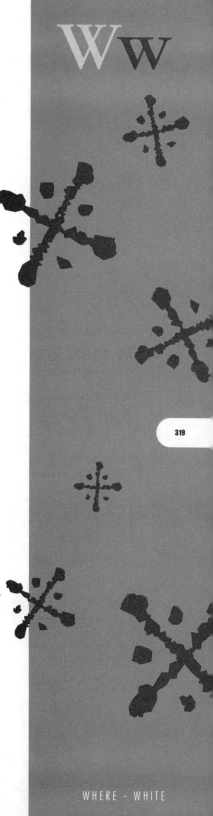

Ww

Isaiah 1:18 as scarlet, they shall be as **w** as snow
Matthew 28:3 and his raiment **w** as snow
Mark 16:5 clothed in a long **w** garment
John 20:12 And seeth two angels in **w** sitting

■ Whole (HOLE)
1. Perfect, strong, healthy.

Matthew 9:12 They that be **w** need not a physician
Matthew 9:21 touch his garment, I shall be **w**
Matthew 9:22 the woman was made **w** from that hour
Mark 2:17 that are **w** have no need of the physician
Mark 5:34 Daughter, thy faith hath made thee **w**
Mark 6:56 and as many as touched him were made **w**
Luke 5:31 They that are **w** need not a physician
Luke 8:48 thy faith hath made thee **w**

2. Entire, all, complete.

Matthew 8:32 the **w** herd of swine ran violently
Matthew 16:26 gain the **w** world, and lose his own soul
Mark 8:36 gain the **w** world, and lose his own soul
Mark 15:33 darkness over the **w** land until the ninth
Luke 9:25 if he gain the **w** world, and lose himself
Luke 23:1 And the **w** multitude of them arose, and led

■ Widow (WID ow)
A woman whose husband has died. Most widows were poor and helpless because they did not inherit any property that their husbands owned when death occurred. God gave Moses some laws to help protect the widows so they could eat. A woman did not work outside the home, so a widow could not get a job.

1 Kings 17:9 commanded a **w** woman there to sustain
1 Kings 17:10 the **w** woman was there gathering sticks
Mark 12:42 And there came a certain poor **w**, and she
Mark 12:43 This poor **w** hath cast more in, than all
Luke 21:2 he saw also a certain poor **w** casting in
Luke 21:3 this poor **w** hath cast in more than they all

■ Widows (WID owz)
Plural of "widow."

Acts 6:1 their **w** were neglected by the daily

■ Wild (WIGHLD)
Not grown by humans; growing without assistance.

Matthew 3:4 and his meat was locusts and **w** honey
Mark 1:6 and he did eat locusts and **w** honey
Mark 1:13 tempted of Satan; and was with the **w** beasts

Wilderness (WIL duhr ness)

A desert, wasteland; a rocky area where little grows; a wild region where few people live.

Genesis 37:22 cast him into this pit that is in the **w**
1 Kings 19:4 himself went a days' journey into the **w**
Matthew 3:3 The voice of one crying in the **w**, Prepare
Matthew 4:1 was Jesus led up of the Spirit into the **w**
Mark 1:3 The voice of one crying in the **w**, Prepare
Mark 1:12 immediately the Spirit driveth him into the **w**
Luke 3:4 The voice of one crying in the **w**, Prepare
Luke 4:1 and was led by the Spirit into the **w**
John 1:23 I am the voice of one crying in the **w**

Will (WIL)

Choose to (do something), going to (do something), decide, want to.

1 Kings 18:1 and I **w** send rain upon the earth
1 Kings 18:24 I **w** call upon the name of the LORD
Psalm 18:3 I **w** call upon the LORD, who is worthy
Psalm 23:4 I **w** fear no evil: for thou art with me
Psalm 23:6 I **w** dwell in the house of the LORD
Psalm 51:13 Then **w** I teach transgressors thy ways
Psalm 55:17 and morning, and at noon, **w** I pray
Proverbs 1:5 A wise man **w** hear, and **w** increase
Matthew 4:19 and I **w** make you fishers of men
Matthew 6:14 your heavenly Father **w** also forgive
Matthew 6:15 neither **w** your Father forgive your
Matthew 16:24 If any man **w** come after me, let him
Matthew 16:25 whosoever **w** save his life shall lose
Matthew 16:25 **w** lose his life for my sake shall find
Matthew 26:39 not as I **w**, but as thou wilt
Matthew 27:63 After three days I **w** arise again
Mark 1:17 I **w** make you to become fishers of men
Mark 8:34 **w** come after me, let him deny himself
Mark 8:35 whosoever **w** save his life shall lose it
Luke 5:5 at thy word I **w** let down the net
Luke 9:23 If any man **w** come after me, let him deny
Luke 9:24 whosoever **w** save his life shall lose it
Luke 9:24 whosoever **w** lose his life for my sake
John 20:15 hast laid him, and I **w** take him away
John 20:25 my hand into his side, I **w** not believe

Wind (WEND)

Any movement of air; a breeze or storm. In the Bible, can also mean a person's breath or spirit.

Exodus 10:13 LORD brought an east **w** upon the land
Exodus 14:21 the sea to go back by a strong east **w**
1 Kings 19:11 great and strong **w** rent the mountains
1 Kings 19:11 but the LORD was not in the **w**

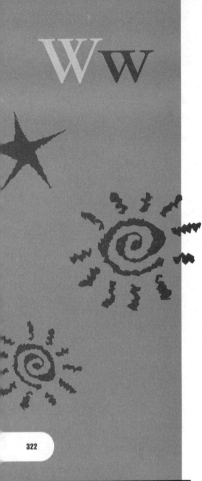

1 Kings 19:11 and after the **w** an earthquake
Jonah 1:4 LORD sent out a great **w** into the sea
Jonah 4:8 God prepared a vehement east **w**
Matthew 14:30 when he saw the **w**, he was afraid (NIV)
Matthew 14:32 come into the ship, the **w** ceased
Mark 4:37 there arose a great storm of **w**
Mark 4:39 And he arose, and rebuked the **w**
Luke 8:23 came down a storm of **w** upon the lake
Luke 8:24 he arose, and rebuked the **w** and the
John 6:18 the sea rose by reason of a great **w**

■ Winds (WENDS)
Plural of "wind."

Matthew 7:25 the **w** blew, and beat upon that house
Matthew 7:27 the **w** blew, and beat upon that house
Matthew 8:26 Then he arose, and rebuked the **w**
Matthew 8:27 that even the **w** and the sea obey him
Luke 8:25 for he commandeth even the **w** and the water

■ Winterhouse (WIN tuhr hows)
Winter is the season between autumn and spring, usually December, January, and February. In Palestine the winters are mild and during these months the rains come. Rich people either had a home built in a warmer area of the land or had certain rooms in their houses that they kept warm. Often these rooms were on the lower floor where they would get the winter's sun, making them easier to heat.

Jeremiah 36:22 the king sat in the **w** in the ninth month

■ Wipe (WIGHP)
To clean, dry, or rub.

Luke 7:38 did **w** them with the hairs of her head
John 13:5 feet and to **w** them with the towel

■ Wisdom (WIZ duhm)
Knowledge or understanding one gets through experiences or learning. Wisdom is a gift from God and should be used in a way to honor God. The book of Proverbs and some chapters in the Psalms speak of wisdom. One who has wisdom and uses it well will have success in his life. One of God's many qualities is wisdom.

2 Chronicles 1:10 Give me now **w** and knowledge, that
2 Chronicles 1:12 **W** and knowledge is granted unto
Psalm 111:10 fear of the LORD is the beginning of **w**
Proverbs 3:13 Happy is the man that findeth **w**
Proverbs 9:10 fear of the LORD is the beginning of **w**
Matthew 13:54 Where did this man get this **w** (NIV)

Wisdom
1 Kings 3:16-28

Luke 2:40 and waxed strong in spirit, filled with **w**
Luke 2:52 Jesus increased in **w** and stature, and in
Mark 6:2 What's this **w** that has been given him (NIV)

Wise (WIGHZ)
1. Able, educated, having knowledge; using knowledge in a practical way.

Genesis 3:6 a tree to be desired to make one **w**
Exodus 7:11 Then Pharaoh also called the **w** men
Proverbs 1:5 A **w** man will hear, and will increase
Proverbs 3:7 Be not **w** in thine own eyes
Proverbs 8:33 Hear instruction, and be **w**
Proverbs 10:1 A **w** son maketh a glad father
Proverbs 13:1 **w** son heareth his father's instruction
Matthew 2:1 there came **w** m from the east to
Matthew 2:7 when he had privily called the **w** men
Matthew 2:16 saw that he was mocked of the **w** men

2. Way or manner.

Luke 13:11 and could in no **w** lift up herself
John 21:1 and on this **w** showed he himself

Withered (WITH uhrd)
Past tense of "wither." To wither is to dry up, weaken, become deformed or twisted, or to shrink (become smaller).

Genesis 41:23 And, behold, seven ears, **w**, thin
Matthew 12:10 was a man which had his hand **w**
Mark 3:1 was a man there which had a **w** hand
Luke 6:6 there was a man whose right hand was **w**

Withhold (WITH hold)
To hold back, not willing to give.

Psalm 40:11 **W** not thy tender mercies from me, O LORD
Psalm 84:11 no good thing will he **w** from them that
Proverbs 3:27 **W** not good from them to whom it is due

Without (WITH owt)
1. Lacking, an absence of, in need of.

Genesis 1:2 the earth was **w** form, and void
Matthew 13:57 A prophet is not **w** honor, save in
Mark 6:4 A prophet is not **w** honor, but in
John 19:23 now the coat was **w** seam, woven from
Philippians 2:14 Do all things **w** murmurings
1 Thessalonians 5:17 Pray **w** ceasing
Hebrews 11:6 **w** faith it is impossible to please God (NIV)

2. Outside, away from the inside.

Matthew 26:69 Now Peter sat **w** in the palace

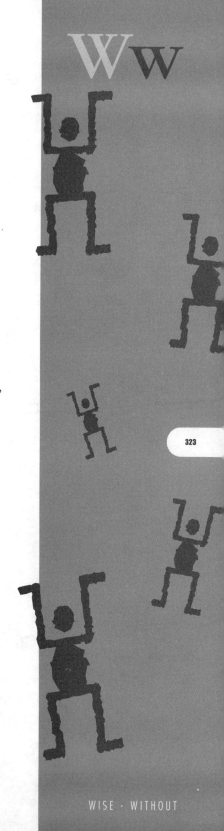

323

John 18:16 But Peter stood at the door ***w***
John 20:11 But Mary stood ***w*** at the sepulcher

Witness (WIT niss)

To observe, see, watch; to know about something because you have seen it for yourself. In a court of law, a witness must tell what he saw or heard. As a Christian, we are a witness for Jesus, and we must tell others what He has done in our lives.

Exodus 20:16 Thou shalt not bear false ***w*** against
Deuteronomy 5:20 Neither shalt thou bear false ***w***
Proverbs 14:5 A faithful ***w*** will not lie
Proverbs 14:5 but a false ***w*** will utter lies
Matthew 19:18 Thou shalt not bear false ***w***
Mark 14:56 For many bear false ***w*** against him
Mark 14:57 and bare false ***w*** against him
Luke 22:71 What need we any further ***w***
John 1:15 John bare ***w*** of him, and cried

Witnesses (WIT niss ehz)

Plural of "witness."

Ruth 4:9 Ye are ***w*** this day, that I have bought
Matthew 26:60 though many false ***w*** came
Matthew 26:65 what further need have we of ***w***
Mark 14:63 What need we any further ***w***
Acts 1:8 ye shall be ***w*** unto me both in Jerusalem
Acts 7:58 the ***w*** laid down their clothes at a

Woman (WOH muhn)

A female human being who is an adult.

Genesis 2:22 LORD God made a ***w*** from the rib he (NIV)
Genesis 2:23 she shall be called ***W***, because she
Ruth 1:5 and the ***w*** was left of her two sons
1 Kings 17:9 commanded a widow ***w*** there to sustain
1 Kings 17:10 widow ***w*** was there gathering sticks
1 Kings 17:17 these things, that the son of the ***w***
1 Kings 17:24 the ***w*** said unto Elijah, Now by this
Matthew 9:20 And, behold, a ***w*** which was diseased
Matthew 15:22 behold, a ***w*** of Canaan came out
Matthew 26:10 said unto them, Why trouble ye the ***w***
Mark 5:25 a certain ***w***, which had an issue of blood
Mark 5:33 But the ***w*** fearing and trembling
Mark 14:3 then came a ***w*** having an alabaster box
Luke 7:37 a ***w*** in the city, which was a sinner
Luke 7:44 And he turned to the ***w***, and said
Luke 7:45 but this ***w*** since the time I came in hath
Luke 7:46 ***w*** hath anointed my feet with ointment
Luke 8:43 a ***w*** having an issue of blood twelve

Luke 10:38 **w** named Martha received him into her
John 20:15 Jesus saith unto her, **W**, why weepest thou

Women (WIM en)
Plural of "woman."

Ruth 1:4 took them wives of the **w** of Moab
Matthew 14:21 thousand men, beside **w** and children
Matthew 15:38 thousand men, beside **w** and children
Matthew 27:55 And many **w** were there beholding afar
Matthew 28:5 angel answered and said unto the **w**
Mark 15:40 There were also **w** looking on afar off
Mark 15:41 and many other **w** which came up with
Luke 24:10 and other **w** that were there with them
Luke 24:22 certain **w** also of our company made us
Luke 24:24 found it even so as the **w** had said

Wondered (WUN duhrd)
Past tense of "wonder." To wonder is to have questions about or to be curious about a thing.

Matthew 15:31 multitude **w**, when they saw the dumb
Mark 6:51 amazed in themselves beyond measure, and **w**
Luke 2:18 all they that heard it **w** at those things
Luke 4:22 and **w** at the gracious words which
Luke 8:25 being afraid **w**, saying one to another
Luke 11:14 the dumb spake; and the people **w**
Luke 24:41 yet believed not for joy, and **w**, he said

Wonderful (WUN duhr fuhl)
Delightful, very good, great.

Matthew 21:15 and scribes saw the **w** things that he did

Wonders (WUN duhrz)
Plural of "wonder." An outstanding or almost unbelievable event; something marvelous. Also, feelings of astonishment or great surprise.

Exodus 3:20 smite Egypt with all my **w** which I will
Exodus 4:21 that thou do all these **w** before Pharaoh
Exodus 11:9 that my **w** may be multiplied in Egypt
Psalm 89:5 the heavens shall praise thy **w**, O LORD
Psalm 136:4 To him who alone doeth great **w**
Acts 2:43 many **w** and signs were done by the apostles

Wool (WUHL)
The thick hair on sheep and other animals. After it is cut off (shorn), the hair is spun into thread. Clothing, blankets, and other useful items were made from it during biblical times. The sale of wool was important to Israel and the nations around them. Wool was referred to in

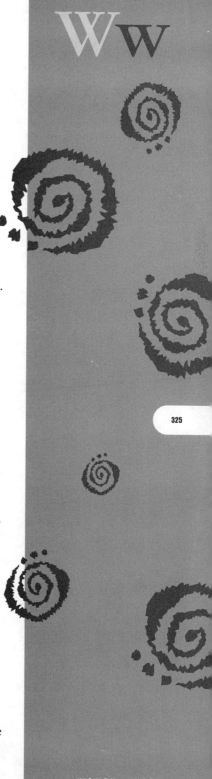

325

Isaiah 1:18 to represent purity and whiteness.

Judges 6:37 I will put a fleece of **w** in the floor
Isaiah 1:18 red like crimson, thy shall be as **w**

■ Word (WURD)
Law, command; promise or vow; written or spoken language. God's Word, the Bible, contains laws and commands, guidelines and promises given by God. God used prophets and His written word to help the Israelites, and us, know what His will is. Also, the Word is Jesus Christ, as shown in John 1.

1 Kings 17:2 And the **w** of the LORD came unto him
1 Kings 18:1 the **w** of the LORD came to Elijah
Psalm 119:11 Thy **w** have I hid in mine heart
Psalm 119:160 Thy **w** is true from the beginning
Jonah 1:1 Now the **w** of the LORD came unto Jonah
Jonah 3:1 the **w** of the LORD came unto Jonah
Matthew 2:8 bring me **w** again, that I may come and
Matthew 2:13 be thou there until I bring thee **w**
Matthew 8:8 speak the **w** only, and my servant shall
Matthew 26:75 And Peter remembered the **w** of Jesus
Matthew 28:8 and did run to bring his disciples **w**
Luke 3:2 the **w** of God came unto John the son of
Luke 5:5 at thy **w** I will let down the net
Luke 7:7 say in a **w**, and my servant shall be
Acts 2:41 that gladly received his **w** were baptized

■ Words (WURDZ)
Plural of "word."

Genesis 27:34 when Esau heard the **w** of his father
Genesis 45:27 they told him all the **w** of Joseph
Exodus 4:28 Moses told Aaron all the **w** of the LORD
Exodus 4:30 Aaron spake all the **w** which the LORD
Exodus 20:1 And God spake all these **w**, saying
Psalm 19:14 Let the **w** of my mouth, and the
Proverbs 15:1 but grievous **w** stir up anger
Matthew 26:44 the third time, saying the same **w**
Mark 10:24 the disciples were astonished at his **w**
Mark 14:39 and prayed, and spake the same **w**
John 18:1 when Jesus had spoken these **w**

■ Work (WURK)
1. To use the hands to get something done; labor, toil.

Genesis 2:2 on the seventh day God ended his **w**
Exodus 20:9 days shalt thou labor, and do all thy **w**
Exodus 20:10 in it thou shalt not do any **w**
Exodus 23:12 Six days shalt thou do thy **w**

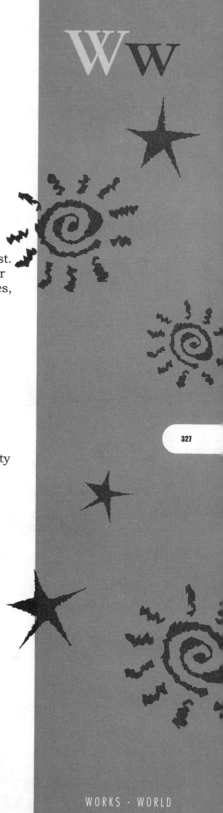

Deuteronomy 5:13 shalt thou labor, and do all thy **w**
Deuteronomy 5:14 in it thou shalt not do any **w**
Psalm 8:3 consider thy heavens, the **w** of thy fingers
Galatians 6:4 But let every man prove his own **w**

2. A deed or action.

Proverbs 20:11 whether his **w** be pure, and whether
Matthew 26:10 she hath wrought a good **w** upon me
Mark 6:5 And he could do there no mighty **w**
Mark 14:6 she hath wrought a good **w** on me
Luke 13:14 six days in which men ought to **w**

Works (WURKS)

Plural of "Work 2." Our deeds and actions show how much faith we have, and whether we do the works of the devil or of Jesus Christ. A Christian will do good works, showing he or she is a believer. God's works show He creates, saves, guides, and cares for His people.

Matthew 5:16 that they may see your good **w**
Matthew 13:54 man this wisdom, and these mighty **w**
Matthew 13:58 he did not many mighty **w** there
Mark 6:2 such mighty **w** are wrought by his hands
Luke 19:37 all the mighty **w** that they had seen
Acts 9:36 woman was full of good **w** and almsdeeds
Ephesians 2:9 Not of **w**, lest any man should boast

Workman (WURK muhn)

A laborer. One who works with skill and ability in order to do a good job.

2 Timothy 2:15 a **w** that needeth not to be ashamed

World (WURLD)

The earth; the places where people dwell; the age in which people live.

Matthew 5:14 Ye are the light of the **w**
Matthew 16:26 gain the whole **w**, and lose his own
Matthew 28:20 you always, even unto the end of the **w**
Mark 8:36 gain the whole **w**, and lose his own soul
Mark 16:15 Go ye into all the **w**, and preach the
Luke 2:1 Augustus, that all the **w** should be taxed
Luke 9:25 if he gain the whole **w**, and lose himself
John 3:16 For God so loved the **w**, that he gave his
John 4:42 indeed the Christ, the Savior of the **w**
John 9:5 as I am in the **w**, I am the light of the **w**
John 12:19 behold, the **w** is gone after him
John 18:36 Jesus answered, My kingdom is not of this **w**
John 21:25 even the **w** could not contain the books

Ww

Worship

328

■ **Worship (WUR shup)**
To show reverence and respect toward another, especially to God. To obey and focus one's attention; to enjoy God's presence; to express honor, praise, and love toward God. It is important that one has time to worship God alone but also as a part of a larger group.

Genesis 22:5 I and the lad will go yonder and *w*
Exodus 34:14 For thou shalt *w* no other god
Psalm 95:6 O come, let us *w* and bow down
Matthew 2:2 star in the east, and are come to *w* him
Matthew 2:8 that I may come and *w* him also
Matthew 4:9 if thou wilt fall down and *w* me
Matthew 4:10 Thou shalt *w* the Lord thy God
Luke 4:7 If thou therefore wilt *w* me, all shall be
Luke 4:8 Thou shalt *w* the Lord thy God
John 4:24 *w* him must *w* him in spirit and in truth

■ **Worshiped (WUR shupt)**
Past tense of "worship." (Also worshipped.)

Genesis 24:26 bowed down his head, and *w* the LORD
Genesis 24:48 I bowed down my head, and *w* the LORD
Genesis 24:52 he *w* the LORD, bowing himself to the
Matthew 2:11 Mary his mother, and fell down and *w*
Matthew 8:2 there came a leper and *w* him, saying
Matthew 9:18 there came a certain ruler, and *w* him
Matthew 14:33 they that were in the ship came and *w*
Matthew 15:25 Then she came and *w* him, saying
Matthew 28:9 held him by the feet, and *w* him
Matthew 28:17 when they saw him, they *w* him
Mark 5:6 saw Jesus afar off, he ran, and *w* him
Mark 15:19 upon him, and bowing their knees *w* him
Luke 24:52 they *w* him, and returned to Jerusalem

■ **Worthy (WUR thee)**
Having worth, value, or excellence. Being good enough; to deserve.

Psalm 18:3 upon the LORD, who is *w* to be praised
Matthew 3:11 whose shoes I am not *w* to bear
Matthew 8:8 I am not *w* that thou shouldest come
Mark 1:7 shoes I am not *w* to stoop down and unloose
Luke 3:16 latchet of whose shoes I am not *w* to unloose
Luke 7:6 I am not *w* that thou shouldest enter under
Luke 15:21 and am no more *w* to be called thy son
John 1:27 whose shoe's latchet I am not *w* to unloose

■ **Wound (WOWND)**
Past tense of "wind" (wighnd). To twist, curl, or turn, as wind the ribbon around the maypole.

John 19:40 and *w* it in linen clothes with the spices

Wound (WOOND)

An injury to the body; a mental or emotional hurt.

1 Corinthians 8:12 and **w** their weak conscience
Revelation 13:3 and his deadly **w** was healed

Wounded (WOON did)

Past tense of "wound" (woond). To hurt the body by cutting or hitting; to have one's feelings hurt.

Isaiah 53:5 But he was **w** for our transgressions
Luke 10:30 stripped him of his raiment, and **w** him

Wounds (WOONDZ)

Plural of "wound." Anything that hurts the body or one's feelings (emotions).

Psalm 147:3 broken in heart, and bindeth up their **w**
Luke 10:34 bound up his **w**, pouring in oil and wine

Wrapped (RAPT)

Past tense of "wrap." To cover something in such a way that no part of it is showing. To wind or fold the covering around an object.

1 Kings 19:13 Elijah heard it, he **w** his face in his
Jonah 2:5 the weeds were **w** about my head
Matthew 27:59 he **w** it in a clean linen cloth
Mark 15:46 and **w** him in the linen, and láid him in
Luke 2:7 son, and **w** him in swaddling clothes, and
Luke 2:12 shall find the babe **w** in swaddling clothes
Luke 23:53 And he took it down, and **w** it in linen
John 20:7 but **w** together in a place by itself

Wrath (RATH)

Rage, great anger, such as that which God shows toward the sin in man's life. When God expresses wrath, He is showing how grieved or sad He is at the things we do. When we tell him we are truly sorry for the wrong things we have done, then he will not be angry. The Holy Spirit will help us overcome the anger we have toward others, so that we do not try and get revenge (get even).

Esther 3:5 then was Haman full of **w**
Esther 7:7 in his **w** went into the palace garden
Esther 7:10 Then was the king's **w** pacified
Proverbs 15:1 A soft answer turneth away **w**
Ephesians 4:26 let not the sun go down upon your **w**
James 1:19 swift to hear, slow to speak, slow to **w**
James 1:20 **w** of a man worketh not the righteousness

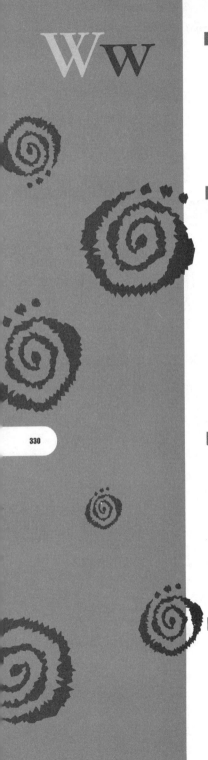

Ww

Write (RIGHT)
To use pencil or pen to form words for others to read.

Exodus 34:1 I will **w** upon these tables the words
Exodus 34:27 LORD said unto Moses: **W** thou these
Jeremiah 36:2 **w** therein all the words I have spoken
Jeremiah 36:17 how did you come to **w** all this (NIV)
Jeremiah 36:28 **W** in it all the former words that
John 19:21 **W** not, The King of the Jews; but that

Written (RIT uhn)
Words that have been placed on paper or other surface by pencil or pen, or that have been scratched into something like stone or metal.

Matthew 4:4 It is **w**, Man shall not live by bread
Matthew 4:6 for it is **w**, He shall give his angels
Matthew 4:10 it is **w**, Thou shalt worship the Lord
Luke 3:4 it is **w** in the book of the words of Isaiah
Luke 4:4 It is **w**, That man shall not live by bread
Luke 4:8 for it is **w**, Thou shalt worship the Lord
Luke 4:10 For it is **w**, He shall give his angels
Luke 23:38 was **w** over him in letters of Greek
Luke 24:46 what is **w**. The Christ will suffer (NIV)
John 19:20 it was **w** in Hebrew, and Greek, and Latin
John 19:22 Pilate answered, What I have **w** I have **w**

Wrote (ROTE)
Past tense of "write."

Exodus 24:4 And Moses **w** all the words of the LORD
Exodus 34:28 **w** upon the tables the words of the
1 Kings 21:8 So she **w** letters in Ahab's name
Jeremiah 36:4 Baruch **w** from the mouth of Jeremiah
Jeremiah 36:27 and the words which Baruch **w**
Jeremiah 36:32 **w** therein from the mouth of Jeremiah
Luke 1:63 and **w**, saying, His name is John
John 19:19 Pilate **w** a title, and put it on the
John 21:24 **w** these things: and we know that his

Wroth (RAWTH)
Angry.

Genesis 4:5 Cain was very **w**, and his countenance
Exodus 16:20 and stank: and Moses was **w** with them
2 Kings 5:11 But Naaman was **w**, and went away, and
Matthew 2:16 mocked of the wise men, was exceeding **w**

Year (YEER)

A time period, usually made up of 365 days; twelve months. During biblical times, the Hebrews did not use a calendar as we do today. At times, the year began in the spring and sometimes in the fall. The spring or fall equinox measured the year. On those days, the day and night each had the same number of hours. Equinox means the day and night are the same length. Oftentimes, the year of a king or ruler marked the date.

Genesis 7:11 In the six hundredth **y** of Noah's life
1 Kings 18:1 the LORD came to Elijah in the third **y**
Luke 2:41 every **y** at the feast of the passover
Luke 3:1 the fifteenth **y** of the reign of Tiberius
John 11:49 Caiaphas, being the high priest that same **y**

Years (YEERZ)

Plural of "year."

Genesis 1:14 for seasons, and for days, and **y**
Genesis 5:5 lived were nine hundred and thirty **y**
Genesis 9:29 Noah were nine hundred and fifty **y**
Genesis 25:7 are the days of the **y** of Abraham's
Genesis 25:7 an hundred threescore and fifteen **y**
Genesis 41:26 The seven good cows are seven **y** (NIV)
Genesis 41:26 seven good heads of grain are seven **y** (NIV)
Genesis 41:27 cows that came up afterward are seven **y** (NIV)
Genesis 41:27 east wind shall be seven **y** of famine
Genesis 41:29 there come seven **y** of great plenty
Genesis 41:30 after them seven **y** of famine
Ruth 1:4 and they dwelled there about ten **y**
1 Kings 17:1 shall not be dew nor rain these **y**
Psalm 90:4 For a thousand **y** in thy sight are but as
Matthew 9:20 with an issue of blood twelve **y**
Mark 5:25 which had an issue of blood twelve **y**
Mark 5:42 for she was of the age of twelve **y**
Luke 2:37 widow of about fourscore and four **y**
Luke 2:42 And when he was twelve **y** old, they went
Luke 3:23 Jesus himself was about thirty **y** old (NIV)
Luke 8:43 having an issue of blood twelve **y**
John 5:5 which had an infirmity thirty and eight **y**

Yoke (YOHK)

A wooden frame placed on the shoulders of two oxen, donkeys, or other animal. The yoke helps them to work together to pull something, usu-

Yy

ally a plow. In Bible times, yoke could mean slavery or hardships of any kind.

Matthew 11:29 Take my **y** upon you, and learn of me
Matthew 11:30 my **y** is easy, and my burden is light

■ Yonder (YAHN duhr)
Beyond, over there, further.

Genesis 22:5 I and the lad will go **y** and worship
Matthew 17:20 this mountain: Remove hence to **y** place
Matthew 26:36 Sit ye here, while I go and pray **y**

■ Young (YUNG)
Youthful, not very old, a few years old.

Leviticus 12:8 two turtles, or two **y** pigeons
Matthew 2:8 and search diligently for the **y** child
Matthew 2:9 stood over where the **y** child was
Matthew 2:11 they saw the **y** child with Mary
Matthew 2:13 Arise, and take the **y** child and his
Mark 7:25 whose **y** daughter had an unclean spirit
Mark 10:13 And they brought **y** children to him
Mark 16:5 saw a **y** man sitting on the right side
Luke 2:24 a pair of turtledoves, or two **y** pigeons
Luke 7:14 he said, **Y** man, I say unto thee, Arise
John 12:14 Jesus found a **y** donkey, and sat upon it (NIV)

■ Younger (YUNG guhr)
Not as old; childish.

Genesis 27:15 and put them upon Jacob her **y** son
Genesis 27:42 she sent and called Jacob her **y** son
Genesis 43:29 and said, Is this your **y** brother
Luke 15:12 And the **y** of them said to his father
Luke 15:13 the **y** son gathered all together, and

■ Yourselves (your SELVZ)
Plural of "yourself." You, your own self.

Genesis 18:4 wash your feet, and rest **y** under the
1 Kings 18:25 Choose you one bullock for **y**, and
Matthew 6:19 Lay not up for **y** treasures upon earth
Matthew 6:20 But lay up for **y** treasures in heaven
Mark 6:31 Come ye **y** apart into a desert place
Luke 17:14 unto them, Go show **y** unto the priests
Luke 22:17 Take this, and divide it among **y**

■ Youth (YOOTH)
A child; teen; a young man or woman.

Ecclesiastes 12:1 thy Creator in the days of thy **y**
Matthew 19:20 these things have I kept from my **y** up
Mark 10:20 all these have I observed from my **y**
Luke 18:21 All these have I kept from my **y** up
1 Timothy 4:12 Let no man despise thy **y**

Zaccheus (za KEE uhs)

The Greek form of the word means "innocent."
A tax collector in Jericho who became very
rich. He was a short man, and when he heard
Jesus was coming to town, he climbed into a
sycamore tree so he could see Him. Jesus
stopped below the tree and said He was going
to eat at Zaccheus' house. Zaccheus believed
that Jesus was the Savior, and he gave back
what he had taken wrongly.

Luke 19:2 there was a man named **Z**
Luke 19:5 unto him **Z**, make haste, and come down
Luke 19:8 **Z** stood, and said unto the Lord

Zacharias (ZAK uh RIGH uhs)

The name means "Yah remembered." He was
the father of John the Baptist. He served as a
priest before John was born. An angel visited
Zacharias as he was serving in the Temple and
told him that he and his wife, Elizabeth, would
have a son in their old age.

Luke 1:13 Fear not, **Z**: for thy prayer is heard
Luke 1:67 father **Z** was filled with the Holy Ghost
Luke 3:2 unto John the son of **Z** in the wilderness

Zarephath (ZAR ih fath)

A town on the coast of the Mediterranean Sea
a few miles south of Sidon. It was governed by
Phoenicia. God sent Elijah to this town after
Elijah had told King Ahab there would be a
drought. A poor widow with a young son took
care of him. She was almost out of flour and
oil when Elijah arrived, but during the
drought, her flour and oil never ran out.

1 Kings 17:9 Arise, get thee to **Z**, which belongeth
1 Kings 17:10 So he arose and went to **Z**

Zebedee (ZEB uh dee)

The name means "gift." He and his two sons,
James and John, were fishermen on the Sea of
Galilee. James and John were two of Jesus'
twelve disciples. Their home was in
Capernaum. Zebedee's wife, Salome, was one

333

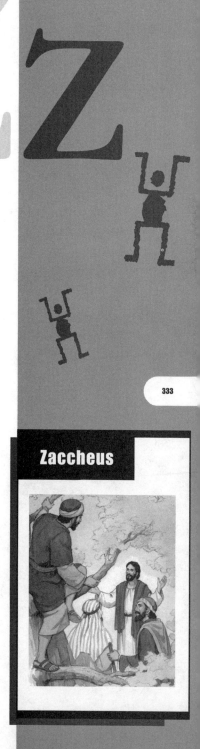

Zaccheus

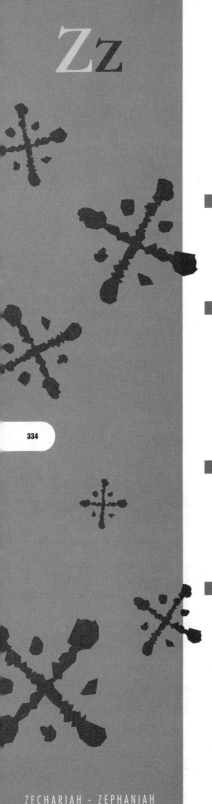

Zz

of the women who went to the tomb of Jesus and found it empty.

Matthew 4:21 James the son of **Z**, and John his
Matthew 4:21 in a ship with **Z** their father
Matthew 26:37 Peter and the two sons of **Z**
Mark 1:19 saw James the son of **Z**, and John his
Mark 1:20 left their father **Z** in the ship
Luke 5:10 also James, and John, the sons of **Z**
John 21:2 sons of **Z**, and two other of his disciples

■ **Zechariah (ZEK uh RIGH uh)**
The name means "Yahweh remembered." He was a prophet in Jerusalem from 520–518 B.C., after the exile. His message was to encourage the rebuilding of the Temple.

Zechariah 1:1 came the word of the LORD unto **Z**

■ **Zechariah, Book of (ZEK uh RIGH uh)**
The eleventh book in the division, Minor Prophets, in the Old Testament. It was written by the prophet Zechariah. The first six chapters tell about visions which Zechariah had, encouraging the people to rebuild the Temple, and make themselves clean from sin so they could worship God. The second part of the book tells about the coming Messiah and the judgment of God at the end of time.

■ **Zephaniah (ZEF uh NIGH uh)**
The name means "Yahweh sheltered or stored up." He was a prophet of Judah during the reign of King Josiah. He may have been a cousin to Josiah. Zephaniah may have lived in Jerusalem since he preached there.

Zephaniah 1:1 The word of the LORD which came unto **Z**

■ **Zephaniah, Book of (ZEF uh NIGH uh)**
The ninth book in the division, Minor Prophets, in the Old Testament. The message of Zephaniah came before the Israelites were taken to Babylonia as captives. He told the people they would be punished for worshiping other gods. The nations around them would also be punished. He encouraged the Israelites and other nations to turn from their sins. The last chapter tells how Jerusalem would be renewed with just a small number of those who honored God.

Zipporah (zi POH ruh)

The name means "small bird" or "sparrow." Her father was Reuel, or Jethro, and she was Moses' wife. She was from Midian. After Moses had led the Israelites out of Egypt, Jethro brought Zipporah and her two sons to meet Moses in the desert.

Exodus 2:21 and he gave Moses **Z** his daughter
Exodus 18:2 Jethro, Moses' father-in-law, took **Z**

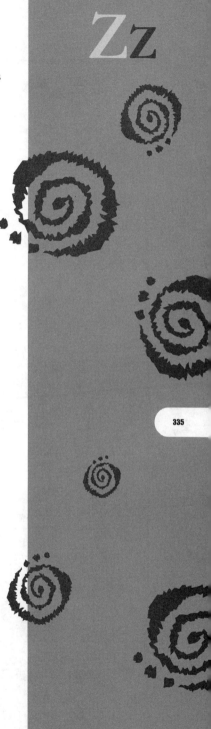

Zz

335

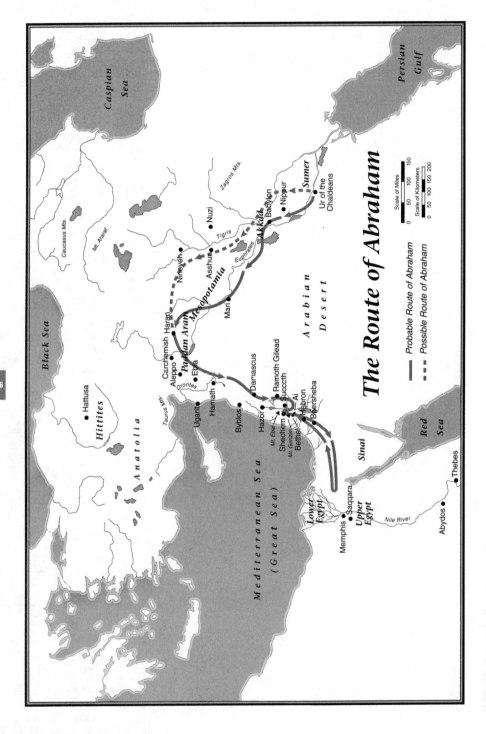

The Route of Abraham

THE ROUTE OF ABRAHAM

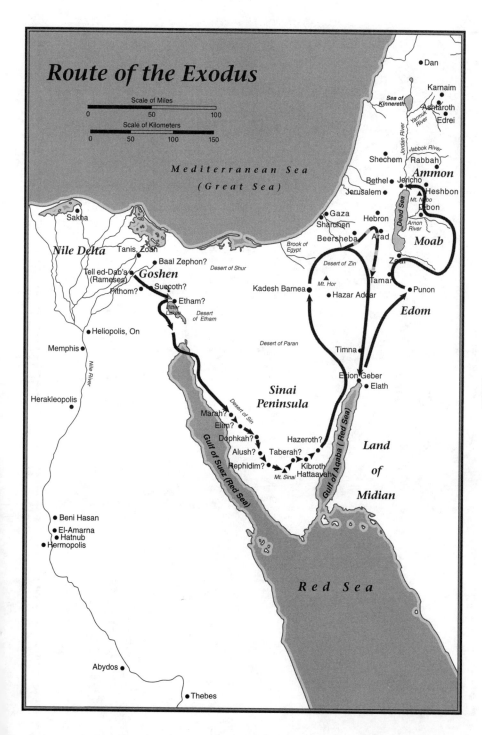

Route of the Exodus

Scale of Miles
0   50   100

Scale of Kilometers
0   50   100   150

Mediterranean Sea
(Great Sea)

Sakha

Nile Delta

Tanis, Zoah

Baal Zephon?

Tell ed-Dab'a
(Rameses)
Goshen

Pithom?

Succoth?

Etham?

*Bitter
Lakes*

*Desert
of Etham*

Desert of Shur

Heliopolis, On

Memphis

Herakleopolis

Nile River

Marah?

Elim?

Dophkah?

Alush?

Rephidim?

Taberah?

Mt. Sinai

Kibroth Hattaavah

Hazeroth?

Desert of Sin

*Sinai
Peninsula*

Desert of Paran

Timna

Gulf of Suez (Red Sea)

Gulf of Aqaba (Red Sea)

Kadesh Barnea

Hazar Addar

Mt. Hor

Desert of Zin

*Brook of
Egypt*

Beersheba

Sharuhen

Gaza

Arad

Hebron

Jerusalem

Bethel

Jericho

Shechem

Heshbon
Dibon

Dead Sea

Mt. Nebo

*Arnon
River*

Moab

Tamar

Zoan

Punon

Edom

Ezion Geber

Elath

*Land
of
Midian*

Dan

Karnaim

Ashtaroth

Edrei

*Sea of
Kinnereth*

*Yarmuk
River*

Jordan River

Jabbok River

Rabbah

Ammon

Red Sea

Beni Hasan

El-Amarna

Hatnub

Hermopolis

Abydos

Thebes

337

Divided Monarchies

Scale of Miles
0   25   50

Scale of Kilometers
0   25   50   75

Mediterranean Sea
(Great Sea)

• Beirut

Phoenicia

• Sidon

Damascus •

Aram

• Ijon
▲ Mt. Hermon

• Tyre

• Dan

• Kedesh

• Hazor

• Acco   Kinnereth

Hannathon •

Sea of Kinnereth

• Ashtaroth

▲ Mt. Carmel

Golan

Yarmuk River

• Edrei

• Dor
Megiddo •

▲ Mt. Tabor

• Lo Debar

Taanach ▲
Mt. Gilboa

Jezreel •

Beth Shan

• Ramoth Gilead

Ibleam •

Jabesh Gilead

Samaria Tirzah

Mahanaim

Socoh •
Mt. Ebal ▲
Mt. Gerizim ▲

Shechem •
Zarethan •

Penuel

Jabbok River

Succoth

Ammon

• Aphek

• Shiloh

Joppa •

Israel

• Rabbah
of the Ammonites

Gezer •

Bethel •

• Gibeon

Jericho •

Heshbon •

Aijalon •

• Jerusalem

Mt. Nebo ▲

• Bezer

Beth Shemesh •

• Medeba

Ashdod •

Azekah •

Bethlehem •

Jahaz •
• Kedemoth

Gath •

Ashkelon •

Mareshah •

• Libnah

En Gedi •

Dead Sea (Salt Sea)

• Dibon

Gaza •

Lachish •

Hebron •

Wilderness of Judah

• Aroer

Philistia

Arnon River

• Arad

Moab

• Beersheba

Wadi el-Arish

Judah

• Kir Hareseth

Zoar •

Tamar •

Arabian

Kadesh Barnea
•

Bozrah
•

Desert

Edom

Desert

of

Paran

Jordan River

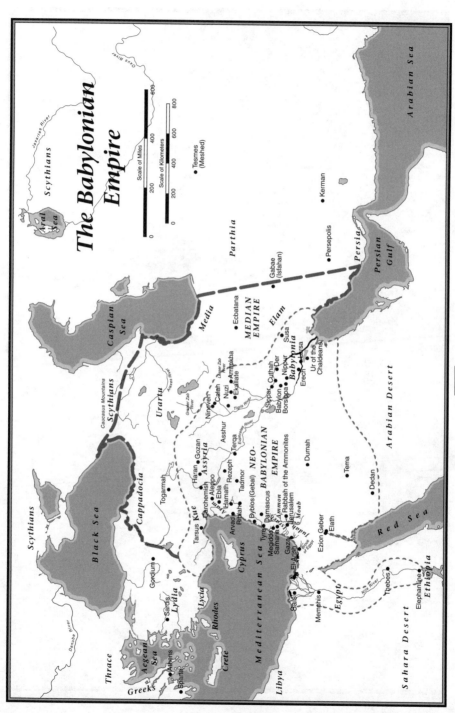

The Babylonian Empire

Scale of Miles
0   200   400   600

Scale of Kilometers
0   200   400   600   800

Scythians

Aral Sea

Oxus River

Jaxartes River

Caspian Sea

Tesmes (Meshed)

Kerman

Arabian Sea

Parthia

Persepolis

Persia

Persian Gulf

Gabae (Isfahan)

Media

MEDIAN EMPIRE

Ecbatana

Elam

Susa

Der

Ur of the Chaldeans

Babylonia

Erech

Nippur

Cuthah

Sippar

Babylon

Borsippa

Arabian Desert

Dumah

Tema

Dedan

Caucasus Mountains

Scythians

Araxes River

Urartu

Greater Zab River

Lesser Zab River

Arrapkha

Ekallate

Nuzi

Calah

Nineveh

Asshur

Tigris River

Terqa

Euphrates River

Gozan

Haran

Assyria

Aleppo

Ebla

Hamath

Rezeph

Tadmor

NEO-BABYLONIAN EMPIRE

Carchemish

Togarmah

Tarsus

Kue

Cappadocia

Black Sea

Scythians

Thrace

Gordium

Sardis

Lydia

Lycia

Rhodes

Aegean Sea

Athens

Sparta

Greeks

Crete

Cyprus

Mediterranean Sea

Libya

Arvad

Byblos (Gebal)

Ribiah

Damascus

Tyre

Ammon

Megiddo

Samaria

Jerusalem

Rabbah of the Ammonites

Moab

Gaza

El-Arish

Ezion Geber

Eliath

Red Sea

Egypt

Nile River

Memphis

Thebes

Sais

Elephantine

Ethiopia

Sahara Desert

339

Palestine in New Testament Times

Scale of Miles
0   10   20   30

Scale of Kilometers
0   10   20   30   40

Mediterranean Sea (Great Sea)

Phoenicia

Sidon

Damascus

Litani River

Mt. Hermon

Tyre

Kefar Dan
Daphne • Caesarea Philippi (Panias)

Raphana

Cadasa

Ecdippa

Thella

Ptolemais (Acco)

Mt. Meron
Korazin
Capernaum • Bethsaida
Heptapegon (Tabgha)
Gennesaret • Gergesa
Magdala • Sea of Galilee
Cana (Taricheae)
Sepphoris   Galilee   Tiberias
Mt. Carmel
Nazareth   Emmatha
Simonias ▲ Mt. Tabor Gadara
Philoteria   Abila
Nain   Agrippina

Hippus

Dion

Edrei

Valley of Esdraelon
Yarmuk River
Jordan River

Dora

Capercotnei

Caesarea Maritima

Ginae

Scythopolis

Salim
Aenon

Pella

Decapolis

Samaria

Geba
Sebaste (Samaria)

Gerasa

Jabbok River

Mt. Ebal ▲ Sychar
Mt. Gerizim ▲ Shechem

Amathus

Apollonia
Antipatris

Anuathu
Borcaeus

Coreae

Joppa

Lebonah • Acrabeta
Alexandrium
Phasaelis

Perea

Gadora

Gophna   Archelais

Philadelphia

Bethel • Ephraim
Neara
Jericho • Abila
Cyprus

Bethennabris

Lydda

Jamnia

Emmaus (Nicopolis)

Jerusalem • Qumran (Essene Community) ▲ Mt. Nebo
Bethlehem • Bethany
Hyrcania

Beth-ramatha   Esbus

Azotus (Ashdod)

Judea   • Herodium

Medeba

Tekoa

Dead Sea (Salt Sea)

Callirrhoe
Machaerus

Ascalon

Betogabris

Anthedon
Gaza

Hebron •
Adora •

En Gedi

Arnon River

Idumea

Masada

Raphia

Malatha

Beersheba

Nabateans

Zered River

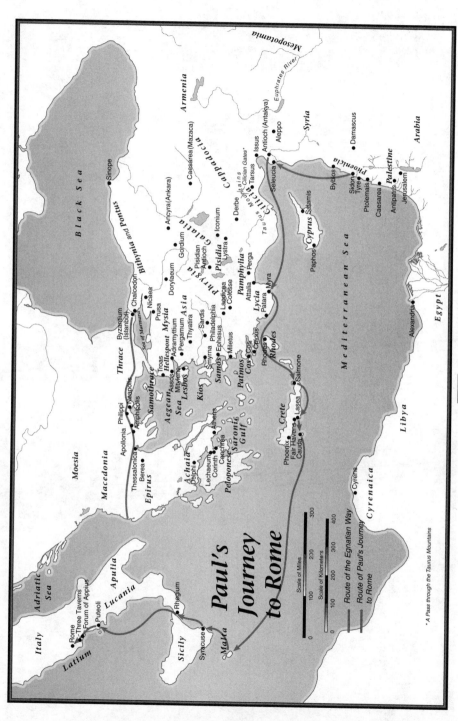

Paul's Journey to Rome

Route of the Egnatian Way
Route of Paul's Journey to Rome

Scale of Miles
0   100   200   300

Scale of Kilometers
0   100   200   300   400

* A Pass through the Taurus Mountains

Bible Bookcase

OLD TESTAMENT

LAW

GENESIS
EXODUS
LEVITICUS
NUMBERS
DEUTERONOMY

HISTORY

JOSHUA
JUDGES
RUTH
1 SAMUEL
2 SAMUEL
1 KINGS
2 KINGS
1 CHRONICLES
2 CHRONICLES
EZRA
NEHEMIAH
ESTHER

POETRY & WISDOM

JOB
PSALMS
PROVERBS
ECCLESIASTES
SONG OF SONGS

OLD TESTAMENT

MAJOR PROPHETS

ISAIAH
JEREMIAH
LAMENTATIONS
EZEKIEL
DANIEL

MINOR PROPHETS

HOSEA
JOEL
AMOS
OBADIAH
JONAH
MICAH
NAHUM
HABAKKUK
ZEPHANIAH
HAGGAI
ZECHARIAH
MALACHI

NEW TESTAMENT

GOSPELS

MATTHEW
MARK
LUKE
JOHN

HISTORY

ACTS

LETTERS OF PAUL

ROMANS
1 CORINTHIANS
2 CORINTHIANS
GALATIANS
EPHESIANS
PHILIPPIANS
COLOSSIANS
1 THESSALONIANS
2 THESSALONIANS
1 TIMOTHY
2 TIMOTHY
TITUS
PHILEMON

NEW TESTAMENT

GENERAL LETTERS

HEBREWS
JAMES
1 PETER
2 PETER
1 JOHN
2 JOHN
3 JOHN
JUDE

PROPHECY

REVELATION

©LATTA

NOTES

NOTES

NOTES

NOTES

NOTES

NOTES

NOTES

NOTES